THE BUILDING SOCIETY MOVEMENT

THE BUILDING SOCIETY MOVEMENT

E. J. CLEARY

ELEK BOOKS
ALL SAINTS STREET LONDON

Published by
ELEK BOOKS LIMITED
2 All Saints Street
London, N.1

and simultaneously in Canada by
The Ryerson Press
299 Queen Street West
Toronto 2B

Printed in Great Britain
by Unwin Brothers Limited
Woking and London
(B 3311)

PREFACE

IN THEIR two hundred years of existence, building societies have been faced with a wide variety of economic and political environments and have succeeded in adapting themselves to these changes with considerable skill. This book is an attempt to trace this process of adaptation; as such it is concerned with what happened, not with what ought to have happened. As independent institutions societies decide what purposes they wish to serve, with legislators intervening from time to time to try and ensure that the purposes chosen are compatible with the public interest, as legislators currently see that interest. In relation to building societies the public is both mortgagor and mortgagee; these are sharply differentiated roles and are likely to lead to rather different views on what constitutes the public interest. In these circumstances neutrality has its attractions even if it is not an attitude that has been maintained with complete consistency by the author.

What follows is a better book than it would have been had I not had the help of a number of people, and that help I gratefully acknowledge. Many improvements flowed from Professor Victor Morgan's reading of a first draft. A number of building society men readily answered my inquiries concerning the origins of their societies. I was able to draw on the considerable store of information that Mr. Hubert Newton has accumulated in his long building society career. Mr. Leonard Boyle and Mr. W. A. Gwilym were generous in making extended loans of relevant publications. Mr. W. C. Rogers gave me details of some early property development societies in Swansea. The Building Societies Association provided details of the inflow and outflow of investment funds for years before their published series starts. Mrs. H. Baird and Mrs. M. Price processed some of the statistical data and my wife helped in dealing with the proofs. To all these, my thanks. I can at least claim that those errors of fact and interpretation that remain are all my own work.

Swansea, 1965. E. J. CLEARY

CONTENTS

Chapter One

THE ORIGINS OF THE MOVEMENT*

THE QUICKENING of industrial growth, which took place in Britain in the second half of the eighteenth century, involved considerable changes in the pattern of settlement. The hands for the new and expanding workshops were found by drawing into the towns people from the surrounding countryside. The change from agricultural to industrial work meant an improvement in wages for most people, but it also involved certain risks which were not entirely familiar to them. Illness and unemployment were substantial risks both in the village and the town, but to be ill or out of work in one's own village was to suffer hardship among one's friends and, more important, one's family. Furthermore, that family, in a settled rural environment, was likely to be a large one. In such circumstances misfortunes were more easily endured.

The migrants were, however, richer in their urban environment and it is not surprising that they should devote some small part of their increased incomes to buying security. These workers found protection by creating friendly societies. The earliest friendly societies began in the late seventeenth century, and they increased rapidly after 1750.[1] Such societies aimed to protect the worker by providing help in times of illness, unemployment or other misfortune. Since they nearly always met at inns, they also provided some social life. Building societies, emerging from the same background, owe something of their origins to friendly societies. Building societies came later than friendly societies, and involved, in the early stages, a much smaller number of people. On quite a small wage a man might find a penny a week for a burial club, but 10s. a month for a building society was a very different matter. Membership of a building society would be possible only for the highly paid worker, and from the beginning small traders and manufacturers played a prominent part.

It is possible that building societies originated also, in part, from the "money clubs", also known as "collecting clubs". Here groups of people agreed to subscribe weekly sums and ballot for the right to borrow the week's proceeds, the winner giving some security as a guarantee of the continuance of his weekly subscription which would repay the loan.

* *Notes on this chapter appear on page 283.*

Something of the idea still persists in the clubs organised in connection with certain mail order businesses.

Little is known of the early history of these clubs, and hence of their relationship to the building society movement. They clearly met a need in providing a means of saving, in the period before Savings Banks, for those items purchased only occasionally: such as furniture and clothes, which would cost more than could be found in any week after buying groceries and paying the rent. Substantially these clubs were forerunners of the hire purchase system. Such groups were numerous in Scotland, known there as "menages", and were seen by Scratchley[2] and (probably following him) by Chambers[3] as forerunners of building societies. However, both these writers pictured the movement as starting in Scotland in 1815 and later spreading to England. Some slight evidence of a connection may be seen in the objectives of the Droylesden Society (1792).[4] Members subscribed to raise a fund "to be laid out in building or purchasing houses or lands, or *otherwise* (my italics) as the said members shall also think proper". Again Article 12 of the St. George's Society, Liverpool (1825) stated that after the Society had reached a certain point in its progress the committee could permit "each and every member who has not previously taken up (i.e. received an advance on) his or her share or shares to have and receive a sum of Sixty Pounds . . . upon his or her own *promissory note* or other personal security".

At a later date such clubs still existed on a considerable scale in Sheffield, lending up to £30 for a subscription of 5s. per month. There they had a long history, the thirty-third in one series of such clubs being founded in 1871.[5]

There were other organisations, developing property, which must have helped in the spread and growth of the building society principle. Groups of people formed associations, other than building societies, to build a few houses for letting, sometimes as a profitable investment,[6] sometimes as a social service. In 1779 the Rev. Miles Bassett, Vicar of Swansea, and four others including Roland Pritchard, an influential Swansea burgess, formed the Union Society to build fifteen dwelling houses to rent. The fact that if vacancies arose through the death of a member, they were to be filled in such a way that at least three of the Society's five members were always to be resident aldermen of the town, probably meant that the Union Society had a charitable element in its make-up.

These associations could have very small subscriptions, and the gambling element of a tontine might be added to attract members. The St. John's Street Tontine Association formed in Swansea in 1791 had a good deal in common with the early building societies. It had 100 members who agreed to subscribe money for five years to build five houses. The houses were to be let and the surviving members shared the income until their number had been reduced to ten. At that point either the houses were to be sold and the proceeds divided among the ten survivors, or they were to continue to divide the income until only five survivors remained, the five houses being then allocated by "casting lots for the choice of such houses each one of which shall remain to them and their heirs for ever". The Association met at the Black Horse Inn on the first Monday of each month and the subscription was "eighteen pence to the box" (to build the houses), "two pence to be spent" (presumably on beer) "and one halfpenny for Clerk's fee and expenses". By the mid-nineteenth century Swansea was an important centre of building society activity.[7] Societies like the Union Society and the St. John's Street Tontine Association must have helped to make the later growth of building societies possible.

The close connection between building societies and property development societies is brought out in the Articles of the Building Association formed in Westminster in 1807. Here 200 shares of £100 each were to be completed by monthly suscriptions of £1, the resulting fund to be invested in property. The articles governing the conduct of the Association, fines, arrears, etc., follow very closely the rules of early building societies, indeed the wording of some articles is identical.

The earliest building society at present known was Ketley's Building Society, which existed in Birmingham about 1775.[8] By 1781 there are four further societies known, three more in Birmingham and one in Dudley. The next decade saw the creation of a number of other societies in the Birmingham area and the spread of the movement outside the Midlands; the Hill House Bank Building Club in Leeds (1785) having pride of place. By 1800 societies are known to have existed in Birmingham, Dudley, Leeds, Droylesden, Rowley Regis, Preston, Horbury (near Wakefield) and Burnley. In the period to 1825, S. J. Price,[9] aggregating the results of his own enquiries with those of earlier researchers, lists sixty-three societies; to these must be added a further six societies,[10] making a total of sixty-nine societies known to have been formed in the fifty years following the formation of the first.

With very few exceptions, these societies were formed in the Midlands and North of England. Table I gives the dates of formation of these sixty-nine societies and Table II gives their geographical distribution.

TABLE I

Dates of Formation of Early Building Societies

	Date									
	Pre-1780	1785	1790	1795	1800	1805	1810	1815	1820	1825
No. of Societies	2	6	1	12	2	0	8	3	8	27

TABLE II

Geographical Distribution of Early Building Societies[11]
Date of Formation

Place	First Society	Subsequent Societies
Birmingham	1775	1779, 1781 (3), 1785 (2), 1786, 1791 (3), 1792, 1794, pre 1795 (3), pre 1820, 1821, 1822.
W. Riding of Yorks	1785	1793, 1806 (2), 1807 (2), pre 1814, 1823 (3), 1824, 1825 (7).
Manchester	1792	1817, 1820 (2), 1821 (2), 1822, 1823, 1824.
Preston	1793	1793, 1798, 1822 (2).
Burnley	1799	1815, 1820.
Stoke-on-Trent	1806	1807, 1816, 1824.
Scotland	1808	1815, 1820, 1824.
Greenwich	1809	
Liverpool	1818	1825.
Carlisle	1824	
Gateshead	1825	1825.
Carnarvon	1825	1826, 1827 (3).

Table I shows that after early growth the spread of the movement is checked, in the 1790s, for about a decade. After 1806 growth starts again and the movement expands rapidly after the close of the Napoleonic War. Table II shows that both in the early years, and in the expansion after 1815, the formation of one society in an area was likely to lead to the formation of others, in the same area. Birmingham and Preston are good examples of this in the early period, and Manchester, Bradford (with eight societies formed between 1823 and 1825) and Carnarvon in the later period.

Given the firm evidence for the existence of sixty-nine societies up to 1825, it can hardly be doubted that in fact many more were formed but have left no trace. From the later history of the movement it is certainly odd that only two societies are known in Liverpool at this date. Liverpool societies were very prominent in the agitation that led to the 1836 Building Societies Act, as were societies in the North-East, an area also poorly represented among the known societies. When the movement spread to London in the 1840s, the new societies were commonly described as being founded according to the "Liverpool plan". The lack of any society formed in Birmingham itself after 1795[12] is also striking. Perhaps the movement did not revive there after the war. There is some support for this view in the complete absence of Birmingham societies from the agitation in 1836. Mr. J. Hosking[13] speaking of those events said, "In fact these societies were utterly unknown in Birmingham at that period."

These early societies have many features in common, but they also exhibit a wide variety of detail, and some development, in their methods of attaining the basic objective of building societies, that is, to enable members to own houses. They were all terminating societies; that is, they aimed to take subscriptions from members until a large enough fund had been subscribed to give every shareholder a house: then the society broke up. Some societies organised the building themselves, purchasing materials and employing craftsmen, among whom might be some members of the society. Northwood's Society (1781, Birmingham) had a brickmaker as an articled servant of the Society.[14] The Rowley Regis Society (1792) empowered its management committee to "employ men to sink wells or do other work they shall think proper to buy timber or other materials they shall think proper for the use of the building and to agree with a mason upon the best terms they are able".[15]

In other cases the work was let out on contract. The Amicable Society (Birmingham, 1781) advertised in a local newspaper that "Any person willing to contract for the building of Ten Houses, may see a plan with the Estimate and all the Particulars, by applying to . . ."[16] Not all societies confined themselves to building houses. The Dudley Arms Society (1786) aimed to build an inn, the Rowley Regis Society showed its connection with the local metal trades by proposing to build houses with nailshops, and rather later, the Windhill Friendly Building Society (Bradford, 1838) planned to build ". . . a large public room wherein the industrious classes might assemble with their wives and families to acquire and communicate useful knowledge and for enjoyment, recreation and rational amusement".[17]

Other societies made advances to purchase existing property. In the Greenwich Union Society (1809)[18] if a member had built a house before his turn came to receive an advance, that existing house could be used as security. By the 1820s it was much less common for societies to build houses: the money was advanced to members either to build their own or purchase existing houses.

Although friendly societies had been granted legal recognition and some privileges by the Friendly Societies Act of 1793, building societies had to wait until 1836 for formal recognition. Without any Act setting out the rights and responsibilities of building societies, the formation of such societies involved a good deal of uncertainty. In particular there was doubt about the liability of individual members for the acts of the society. During the Napoleonic War years, the government did not look with favour on associations which did not have its legal approval, and severe penalties were imposed on secret societies. Societies were formed by groups of people meeting and drawing up articles of agreement and in signing these, members agreed to abide by those articles. Usually, following the friendly society pattern, societies carried on their business through trustees, indeed the founder members were sometimes themselves the trustees.

Given the legal uncertainties under which societies operated, it could be a very serious matter for the members if the affairs of the society did not run smoothly. Some fear can be sensed in some of their articles of agreement, and the search for forms of words which at least give the appearance of binding the group irrevocably together. The elaborate form of the introduction to the rules was repeated in the covenant at the end which the members signed. The sixteen articles of the Nelson's Union Inn Society were:

"... indented, made, concluded and fully agreed upon ..." by the six founder members, who "... mutually, reciprocally, jointly, separately and distinctly covenanted, declared and agreed, etc." The St. David's Society's seventeenth article was the following covenant, "And for the true and faithfull observance and performance of all and every the said above articles, rules and regulations the said several subscribers to the said club or society, who have hereunto set and subscribed their names and have become members of the said society, do each and every of them hereby, for himself, herself or themselves and for his, her or their heirs, executors, administrators and assigns, separately and not jointly, and for himself, herself or themselves only and for his, her or their own deeds only, covenant, promise, declare and agree to, and with the other and others of them the said subscribers to the said club or society, that he, she and they, and his, her and their executors, administrators and assigns shall and will faithfully and truly observe, perform and keep all and singular and every of these rules, articles and regulations herein before mentioned, expressed and contained and which are on his, her and their part or parts and behalf to be observed, performed, fulfilled and kept. As witness our hands this ... day, etc."

A second line of defence was to levy heavy fines on anyone not complying with the articles of agreement in any way. In many societies everyone had to take his turn in occupying the official positions, with changes made every six months, and a fine for anyone who refused. This rotation had the dual function of involving members more closely in the society, and of enabling them to check on the activities of their fellow members from a variety of viewpoints.

A few societies registered themselves as friendly societies. This made their legal position clear and extended to them the exemption from stamp duties granted to friendly societies by the 1793 Act. However, that Act and its successors up to the Friendly Societies Act of 1834 only made it lawful "to establish ... societies of good fellowship, for the purpose of raising from time to time, by subscriptions . . . a stock or fund for the mutual relief and maintenance of all and every the members thereof in old age, sickness and infirmity or for the relief of the widows and children of deceased members. . . ."[19] Clearly it might be represented that having a share in the mutual fund of a building society was some protection against such contingencies.

The Bradford Union Building Society, which from the details given by Naylor[20] was an ordinary building society, had as its first rule, "Resolved that we whose names are hereunder subscribed do form ourselves into a Society and by contribution of our own savings to a common fund and on the principle of mutual insurance for the maintenance of ourselves, wives and children in sickness, infancy, advanced age or any other natural state or contingency, we do hereby undertake to build 33 cottages or dwelling houses." With these noble aims the society succeeded in obtaining registration as a friendly society on July 15, 1824. The Barkerend Society (also of Bradford) had obtained registration some three months earlier.

The Friendly Societies Act of 1834 greatly widened the purposes for which friendly societies could be formed, adding to the detailed list above, "or for any other purpose which is not illegal".[21] Given the benefits which registration as a friendly society conferred, it is probable that many societies took advantage of the change. The widespread protest from building societies at the possibility of the withdrawal of one privilege, the exemption from certain stamp duties, in the 1830s, supports this view. Indeed it was these protests that led to the Building Societies Act of 1836.

The legality of building societies registering as friendly societies does not appear to have been tested either before or after the 1834 Act. However, in 1812 the question of whether building societies were in themselves illegal, was raised by the defendant in the action *Pratt v. Hutchinson*.[22] Hutchinson had stood guarantor for an advance that the Greenwich Union Building Society had made to a member. The member having fallen behind in his payments Pratt, the society's treasurer, sued Hutchinson. The defence offered was "That the Society was formed for raising a joint stock by small monthly subscriptions and making transferable shares of the same, and that in as much as the right of transfer of shares was of a limited nature, the society was a mischievous and dangerous undertaking and should be declared a public nuisance and grievance within the Statute, 6 Geo. I, c. 18; [The Bubble Act, 1720]. That the Society was not established either by Act of Parliament or Charter, or other legal authority, and that the obligation declared on was void in law by force of the said Statute."

The Society's article 30 said that every member should have full power to sell his shares privately provided the purchaser became a member and ". . . should on his admission become a party to the articles and duly execute and observe the same and no person should be permitted to purchase any share until he should have been first proposed and approved at a meeting of the said society by at least three-fourths of the members present".[23]

When Lord Chief Justice Ellenborough suggested that these very restrictive conditions of transfer took the case outside the Bubble Act, the defence changed its ground. It was then suggested that while the case did not come within the Bubble Act on the transfer issue, it did in terms of purpose. "Raising a sum by small subscriptions to build houses was one of the very speculations mentioned in Anderson's *History of Commerce* as one of the bubbles of the day that gave rise to the Act."[24] The Court found for the society without calling for an answer to the points raised by the defence. Thus, while building societies had no legal recognition from the State, at least their activities were held by the Courts to be not illegal in themselves.

What sort of people were the members of these early societies? We can infer something from the rates of subscription that were charged, for these are known for many societies. By far the most common subscription was 10s. per month. A few societies, such as John Arrowsmith's Society of Preston (1793) and the Tunstall Society (1816), charged £1 or a little more, the highest subscription being that of the Greenwich Union (1809), £2 per month. In addition a borrower would have to pay rent or interest to the Society of 6s. to 10s. per month in most cases, making a total outlay of nearly £1 per month. The earnings of building craftsmen were about £3 per month in the late eighteenth century, rising to a little over £4, against a background of war and rising food prices, in the period 1800–1820.[25] Bowley[26] estimated the wages of town labourers at 12s. per week in 1795 rising to 16s. in 1824; agricultural labourers 9s. in 1795 and 9s. 6d. in 1824. Artisans fared better; in 1795 in London 25s., and in the provinces, 17s. In 1824, 30s. in London and 24s. in the provinces.

It seems unlikely that many below the ranks of the better paid workers could afford membership of a society, given the wage rates at that time. Such a conclusion is strengthened when the danger of sickness and unemployment is borne in mind, because members in arrears were dealt with rather severely; and this view is confirmed by the known occupations of members. The six founder members of the Nelson's Union Inn Society, Manchester (1821)[27] were two shopkeepers, a joiner, a silk manufacturer, a fustian cutter, a merchant, a tailor and a milkman. The founder members of the Carnarvon Society (1825) were a draper, a chandler, a brazier and an architect. Other occupations listed in various societies are: cotton spinner, clogger, weaver, bricklayer, stonemason, travelling dealer, ironmonger, flour dealer and schoolmaster. In the Longridge Society,[28] Preston, nine of the twenty members were described as yeomen.

Clearly building societies were not wholly working class in their origins. From the first, the lower middle classes were well represented among the membership, and in a society like the Greenwich Union with high monthly subscriptions, they must have been dominant. The fact that the Droylesdon Society (1792) collected subscriptions quarterly scarcely suggests that its members were weekly paid workers. Even with the higher earnings of workers in the 1840s, and 10s. per month still the usual subscription, contemporary commentators had no doubts about the part the middle classes were playing. Tompkins states that building societies "have as their object the improvement of the middle classes by the best of all means—viz. their own unaided efforts".[29]

How far the early societies were building for owner occupation and how far for letting is an open question; at least they were not entirely concerned with owner-occupiers. The rules of Deritend Society, Birmingham (1781), state[30] "That each Subscriber for three [or, in fact, two] shares shall have One or more houses built." The Amicable, Birmingham, also had provision for members to take more than one share. When a member of the Longridge Society had been allocated a house by ballot he was at ". . . liberty to enter upon his own House, or put a tenant therein . . ."[31] Two members of that Society held more than one share and during its life, some members also took shares in another society. The frequent presence of shopkeepers and innkeepers among members suggests investment rather than occupation as the objective, as does the founding of a society in Dudley (pre-1895) by a prominent local master builder, Isaac Badger, and one in Birmingham (1791) by a local timber merchant, John Pritchett.

All the early societies held their meetings at inns, indeed there were few alternative places, and frequently the society took its name from the inn at which it met. In this respect building societies were following the friendly society pattern, with subscription night becoming something of a social occasion. The innkeeper played an important part in many societies. He was frequently custodian of the books, securities and unbanked money. Article 12 of the St. David's Society, Manchester, read, "That there shall be a box provided with four locks and four keys; the keys shall be kept by the landlord, president and stewards. The box shall at all times contain deeds, writings and books belonging to the society and all cash not deposited at the bank; the landlord shall give security to the satisfaction of the Society for the box and its contents."

Rather than pay rent for a room, societies normally undertook to consume some minimum amount of liquor. Article 8 of the Carnarvon Building Society illustrates the system. "That there shall be two persons appointed for three months ensuing to deliver to each member as he pays his subscription a Ticket which shall entitle him to the amount of Fourpence in malt liquor which Ticket shall be produced by the Landlord at the close of the evening's accounts, the duty to be taken alternately, the account paid by the Trustees."

As with other offices, the efficiency of drink stewards was ensured by fines. The Nelson's Inn Society[32] is a typical example. If a man refused to serve his turn as drink steward he was fined 2s. If a drink steward was not in the room for the start of the meeting at 7.30 p.m. he was fined 3d., which became 6d. at 8.00 p.m. If he had not arrived by 8.30 p.m. thirsty members showed their disapproval with a fine of 2s. 6d. The amount spent on drink was usually 3d. or 4d. per member, but in the Netherton Society it was 8d. The question, important to the landlord, of whether members with more than one share, should have to spend proportionately more on drink, was usually resolved in the member's favour. Thus the Bradford Building Institute (1825) had a rule that 4d. was to be spent on liquor, but no member was compelled to spend more than 4d. no matter how many shares he held.[33] In some societies where the officers were unpaid, they might be rewarded with spirits, paid for out of the society's funds, rather than the staple beer.[34]

In case members got too convivial, the societies armed themselves with appropriate powers in the rules. A rule, such as Article 14 of the St. David's Society, Manchester, was to be found in most societies. "If a member attends during club hours, or during the time business is transacted, disordered in liquor, he or she shall not be permitted to remain in the room, the President shall order him or her to withdraw, and if he or she does not immediately comply, he or she shall be fined 1s. and again be ordered to leave the room, and for every refusal be fined 2s. Any member who shall use offensive language to any member or members, shall be called to order by the President and if he or she does not desist from such discourse he or she shall be fined 2s. If any member fights or strikes another member in the club room, the member so offending shall be fined 5s."

In spite of the inclusion of women in the rule above as potential inebriates, blasphemers and pugilists, the fact that the societies did meet at inns raised difficulties for female members. A simple solution was found in some societies by absolving them from the duties of holding office or attending meetings. The Burslem United and Amicable Society ruled "that all female members shall be exempt from serving offices and attending meetings". The Amicable Society, Birmingham, had a rule, "That any member of the Society who shall Act for Women and Children shall only do the duty of one Share as a Committee Man".

The annual general meeting of a society could be quite a social occasion for the members, and rules sometimes provided for an extra yearly levy to cover the cost of the more lavish entertainment on that occasion. Also some important event in the progress of a society might be marked with a dinner. The Rowley Regis Society agreed on June 3, 1795[35] "To have a Bed of Beef cooch'd the next club night for the workmen and members as a Rearing with cabbage to it to be ready at 7 o'clock". This was probably to celebrate the completion of four houses, which, according to a contract signed earlier, were to be completed by June 10th.

The fact that societies met at inns must have helped in spreading knowledge of the principles and benefits of building societies. This is perhaps more obvious in the mid-nineteenth century, especially in the North of England, where a single inn would organise a succession of societies, as more people wished to join than could be accommodated in one. Yet as early as 1795 there were three societies all meeting at the Dudley Arms.[36]

The great strength of the early societies was that they were fully mutual; everyone had an equal interest as borrower and lender, or would have by the time the society terminated. Thus there was no need, at least in principle, to dispute about the terms on which advances were made, for everyone would in due course take an advance, and be subject to the conditions agreed. At the termination of the society each shareholder got his proportionate share of the accumulated property of the society. This did not eliminate disputes about details; these existed and were hotly contested. The Longridge Society, which aimed at building a house for each shareholder, after building and allocating the first four houses, decided to make some small improvements in the second four houses to be built. The members who had been allocated the first four houses felt aggrieved and took legal advice, which resulted in a letter from their solicitor to the society. Matters must have been settled amicably for the society proceeded smoothly to its termination.[37]

The difficulty of building identical houses for upwards of about twenty members is obvious and various methods were adopted for meeting this problem. Members' ideas on how the houses should be finished internally were likely to conflict, for complete uniformity would hardly be in keeping with the spirit of independence and self-sufficiency which was one of the drives leading people to join building societies. As long as the society organised the building, the simplest solution was that of the Bradford Union. Here, though houses were of uniform size, they were balloted for before erection so that members might make such alterations in the interior as they desired, presumably at their own expense.[38]

The Dudley Arms Society chose a different solution. At its termination all the houses built were put in good repair and a value placed on each house. The houses were then numbered and a ballot took place to allocate the houses. The members receiving houses with high valuations paid into a pool the difference between the value of their house and the house with the lowest value. This pool was then shared equally among the members. The result was that, taking the value of the house plus the net receipts from the pool, every member was treated equally.

The Burslem United Society (1807) took account of the varying preferences of members by creating three sorts of share, with subscriptions of 20s., 15s. and 10s. per month. The corresponding houses varied in the size and number of rooms, the largest being semi-detached.[39] The Greenwich Union allowed members to build to their own specification, provided they employed craftsmen acceptable to the society in the construction. If the house built was not sufficient security for the advance of £210 made on the shares, additional security had to be given.

Often, as with the Longridge Society, the group must have settled for building houses as nearly alike as possible and allocating them by ballot. By this means an equal chance of being allocated a slightly better house became a substitute for exact equality of the houses themselves. The difficulty of building identical houses seems the probable reason why societies gave up building operations. To make an advance in terms of money, allowing the member to provide security for it by building a house to his own specification, or purchasing an existing house, was a much easier solution. Thus towards the end of the period under discussion, a rule to that effect was to be found in most societies.

If a terminating society depends entirely on the fund raised by subscriptions, to fulfil its purposes, then in the early stages it will make slow progress. If twenty people subscribe 10s. per month it will be almost ten months before an advance of £100 can be made, and even with the interest on the first advance swelling the funds, it will be nearly as long again before a second £100 can be advanced. Later, of course, when the funds are being swelled by the interest on a large sum already advanced, new advances can be made more rapidly. The aim of members in joining the early societies was to get an advance, and any delay would be irksome.

It was soon realised that such delays could be reduced if the society could borrow money from outsiders, or if the richer members were prepared to lend money to the society, or pay their subscriptions in advance. The first year's income of the Longridge Society shows that share subscriptions yielded £155 18s. 6d. while the larger sum of £255 10s. was borrowed. A solicitor lent £500 to Hawker's Society, Birmingham (1794), in its first year of operation.[40] Rule 15 of the Bradford Union Society[41] was "That the President and Stewards for the time being shall be authorised to borrow by Notes of Hand or Bond such Sums of Money as may be wanted for the purposes of the Society". The frequent practice of charging an entrance fee, seldom more than £1, also helped a little in increasing the societies' funds at their inception.

To decide the order in which members were to have their advances—in many cases this meant the order in which they would occupy the houses built by the society—a variety of procedures was used. One method was to hold a ballot using dice or numbered cards. Towards the end of the period, the selling of advances to the highest bidder became more popular. In Nelson's Union Inn Society, when sufficient money was accumulated to make an advance, members marked on cards the amount they were prepared to give for the money. The result of these first bids was made known, the cards were then distributed for a second and third round of bidding, and the highest bidder got the advance. There are references to "three biddings" in a number of rules, which probably refer to this procedure.

Another method was to make advances to members in the order in which they joined the society, but such a method had the great disadvantage of discouraging members from joining the society after it had started business. The problem might be avoided altogether as in the Amicable Society, Birmingham. Rule 14 stated[42] "That as soon as the said houses are erected, they shall be let by the committee for as much Money as they can get for the same and that the Treasurer for the time being shall receive the Rents for the benefit of the said Society". The rents would, of course, swell the funds of the society, speeding the day when, its objective achieved, the ownership of the houses built would be transferred to the individual shareholders.

The ways in which borrowers paid their fellow members for the advantage of getting a loan varied. Basically there were three slightly different methods. Sometimes the modern solution was adopted, with the borrower owning the house, mortgaging it to the society and paying interest on the loan; the repayment of principal being taken care of by his subscription to the society. The Droylesden and Greenwich Union Societies both adopted this system, charging interest at 5%. The most common method of operation, and a reason for adopting it, is given by Tompkins,[43] thus, "At first the mode . . . appears to have been for the Society to purchase a plot of ground, which, after being built upon by the Society's funds, the tenements were then let by the Society to members or others, as tenants only, who paid a fair rent for the occupation; and this continued until the Society was in a condition to allot a tenement, or give to each member his share in full. This proceeding, it is very probable, was partly caused by the uncertainty, in a legal point of view, which attended a title when given from a Society which was still in operation and not legally recognised."

Under this system rent takes the place of interest, in equalising the position of those who obtain an advance early in the Societies' operations, compared with those who have to wait a long time for their advance. Low rents would be to the advantage of those getting early advances, high rents having the reverse effect. In some societies no rent was fixed, but bidding took place to see who was prepared to pay the highest amount. Thus the Carnarvon Society (1825) speaks in article 4 of "the highest bidder at 3 biddings for the rent". In the Longridge Society, after about eight years when its contemplated twenty houses must have been all erected, the receipts from rents were £80 per year, that is £4 per house. Since the houses cost about £90 to build, this is equivalent to a rate of interest of nearly 4½%. In Northwood's Society, Birmingham,[44] the secretary was accused, among other things, of negligence in failing to get eight houses completed on time. He thus lost the society a half-year's rent on each, which it was claimed amounted to £3 5s. per house. The society's shares were for £120, so that rent of £6 10s. per year would be the equivalent of interest at 5¼%.

A third method was to charge what later became known as redemption money. Here the monthly subscription was raised when a member had received an advance. In the Bradford Institute Society,[45] with shares of £120, the 10s. per month subscription was thus raised to £1. This is equivalent to interest at 5%. It is perhaps a reflection on the members of the society that a later rule should state "no interest is allowed or charged". Nelson's Union Inn Society similarly raised the subscription from 10s. to 18s. 4d., but since advances here were sold by bidding one cannot state a definite rate of interest. It would not need a very high premium to be paid for the advance, to raise the effective interest rate above 6%. The above evidence, admittedly fragmentary, shows that the rate of interest charged in these early societies was usually around 5%.

Mention has already been made of certain fines levied by societies, and of their importance as a means of ensuring the smooth running of the society. Where official positions were unpaid and the duties taken in rotation, fines were levied on those refusing to take office; this was true in some societies even where offices were filled by election, e.g. the Medlock Friendly Society, where to refuse to serve as Trustee if elected cost a fine of 5s. unless the member had held the office in the previous twelve months. Trustees, because they had keys to the society's box, were fined heavily; up to 5s. for being late at meetings, and 10s. for failing to send the keys, or for absence. If a member wished to obtain an advance, it was his duty to summon the survey committee to survey the property. Failure to give due notice to each member of the committee meant a fine of 10s. 6d. in respect of each member not notified. Any member of the survey committee who did not attend was also fined 10s. 6d. In one society, St. George's, Liverpool, there was even a fine of 5s. for smoking during the society's meetings.

The chief threat to the success of a society came from the failure to pay subscriptions and rents or interest regularly, and the fines imposed for such failures were generally heavy, though there were exceptions. Fines in the Medlock Friendly Society were high: one month in arrears, a fine of 1s. on both the subscription and the rent, rising to 4s. on both for the fifth month. The total fines for five months in arrears was thus £1 3s. 0d. At the other extreme was the Carnarvon Society: one month's arrears brought a fine of 6d., a second month 1s. and each subsequent month 1s., with the fines halved for additional shares. Fines were not the only sanction. When a member was in arrears for a given period, sometimes as low as three months, though more usually twelve, he ran the risk of being excluded from the society. In that event his share would be sold and he might receive, at best, the proceeds of the sale, after deduction of the fines that were due and a transfer fee of a guinea—at worst (e.g. with the Bradford Union and the Longridge Societies), nothing at all.

Even if all dues were promptly paid the success of a society depended a good deal on the quality of its officers. Where the society organised its own building operations the secretary's office in particular must have involved a great deal of work. In such circumstances filling this office by rotation would not be satisfactory, especially at a time when the ability to read and write was far from universal.[46] The secretary frequently held office longer than other officers, and usually received some payment, either occasional sums voted to him or a small salary. A salary of two guineas for the first six months, with a later increase, was a usual rule. The survey committee frequently divided the survey fees paid by the prospective borrowers, usually 5s. to 10s. More rarely the management committee received a small payment for each attendance—in the Longridge Society it was 6d. per meeting.

Since a member was likely to be excluded from the society, and perhaps forfeit his interest entirely, if he fell into arrears, it must have been a very serious matter for many people to commit themselves to a monthly subscription for a period of ten to fifteen years. With illness or unemployment as a constant possibility the risk involved was considerable, and must have been a serious brake on recruitment. The society's position was also insecure, if members were allowed to withdraw. Even a few withdrawals, in the early years of the society, might leave the remaining members liable for loans, and contracts for buildings, beyond their ability to pay.

A way out of this dilemma was found by allowing shares to be transferred. Thus a person could withdraw, provided he found someone to take over his obligations to the society. The amount a withdrawing member would lose would then depend on the price he received for his share. The market for such shares must have been a narrow one, and it was probably difficult to withdraw without some loss, in addition to the one-guinea transfer fee. The method of transferable shares was a reasonable compromise. The member did not lose everything if he fell on hard times, and the numbers in the society were maintained.

Many societies adopted a further safeguard, permitting shares to be sold only to persons acceptable to the members. For example, article 18 of the St. George's Society, Liverpool, allowed the sale and transfer of shares "unless there be an objection made by any Member or Members to the admission of such purchaser or transferee as a new member of the Society, and in that case it shall be left to the Committee to determine as to the propriety of admitting such new Member". Transfers in the Greenwich Union could take place only with the consent of three-quarters of the members present at a general meeting. Such a restriction seems reasonable in view of the close-knit nature of the societies and their social and economic functions.

In some societies withdrawals were allowed freely, as long as there were ample funds to meet all the advances which had already been allocated. Only rarely would any interest be allowed on withdrawals,[47] so that it would usually be in the member's interest to sell the share. Transfer fees were also payable when a share passed to an heir on the death of a member, the transfer being made only if the heir undertook all the obligations of membership.

With terminating societies it was not easy for a new member to join once the society had been in existence for a year or so. If members were to participate equally in the division of property at the society's winding-up, then all members would need to subscribe not only the same amount, but subscribe it at the same dates. A new member joining a society with a subscription of, say, 10s. per month, when it had been in existence for two years, would clearly be at an advantage if he paid only the back subscriptions of £12. He would have had the use of that £12 for the previous two years, while founder members' subscriptions were tied up in the society. Since rates of interest, as we have seen, played no formal part in most societies, it was difficult to decide the correct amount that a newcomer should pay, in addition to back subscriptions.

The Amicable Society, Birmingham, with twenty-eight founding members, stated in article 18, "That this Society shall not consist of more than fifty members" but no clue is offered in the articles as to the terms on which the twenty-two latecomers would be admitted. A number of societies founded towards the end of the period had a rule similar to the Medlock Friendly Society's article 6, "and any member who may enter after the receipt of any rent, shall not only pay up the amount of his subscription from the day of the date of these presents [i.e. the date the society was founded], but such other sum as each individual share may have gained or be deemed worth, or such sum or sums of money as the Trustees for the time being think proper". The Bradford Building Institute was more succcinct: newcomers were to pay whatever sum was "considered proper to make them equal with the older members".

Most societies did not consider this question when drawing up their rules—perhaps a reflection of the fact that few people would be able to afford the weight even of back subscriptions. To make accurate rules on the matter would have raised problems of an actuarial complexity beyond the abilities of most of the early managements. Indeed to consider new entrants would, to a degree, have been foreign to their nature. They were essentially small groups with social as well as economic ties, setting themselves a clear and limited objective. In some ten years they would achieve their purpose of giving each member the security that ownership of property brings: then they wound up. Frequently as the society drew towards its close, and the prospect of ownership became more immediate, subscriptions were raised. Thus the terminating day would be brought nearer, when the properties would be conveyed to the members.

While there are close similarities between the societies of the 1780s and those of the 1820s some developments had taken place. The methods of societies changed as experience pointed to certain weaknesses in the original pattern of organisation. Few of the later societies engaged in building their own houses; they were deterred by the administrative problems and the frictions which might arise between members. Determining the order in which members were allocated advances by the order in which they joined the society, was a hindrance to recruitment. The later societies avoided this by giving the advance to the member who was prepared to offer most for it. The difficulty of withdrawing from a society if a member's financial circumstances changed must have seriously affected recruitment to the earlier societies, and here again the later ones show some adjustment, making withdrawal easier and even in one case paying some interest to those withdrawing.

Chapter Two

THE BUILDING SOCIETIES ACT, 1836*

When the 1834 Friendly Societies Act extended the purposes for which such societies could be formed, by adding to the list of specific purposes, the words "or any other purpose which is not illegal", the way was open for societies to obtain legal protection. That building societies were not illegal in themselves had been established in 1812 in *Pratt v. Hutchinson*. However, the period during which they could register under the 1834 Act was short, for in 1836 a separate Act was passed specifically to encourage and protect benefit building societies.

Accounts of the events leading to the passing of the 1836 Act are somewhat conflicting, but the issue that created building society pressure for a separate Act, was the transfer of shares in societies. Penalties for default in paying subscriptions were heavy, though justifiably so. Fear of incurring these penalties, given the normal uncertainties about health and employment, would have severely handicapped the growth of societies, if they had not wisely provided that members could escape such penalties by transferring their shares. Clearly the ability of members to transfer shares freely was important to the movement.

The immediate cause of building society alarm was a threat to impose a stamp duty on the transfer of shares. The imposition of such duty, according to the St. Stephen's Society, Salford, would prevent "the more humble part of the community, when overtaken by adverse circumstances, from disposing of their shares, except to great disadvantage".[1]

In evidence before the Royal Commission in 1871,[2] Mr. J. Hosking, a leader of the movement in Liverpool, said that some legislation in 1835 about taxing the transfer of shares had alarmed societies, and a deputation representing societies in Liverpool and Manchester waited upon the Hon. Thomas Spring Rice (later Lord Monteagle) the Chancellor of the Exchequer. They explained the working of building societies to him and he was sufficiently impressed to say that he thought such societies deserved encouragement and should have a special Act to regulate them. Naylor agrees the date, 1835, but gives a different cause for alarm, "A legal decision in 1835 that threatened to deprive them of some portion of

* *Notes on this chapter appear on page 284.*

the exemption from stamp duty, stimulated action on the part of those interested in Building Societies."[3] An examination of the High Court's decisions for 1835 does not reveal any decision likely to raise alarm on this issue. According to Mr. Hosking's account, after the return of the deputation, a Manchester solicitor, Mr. Hewitt, drafted a Bill, covering the points that led to disquiet, which was not passed in 1835, but the Government did pass (this much at least is certain!) an Act in 1836.

Mr. Hosking's date, 1835, may be open to challenge; it is known that a government measure, reforming stamp duties, introduced in March 1836 would have affected share transfers. However, the fears of building societies may have been quite unjustified, for Spring Rice intended no substantial change in the law. He said in debate, "By the law as it stood an *ad valorem* duty was chargeable on the amount of consideration for the transfer of shares in Joint Stock Companies—such as railroad, canal and banking shares. With this he did not mean to meddle, but he intended to super-add a small tax upon the first issue of those shares".[4] Given the brief interval between the introduction of that measure and the introduction of the Building Societies Bill, just over two months, it seems unlikely that the Liverpool and Manchester Societies would have drafted a bill themselves.

Whether the Liverpool and Manchester delegation was a response to the government measure of March 1836, or whether it had taken place a year before, that measure led to other protests from building societies. Between May 2 and May 16, 1836, eleven petitions were received, all from Manchester and the surrounding district.[5] They included petitions from the Manchester and Salford District Building Association and the Pendleton Building Association. This suggests that building societies were forming associations to take joint action, but it must be remembered that at this time some ordinary building societies called themselves building associations. The Pendleton Association may have been of this type; the Manchester and Salford was more likely a true association for joint action. The arrival of three petitions from building societies in Bury on the same day, May 11th, also suggests some sort of local co-operation.

Whatever the date of the interview with the Chancellor of the Exchequer, he kept his word and on June 14, 1836, the House of Commons Journal records that leave was given by the House to bring in a Bill for the Regulation of Benefit Building Societies, the Bill to be prepared by Mr. Poulett Thompson (President of the Board of Trade) and Mr. Chancellor of the Exchequer. Mr. W. L. Harle said[6] that the originator of the bill was in fact Mr. W. O. Ord, the Member for Newport, Isle of Wight.

Part of the government's support for building societies derived from their experience with savings banks. Such banks for small savings were established under an Act of 1817,[7] and gave the depositors a rate of interest, 3d. per cent per day (slightly above 4½% p.a.) so favourable that the Exchequer lost money on their operations. The government's hope was that by encouraging building societies, small savers would use those institutions, with no government guarantee, in preference to savings banks, with a consequent saving to the Exchequer. Hosking quoted Spring Rice as saying, in introducing the Building Societies Bill, "We lose every year by the Savings Banks; and if we encourage these societies, we shall benefit the Government funds by getting the people to save in these Societies instead of in Savings Banks".[8] The 1817 Act had given friendly societies the privilege of investing their funds in the savings banks. The 1834 Friendly Societies Act extended the privilege to building societies.

The government's motives in passing the 1836 Act are revealed in Section 6. The right to deposit funds in savings banks was the one privilege of friendly societies which was not conferred on building societies. Section 6 reads, "Provided that nothing herein contained shall authorise any benefit building society to invest its funds or any part thereof in any Savings Bank or with the Commissioners for the reduction of the National Debt".

Section 8 allayed building society fears about stamps on share transfers; it stated "That no rules of any such society or any copy thereof nor any transfer of any share or shares in any such society shall be subject or liable to or charged with any stamp duty or duties whatsoever". In fact, the question had already been dealt with in Section 4 which extended to building societies all the privileges of friendly societies, and these included the wide exemption from stamp duties of the 1829 Friendly Societies Act (10 Geo. IV, c. 56, s. 37).

This concentration on the question of stamps on share transfers rather than on consideration of the wider privileges granted under the Friendly Societies Acts, was to put many societies to needless expense for some years. Many societies seem to have been unaware that they could claim exemption from stamps on such documents as mortgages, until the mid-1840s (see below, p. 81).

The Bill quickly passed the Commons without any sustained discussion on the floor of the House; the third reading was on June 23rd. Its passage in the Lords was almost equally swift, with the Commons receiving the Bill back from the Lords, without amendment, on July 5th. The swiftness of Parliamentary action rather defeated the purpose of five petitions in support of the Bill from Newcastle-upon-Tyne, for the first of these did not arrive until July 4th and the remaining four until July 8th.[9] While the speed of the Bill's passage must have been encouraging to its sponsors and protagonists, it had drawbacks. The Act was drafted without substantial discussion among the interested parties and passed too quickly for detailed discussion in Parliament.[10] The result was that the Act was ill fitted to carry out the purposes envisaged in its preamble. Indeed its bad draftsmanship became a byword among legal commentators, to say nothing of the time that the courts were to spend elucidating its obscurities.

The preamble to the Act recognises the existence of building societies "principally among the industrious classes for the purpose of raising by small periodical subscriptions a fund to assist the members . . . in obtaining a small freehold or leasehold property", and states that the purpose of the Act is to protect and encourage such societies.

Section 1 grants the privileges of the Act only to societies with shares not exceeding £150 and subscriptions £1 per month per share. The apparent intention of encouraging only small societies was negated by the lack of any restriction on the number of shares an individual could hold.[11] Members were free to make legally binding rules governing the affairs of the society and to "impose and inflict such reasonable fines, penalties and forfeitures" upon members breaking the rules "as the members think fit". No member was to receive "any dividend or interest by way of annual or other periodical profit upon any shares . . . until the amount or value of his or her share shall have been realised, except on the withdrawal of such member".

Section 2 exempted interest charged by societies on their advances from the provisions of the Usury Laws. Societies were free to decide, under Section 3, the forms of documents they required—transfers, agreements, etc.—and these were to be annexed to, and certified with, the rules.

Section 4 gave rise to more difficulties than any other. It expressly re-enacted the Friendly Societies Acts of 1829 and 1834 "so far as the same or any part thereof may be applicable to the purpose of any benefit building society. . . ". There was no hint of guidance to help in judging the circumstances in which those Acts would be regarded as being applicable to building societies.

Section 5 enabled mortgages to the society to be discharged by a receipt of the trustees, without the need for reconveyance, thus saving members a good deal of money at the termination of a society.

Section 7 extended the Act to cover all societies established before June 1, 1836, on the certification of their rules, as directed in the Friendly Societies Acts adding "and that no such Society shall be required to alter in any manner the rules under which they are now respectively governed". Existing societies could scarcely have hoped for more generous treatment.

Altogether the Act granted substantial privileges to societies, while placing practically no clear restrictions on them. The phrasing of the preamble to the Act, and the Act's close relationship with the Friendly Societies Acts, suggests, as the Royal Commission of 1871 inferred, that Parliament was concerned to assist the "industrious classes" to become owners of small properties. The Friendly Societies Acts were frequently reviewed, with new Acts in 1840, 1846, 1850, 1855, 1858 and 1860, and these Acts show two things: first, a fairly continuous movement to central control, with the powers of the certifying barrister,[12] later the Registrar, gradually enlarged; second, a determination to confine the privileges granted to friendly societies to the "industrious classes". For instance, the Act of 1840 excluded societies granting individual insurance policies in excess of £200. This exclusion was aimed at the mutual life insurance offices, which had been registering as friendly societies in order to obtain exemption from stamp duties.[13]

With building societies things were different, and Parliament did not concern itself with them again, except marginally until the 1870s. During the intervening years they were to change considerably in both size and organisation. The large societies of the 1870s did not have much in common with the sort of society that the legislature seems to have had in mind when it passed the 1836 Act. As the pattern of building society organisation changed, in default of guidance from the legislature, the societies came increasingly to depend on the courts for guidance.[14] Case law had to be created to cover the many contingencies not foreseen in 1836. Such a situation gave the societies considerable freedom to respond to the opportunities of the times, but such freedom was expensive in terms of legal fees. In some ways, at least, the clearer definition of their powers which successive Acts gave to friendly societies would have been very welcome, and advantageous to building societies.

The 1836 Act got itself a bad reputation in both legal and building society circles. The Royal Commission of 1871 said of it, "Again the Benefit Building Societies Act itself is probably one of the worst drawn which yet remain on the statute book. The language of its first and leading section is incapable of grammatical construction and the Act so bristles throughout with doubts that, to use the words of a witness, 'almost every line of it has to be brought to the test of judicial interpretation'."[15] A legal commentator, in 1851, held that new legislation was required "... to avoid the doubts alluded to and the great inconvenience of frequent references to other statutes, containing numerous provisions inapplicable to building societies; which is a very clumsy plan of legislation, and can only be attributed to a ridiculous economy and the usual indifference exhibited . . ., in the preparation of Acts of Parliament".[16] A Lord Chancellor commented ". . . the whole language is so excessively confused that, in truth, looking at it grammatically it is unintelligible".[17] These judgements are not unfair but there were other ingredients in the mixture, for the certifying barrister, the Courts and the societies themselves, in drawing up their rules, all added their portion of confusion to the history of the following forty years.

To take the certifying barrister first. His powers were very limited under the law; societies were to be certified provided that their objects came within the scope of the Act, and that their rules in no way contravened the law. There were three barristers, one each in Dublin, Edinburgh and London. Only a handful of societies were formed in Ireland so the Dublin registrar's work was unimportant. There were more societies, though no great number, in Scotland, and at Edinburgh great laxity was the rule. The Royal Commission's view was that, "The so-called register of friendly societies for Scotland is in fact a mere waste book of the most insufficient description and most wretchedly kept . . . Latterly it never distinguished the nature of the Society registered, except in so far as it can be guessed from the title. It is in such a state that the law cannot possibly be carried out."[18]

Again they found the Registrar, Mr. A. C. Ritchie, who had no reserve in throwing his office open to them, a man of courteous manners and benevolent character, but "Mr. Ritchie is now perfectly incompetent for the fulfilment of his duties. He does not in fact fulfil them . . . In respect of building societies especially, bodies have received the Registrar's certificate which appear to be entirely out of the purview of the law, and indeed Mr. McKenzie [Ritchie's assistant] (who it must be remembered is the real interpreter of the law in Scotland) on his examination before us appeared to be perfectly ready to sanction any rule approved by a general meeting."[19]

In England, things were different, Mr. Tidd Pratt, the certifying barrister from 1834 to 1870, was a strong character, steadfast in his concern for the law. However, his view of what was legal under the Act changed, on occasion somewhat erratically, during his term of office; since his power was limited to certifying rules and changes therein, this did not make for uniformity as between societies. Many rules accepted in early societies were struck out of the draft rules of later applicants. His efforts to keep the growing movement narrowly within the confines of the 1836 Act were unsuccessful. His only real control was over new societies as they registered, or existing societies when they submitted alterations in their rules, and this was insufficient to meet the case. Though his purpose may have been consistent, it did not appear so to the societies. New societies understandably objected to having proposed rules struck out, which would have given them powers which all their local neighbours—

registered earlier—possessed. A letter to *The National*,[20] a weekly devoted to building society matters, asked "What was the use of trying to register rules with Mr. T. Pratt if the week after he has enrolled one on a certain principle he turns tail and refuses to do the same for others . . ." In his efforts to control societies he seems at times to have exceeded the powers granted to him by the Act.

The following are some of the views that building society officials gave to the Royal Commission about the Registrar. "The Registrar has this arbitrary power, that even supposing that a clause was inserted in the rules, and that there was nothing antagonistic to it in the Act, he has still always held that he had the power of striking it out."[21] A clause concerning the method of winding up a society approved in a number of cases was struck out and "he [the Registrar] said 'It is not because it is not in uniformity with the Act, but I do not think it is a good rule'." Mr. Higham, discussing another occasion, added, "He acted in a dictatorial and arbitrary manner".[22] Another witness, Mr. Peacock, said, "You may send one rule one day and it is certified and you may send another rule another day and it is refused. It was frequently so in the later part of Mr. Tidd Pratt's day."[23] Mr. Ingle's view concerned the office itself. "If you ask me my opinion of the duties of the Registrar, I think they are a perfect farce."[24] As early as 1849 Scratchley complained of the lack of authority to guide societies, which, in his view, "has been the cause of considerable mischief".[25]

In spite of Pratt's efforts the rules of building societies were often badly drawn. The movement was growing too rapidly for effective supervision, and managers frequently had little legal knowledge or experience. Perhaps the Lord Chancellor Lord Cranworth's comments in 1854, on the rules of the Camberwell Society, suffice to show that neither the Act nor the Registrar's rulings were the sole source of confusion. "I do not know whose duty it was or is, to have framed proper rules for this Society; but on whomsoever that duty did devolve, I think the party has very much misunderstood his duty. I have been endeavouring to interpret and execute the rules, but it is quite obvious that no one could have meant such rules as are here introduced; and it is very much to be hoped, if these Societies are to continue, that some person will frame rules which can be carried into due operation without manifest injustice."[26]

To the judiciary the decisions of the Courts no doubt showed consistency in the interpretation of the Statutes, but the managers of building societies did not always agree. The result was criticism of the Courts and a strong demand for new legislation to put an end to the doubts raised by judicial decisions, a demand which was ultimately (in 1874) successful. Mr. Ingoldby, chairman of the Planet, at that time one of the largest societies, said, in 1871, "The legal decisions have been so conflicting during the past four or five years, that the uncertainty has led to a sort of panic amongst the members".[27] Dr. von Plener summed up the position as follows, "In addition to these enactments (the Building Societies and Friendly Societies Acts) there have been many, often contradictory decisions of the courts, which in almost every instance, have been evoked by the obscurity of the law, and the frequently incomprehensible nature of the societies' own rules."[28]

A major source of confusion was section 4, which expressly re-enacted the Friendly Societies Acts of 1829 and 1834. These two acts were, as noted above, amended a number of times and finally repealed by an 1854 Act, to consolidate and amend the laws relating to friendly societies (13 & 14 Vic. c. 65). A basic question was whether the various amendments to the Friendly Societies Acts of 1829 and 1834 and their repeal also affected those acts as they were incorporated in the 1836 Building Societies Act. The legislature sometimes intended that they should be. Section 12 of the 1846 Friendly Societies Act (9 & 10 Vic. c. 27) amending the procedure for certification, was to cover all registrations made under the 1834 Friendly Societies Act "or to which the provisions of that Act have been extended and made affiliate". Though this precise point was not raised, the Courts took a different view; any amendment of the Friendly Societies Acts, for the purpose of regulating friendly societies, did not affect those Acts insofar as they were part of the 1836 Building Societies Act. The point was raised in *Walker v. Giles and Fort* in 1849. The case concerned, incidentally, the applicability of the exemptions from stamp duty, granted in the 1829 Act, to building societies in the light of amendments made by the 1840 Friendly Societies Act. Chief Justice Wilde held[29] that "Before the 3 and 4 Vic. c. 73 (the 1840 Act) passed, the exemptions in the 10 Geo. IV. c. 73 (the 1829 Act) were incorporated in the 6 and 7 Will. IV. c. 32 (the 1836 Act) as if they were expressly re-enacted; that being so the subsequent Act could not limit the exemptions, without taking notice of any other than the Friendly Societies Act".

This judgement came too late to help the Certifying Barrister. Besides changing his title to Registrar the 1846 Friendly Societies Act had altered the procedure for registering societies. Formerly a society had to send two copies of the rules to the Certifying Barrister. When these had been certified, one copy was returned to the society and one sent to the local clerk of the peace to enter on the Court rolls. Now one of the two copies was to be returned to the society and the other retained on file by the Registrar. Was the change to apply to building societies? Mr. Tidd Pratt in London decided it should and acted accordingly. From 1846 to 1850 he followed the procedure of the new Act. The Friendly Societies Act

1850 called for a reversion to the earlier procedure, and in 1850, he reverted to it, but whether he did so because he now regarded the 1850 Act as the relevant one, or because he, in the light of the judgement above, thought he should never have made the change is not known. The Registrar in Edinburgh, having made the change in line with the 1846 Act, continued with that procedure, rather illogically ignoring the call in the 1850 Act to revert to the original procedure. The Registrar for Ireland, showing the keener appreciation of his race for the cross currents of the British Parliament, covered himself against all eventualities by illegally demanding three copies of the rules from new societies after 1846. One copy he returned to the society, one was sent to the clerk of the peace, the third was filed.[30] Surveying this confusion the Royal Commission commented, "Hence it is to be doubted whether at the present day there is any valid registration since 1850. A legal doubt of such magnitude quite overshadows all the lesser ones which flow in individual cases from the many fluctuations in practice of the late registrar for England."[31]

The confusion did not end with the Registrars but spilled over into the lower courts, as the Secretary of the Temperance Society found. "I thought Mr. Pratt Taylor was going to commit me to prison, for I directed his attention to certain sections of the Act of Parliament of 10 Geo. IV [the 1829 Act] and he said, 'You must not direct my attention to this, Sir, this is a repealed Act' and he would not believe me but what that was the case."[32]

Whether or not societies had the right to borrow money was an issue of central importance to the movement, and one about which doubts were raised. We have seen that the early societies did borrow money and this was very helpful in allowing members to get advances more quickly than would be possible from subscriptions alone. The 1836 Act made no mention of borrowing powers, but in 1838 the Treasury issued a booklet, *Instructions for the Establishment of Benefit Building Societies*, which contained a set of model rules prepared by Mr. Tidd Pratt[33] and included a rule which dealt with borrowing powers. It was narrowly drawn, allowing short-term borrowing from the society's bank.

Earlier societies had exercised wider borrowing powers than this, borrowing from members and the public. Societies extant at the passing of the 1836 Act could have their rules certified without being required to alter them in any manner (s. 7). Thus from the beginning rules giving wide borrowing powers had been certified.

Early commentators had no doubts about the legality of borrowing. In 1845 Tompkins stressed the importance of the power to borrow in the early years of a society.[34] Stone, in 1851, saw nothing wrong with borrowing so long as a limit was placed on it. "The provision in the statute which enables the members to make rules and regulations for the government and guidance of the society, legalises the usual rule which gives the directors authority to borrow money for the purpose of advancing it to a borrower, *not exceeding the prospective amount of six months receipts*, because such a course is perfectly consistent with the object of these societies, and the general provisions of the statute, and is kept within moderate bounds."[35]

In the early 1850s the Registrar began to review rules on borrowing more closely. While terminating societies had only a limited use for borrowed funds, permanent societies might usefully borrow much larger sums, indefinitely, and the change in the Registrar's attitude may have been a response to the emergence of permanent societies. Another possible cause for his concern was the decision in *O'Connor v. Bradshaw* in 1850.[36] Here what was in effect an unregistered building society had established a bank for receiving deposits on the security of the society's property. This was held to be contrary to the Bank Act, and a similar sort of business was beginning to emerge among some building societies with deposit departments.

Whatever the cause of the Registrar's change of view, by 1853 he was certainly refusing to certify the borrowing rules of some societies. Mr. Warner submitted a borrowing rule in 1853 which was struck out, though a similar rule submitted in 1856 was allowed.[37] The response of societies was varied; some, such as the Burnley Society, "tried to do without borrowing for four or five years, but it [the Society] didn't progress, it went back".[38] Another attempt by the society to get borrowing powers, in 1863, was not allowed. Other societies, unable to get sanction for borrowing powers, none the less went ahead and borrowed.[39] One effect of the Registrar's action must have been to inhibit societies with approved borrowing rules from making any change in their rules, however necessary, for fear that in the process of registering their new rules they might lose their borrowing power.

In 1857 the Registrar began to have doubts about the more severe attitude he was adopting and on July 6th he took the opinion of the Attorney-General, Sir Richard Bethell (later Lord Westbury). The opinion read thus, "I am of the opinion that a rule authorising the raising of money for the purposes of a society would be repugnant to the fundamental principles of a society and it cannot be certified as a rule in conformity to Law and with the previous provisions of the Statute."[40] In the light of this opinion the Registrar refused all borrowing rules; at least that was the general view of those giving evidence to the Royal Commission. But the refusal was not quite universal. The Durham County

Society had no borrowing power when it was formed, but in August 1867 it submitted some alterations to its rules, including an unlimited borrowing rule, and these were registered.[41] Maybe this was just an isolated case, illustrating the inconsistency with which several witnesses had charged the Registrar.

The general situation was very unsatisfactory; some existing societies with borrowing rules certified earlier had received very large sums on deposit; if borrowing was not legal, what redress did lenders have? The position of depositors in societies without borrowing rules was even more dubious. It says much for the confidence of the public in building societies that these questions were not raised in the courts, at least not for some years. In the words of the Royal Commission, "Although the word 'deposit' is according to the practice of the registrar's office invariably struck from building society rules, the excision of the word is at all events nugatory, since the sums of money deposited with building societies are in not a few cases of enormous amount. So great indeed is the confidence of the public in these societies that many of them have to resort to various means to check the influx of deposits."[42]

The confidence of the public was all the more surprising in the light of a case[43] concerning the Kent Benefit Building Society (1860). Here the trustees of a building society had borrowed money to illegally purchase land,[44] giving a mortgage on the land as security. Interest on the loan not being paid, the mortgagee sold the land, and since the proceeds were insufficient he sued the trustees for the difference which they then paid. The trustees then claimed this money from the society. Their claim was disallowed. It was held that the society, through the trustees, had borrowed for an illegal purpose. This should have raised the further question of the position of the trustees, when the borrowing itself was illegal.

The next move came from the societies, who found a way round the Registrar's refusal of borrowing powers. They achieved their object by creating realised or paid-up shares. The Act of 1836 stated in section 1, that "No member shall receive or be entitled to receive from the funds of such society any interest or dividend by way of annual or periodical profit upon any shares in such society, until the amount of value of his or her share shall have been realised, except on the withdrawal of such member . . .". Shares were created with very low values, £10 and less, although the Act mentioned shares of £150 and implied a value at least great enough to build a house. A share of low value would soon be completed, or could be paid up outright, and the intention of the Act regarding the payment of interest could thus be evaded. James Taylor, of Birmingham, manager of a large group of societies, said, "This section of the Act is evaded and everybody knows it".[45] The secretary of the

Burnley Society admitted that they called their deposits paid-up shares (£10).[46] The Registrar resisted such moves at first, but later acquiesced, as long as interest was only paid annually.[47]

Even this latter restriction was evaded in one case. J. B. Reay of Liverpool conducted two permanent societies. Both paid interest annually, one at Christmas, the other in June. Both had small paid-up shares, so that by splitting his investment between the two, the shareholder could effectively get half-yearly interest payments.[48] The way for these practices had been made easier by a decision in a case in 1847,[49] where it was held that a member could hold more than one share. Ultimately the Registrar refused to accept rules involving such shares. "The other forms of loans, viz. paid-up, preference or realised shares, although sanctioned for some years by the registrar's office and therefore practised by many important societies, is now held by the Registrar, on the strength of an opinion by Sir Roundell Palmer, to be illegal."[50]

The whole question of borrowing powers was eventually cleared up in a series of court cases. The most important of these was *Laing v. Reed*[51] heard on November 4, 1868, which was brought as a test case. It concerned the Northern Counties P.B.B. Society and turned on the legality of a rule which empowered the trustees of the Society "from time to time as occasion should require, to borrow money at interest not exceeding 5%, for which they might give their own personal security and they should be indemnified out of the first funds of the Society, which should be received, provided that the total amount of money so borrowed should not at any time exceed two-thirds of the amount for the time being secured by the mortgages of the Society". The Court held that there was nothing in the rule repugnant to the Building Societies Act or contrary to the general law of the land and that the rule was valid.

It will be noted that the rule is precise in stating a limit to the borrowing of money, and only temporary borrowing was envisaged. The latter point was not important, but the precise limit was: the Lord Chancellor said, "If the rule had authorised the trustees to raise an unlimited sum of money wholly regardless of the contributions which might be made by members, that no doubt would be contrary to the interest and scope of the Act."

After this judgement the Registrar was prepared to accept borrowing rules, provided they stated a limit not above two-thirds of mortgage assets. This judgement gave some comfort to the societies. Nevertheless, some incidental remarks of Lord Giffard, in supporting the Lord Chancellor's ruling in the case, must have given cause for anxiety to a number of societies which had created something like savings banks in connection with their building society activities. He said that if a society's rules had made it into a banking company that would have been repugnant to the 1836 Act and hence illegal. Many societies hastened to certify alterations in rules to bring them into line with sanctioned rules, to protect their trustees and depositors. This protection proved to be very important in the light of a series of later cases.

The first[52] of these, heard later in the same year as *Laing v. Reed*, concerned a person who had lent money to the National Provincial Society. Unable to withdraw the money loaned, he petitioned in the Chancery Court to have the Society wound up. The directors of the Society were not empowered by the rules to borrow money at all. In the light of this the Court decided that the petitioner had no legal or equitable claim against the society.

The second case, in 1870, involved the Victoria Society[53] which had a rule authorising unlimited borrowing. Although depositors were regarded as members of the Society, "persons merely joining the Society to invest or deposit money should not be called upon, or entitled to take any part in the management of the Society". The Society was in financial difficulties and the depositors were trying to enforce their claims against the shareholders. The court held that the rule authorising the taking of money on deposit without limit was invalid and that the depositors were not entitled to have any call made upon shareholders for the repayment of their deposits. The depositors also claimed that because they were excluded from the management, they were not members and so were not bound by certain other rules. In considering this the court held, incidentally, that the directors had no power to take deposits from persons not members. This judgement naturally created a good deal of anxiety among the depositors in many societies.

In the case of *Richardson v. Williamson and another*[54] in January 1871, these matters were carried a stage further. Mrs. Richardson had lent money to the Imperial P.B.B.S. and was given a receipt by Messrs. Williamson and Lawson, two of the society's directors. Mrs. Richardson wanted to withdraw her money and, with the Society in financial difficulties, she could not. The Society had no borrowing rule. In the light of the National Provincial case above, "The plaintiff was advised that the Society had no power under the Benefit Building Societies Act to borrow money and that her only remedy was against the defendants, not the society". Lord Chief Justice Cockburn found for Mrs. Richardson, remarking, "The defendants apply for loans without taking the trouble to ascertain whether the Society which they represent, has any authority to borrow money, and by doing so, it cannot be doubted that they represent that the Society has this authority."[55] In the light of this decision many building society directors were placed in an unenviable position for they were being held personally liable for any deposits taken without authority in the rules. This series of decisions certainly added urgency to the efforts that building societies were already making, for other reasons, to get some amendments to the 1836 Act passed by the legislature.

The manner in which building societies might legally be wound up was another issue giving rise to confusion. If the society's affairs proceeded smoothly, there was no difficulty, for the rules of terminating societies set out the way in which assets were to be distributed, at termination, and in permanent societies the question did not arise. If, however, things did not go according to plan, and a society wished to discontinue, there were difficulties. Under section 26 of the Friendly Societies Act, 1829, a society could be dissolved with the approval of five-sixths of its members. This was one of the sections of the Friendly Societies Acts thought to be "applicable to the purposes of building societies", though some features of it did not fit building society practice very well. In the period 1838–48, according to W. L. Harle[56] many societies were wound up outside the courts, presumably under section 26, "in circumstances which were partially disastrous to themselves". This is probably a reference to the strong bargaining position of advanced members in societies trying to wind up. They were legally bound only to repay their loans over a period of years. If the society wished to realise its assets at once, such advanced members might force the society to accept a good deal less than the nominal debt, in settlement of the advance.

The situation changed with the passing of an Act in 1848 governing the winding up of companies. In a case in 1851, concerning the Sherwood Loan Society,[57] it was held that, although registered as a friendly society, because its object was profit, the provisions of the Winding Up Acts and not section 26 of the Friendly Societies Act 1829 should govern its winding up. The Sherwood Loan Society had much in common with building societies, except that it made loans to members on the security of other assets than real estate. The fact that it was registered as a friendly society was held to be unimportant by Vice-Chancellor Kindersley, "I cannot see any such distinction between loan companies and societies of this nature to induce me to say that they do not come within the Winding Up Acts". This suggested that the Winding Up Acts would also be applicable to building societies, a suggestion that was confirmed in 1856.[58] It was held that societies registered under the Building Societies Act came within the operation of these Acts; hence they could not be wound up outside the courts. The expenses involved in winding up under court supervision would be likely to take most of the assets of a small building society.

There was some hope that the simpler procedures for winding up of the Industrial and Provident Societies Act, 1862, might apply to building societies; in one case this was held to be so, *In re The Midland Counties B.B.S.* 1864.[59] However that decision was overruled,[60] and it was now held that building societies came under the Companies Act, 1862, sections 199-208. These sections applied to companies which though not registered under the 1862 Act, may be wound up according to its provisions, but only compulsorily by the Chancery Court. There was an alternative, but a very difficult one, considered by Scratchley in these terms, ". . . an arrangement to dissolve by the express consent of every individual concerned whether as unadvanced or advanced shareholder cannot easily be made; as it is always difficult and frequently impossible to obtain such consent, since the various classes of members have diverse interests. The ruinously costly process of compulsory winding up by the Chancery Division of the High Court is unsuited to the case of an insolvent Building Society. . . . In a few cases winding up has involved not merely the loss of past investments, but also contributions to the claims of outside creditors".

Messrs. Higham and Hoare in evidence to the Royal Commission said they did not know what was the law in this respect. All attempts to frame rules covering voluntary dissolution were struck out. Hoare said they went to the Registrar and asked him what they were to do, and his answer was, "I cannot tell you".[61] The lack of rules concerning dissolution could be expensive in another way, with disaffected members presenting bills in equity demanding dissolution of societies, and this involved societies in the expense of defending such actions.

There were many other matters, besides borrowing powers and winding up, in which the legal position was only slowly defined by court decisions; one of these was the redemption of mortgages. Rulings regarding redemptions were at first very disadvantageous to the borrower. For a time it was held that an advanced member of a terminating society could redeem his property only by paying to the society, without any discount for early payment, the sum of all future payments of subscriptions and interest that would become due during the expected life of the society. If, in the event, the society did not terminate at the expected date, he would be liable for further payments until the actual termination, in spite of the fact that he would have had no voice in the society's affairs in the interim.[62]

In 1854 there was a ruling that he could claim, as a deduction, the same bonus as would be paid to a withdrawing member,[63] though he was still liable to extra payments if the society did not terminate at the expected date. Some societies attempted to ease the position by setting a definite date for termination in the rules, rather than setting some monetary objective, which would fix the termination date. Eventually a carefully drawn rule of this type satisfied the court in 1870.[64]

An alternative solution was to give special powers to the society's directors. "Where, however, the rules expressly empowered the managers to determine the amount of money to be paid by any mortgagor in full for the claims of the society upon his property, on payment of which the share or shares, in respect of which the security was made, were wholly extinguished, it was held that the payment of the sum fixed and the receipt endorsed upon the mortgage was a total extinguishment of the shares and that the member was not liable to pay any further subscriptions. *Priestly v. Hopwood* 12 *Weekly Rep.* 1031."[65] Not all societies would be prepared to give their directors such great power. In the permanent societies, since there was no question of termination, redemptions could be calculated without these uncertainties, and this was one reason for their growth in popularity.

The 1836 Act gave some nominal guidance regarding fines. It allowed societies to impose "such reasonable fines, penalties and forfeitures" upon those breaking the rules "as the members think fit". The question of what was in fact reasonable came before the courts. The general view was that, provided the fines were stated in the rules, the court would not interfere. Rule 33 of the Guardian Society, London, deprived a member who had not yet received his advance of his whole investment if he was six months in arrears with his subscription. (Such a rule was fairly common, but after twelve months rather than six.) Such forfeiture was held reasonable in 1857, in spite of the fact that in the particular case the member had offered and the secretary had accepted a cheque for the whole arrears a little after the six months had elapsed.[66] A fine of 1s. per pound per month was held reasonable;[67] as indeed it was compared with fines levied in some societies.

Eventually, in 1877, the courts did find certain fines unreasonable. The Birkbeck Society had a table of fines on unpaid subscriptions increasing from 6d. per month in the first month to 5s. for the sixth month, making a total of 15s. 6d. for the six months. The society claimed[68] that according to their table, for periods beyond the sixth month, fines should continue to increase, 10s. for the seventh month and so on. Lovejoy, having borrowed £1,400 on twenty-eight shares in 1868, fell into arrears and in 1871 the Society took possession. In 1876 Lovejoy sought to redeem the property and the Society claimed £4,687, consisting of £1,747 principal and interest and £2,940 fines. The Master of the Rolls, allowing no fines beyond the six months stated in the table, awarded only 15s. 6d. fines per share, adding "If building societies cannot get along without fines such as these, the sooner they are destroyed as common pests the better". The Society appealed, and was awarded fines of £420, arrived at by allowing fines for each month beyond the sixth month, at the same rate, 5s., as for the sixth month.

In an effort to save societies expense, the 1836 Building Societies Act, via its re-enactment of the Friendly Societies Acts, had given societies power to settle internal disputes with its members by arbitration. A number of attempts were made, both to force matters covered in the rules by arbitration procedures into the courts,[69] and to resist suits brought by societies in the courts, on the ground that the claims in dispute (such as taking possession when a mortgagor defaulted) should be settled by arbitration.[70] However, the courts held very strictly to the intent of the Act, to save societies from costly litigation. In one instance[71] Vice-Chancellor Bacon remarked, "If I were to decide in favour of this bill and against the demurrers, I should open the floodgates of litigation and ruin many and distress more of the existing societies".

Since the 1836 Act had not stated specifically which persons could be members of a building society, or the number of shares a member might hold, it fell to the courts to decide these questions. Joint stock companies were not allowed to hold shares in building societies.[72] An important case in 1848 determined that the Friendly Societies Act, 1840, which limited the interest of any one member in a society to £200, did not apply to building societies.[73] This decision paved the way for a ruling that members could hold more than £150 in shares in a society,[74] a limit that many thought had been implied by section 1 of the 1836 Act. Had such a limit in fact been held to apply, it is certain that the movement would not have expanded as rapidly as it did. This expansion was further helped by a decision[75] that societies could lend to strangers as well as to their own members.

Altogether building societies suffered a good deal as a result of the speed with which the 1836 Act was passed. Even if there had been an adequate enquiry into the nature of building societies, and extended consultation with interested parties, it is doubtful if the Act would have been much more satisfactory. At the time the Act was passed societies were on the threshold of considerable expansion and change. If the 1836 Act had been narrowly drawn it would have been in terms of the behaviour of societies as they existed in 1836 and the later expansion would certainly not have been on the scale that in fact took place. If, on the other hand, the legislature had tried to forecast the future needs of societies, it might not have been very successful, for the changes of the 1840s were, as we shall see, very extensive. The situation called for the sort of continuous reform that we find in friendly society legislation, with the legislature frequently redefining the powers and purposes of societies as they adapted their forms of organisation to the changing economic and social environment.

Chapter Three

THE GROWTH OF BUILDING SOCIETIES AFTER 1836*

AFTER THE PASSING of the 1836 Act the movement grew rapidly both in the number and the geographical spread of societies. It is not possible to describe this expansion precisely because the 1836 Act did not require societies to make any return of their activities to the Certifying Barristers; worse still, those officials did not keep any register of societies formed. In 1859 the Home Office published a return, but its form showed a singular lack of understanding of the sort of information that would be valuable, or indeed of the sort of information societies could provide. There was no compulsion on societies to complete the forms on which the return was based. At that time societies were suspicious of the government's possible intention of extending their liability to pay stamp duties, and hence feared that any information revealed might be used against them. The result was that only 198 returns were completed, although the number of societies was much larger than that. Further, the questions asked were understood by secretaries in a variety of ways, so that the results were of little value. The return did show something of the wide geographical distribution of societies, but this had already been shown by published building society directories, with much wider coverage than the official return.

The local clerks of the peace in England and Wales should have been able to give information about the number of societies, for the court rolls were the repository of certified copies of the rules of all societies formed. When the Royal Commission of 1871 sought this information it was found that many clerks of the peace did not distinguish, on their rolls, entries signifying the creation of a new society from entries that resulted from changes in the rules of the existing ones. The Commission's investigations do, however, give a fairly firm figure for the number of societies which had been registered during the period 1836 to 1869: about 3,500.[1] This throws little light on the growth of the movement during a period in which terminating societies were continuously being formed, completing their lives and disappearing. Current commentators are not very helpful: their estimates vary so widely.

* *Notes on this chapter appear on page 286.*

Tompkins[2] in 1845 estimated 300 societies, with an annual income, assuming 300 members each (this is certainly too high) of £540,000. Scratchley,[3] only four years later, puts the number at over 2,000 and the annual income not less than £2,300,000. Stone,[4] in 1851, talks of 2,050 societies registered and adds "the yearly income must now amount to £4,000,000". In 1869 Scratchley wrote,[5] "As proof of their numbers it may be stated that up to the present time there have been registered in the United Kingdom over 7,000 societies and they are increasing every year. Of these there is evidence to show that above 3,000 are still in existence". Unfortunately none of the commentators give any details of the basis on which their estimates were formed, so these estimates are best treated as guesses. A statistical note on page 286 sets out the basis for my own estimate, that the total number of societies formed up to 1869 was about 3,500. The number of societies in existence probably rose to about 1,500 in 1850 or thereabouts, following the rapid expansion of the movement in London in the 1840s. It seems unlikely that the total number of societies in existence at any one time, up to 1869, greatly exceeded 1,500.

A *Building Society Directory*, edited by Henry Brooks, though no doubt incomplete, gives some idea of the rate of growth of societies. The ninth edition of this directory—presumably an annual—was published in London in 1854; the tenth in 1855. This directory notes the date of formation of the majority of the societies catalogued in it. Bearing in mind that terminating societies usually had a planned life of about ten years, this directory should give a reasonably accurate picture of the rate at which societies were being formed during the decade 1843-1853. Since this was a London directory we may assume that information concerning London is more complete than that for the provinces. The directory distinguishes terminating and permanent societies. Permanent societies being on the whole larger than terminating societies, it is probable that the directory gives a more complete list of permanent than of terminating societies.

Table III brings out clearly the explosion of the movement in the mid-1840s, particularly in London. Once that was over, new formations continued at a surprisingly even rate. No doubt the severe financial crisis of 1847 helped to check the rapid growth of the movement. As Table III shows, permanent societies began to gain ground, though only slowly, after 1845. A letter in 1847 states, "The basis of a *permanent* society appears to be gaining considerable favour with . . . promoters and the public, which, when more readily understood, will very much facilitate their objects".[6] Up to 1845, there is at least one entry for each of twenty-eight towns; by 1850 this had increased to eighty-one towns, and by 1853, the number rises to 138 including forty-five towns with societies for which no formation date is given. The following ten towns, excluding London, had at least eight societies, as shown: Manchester, 87; Liverpool, 61; Birmingham, 22; Sheffield, 12; Preston, 10; Bristol, Chester, Southampton and Swansea, 9 each; and Leeds, 8. By 1850 there were certainly societies in every English county except Huntingdon, Lincoln, Norfolk and Rutland. In Wales there were numerous societies in Glamorgan and Carnarvon, with Denbigh and Monmouth also represented. As the Royal Commission confirmed twenty years later, the movement was much less widespread in Scotland and Ireland.

Something of the progress in the next quarter-century is shown by entries in a directory for 1873.[7] This lists over 1,500 societies, and is probably a fairly complete record of societies at that date. The geographical distribution of societies in Brooks' directory and the 1873 directory are given in Table IV. By 1873 there were more than twenty societies in each of thirteen counties outside London; these were Lancashire, 445; Durham, 87; Yorkshire, 86; Northumberland, 54; Stafford, 42; Glamorgan, 31; Cheshire, 28; Sussex, 27; Gloucester, 26; Warwick, 26; Carnarvon, 25; Kent, 22; and Lincoln, 22.

TABLE III

Date of Formation of Building Societies listed in Brooks' Directory, 1854

	Before 1843	1843	1844	1845	1846	1847	1848
Provincial							
Terminating	14	5	13	19	46	33	23
Permanent	0	0	0	1	0[8]	3	4
Metropolitan							
Terminating	2	16	19	64	56	40	15
Permanent	1[9]	0	1	2	0	2	5
TOTAL	17	21	33	86	102	78	47

	1849	1850	1851	1852	1853	No Date	Total
Provincial							
Terminating	14	19	11	18	17	176	408
Permanent	6	4	4	8	4	12	46
Metropolitan							
Terminating	10	10	14	11	21	81	359
Permanent	2	5	6	3	4	4	35
TOTAL	32	38	35	40	46	273	848

Bearing in mind that the data for 1853 are incomplete, especially so for terminating societies outside London, Table IV shows that the permanent principle was making rapid headway and accounted for a large part of the growth. Indeed in London and the South-East there is an actual decline in terminating societies. Even in the Midlands and the North, where there may have been some increase in the absolute number of terminating societies, the proportion of the movement's total assets in such societies was declining. Not only was the number of permanent societies growing more rapidly than that of the others, but also permanent societies were individually larger. Lancashire was something of an exception to this pattern. Here, in spite of the progress of permanent societies, terminating societies were still very important; in 1873 there were 300 of them compared with 145 permanent. In some Lancashire towns the permanent principle was very slow to become established. In Oldham in 1873 there were still thirty-four terminating societies (twenty-nine of them still meeting in inns) and only three permanent; and in Rochdale the respective figures were twenty-eight and two. Liverpool had 124 and Manchester 123 terminating societies, though in these two towns the permanents had made substantial progress. The importance of terminating societies in Lancashire was later reflected in the opposition to the reforms of 1874.

TABLE IV

Growth of Building Societies, 1853-1873

	1853			1873		
Region	Terminating	Permanent	Total	Terminating	Permanent	Total
North	258	15	273	475	234	709
North Midlands	37	7	44	50	36	86
South Midlands	17	1	18	38	21	59
East	14	3	17	35	21	56
London and South-East	390	39	429	266	168	434
South-West	34	14	48	35	32	67
Wales	9	1	10	52	21	73
Scotland	5	1	6	6	2	43[10]
Ireland	1	2	3	2	5	7
TOTALS	765	83	848	959	540	1,534

The rapid growth of societies in the mid-1840s, especially in London, is emphasised by the emergence about that time of a group of periodicals dealing specifically with building society matters. *The National*, subtitled A Weekly Family Journal of Politics, Literature, the Fine Arts and Record of Building Societies, started publication on March 14, 1846. It was increasingly devoted to building society matters, carrying reports of meetings, discussions of legal matters, and a section reporting the premiums that were currently being paid for advances, in those London societies which allocated advances by means of competitive bidding. Its central place in the building society world is reflected in its close association with the efforts made in 1848 to create a central organisation of societies.[11] *The National* probably ceased publication in February 1849; the British Museum Newspaper Library's file ceases at that date, and in April 1849 *The Reporter* was claiming for the first time to be the only journal devoted to building society affairs.

The first issue of *The National* notes the existence of another publication, presumably the first building society journal, *The Building Society Record*. This was a monthly publication which ceased its separate existence in March 1847 when it was joined with *The National*. In 1848 *The Reporter* entered the field. This was a monthly journal with a rather wider coverage of the general political scene than *The National*, but it also devoted a substantial amount of space to building society matters.

The Freeholder was the vehicle of the freehold land society movement. The first number appeared on January 1, 1850, and it continued as a monthly until March 1852. By that time it was losing money and in a last effort to build circulation it began weekly publication on March 1, 1852. This move proved unsuccessful and it ceased publication on August 28, 1852. *The Freeholder* confined its attention very closely to the freehold land societies, reporting their activities in great detail; including maps of new estates purchased, showing the streets named after leaders of the movement and its ideals—e.g. Taylor Street, Franchise Street, and Scholefield Street.

The idea of permanent societies was introduced in 1845 by James Henry James, an actuary. He published a pamphlet entitled, "Benefit Building Societies, their Advantages if Legitimately Constituted, the Defects of Principles generally Applied to their Establishment, with Suggestions for their Improvement and their Profitable Union with Life Assurance Societies, practically considered." A reviewer commented,[12] not unreasonably, "Mr. James appears to have framed his title with the express purpose of deterring people from reading his work", adding, "Mr. James' plan is at present mere theory which might or might not in practice work well". The pamphlet was received with something less than eager attention, for although *The National* claimed in its sub-title to be a *Record of Building Societies*, it did not review James' work until a letter from James called attention to it.

He wrote ". . . In a pamphlet on Building Societies recently published at 128 Chancery Lane, it will be seen that I am opposed to the plan of dissolving such associations at a period when all the shares have been realised, because it prevents many persons joining after the first establishment of the society; to promising a profit on shares equal to the payments made for them [the early terminating societies in London made such promises] and to the allowance of premiums on shares advanced;

because the payments of members are thus rendered indefinite as to the amount and duration, involving the necessity also of mortgagors giving too large a return for loans and charging their property with a debt which in fact actually doubles the sum lent on the same. [The amount actually advanced on £120 shares in terminating societies averaged about £60.] In the constitution of the Metropolitan Equitable Investment Association these defects are obviated, the Society itself being permanent the payments alone being limited; the monies secured on mortgage bearing no reference to the shares taken".[13] The Metropolitan Equitable (1845) seems thus to have been the first permanent society, offering advances for terms of three, five, seven, ten, twelve and fifteen years; it was soon followed by the National Equitable which was in being by June 1846.[14]

James felt the reviewer had done less than justice to his innovation and wrote again on May 16th setting out its advantages.[15] Permanent societies enabled members to take shares at any time. The duration of borrowers' payments was fixed and certain and this made it easy to calculate the sum a borrower would have to pay at any time to redeem his mortgage. James also advocated setting aside "a portion of the fees, fines and forfeitures to a 'Benefit or Casualty Fund' for shareholders". James' strictures on the existing societies led to an acrid correspondence between himself and J. R. MacArthur, author of *Building Societies Simplified and Improved*, who was manager of one of the largest London societies, the British Building and Investment Association, and a leader of the movement in London. He claimed that James was "waging war on Building Societies as at present constituted", merely to build up his own society.[16]

The legality of James' principle was challenged, notably in an article by Lord Kenmore in the *Building Society Record* of July 5, 1846. Some felt, not unreasonably, that the wording of the Act implied the termination of societies. Kenmore's objection was to the annual division of profits deriving from the conception of paid up shares, which he felt to be contrary to Section 1 of the 1836 Act.[17] Tidd Pratt seems to have had some misgiving, "The draft rules of a society on the above permanent system was prepared and submitted to the Government Barrister and was, after some delay, returned approved".[18]

Arthur Scratchley has been generally acknowledged as the originator of the permanent principle. This probably arises from his own reference in the 1867 edition of his *Treatise on Benefit Building Societies* to "The Permanent plan which we devised in 1846".[19] No such claim to innovation was made in the first edition of that work whose preface is dated May 1849. By that date he was aware of existing permanent societies; referring to building societies he says, "They are now divided into two distinct categories; the one terminating, the other permanent".[20] Scratchley was the founder of a permanent society in 1848, the London and Metropolitan Counties Society.[21] It seems difficult to believe that Scratchley was not aware of James's ideas. James wrote a second work in 1849, published a month or so after Scratchley's book. In this, *Guide to Benefit Building Societies*, James wrote, ". . . the idea of forming societies on a permanent basis, so that their operations might continue for an indefinite period, the term of individual membership only being restricted, was first suggested by the author in 1845, which principle is now being successfully carried out".[22] This claim is confirmed by the correspondence in *The National*, referred to above, early in 1846, and Scratchley did not graduate from the University of Cambridge until 1845.

The fact that Scratchley[23] did not originate the idea of permanent societies does not greatly diminish his importance in the development of the building society movement. In 1849 when his Treatise was published, permanent societies, though not new, were few, and that book must have been very influential in spreading the permanent principle. It is a much clearer exposition of the principle than is to be found in James's work, not least because the latter's style was so involved. Further, Scratchley's repute as an actuary (he was actuary to the Western Life Assurance Society) brought him in touch with societies in many parts of the country as consultant, and he catalogued the weaknesses of the typical terminating society in vast detail.

Another powerful influence in the spread of the permanent principle was its use in connection with freehold land societies. These societies were first formed with the object of assisting people to acquire sufficient property to qualify for a vote at parliamentary elections. By an Act in 1430 (8 Henry 6, c. 7) owners of freehold land of an annual value of £2 were qualified to vote in county constituencies, provided their land was not mortgaged. This restriction was removed in 1696 (7 and 8 Will. 3, c. 25) after which the owner of mortgaged land could vote provided its annual value was £2, net of all charges. The Reform Act of 1832 extended the vote to lease- and copyholders of land with an annual value of £10 in the counties and owners of houses of an annual value of £10 in the boroughs.

During the agitation for reform of the suffrage in the early 1840s, some small groups of half a dozen or so persons purchased land, to be then split among the members so as to qualify each for a vote. The refusal of the Revising Barrister to place these new freeholders' names on the electoral register, or the contesting of his action by interested parties when he did so, led to a series of law suits. The main point at issue arose from the above mentioned statute of William III, section 7 of which enacted that "all conveyances in order to multiply voices and divide the interest in any house or lands among several persons to enable them to vote at the election of members to serve in Parliament are hereby declared void and of null effect". It was not unknown for property to be conveyed to a person to enable him to vote (for the right candidate of course!) for a nominal sum on condition that it was reconveyed to the real owner after the election. A number of statutes were passed to try and prevent this practice. One dated 1712 (10 Anne, c. 23) states its intention clearly in its title: "An Act for the more effectual preventing fraudulent conveyances in order to multiply votes for electing Knights of the Shires to serve in Parliament."[24]

In February 1845 the Courts decided that a Mr. Bowen and his five associates should have votes at Lichfield.[25] They had jointly purchased a house there in order to qualify as electors. The Courts' view was that since the vendor was not aware of the motive of the purchasers and the conveyance was genuine it was not void. The same position was taken by the Courts in 1846 when W. F. Hoyland and seventeen other members of the Anti-Monopoly Association acquired votes in the S. Lancashire constituency by purchasing some houses and land at Newton.[26] They acted through a Manchester house agent, and again since the vendor knew nothing of their intentions, the conveyance was held to be legal.

In a series of cases in 1846 the vendor was clearly aware that the purchasers were making their purchases in order to acquire votes. In the leading case[27] the agent of one of the political parties in Huddersfield was openly advertising for people prepared to sell land to would-be voters, and offering his services as intermediary to those wishing to acquire votes. Alexander asked the agent to get him a vote as cheaply as possible. The agent found property of sufficient value to obtain votes for thirty-five people and this was bought jointly by Alexander and thirty-four others. The vendor was aware of and sympathetic to the intentions of the buyers, but as he could not afford to subsidise their objective, the sale took place at the full market price. The court held that these acts were legal, because there was no element of fraudulent intent. It was a *bona fide* purchase for an adequate monetary consideration and there were no secret trusts.

Stone, in the light of these cases, concluded, "It may be considered as clearly established by these decisions that a *bona fide* conveyance for a valuable consideration and without any secret trust or fraudulent intention, will be valid; although it may have been made with the express intention of multiplying votes or splitting interests in property for the purposes of increasing the number of votes for members of parliament."[28]

These decisions, plus the idea of permanent societies, opened the way for land societies. The 1836 Act forbade building societies to own land, but in September 1847 James Taylor of Birmingham[29] thought of a way round this prohibition. If a group of interested people were prepared to put up the money to buy an estate, and agreed to sell plots with an annual value of £2, then what was legally a building society could advance the money to members to take up these plots. The original purchasers of the land were, at least in the scheme's conception, only dummies, though in the nature of the case they were likely to be politically interested dummies. "Some difficulty was at first experienced in registering it [Taylor's society] but Mr. Tidd Pratt at length found it practicable to certify it."[30] Taylor continued the operation of the Birmingham Freehold Land Society with his group of normal building societies, the first advancing money to buy the plot of land, the second to erect a house upon it. The land society laid out estates in plots, put in roads and drains and exercised some general control over building; building lines were set, no public houses allowed and the number of shops controlled.[31] At the start plots were allocated to members in rotation, but the considerable success of the society led to long waiting lists and this hampered further progress. To offer a greater incentive to new members, in 1851 a proportion of plots were allocated by ballot and eventually all plots were allocated in this way.[32]

Brooks' Directory gives some information on the progress of these land societies, which is brought together in Table V. The movement did not start in London until 1849. In London, as in the provinces previously,

TABLE V

Formation of Freehold Land Societies

	1847	1848	1849	1850	1851	1852	1853	No Date	Total
	(Date of formation and number formed)								
Provincial	4	3	18	19	0	1	2	22	69
Metropolitan	0	0	3	1	0	10	28	2	44
TOTAL	4	3	21	20	0	11	30	24	113

there was a gap of a few years after the first society was founded, before the main body of societies appeared. The first society in London was the National Freehold Land Society, started in June 1849 in the Liberal interest. Richard Cobden gave a famous address to its first public meeting,[33] and John Bright was a director as were other prominent Liberals. The Tories replied with the Conservative Freehold Land Society and these two societies, with the Birmingham Freehold Land Society, were much the largest of the such societies. The Conservative Society was formed in 1852, when it was felt that the existence of land societies in the Liberal interest had contributed to the Conservatives' losses at a general election.[34]

Given their political orientation, the land societies naturally had a greater sense of common purpose (or two purposes!) than building societies; they also had ready made national leaders. Societies in the Liberal interest in the Midlands formed the Midland Freehold Land Association, with Taylor as its secretary in 1847, and the first national conference was held in Birmingham in November 1849. In November 1849[35] a national organisation, the Freeholders' Union, was formed and at its fourth national conference in London in 1853[36] the following results were noted: an increase of thirty societies in the previous year to a total of 130; total membership, 85,000 holding 120,000 shares. 19,000 allotments had been made from the 310 estates purchased so far, total receipts, £790,000.[37]

The question of whether balloting for plots constituted a lottery considerably exercised the conscience of the conference. "Those societies which followed the rotation system had not increased while those which had adopted the ballot had been greatly augmented." Revising Barristers were still proving reluctant to register newly created freeholders; one resolution carried stated, "That the conflicting decisions of Revising Barristers are a great and growing evil, which should be brought to the notice of the Lord Chief Justice and the House of Commons at the earliest opportunity". In the face of these legal difficulties, members in some cases received help from their society. "Legal aid was provided by the Society for members of the National who met with resistance when endeavouring to register as qualified voters."[38]

There were other difficulties. Political opponents of the new movement "sought to discredit the newly formed societies in every possible way. An obvious form of attack was to attempt to arouse uneasiness in the minds of members by disquieting press articles".[39] In 1850 the movement began publication of its own journal, *The Freeholder*, but it was soon making heavy losses, of £1,000 a year,[40] and was discontinued in August 1852.

The movement reached its peak in the mid-1850s. With the passing of the Company Act, 1856, a more direct and convenient form than building societies was found for carrying out these enterprises. The legal necessity of acting via trustees ". . . was an unending source of minor difficulties, and when the Companies Acts of the mid-fifties presented an opportunity for a more satisfactory procedure, it was eagerly seized upon. The National forthwith formed a subsidiary company."[41] (The British Land Company.)

Societies like the National and the Conservative turned increasingly to ordinary building society business. Competition for estates near towns tended to raise prices and this checked progress. The enthusiasm of the politicians also probably flagged, brought face to face with the age-old instability of the electorate. As an American politician put it, "It's easy enough to buy votes, the difficulty is in seeing that they stay bought." The British version was given to the Royal Commission by H. J. Phillips (Temperance Society). "At one time it was considered there was a strong desire to get a plot of land in order to obtain a vote and we went to considerable expense in getting allottees on the Register in S. Essex . . . on another occasion provision was made to carry them to the poll and not half of them would go."[42] Worse still people who got land to vote Liberal, having obtained it, voted Conservative.[43] Lastly it was not only the voters who refused to "stay bought". In one case a trustee having bought the land and agreed to transfer it to the members of the land society at a given price, received a better offer from elsewhere and refused to sell to the land society's members.[44]

By the mid-1860s the creation of votes was "now quite a matter of secondary importance"[45] and the changes in the franchise in 1867 removed much of the remaining political incentive behind the movement, which disappeared altogether with the Reform Act of 1884. Land societies still had a function in providing small freehold building plots to prospective owner occupiers. In terms of getting people on the electoral register, building societies, because of their greater number, were more important than land societies. They enabled many people in the boroughs to acquire a house of £10 annual value. There were considerable legal battles here, too. The £10 had to be net of mortgage charges and revising barristers held this to include all payments on the mortgage, not simply the interest element. Eventually the question was decided thus. Take from the value of the property mortgaged the sum needed to redeem the mortgage. If the difference would yield £2 annually, using the same interest rate as in the calculation of the present value of future payments to establish the sum needed to redeem, the mortgagor was entitled to vote.[46]

Freehold land societies benefited the building society movement in a number of ways. The rapid growth of land societies and their dependence on the permanent principle was an important factor favouring the spread of the permanent principle. The land societies were essentially political creations and this meant that many people prominent in politics found themselves engaged in building society work. The fact that people of the calibre and repute of Richard Cobden and John Bright were to be found on the directorate of a building society must have helped to strengthen public confidence in these institutions. A number of other M.P.s were active in the movement. Sir Joshua Walmsley and Charles Gilpin were successively chairmen of the National Society. By their association with land societies many politicians and others gained some knowledge of the ways of building societies, and this knowledge could be important during public discussion of building society matters. The outcome of the government's attempt to impose certain stamp duties on building societies in 1855 (see below, pp. 84-86), might have been different but for the work of Mr. W. Scholefield, M.P., and he had been chairman of the Birmingham Freehold Land Society.

With the decline in political interest in land societies many prominent people left the building society movement; some stayed, however, to its permanent benefit. Charles Gilpin, for example, remained chairman of the National Society until 1874. Further, some of the societies that had achieved rapid growth partly as a result of their political connections became straightforward building societies when political interest declined, and remained to impress the public with their size and stability; three such were the Conservative and the National Freehold Land Societies and the Bennett's Hill group of societies which had grown around the Birmingham Freehold Land Society. The freehold land societies owed their origin to building societies, but they repaid that debt, for the building societies movement in turn gained a good deal.

Chapter Four

CHANGES IN ORGANISATION AFTER 1836*

IDEALLY a terminating society was a completely mutual organisation; everyone contributed equally to its funds and everyone shared equally in the distribution of the society's assets when it terminated. The system had three basic weaknesses. First, the fact that all members had to contribute equally made it difficult to attract new members after the society had been in existence for a year or two. To be on an equal footing with founder members, late entrants faced a heavy burden of back subscriptions and this was a considerable barrier to recruitment. Second, if members had to depend on their own subscriptions to raise the fund from which advances were made, then the progress of the society would be slow and some members would have to wait a long time for their advance.

This difficulty could be met in two ways. The fund from which advances were made could be increased, without increasing the demand for advances, by borrowing money or by having some members who would receive a lump sum instead of advances when the society terminated. But these remedies for the second weakness created a third. If a sufficient fund was built up in the first few years to satisfy all demands for advances, then for the remainder of the society's life subscriptions would be flowing in, and there would be no use for them. Borrowed funds, depending on the nature of the contract with the lender, might be repaid but the investing member, very welcome in a society's early years, was an embarrassment later on.

"To remedy this evil," wrote Stone in 1851,[1] "the *Ballot rule* was framed, by which it is provided, that when there is a balance at the banker's beyond a certain amount, which is not wanted for advances or other claims, the directors may require the investing members to withdraw, by ballot, the value of as many shares as will be sufficient to exhaust such portion of the monies in hand as they shall think proper. The investing members on whom the ballot falls will receive the value of their shares, including compound interest at the rate on which the society has been formed." That such a rule was not universal is shown by the additional comment, "Nothing would be more likely to cause a society

* *Notes on this chapter appear on page 290.*

(including permanent societies) to fail to meet its engagements than the omission of the ballot rule which operates as a safety valve to dispose of the surplus funds when necessary." Such a remedy had its dangers, for it diminished the number of the society's members, and, as Scratchley[2] put it, "Thus the society which might otherwise have succeeded, declines rapidly in importance; and its expenses or any deficiency of funds which may afterwards be discovered, instead of being spread over a large body, have to be borne by the few who are unlucky enough to remain to the end."

The main organisational change in the terminating system was aimed at meeting these weaknesses. When a society had reached the stage where back subscriptions were a barrier to new members, the directors of the society would start a second society. Then, instead of paying back subscriptions to the first society, the intending member could join the second society as a founder member. The early need of the second society to borrow, to speed up the making of advances, was met from the surplus funds of the first society. By the time the second society was running into its period of surplus funds a third society would be founded. Thus the same group of directors would found a series of societies, interlocked by a chain of lending and borrowing. This answer to the weaknesses appeared in the early 1840s and took the movement a long way towards permanent forms of organisation. The Gould Square Provident group formed six societies between 1844 and 1847.[3] "To enable members to join [the Chelmsford and Essex Society] after the commencement without payment of arrears a new series of shares is issued every two years, the second series dating from 13 September, 1847."[4] The system sometimes became so formalised, as with the Ryde, Isle of Wight societies, that a new society was formed each year, the size of the society varying with the demand for advances in the year in which the society was formed. In Sunderland there were nearly 40 societies founded in the one group, the Sunderland Working Men's Societies.

In the early years of this procedure the various societies in a group were kept completely separate in their operation, with a declaration of profit each year for each society. This must have made their operation quite complicated. A further development tied the societies closer together. It was an arrangement "whereby the society could be of a permanent character but the membership terminating subject to the uncertainty about the duration of their membership. . . . Shares were issued in series, each series being distinct from the others, although with the others sharing in the general profits of the society. The society issues so many shares in the first year making advances in the customary manner. At the end of the first year total assets are divided by the total shares in the first issue to get their value. Thereupon a new series of shares is issued. At the end of the second year the sum total of the income of that year is divided by the total number of shares in force in both series and their value again ascertained. The shares of the first issue will be found to have a value of two years' subscriptions to which is added the profit by way of interest during the two years, on each share; while the value of the shares in the second series will be worth one year's subscriptions and the one year's profits. So the process goes on year by year, the sum total formed by subscriptions plus interest being divided at the end of each year by the number of shares of all series. By . . . twelve or thirteen years the first series reaches its ultimate value and those not having had advances are paid in cash; the rest get their mortgage deeds."[5]

A further weakness of the terminating system was that members did not know how long the society would need to continue to achieve its object. We have seen that this uncertainty bore very heavily on an advanced member who wished to redeem his property, but it affected the investing member too. On joining he committed himself to a monthly subscription for an unknown term of years. Not all uncertainty could be eliminated: so much depended on whether the society was successful or not, and no system of organisation could guarantee success, but the form of the uncertainty could be changed. This was done by fixing the life of the society in terms of a period of time, rather than of value for each share. The members now knew for how long they were committed to paying subscriptions; the uncertainty involved what they would get for those subscriptions, and this, of course, depended on the progress of the society. For redeeming members this could be a great improvement. Difficulties could arise at the termination, for if all had not gone according to plan the value of investing shares might be less than the advances made on borrowing shares, and the assets of the society had to be equally divided.

To take an example, if a society with subscriptions of 10s. per month can invest the money at 5%, each share will be worth £120 after nearly fourteen years. In such a society a borrowing member getting an advance at its commencement will get £60 cash—the present value of a stream of 10s. monthly subscriptions for fourteen years. Members getting advances at the end of the first year will get a little over £66 and so on for later advances. The investing members will get £120 in cash after the fourteen years, and thus, if everything went smoothly investing and borrowing members would be treated equally. Whether the society has set its termination in terms of money (£120 per share) or time (fourteen years) will make no difference. This would not be the case if the society made losses. Suppose the losses are such that at the end of fourteen years funds are only sufficient to pay investing members £100, then if the society has set itself a monetary objective it must clearly endure beyond the expected fourteen years. If the rules, in order to avoid the uncertainty mentioned above, state that the society is to terminate after fourteen years there is trouble. If the total funds are given to investing members they get £100 each, while the borrowing members would have had the equivalent of £120. Clearly to distribute the society's assets equally creates difficulties; you could scarcely give each investing member £100, plus legal title to one room in a borrowing member's house!

The difficulty might be resolved by bargaining between the investing and borrowing members. In the example above, if there were equal numbers of investing and borrowing members justice would be satisfied if each borrowing member agreed to pay an investing member a lump sum of £10. In practice it was not always as simple, for borrowing members having had their advance were in a strong position. The Royal Commission of 1871 was told that "In some cases societies are dissolved when a given amount is realised and in societies more recently established the payments cease on a certain day. My last terminating society was to cease on the first of February 1870 and the money was forthwith distributed among the investors. If the Society wants to close it must come to terms with the Mortgagors." [Mr. J. Higham] "They were compelled to make a compromise with the mortgagors; it was the only way of arranging the matter, and they drove a very hard bargain about it." [Mr. Hoare][6] An example of such bargaining is provided by the Liverpool and West Derby Society, which had aimed at paying £100 to shareholders in return for subscriptions totalling £50 over ten years. Results were falling behind expectations and, after nine years, the rules were changed. "That for the purpose of bringing the Society to an immediate termination each non-purchased [i.e. investing] member be paid £19 as a bonus in addition to the subscriptions paid in and that the purchased members do pay a sum per share sufficient to meet the required amount."[7]

The greatest change in organisation was the creation of the permanent societies. The Royal Commission took no note of these developments in terminating societies and in consequence stated the advantages of permanent societies as follows: "In a permanent society the investors can always ascertain the exact length of time during which they will have to pay their subscriptions, if the regular amount be enforced by fines; it is always comparatively easy to ascertain the amount to which any investing member, who may wish to withdraw, is entitled. . . . But it is to the borrowing members that the permanent society holds out the greatest inducements, for it enables him to extend his repayments over any fixed number of years at his own choice with the absolute certainty of clearing his property from the encumbrance and freeing himself from all further liability at the end of that time, and to feel when he mortgages it that he can redeem it at any time on payment of a sum easily calculated, and that whether the society prove successful or no."[8]

Not all permanent societies gave all these advantages, and in the eyes of some people they were advantages too dearly bought for the movement as a whole. The insulation of the borrower in permanent societies from the success or failure of the society was an important change. If the investor was to bear the risks it was not surprising that he should regard the society as "his". In the early societies since all members were both borrowers and subscribers, mutuality was ensured. The change began with the emergence of the investing members. The investing member was not the creation of the permanent societies; as we have seen terminating societies accepted members who had no intention of borrowing money from the society. The growth of permanent societies only speeded up this development; it was taking place anyway. However, many people regarded the permanents as the villains of this particular piece, destroying the ideal of the small mutual society. Since the third quarter of the nineteenth century was a period when many people saw the solution to economic problems in terms of cooperative effort, some hostility to permanent societies was understandable.

With the permanent system a fund was raised from one group, the investing shareholders, and the money advanced on mortgage to another, the borrowers. The two groups could be, and often were, quite distinct. As the society did not terminate in a distribution of the assets equally among members, it was no longer necessary for the obligations of all members to be the same. The terms on which investors subscribed money to the society could be varied to suit differing needs. The terms on which money was advanced to borrowers—especially in regard to the duration of the mortgage—could also be varied.

If the borrower was not to bear any of the risk, it was not unreasonable that he should be excluded from the profits of the society, but there was nothing in the "permanents" which made this exclusion necessary. Many permanent societies, having paid investors the interest rate agreed, used the remaining profit to make bonus payments on all shares—investing and borrowing. The Leeds Permanent, one of the most successful of the early permanent societies, did this. In at least one society it was the investors who could reasonably complain of the lack of mutuality: "This society [the Wolverhampton and District Permanent] differs from most societies in the way of profits, 5% interest is credited to investing shareholders and borrowers have the rest, the profits for the last two years have been 12½%."[9] But in general the permanent societies were from the start not mutual. In 1851 Stone wrote, "In permanent societies this complete equality and mutuality has not hitherto existed."[10] *The Building Societies Directory*, 1874, pleaded for a return to mutuality as a way of overcoming public hostility.[11]

The growth of the permanent system changed the nature of the societies: "they became agencies for the investment of capital rather than for enabling the investors to provide dwellings for themselves".[12] "When the mutual relation of advance and share had disappeared, it was only a step further to bestow the former without reference to the latter, so the borrowing member became simply a mortgagor of the society . . ."[13] Some societies carried the isolation of borrowers to the extreme by excluding them from membership altogether. The Chairman of the Planet Society favoured such a move in his evidence to the Royal Commission.[14]

The early societies had borrowed money to speed up the granting of advances to shareholders. The advent of investing members, who had no intention of taking an advance, could have made borrowing unnecessary, for those wishing to lend to societies could do so as investing members. In fact societies continued to borrow money, because many people were reluctant to become investing shareholders. James Taylor put the position thus, "They do not want to be called shareholders, they think there is some liability and . . . would prefer being depositors and having the money whenever they thought proper" and "In old societies they do not like things altered; you have to be very careful with working men."[15] Perhaps if societies had remained true to the letter of the 1836 Act, these attitudes might have been overcome without any restraint on the growth of societies. This hypothesis was never tested, for societies quickly created securities—deposits and preference shares—which did not involve as much risk or uncertainty as investing shares.

It is doubtful whether holding deposits, in some cases, did much to reduce risk. Where more than 90% of a society's liabilities were deposits and a proportion of its assets mortgages on factories, the depositor had very little extra safety compared with the shareholder. The chief advantage of deposits was probably ease of withdrawal, though when a society made temporary loans against investing shares, this advantage was slight. Up to £50 would frequently be withdrawn on demand, with a month's notice required for larger withdrawals.[16] Stated interest rates on deposits were usually about 1% lower than on shares, but actually the gap was wider as a result of bonuses paid on shares. Interest rates on deposits fluctuated a good deal depending on the supply of money, though this was less common in the North.[17] With shares much less use was made of interest rate changes to restrict the inflow of money; share lists were temporarily closed. Interest rates on larger deposits, usually of more than

£100, and withdrawal notice, were settled by negotiation.[18] The deposit facilities of building societies particularly attracted the small saver; the depositor tended to be the less well paid worker, and the shareholder the skilled man or small trader. Towards the end of the period the deposit departments of some of the larger societies took on more and more of the appearance of banks. In some cases cheque books were issued to deposit holders,[19] and where this was not so, cheques could be obtained from the society to make particular payments. The result was sometimes severe competition with banks. The Royal Commissioners found "The competition of Building Societies with banks is, in Newcastle, very severe; nor is it difficult to see that a building society, with all its money secured on freehold or leasehold property, and a constant incoming of repayments by monthly instalments, may fairly be preferred by a portion at least of the public, as a field of investment"[20]. To the Royal Commission's question "And the operations of building societies generally and in London particularly have been for some years to make them more banks of deposits than building societies as contemplated in the original Act?" E. W. Brabrook replied, "Precisely so; they are investment associations; only the nature of the investment is restricted by the Act to loans upon mortgages and other prescribed securities."[21] Regarding London the reply was not strictly accurate, for as the figures below show, the deposit system played a smaller part in building society operations in London than elsewhere. Mr. Higham gave evidence[22] to the Royal Commission of the liabilities of London societies excluding the two largest. There was, in 1870, £2,516,000 to the credit of investing members and £1,515,000 to depositors; thus depositors held 38% of the total. The Building Societies Protection Association gave the figures[23] for the liabilities of 124 societies, including the London figures above. Deposits as a percentage of shares plus deposits for these societies was 40%. For the Birmingham societies the figure was 60%. T. Y. Strachan gave more detailed figures for the Newcastle area, from which Table VI has been constructed.

TABLE VI

Deposits of Societies in Newcastle-on-Tyne and Gateshead

		Deposits as a % of Total Liabilities				
		under 60	—70	—80	—90	—100
Number of	Newcastle	1	4	5	8	6
Societies	Gateshead	0	1	4	3	1

The highest percentage was 95 in a Newcastle society.

In the light of these high figures for deposits, which might in many societies be withdrawn at short notice, it is remarkable that societies, at least on the evidence of witnesses to the Commission, took no active steps to safeguard their liquidity position. All the funds were generally regarded as available to lend on mortgages, and the inflow of money from repayments and new deposits was left to take care of withdrawals. As long as societies were expanding rapidly, this was perhaps a safe assumption, provided there was no shock to depositors' confidence. The legal decisions, noted above, p. 37, in the late 1860s gave this shock and, in the light of the figures for deposits, the concern of societies to know precisely their legal position is quite understandable.

By the 1840s the system of bidding for advances, not unknown in the early societies, was ousting balloting or rotation as the usual means by which advances were allocated. Both balloting and rotation had their drawbacks. A person might have a favourable opportunity to purchase property before he obtained an advance, and in addition, rotation would clearly inhibit new members from joining once the early places on the roll were filled. In terminating societies the bidding took the form of finding who would take the lowest present advance on his share. Thus a man might agree to take £60 cash on his nominal £120 share in the first year in satisfaction of the claims created by his agreement to contribute 10s. per month for the life of the society. That this system of bidding did not become universal is suggested by the following comment in 1874: "The system of open competition or sale has probably secured more general favour than either of the foregoing"[24] [balloting and rotation]. With permanent societies competition took different forms. Where a fixed rate of interest was charged, it was usually a question of who was prepared to repay, in addition to the interest, the highest sum per £100 advanced; or sometimes, who would accept the lowest sum per nominal £100 advanced. The bidding might be conducted openly at meetings (the Queen's Society, Birmingham used the three ticket system)[25] or, as in the Temperance Society, by sealed tenders for the money that was declared to be available each month.[26]

There was an added reason for adopting bidding rather than balloting for advances, "in consequence of members sometimes making it a practice to apply for advances [when they had no intention of purchasing property] in the hope that, if successful, in the application [in the ballot] they may make a profit by transferring their right to another member. . . ".[27] In such circumstances it was only reasonable that any profit should go to the Society, and this would be achieved if the advance was made by auction.

Attractive as this system of selling advances was, it did immense damage to many societies and proved the downfall of some. To take an example, a society with a subscription of 10s. per month, if the subscriptions were continuously invested at 5% interest would yield £120 for each member after nearly fourteen years. Discounting £120 at 5% over the same period gives a present value of £60 and if all advances were sold at this rate of discount the society would just achieve its objective, borrowing members would have had their advance and at termination would get their deeds, while investing members would get £120. Suppose that advances are sold, and instead of getting £60 a borrower was prepared to take £50, clearly the society will meet its obligations and show a profit of £10 at its termination. This borrowing member's 10s. per month can be divided into two elements, one repaying the advance and the second enabling the society to slowly realise its £10 profit. Unfortunately this is not the way many societies treated the transaction. The tendency was to take the £10 into the accounts as profits realised in the year in which the advance was made. Some societies went further. "The main source of error consists in the practice of inserting the whole nominal amount of the share, for instance £120 as having been lent in cash to a borrowing member, when he has probably only received £55 or £60."[28]

The mass of managers of the small societies had little knowledge of accountancy and less of actuarial science. They worked from standard tables, those of Theodore Jones being very popular. These tables set out the value a person's subscriptions would have, accumulated at various rates of interest, over the life of the society. Thus the amount to be paid to a member withdrawing at any time could be read off, in the light of the rate of interest on which the society was working. Where advances were made by ballot or rotation the amount to be advanced could be similarly read off. As stated above, in a 5% society with 10s. monthly subscriptions the advance would be £60 at the start of the society, £66 3s. 0d. after one year, rising to £108 10s. 0d. if the advance was not made until the thirteenth year. These tables could also be used to decide the amount a member should pay if he wished to redeem his property. As long as advances were made by rotation or ballot, such tables served well enough—though some of them were not accurate. "As regards the prospectuses in numerous instances the promoters either from inattention, or not being sufficiently acquainted with the subject, have merely copied an early form of one which by calculation and experience will be found to be erroneous in many particulars. . . ."[29]

Once advances were sold the society's figures ceased to fit the standard tables. This would still not have mattered if societies had made no distribution of interest before termination, but in the case of withdrawing members most of them did so. Many societies went further: although the 1836 Act forbade distribution of interest before termination, the law was ignored.[30] Scratchley[31] gives some examples of societies' accounts where discounts on advances were regarded as immediately realised profit. One society showed an income of £2,649 from subscriptions, etc., in the first year; this was advanced to members who received on average a little less than £60 cash. The nominal value of shares was £120 and the difference was included in the society's assets which came to £5,460. Hence a net profit of £2,739 was declared, and presumably any member withdrawing a share on which he had paid only one year's subscription, £6, was entitled to the present value of his share, which was given as £12 0s. 9½d. If no further advances were made the society, having made 100% profit in its first year, would make no profit for the rest of its life; and if the shareholders became disillusioned with its later lack of success, one could scarcely blame them, especially after such a dazzling start!

The comments of the directors of that society, on the accounts, were revealing: "The directors congratulate the members on the success of the society during the past year, a success which verifies the correctness of the prospectus. The balance sheet shows the superior advantage of building societies over other modes of investment, for if the amount received had been placed in a savings bank, the profit would have been £43 or 1s. 10½d. per share, while by the legitimate operations of the society the profit secured has amounted to £2,738 18s. 8d. or £6 0s. 9½d. per share." Some directors clearly went to great length to live up to the promises made in prospectuses. "So much do they depend upon premiums that they will not hesitate, sometimes just before a report is issued, to borrow from the bank on a promissory note at 8% to get the premium for the re-lending of it into the report."[32]

In a period of rapid expansion, especially in the 1840s, the shortage of able directors must have been considerable. Further, the lack of accountants and actuaries meant a lack of skilled advice. The friendly societies were suffering in the same way. The result was that many societies, failing to live up to their early promise, lost members and ran into difficulties. At the same time new societies were advertising their wares in strident tones, and the image of building societies became rather tarnished. A violent correspondence occupied the columns of *The Times* in September and October 1844. *The Times* had carried an article favourably discussing a pamphlet by John Bowen of Bridgwater, *A Joint Stock Building Societies Bubble*.

The article stated, "The Bridgwater Society both lends its money at the easiest rate and also receives the most enormous interest at the same time. . . . This is done by a sort of legerdemain. One set of figures appears in one part and reappears in another with just a little alteration that would hardly be observed but which, when it sums up and is multiplied by four or five shares, makes all the difference. Thus they coolly start by telling the borrowing member of the Society that he pays for his ready money with a deduction averaging, according to the experience of similar societies, from £50 to £65 per share [of £120 nominal value] . . . now when they come to catch the eye of the needy borrowing man they of course made the smallest deduction—£50. Mr. Bowen simply takes their highest and that makes all the difference. . . . The difference between £50 and £65 to begin with makes a difference of between £70 and £300 in the event." Mr. Bowen himself had been still harsher in his remarks on building societies. "Can anything more detestable, in principle more degrading to our common nature, be presented to the world than this nefarious scheme for transferring the little savings of the frugal poor, into the pockets of ravenous capitalists? Here are the inexperienced, the sanguine and the needy encouraged to bid against one another. . . . Ignorance, misfortune, and distress are converted into a pretence of 'opening a channel for the fruits of industrious labour' and of 'affording a rich reward to economy and prudence'."[33]

Building societies had their defenders. A letter addressed to *The Times* [but not published] stated, *inter alia*, "I have no small share of respect for your sentiments and decisions but the mere circumstance of even *your* stigmatizing the Societies as 'swindling bubbles', 'self evident mare's nests', 'conducted by sleight of hand and legerdemain' would not deter me from exercising my own judgement in the matter."[34] "There certainly may have been instances of speculating borrowers consenting to submit to exorbitant reductions. . . . The greatest deduction made in the society to which I belong never amounted to £58 and the deduction has been very regular at £50 to £55."[35] "*The Times* newspaper having originally discountenanced Building Societies from ignorance must continue to do so for consistency."[36]

Tompkins in 1845 noted that prospectuses contained ". . . promises which could not be fulfilled with justice to all parties concerned; and as all state a probable period of the society's termination, which period differs in various announcements, and it is no doubt from these causes in conjunction with want of sufficient knowledge of the subject that a spirit of partial opposition has arisen against building societies, which when conducted on sound principles, they do not deserve".[37] Arthur Scratchley probably did more than any other single individual to further these sound principles. He continually stressed that the assets of the society consisted of a series of promises to pay sums of money at future dates, and it was the present value of these future payments that was the important thing, not their ultimate value. Profit was only realised as these payments were in fact made. J. McFarlane Gray put forward an ingenious solution: "It would not be difficult to construct a *mechanical actuary*. A set of ivory scales, divided logarithmically, as in the common slide rule, but finely divided and of a good size to enable figures to be read off and constructed especially on building society scales, would enable the auditors to read off the [present] value of all the mortgages in a few hours, with sufficient accuracy. One set of scales might well be used for all the societies in Liverpool [since they were run on the same plan] and they could well afford to pay for first class workmanship on it."[38]

The *Building Societies Gazette* commented on building society prospectuses as late as 1869:[39] "There is room for reformation in the wording and general construction of these documents. They are not written with a deliberate intention to deceive, *only* to stimulate 'business'. But one talks bravely of the profits being enhanced by the peculiar principle of *that* society and is issued with a balance sheet which actually has a balance on the *wrong* side of ten pounds. Another offers money on approved security at 5% interest, and borrowers find, all too late, that a premium is charged the first year in *addition* to the 5% interest and actually deducted from the advance, although there is not so much as a whisper of it, or any other charge indeed, beyond the 5% in the prospectus. A third advertises money at 4%, whereas £4 is charged every year, the last even as the first, for each hundred borrowed." Shades of modern hire purchase finance!

In 1871 the Planet, at that time the third largest society, was in difficulties as a result of charging low interest rates but high premiums to borrowers. These premiums were treated as realised profit and high bonuses were paid out of them. When new advances fell off the high bonuses could not be maintained.[40] In the years after the passing of the 1874 Building Societies Act, which forbade the inclusion of premiums in the realised profit declared by societies, the Registrar noted that a number of societies, large and small, persisted in the practice.

The premium system raised other issues. Societies would be tempted to lend on poor securities because the potential borrower, perhaps a speculative builder already in financial trouble, was prepared to pay a very high premium. This temptation would be still greater if the society itself was in difficulties. As with any other auction, those interested in the proceeds of the sale, though not themselves potential buyers, may bid to force up the price to potential buyers. "People bid against members wanting advances to raise the premium, although they have no intention to build, and if they get it cheap, they resell."[41] It seems to have been one of the responsibilities of directors to bid to prevent premiums falling too low. "Some parties paid a premium of £62 or £63 per share and others, perhaps on the next monthly night, £54, especially if the party bidding was known to the directors and they did not like to bid against him."[42]

With the emergence of the permanent and serial terminating societies, public houses ceased to be the main meeting places of building societies. Many now had permanent offices, which were open daily, making it much more convenient for members to pay subscriptions. The following is a description of the offices of the Birmingham Freehold Land and Building Societies in the 1860s. "This office might be called a shop for the sale of land and houses. Fitted up with a counter and desks, and provided with clerks and other officials, it is an establishment at which at suitable hours anyone may call to make enquiries, pay in money or transact other business connected with the societies. Around the walls are hung maps and plans, showing the estates which have been purchased and the way they are to be sectioned off into streets and building plots with a list of prices. Besides these plans there are drawings in water colours representing the elevations of different classes of houses, . . . of various dimensions and style of finish."[43]

In such circumstances the social aspects of building society membership could not continue. However the permanent societies did not dominate everywhere; and especially in Lancashire, South Wales and the North East, terminating societies continued to thrive, sometimes not too far removed from the old pattern. Oldham in 1873 had thirty-six terminating societies, twenty-nine meeting at inns. The temperance movement played its part in breaking the connection between building societies and the trade, though not always successfully. The 4th Swan Society meeting at Ashton-under-Lyme paid 3d. per member for its meeting place, an inn, but got a chit for 3d. worth of drink for each member. To placate a new chairman, the rules were altered so that each member paid only 1d. for the use of the room. But attendance fell off and the subscriptions did not come in, so the new rule was rescinded.[44] "I once formed a society in what was called a Rechabite tent, with a view to another class of persons, who were teetotallers, and that society did not succeed."[45] A similar attempt in Oldham was, in spite of the environment, more successful.[46] Of a group of Manchester terminating societies it was said in 1871 "We charged the members 3d. or 4d. a night each, that they might drink at the public house, instead of paying rent. We now pay £6 a year rent to some chapel keeper. . . . The members come less to meetings now."[47] But increasingly societies took heed of Scratchley's advice: "No meeting of the society should ever be held at any tavern or public house. The members may save much money by the adoption of this rule . . . and deliver themselves from the temptation to form habits of intemperance and useless expenditure, which well might counterbalance all the advantages to be derived from these institutions."[48]

Chapels, parish rooms and mechanics' institutes were increasingly the meeting places of small societies. An advertisement in the second issue of the *Building Societies Gazette*[49] called attention to a proposed Building Societies Hall, containing a small hall for meetings, a board-room and subscriptions room in a prominent position near Islington Church "if sufficient societies will avail themselves of the advantages which such a building offers, at a rent they now pay for inferior accommodation".

While societies were small their management was clearly a part-time business, though experience might be preserved by the same secretary taking over a second society when the first terminated. With the growth of large permanent and serial terminating societies, a new group of professional managers emerged, who were to play a leading role in deciding the movement's future. Many of these men had their first contact with building societies via their previous occupations such as solicitors' clerks, printers, surveyors and seal makers. The emergence of such a professional group, together with directors of growing experience, raised the standard of management. The Royal Commission noted "that the directors were from the working class or those near them in point of station" in the early terminating societies but the permanents were invariably under middle class direction.[50]

The usual method of forming a society was for a person or group to find a nucleus of people prepared to invest money, and a group of interim directors to agree some interim rules. The embryo society then advertised for shareholders and called a general meeting to adopt the rules and appoint directors under those rules. Mr. Campbell, manager of a large Sunderland group, put the expenses of formation "—publishing bills, newspaper advertisements, certifying rules, rule books, forms, penbooks and account books—at about £100".[51]

Managers were usually paid, wholly or partly, according to results, "In accordance with the number of shares taken and the amount of business done".[52] On his appointment as part-time secretary of the newly formed Temperance Society in 1853, H. J. Phillips was paid 3% of total receipts with a maximum of £200; this gave him an income of £51 in the first year.[53] James Higham of the Fourth City Mutual Society and his four clerks received between £600 and £700 in 1870, when the Society's income was rather more than £10,000.[54] T. Y. Strachan gave the Royal Commission details of the total management expenses of a large number of societies in Newcastle-upon-Tyne and Gateshead, which have been grouped in Table VII.

The table shows the economies of scale well enough among both terminating and permanent societies. Expenses for the large London societies were distinctly higher than those in Newcastle. Warner put the expenses of the Sun Permanent at 3% to 4% of turnover.[55] For the London and General Society the figure was about 2%[56] and for the Fourth City Mutual about 1%.[57] Details of management expenses in Scotland were given in the report of the Assistant Commissioner;[58] unfortunately they can only be related to mortgage assets and not turnover. Details are given in Table VIII.

TABLE VII

Management Expenses as a % of Annual Turnover

	Permanent Societies		Terminating Societies	
	Average expenses %	No. of Societies	Average Expenses %	No. of Societies
Turnover				
Newcastle				
under £10,000	1·35	7	0·94	3
— £20,000	0·68	8	0·34	1
over £20,000	0·63	9	0·31	1
Gateshead				
under £10,000	1·38	5	0·84	3
— £20,000	0·43	1	—	—
over £20,000	0·83	1	—	—

TABLE VIII

Management Expenses as a % of Mortgage Assets, Scotland

Mortgage Assets	Permanent Societies		Terminating Societies	
	Average Expenses %	No. of Societies	Average Expenses %	No. of Societies
under £10,000	1·27	3	2·02	4
— £50,000	0·62	4	0·28	2
over £50,000	0·38	2	—	—

The same pattern emerges in relation to size as in Newcastle, except that small terminating societies in Scotland had distinctly high management expenses. It is possible to derive from Strachan's figure for Newcastle and Gateshead a figure of management expenses related to mortgage assets for all permanent societies taken together. This comes to 0·29% for Newcastle, 0·56% for Gateshead. The comparable figure for Scotland is 0·47%.

The lower expenses of many terminating societies was probably the result of greater use of voluntary labour; directors and other officers associated with some cause or institution, or from motives of public service, giving their services for nominal returns. One would expect this to apply especially to small terminating societies but in fact the large terminating societies had lower expenses. The treasurer of the substantial Landore series of societies in Swansea received only £4 10s. per year.[59] In Oldham the directors received ". . . a glass of spirits that is their perquisite in the matter, they give their time".[60]

In the large societies directors' duties would be more onerous and payment was the rule. The seven directors of the Fourth City Mutual split £250 between them for their weekly attendance at meetings.[61] The directors of the Greenwich Industrial Society divided a quarter of the society's profit for their fortnightly attendances of about two hours. The directors' income was increased by survey fees. Surveys were usually carried out by a committee of the board, sometimes with the help of a professional surveyor. The Fourth City Mutual paid 7s. 6d. for each visit, to the three members of the Survey Committee, for their two reports: one on the character of the neighbourhood, one on the structure of the house. Such fees averaged £10 per year per director.[62]

Survey fees tended to vary with the distance the directors had to travel. The Sheffield and South Yorkshire Society charged a 10s. 6d. survey fee provided the property was within three miles.[63] The Sun Permanent's fee was 15s., or 17s. outside the metropolis, but these surveys were subsidised: the three directors receiving a guinea between them and the professional surveyor one guinea on the first £100 value of the property and 5s. per £50 thereafter.[64] Some societies had special arrangements with surveyors whereby surveys were undertaken for members at reduced fees. In a Scots society the surveyor reduced charges by 50%[65] and in an Irish Society, if the member's application was unsuccessful, only half the survey fee was charged.[66] The Landore Society's survey fee was 4s. per visit.

As societies grew a building society connection was important to solicitors. Frequently all a society's work would go to one solicitor, the work being done on a fixed scale of charges lower than the normal charges. In the Sun Permanent, the solicitor executed all assignments at four guineas each, exclusive of stamps, and the society charged the member three guineas for the first £100 and half a guinea per £50 thereafter, the solicitor's fees being lent by the society and repaid over time. In most societies the borrower paid the solicitor's charges in cash.[67] The scale of legal fees for the London General Society was—up to £200, three guineas; up to £750, four and a half guineas and over £750, six guineas. The Landore societies charged £1 10s. solicitor's fee per £80 share.

At a time when the leasehold system was rapidly growing, with varying conditions attached to leases, societies needed to beware, and the choice of solicitor was very important. A barrister warned societies,[68] "And with reference to conveyances from sub-lessors—which in and around the metropolis are very numerous—and such as railway and other large companies would palm upon their under tenants, who may be so readily tempted to sacrifice their future interests to the present advantages which local situation may seem to afford, great and stringent precautions are at all times requisite, for with nothing less than a clear, tangible and saleable title can building societies fairly deal." He was not alone, Scratchley stated that "The security offered to building societies is one of peculiar liability to be of an unsound nature."[69]

On the question of reserve funds, societies were divided. Scratchley put the lack of provision for losses through bad investments as one of the causes of the failure of societies and in his model rules prescribes that one-third of surplus profits "be carried to the credit of a permanent guarantee fund to meet any loss which may arise", adding that the proportion may be varied in the light of experience over the first ten years.[70] The opposite view was put by Mr. Campbell of Sunderland to the Royal Commission, "We might as well suffer a loss when it occurs as provide a reserve fund."[71] It might be held that such a view was reasonable for a terminating society with a stable membership, but if a permanent society had suffered a loss, it was unlikely to attract new members. One of the largest permanents, the Leeds Society, had no reserve fund.[72] The Halifax Permanent on the other hand started such a fund at its inception.[73]

Detailed evidence concerning reserve funds is available for permanent societies in Newcastle and Gateshead, again thanks to T. Y. Strachan's evidence to the Royal Commission. The Assistant Commissioner in Scotland collected information but only six of the fifteen societies from which he obtained details had reserve funds, and the ratio of reserves to mortgage assets varied widely from 2·6% to 16·2%. Table IX shows the figures given by Strachan. All the societies, except one in Gateshead, had a reserve fund, and while the largest societies had rather stronger reserves, there is remarkably little variation between size groups.

TABLE IX

Reserve Funds as a Percentage of Mortgage Assets, Permanent Societies

Mortgage Assets	Newcastle-on-Tyne Average Reserve Ratio	Newcastle-on-Tyne No. of Societies	Gateshead Average Reserve Ratio	Gateshead No. of Societies
under £10,000	3·4	4	3·0	4
— £100,000	3·5	18	3·0	3
over £100,000	4·3	2	—	—

Judging from the evidence given to the Royal Commission relatively few societies employed the services of actuaries either in checking their tables of payments or in valuing future subscriptions. Of the large London societies that gave evidence to the Commission, the Monarch was alone in having an actuary to verify its tables, though J. S. Parker was actuary to twenty-three small London societies.[74] Arthur Scratchley was consulted by some London societies and was retained by some provincial societies, the Bristol and West of England Society among them, to carry out valuations triennially or at longer intervals. The Leeds Permanent was fortunate in having an actuary, Thomas Fatkin, as its chief official.

Auditing left much to be desired, in many societies, as we have seen. It was almost universally an internal matter, with one of the ordinary members appointed to represent the body of the society's members at the audit. While such an informal approach might be acceptable in small societies, it involved serious risks for the societies that grew large; just how serious these risks were was later demonstrated in the case of the Portsea Island Society. Davis commented, "... in too many societies no accurate system of keeping the books is adopted, and in consequence balance sheets are ... perfectly untrustworthy".[75]

It was the Northern societies which gave the lead in the matter of branch organisation. In 1871 James Higham stated that only one London society (it was in fact the Temperance) had agents.[76] In the north the practice of opening branches and appointing agents was developed early. The Freeholders Society, Manchester, allowed any district with fifty members to petition for the appointment of a local treasurer to receive subscriptions. In 1846 this society had branches in Bolton, Rochdale, Oldham, Heaton Norris, Bury, Patricroft, Wigan, Ashton-under-Lyne and Farnworth.[77] The Halifax Permanent, in its first year, 1853, opened offices at Sowerby Bridge, Thornton and Queenshead. In 1854 a branch was opened at Brighouse and two years later at Hebden Bridge and Stairland. All these were in the area close to the head office, as were others founded later. A larger step was taken in 1862 with the opening of a branch at Huddersfield "with its own 'directory' of a chairman, vice-chairman and ten members".[78] The Queen's Society, Manchester, had ten branches in neighbouring towns, and persons were appointed "in other towns where we have a large number of members and who receive their subscriptions".[79] The Leeds Permanent had, in 1871, eighteen branches, some fairly far removed from Leeds, such as those in Hartlepools and Sheffield.[80] Only investment business was conducted at branch offices, mortgage business being transacted from Leeds. The Leeds Provincial and the Bradford societies had branches. These early moves of the Yorkshire societies to create branches must have done much to help their rapid growth, and to lay the foundation for their importance in the development of the movement.

The period after 1836 saw a decline in the extent to which building societies actually built houses themselves; lending money to purchase existing houses, or to finance the building of houses, now became their chief function. Had this change not taken place, then as the movement grew it would clearly have been active in deciding the sort of houses that were built, and in determining housing standards generally. However, their role, in general, became a passive one; provided a house gave adequate security for the loan, that satisfied the society. There were exceptions; some societies still engaged in building, and some attempted to influence housing standards positively.

The Royal Commission's view was that "building societies do not build; they simply make advances on building . . . The few exceptions in England appear to arise chiefly where money has been advanced for the purposes of building, which the borrower fails to carry out and which the Society is compelled to take in hand and complete".[81] Such a judgement is not wholly supported by the evidence the Commission heard; among the societies which stated they had engaged in building were the Fourth City Mutual, Burnley, Temperance, and Landore. The term "building clubs" was generally used to designate small societies which built houses as against "building societies" which advanced money.[82] The Bennett's Hill Societies in Birmingham exercised some control of building, though not in detail. No "back to back" houses were allowed. Borrowers were tied to a building line, though not a style. There were some experiments in Halifax to improve the quality of working class housing, in association with building societies, though the societies' role was not much removed from their usual function as lenders.[83]

The movement was very much divided in its attitude to speculative builders. For some, advances to builders was their main business. "Yes, it is the general practice in our business to advance to builders"[84] (C. L. Gruneison, Conservative Land Society). "I should think the bulk of our advances are made to builders"[85] (H. J. Phillips, Temperance Society). There were equally strong views on the other side. "I saw that builders tried to introduce business into it [his society] for the purpose of building . . . and I discountenanced anything of that sort"[86] (J. Ryalls, connected with a number of Sheffield societies). Mr. T. F. Peacock was against lending to builders: advances should be made only on houses already built.[87] Lending to builders had its dangers; Mr. G. Watson, an Edinburgh solicitor, spoke of "Men of straw who have never been heard of in the trade, suddenly become builders on a large scale, and after a time disappear".[88] In Sheffield "In one street there are forty-one houses only three of which are let, all have been built out of building societies' money with heavy ground rents to pay".[89] Societies protected themselves against being left with unfinished houses, when a borrowing builder failed, by not lending in advance of construction. The Planet Society made no advance "until the buildings are covered in, and seldom even then".[90] The National Society advanced two-thirds of the value when the building was roofed.[91] The Cork and South of Ireland Society had a more dangerous practice. When one-third of the money required to build a house had been spent, the society could advance the remaining two-thirds.[92] The Temperance Society advanced money to builders and when the house was sold the builder's obligations were transferred to the buyer.[93]

Large societies were sometimes unable to find a sufficient demand for mortgages locally, and lent on properties distant from their home town. This created difficulties with valuations. The directors might still survey, picking up "the knowledge in the best way they can from enquiries on the spot".[94] This was clearly a dangerous method of doing business and could lead to losses. "In seeking profitable employment for surplus funds the society [the National] was led to make advances in the North of England, an adventure into alien fields that proved expensive."[95] One solution was to employ a local valuer, but this too had its risks, for with an unknown valuer there was the possibility of collusion between him and the potential borrower.[96] In 1849 Scratchley commented on such collusion, "False estimates are . . . not always the fruits of incapacity and inexperience. Cases have occurred of compacts between the surveyor and the vendor or purchaser of property, or even some officer of the Society, to share between themselves the profits of an unfair valuation."[97]

Advances were made on a variety of property, though freehold and leasehold houses were the main business. Doubts were at one time held about the legality of advances on copyhold property. Tidd Pratt informed the Dunmow Society in 1846[98] that "Opinions have been given by conveyancers that copyholds are not within the meaning of the words 'Real or leasehold estate' mentioned in 6 & 7 Will. IV, c. 32; in addition to which I do not think it advisable to take a mortgage on copyhold property as it would require the trustees to be admitted as tenants on the Court Roll", a matter of some expense. Court rulings that copyhold property constituted real estate overcame these doubts[99] but Pratt's other objection remained.

By the 1850s societies were lending on other security than house property and by the 1860s some societies were concentrating on more speculative property to a dangerous degree. The Sheffield and South Yorkshire Society had, by 1871, advanced amounts of £10,000, £12,000 and £30,000 to owners of factories. Mr. Allott, its secretary, said in 1871, that the practice had grown up during the last eight to ten years, and he saw no danger in it provided there was an ample margin of security and the personal security of the owners was pledged. This society, as a result of just such advances, was to provide one of the spectacular failures of the 1880s. Allott's answer to the question, "But your society has been conducted with great prudence and care?" was thus prophetic, "I think that it has been so far".[100] The practice was not confined to Sheffield; Mr.

Cully the Assistant Commissioner for Scotland referred to many Glasgow societies getting into difficulties by lending on factories.[101] However, it was at a later period that such lending became a danger to the movement.

There were those who wished to extend the range of securities that building societies might take. In 1851 Stone put forward a plea to allow advances against personal property. "All the legislature need do, to make personal property a good legal security to building societies, is to modify in their favour that portion of the bankruptcy and insolvency laws before alluded to; and to extend their power to make advances on personal as well as real property, with the addition of a clause for the registration of such securities and to make fraudulent dealing with or removal of personal property when mortgaged a misdemeanour and punishable as such. . . ."[102] Mr. Allott complained to the Royal Commission of having to turn down applicants who offered adequate security (other than real estate) and gave as examples debentures on companies with a personal guarantee of the directors, and railway debenture stocks with three, four or five years to run, from people who did not wish to realise the stocks but needed money.[103] The range of securities was in fact extended, not directly, but in the form of collateral security. The Sun Permanent in many cases advanced the full value of a property, making a second person security for twelve or more months' subscriptions by which time the outstanding loan was below the normal limit and the collateral security would be released.[104] The Fourth City Mutual occasionally took life insurance policies as collateral.[105] Some societies made loans against the security of their own shares. To withdraw shares usually involved some period of notice and could mean a sacrifice of interest, loss of one's place in the queue for advances or some withdrawal fee. In such circumstances, members in temporary difficulty could sometimes obtain a loan by pledging their shares as security. The London and General, Birkbeck and Sheffield and South Yorkshire societies provided this facility.[106] Societies often invested surplus funds in ordinary mortgages in the open market.[107]

The Royal Commission heard much evidence concerning the percentage of the value of a property societies would advance on mortgage. J. D. Smith of Edinburgh summed the matter up in saying that while he would like a margin of one-third he often had to take a margin of only one-tenth.[108] The normal advance on house property was 75% to 80% of the valuation, with some societies lending over 80% and even 90%.[109] The early terminating societies aimed to wind up after ten years or a little longer and mortgage terms were generally the same in permanent societies. However, longer term mortgages were to be found. J. Hosking reported doing the bulk of his business in Liverpool on a twenty-five year term,[110] and in another Liverpool society the normal term was twenty years.[111] The Northern Counties Society, Newcastle, also made advances for over twenty years.[112] This suggests that terms may have been rather longer in the North than in the South. The Temperance Society gave advances for fifteen years on freehold property but only for twelve years on leasehold.[113] The evidence given about the size of advances suggests an average figure of about £400.[114] Advances over £1,000 were uncommon, unless a society was making advances on non-house property. The distribution of mortgages for the Union Society, Belfast, was, under £200, 50 mortgages; —£500, 80; —£1,000, 100 and 70 mortgages of over £1,000.[115] This society made many advances on factories and mills, so the average size of advances would be larger than that for the movement as a whole.

For a period in 1849 Tidd Pratt refused to certify rules if advances greater than £150 were to be granted. The 1836 Act placed a limit of £150 on any one share, and the question of whether more than one share might be held if the total value exceeded £150 was raised in the case *Cutbill v. Kingdom*,[116] though not clearly decided. Tidd Pratt's refusal to sanction rules giving power to advance more than £150 was the result of some remarks of the judges in the case referred to.[117]

The following precepts were consciously observed, in at least some societies, in the conduct of their mortgage business:

If a potential borrower says he can put up £50, asks for an advance of a further £200 and the security is felt not to justify such an advance, no smaller advance should be offered. It may tempt the potential borrower to overstrain his finances to meet the shortfall and consequently get into difficulties.

Attention must be paid to the borrower's income as well as the adequacy of the security offered.

It is dangerous to commit a large proportion of the society's funds in a narrow area; a local fall in property values would leave the society in a dangerous position.

Special care is needed in approving advances in areas where the society has little experience of property values.

Resist the temptation to lower security requirements when funds are plentiful.

It is difficult to give any accurate picture of the rates of interest charged to borrowers; premiums on advances often confuse the picture and where these premiums were the result of bidding, the true rate charged by a society was likely to vary from month to month. A few features do emerge. First, that in permanent societies rates did not vary widely over time, and where variations were made it was only on new advances. Second, rates were distinctly higher in the South, especially around

London, than in the North. Thus in the period from its foundation in 1853 to 1884, the rate charged by the Halifax Permanent Society varied between 4½% and 5%, the rates quoted by London societies varying between 7% and 9%.[118] As borrowers became more familiar with building society operations the very high rates of interest that were charged in the 1840s declined; they realised that a rate of say 5% on the whole advance for the whole term, was not, in fact, a loan at 5%, and this "... fraud upon the borrower ..." was not practised "... as much as it used to be some years ago."[119]

The permanent societies were able to be much more flexible in the terms offered to borrowers (and indeed to investors). As Naylor puts it in describing the development of the Bradford Third Equitable Society, "The principle of shares was more and more departed from in order to give greater freedom and more equitable conditions to both investor and borrower. It was the 'amount' on which interest was calculated; it was the 'amount' which was deposited or withdrawn, not the share or aliquot part of a share; it was the 'amount' which was advanced on mortgage not the 'shares', so that the share remained in theory rather than in practice. As a consequence tables were discontinued and it became possible to make arrangements to suit individual requirements and each investor and borrower could ascertain from his private statement what rate of interest he was being allowed or being charged."[120]

James Higham gave the Commission a representative view of the societies' attitudes to fines: "... we are obliged to keep them heavy in the interest of the shareholders, because if they were lower it would lead to laxity in payments, and with the working classes it is very important ... to induce them to keep up their payments regularly. For that reason we charge 4d. on 14s. per month."[121] (About 30% per annum.) In fact this was a moderate figure: 60% was said to be the universal practice in Liverpool.[122] The practice of increasing fines as the period of arrears increased was fairly common, at least over the first few months. In a Manchester society[123] the fine rose from 1s. for one month's arrears on a 10s. subscription, to 8s. for the fourth month. The Bradford Third Equitable rose from 3d. for the first month to 1s. for the fourth on a monthly subscription of 15s.[124] In some societies directors had power to suspend fines in cases of accidents or unemployment,[125] but "generally directors hold to enforcing a heavy fine".[126] Fines tended to be lower in permanent than in terminating societies.

Regarding foreclosures Higham told the Commission that in over twenty years as a manager he had had only thirty to forty defaulting borrowers.[127] These were mostly cases where the borrower had built property, and the cost exceeded expectation. "I do not think I ever knew a working man or party who had not had experience, engage in a building transaction without finding that the house cost him considerably more than he expected".[128] Some large societies, such as the Queen's of Birmingham and the Bradford Third Equitable reported that they had never had a default. The Burnley Society took possession when the borrower was three months in arrears,[129] but most societies waited longer; six or nine months. When a society was forced to sell a property, the borrower was usually harshly treated as a result of the inequitable redemption rules referred to above. E. W. Brabrook stated that sales were frequently a cause of hardship. To redeem, the total of future subscriptions, without any discount, had to be paid; and this, together with fines and costs "usually swallowed up the whole of the property".[130]

The need to continue to act through trustees was irksome to some societies, and the lack of a public record of the names of trustees had one great drawback for the members. Mr. Ingoldby of the Planet Society explained it as follows: "Some times these matters [mortgage repayments] may go on for ten, twelve or fourteen years, according to our rules. During that time the trustees originally in the deed may have changed repeatedly and it is a great hardship on the borrowing member, they have to prove the appointment of successive trustees in order to get an adequate release. It is very well for him to have a receipt according to the rules of the society for the purpose of holding his property; but in the case of people who buy of him, he has to furnish a proper document of release and we have found that in very many instances to be a very great hardship upon borrowers."[131] Scratchley wrote, "The trouble this causes is sometimes so great that many solicitors advise their clients to have nothing to do with property that has passed through the hands of a Benefit Building Society."[132]

Some people saw an advantage in the necessity for trustees, for their presence would restrain boards of directors from dangerous speculations. The Assistant Commissioner for Ireland felt the hostility of certain boards to the legal necessity for trustees arose because the trustees were capable of independent judgement. He held them to be a valuable restraining influence.[133] Referring to the doubtful practice of the deposit of deeds by a society as security for borrowing, Mr. Brabrook thought that management committees would be more likely to resort to such methods when in need of money if there were no trustees.[134]

The objections of some societies to acting through trustees were founded on bitter experience. "When a society gets hold of a trustee . . . who will not act it is most difficult. . . . The trustees in one case were positively bought out in order to get rid of them."[135] Changes of trustees involved the society in expense and such changes could be frequent. Asked if these changes were the result of the duties the office entailed, Mr. Ingoldby replied,[136] "I think that they objected rather to the non-remuneration for their services." He agreed that it was an annoyance to trustees to have their names continually before the public as plaintiffs in the courts, for all actions by a society were brought in the names of the trustees.

In the period from 1836 to 1874 building societies travelled a long way in terms of organisation, but not all societies travelled the same distance. Indeed in 1874 there was a very wide variety of building societies still in existence. In some towns such as Oldham, there were societies operating in exactly the same way as societies in the earliest days of the movement. Only a few miles away in Manchester the Queen's Society was one of the largest permanent societies of the day. In London also large permanent societies were to be found alongside small terminating societies, and by 1874 the first wave of Starr Bowkett societies was already attracting attention in the metropolis. Yorkshire was already established as a stronghold of the movement with large permanent societies in Leeds, Halifax and Bradford and a host of smaller permanent societies, including the oldest Yorkshire permanent society, at Wakefield. The North East, like Lancashire, was a stronghold of both permanent and terminating societies; in South Wales, while permanents existed, the terminating societies were still dominant. In addition to building societies, freehold land societies, though beyond the first flush of youth, were still operating in many places. However, by 1874 the land societies were motivated by a desire to provide plots of land on which to erect houses, rather than to provide votes.

A large part of the movement had grown away from the simple conception of the 1836 Act; there had been no guidance from Parliament and only intermittent guidance from the Registrar and the Courts. In the main, building society managers followed their own judgement in creating securities to meet the public's need and in deciding what securities were acceptable.

Many of the innovations in organisation were beneficial to the movement and the 1874 Act was a first and none too successful attempt to translate the best of building society practice into legal requirements. Nowhere was the growth of the profession of "building society manager" more clearly shown than in the events which led to the passing of the Building Societies Act of 1874.

Chapter Five

JOINT ACTION AND THE BUILDING SOCIETIES ACT, 1874*

THE ISSUE which had induced building societies to take the limited concerted action which produced the 1836 Act, was the threat to their exemption from stamp duties. It was this same issue that continued to be the main force leading to joint action, intermittently at first, but eventually creating a permanent organisation for mutual protection. This organisation was to play an important part in bringing about the Building Societies Act, 1874. Thus the issue of stamp duty exemptions led also to the 1874 Act and it is ironic that during the bargaining preceding that Act, societies agreed to abandon their claim to special privileges in regard to these duties.

The agitation in 1836 did not produce any permanent central organisation, and no such organisation was to emerge until 1869. On particular occasions societies took joint action in defence of their privileges, then co-operation lapsed until the next threat appeared. At a time when terminating societies dominated the movement it was perhaps natural that these, viewing only a limited future, should not think very seriously about the problems of the movement as a whole. The change to the permanent system created a class of managers whose building society activities were their professional lives. With the emergence of this group, problems affecting the movement as a whole could no longer be so easily ignored.

It is therefore not surprising that when the terms of the 1874 Act were being discussed, the terminating societies were less influential than their numerical strength would suggest.[1] The resulting Act was unfavourable to their continued existence; they paid a heavy price for their neglect of general questions.

The 1836 Act extended to building societies such portions of the Friendly Societies Acts as were applicable to their purposes. Clause 37 of the 1829 Friendly Societies Act exempted such societies from stamp duties on all documents needed to conduct their business. The possibility that this Clause was applicable to building societies seems at first to have been

* *Notes on this chapter appear on page 293.*

ignored; building society mortgage deeds continued to be stamped as they had been before 1836. W. L. Harle told the Royal Commission of 1871[2] that in the years before 1836 building societies were never mentioned in preparing securities, everything was done in the name of the trustees, ". . . because at that time conveyancers thought it not desirable to introduce any reference to a society. That went on for some years. Until a decision of the Court of Common Pleas [1849] which released societies from stamp duty, the whole matter was treated as a private mortgage". This was a fair statement of the situation, but not wholly accurate.

The question was first raised in 1843 when the Mutual Society of Stepney had enquired of Tidd Pratt whether mortgage deeds required stamps. His reply, dated August 9th, stated, "I am clearly of the opinion that all mortgages of Building Societies require to be stamped".[3] In 1846 the matter was raised with the Stamps Office. Mr. Pavey (Commercial and Foreigners, London), having obtained a barrister's opinion favourable to exemption, sought confirmation from the Board of Commissioners for Stamps and Taxes. They refused to commit themselves, Pavey receiving the somewhat tart reply, "It appears to the board that the question is one in which much difficulty is involved, and if the opinion is not sufficiently satisfactory to the directors [of the society] the board think they had better adopt the alternative course of stamping the deeds".[4]

The question was clearly under active discussion in 1846. In its first issue, on March 14th, *The National* had published opinions from two barristers, who "with the proverbial uncertainty of the law had delivered diametrically opposite opinions". On June 20th *The National* published five more opinions, three against, one for, and one uncertain. A solicitor, W. Taylor, probably summed up the current practice when he wrote, "I am aware that some eminent counsel have given their opinions pro and con, but whilst there is any doubt on the point no solicitor could safely or wisely advise a society not to stamp their deeds of security."[5]

Building Societies began to organise to secure this privilege. The second British Building and Investment Society, one of the largest in London with the forceful J. McArthur as its secretary, started collecting signatures for a petition to Parliament. This drew attention to clause 37 and continued, "Nevertheless your petitioners are informed by the proper authorities at the Stamp Office that under the legal construction of the said Acts mortgages to building societies are not exempt. . . ".[6] On March 21st *The National* reported "A meeting of Secretaries of Building Societies was held last Tuesday at Newton's Eastern Coffee House, High St., Whitechapel, to take into consideration the repeal of the duty on mortgages to Building Societies."

Nothing further came of this meeting until July, but in May, B. Hawes, M.P., presented petitions against the stamp duty from three Bowkett Societies.[7] In June delegates from the six existing Bowkett Societies formed a committee with a Mr. Peacock as secretary, to collect signatures and prepare for parliamentary action in the next session; Hawes agreed to assist in this.[8] This committee met monthly, usually under the chairmanship of Dr. T. E. Bowkett, at least until the end of 1846. An effort to extend the organisation outside London received little support, though there were letters of encouragement from Frome and Preston.[9] The Committee were pressing for the exemption of duty on mortgages up to £200, a limit suggested by the Friendly Societies Act, 1840.

On July 10, 1846, a meeting was held at the Albion Hall, Moorgate,[10] "numerously attended by parties connected with Metropolitan Building Societies". The legal position on stamps was outlined and a resolution passed that, "It is desirable to form an association with requisite power to obtain such an alteration of the Building Societies Act as will effect the object in view." The body was to be called "The Building Societies Association for Procuring the Amendment of the Building Societies Act". The annual subscription was to be one shilling. The officers, W. Farmer, chairman, T. H. Gorse, secretary and J. Dobson, treasurer, headed a committee of thirty members. This association seems in fact to have been stillborn; the size of its committee was scarcely an advantage. Throughout 1847 *The National* carried letters and editorial comment on the lack of activity by the committee. While the Association and its committee were idle, some of its members were not, for a number of commitee men were at the head of a new organisation which was formed privately in February 1848 and held its first public meeting in March. This was the Building Societies Institute, with James Brewer as its chairman and R. Jesserun its secretary.[11]

About the same time *The National* reported that an influential member of the legal profession had prepared a bill that had the approval of the Registrar to amend the 1836 Act. It suggested that the bill be examined by a committee of leading building society officials and the Building Societies Institute did in fact take over the bill. The Institute was closely associated with *The National*, using the latter's office as its postal address. The formal objectives of the Institute were to promote and protect the interests of building societies; to provide general information on their progress for the use of members and others and to amend the 1836 Act. The Institute met fairly regularly, and clearly achieved some standing in the movement, since its committee sometimes acted as adjudicators in disputes. When the arbitration procedures of a society were overridden in a County Court, the Institute acted swiftly and was successful in getting the original judgement against that society reversed.[12]

In January 1849 the terms of the Institute's proposed Bill were published. Conferences had been held "with members of the government and Mr. Tidd Pratt and they confidently hope that during the next session their object will be gained".[13] Pratt had said that nothing short of a new Act would meet the difficulty. The terms of the Bill allowed societies to take collateral security in addition to mortgages; allowed borrowing by societies on the security of mortgage deeds; fixed stamp duty on mortgages at 35s., irrespective of the value of the property mortgaged; granted exemption from all other stamp duties and property tax and limited the size of individual advances.

On February 9th the Bill was considered at a meeting of the Institute with sixty members present.[14] Discussion centred on the proposed limitation of individual advances. Limits of from £600 to £2,000 were suggested and, lacking agreement, the clause was dropped. A deputation was appointed to discuss the Bill with the President of the Board of Trade. Presumably as a result of this delegation, *The Reporter*, in its issue for March, said it was anticipated that a committee of enquiry would be set up. This anticipation was not fulfilled, because of events in the Courts.

The action *Walker v. Giles*,[15] heard in May and June 1849, raised the question, among others, of the stamping of building society mortgage deeds. Chief Justice Wilde held clause 37 of the Friendly Societies Act 1829 to be one of those applicable to building societies. This was not quite the end of the matter. "The decision created much discussion and its correctness was impugned; but in the subsequent case, *Barnard v. Polsworth*,[16] November 3, 1849, the Court of Common Pleas confirmed the former decision on this point; and in one report of the case Maule, J., is stated to have said that he had noted the strictures on the former decision but he saw no reason to alter it."[17] Not everyone was convinced. "It seems that conveyancers are not reconciled to this decision; and it is possible that the question will again be discussed under the new stamp Act [1850]. In the meantime it is probable that the above decision will be acted on, and it cannot be doubted that the legislature would provide a remedy in the event of *Walker v. Giles* being overruled."[18]

With the question of stamp duties settled, interest in the Institute languished though it continued to meet, now at the Sun Tavern. In December 1849 it was decided to meet quarterly. The Committee continued to act as arbiter and adviser on matters of professional practice; at the meeting in December 1849, ". . . a number of questions were discussed and replies agreed to".[19] In June 1850 the Institute was in touch with Mr.

Slaney, M.P., Chairman of a Commons Committee on the Savings of the Middle and Working Classes, regarding registration.[20]

At the formation of the Building Societies Protection Association in 1869 James Higham stated that, "It was now more than twenty years since a few officers of Building Societies met periodically at the Sun Tavern to consult together in reference to the general interests of those Societies".[21] Higham must have been referring to the Building Societies Institute, certainly he was often reported as among those attending its meetings.[22] Just when the Institute ceased is doubtful. A meeting in January 1851 is the last mentioned in *The Reporter*, which normally carried a brief account of these meetings.

The agitation concerning stamp duties by building societies no doubt contributed to the reduction of these duties in 1850: not that the reduction was of any immediate interest to societies, in view of the legal decisions in 1849. In 1850 the Chancellor of the Exchequer, Sir Charles Wood, reduced the duty on mortgage deeds to 2s. 6d. per £100 from the old progressive scale under which mortgages up to £50 required a stamp of £1, increasing by 10s. 0d. per £50 up to £200, then rising more slowly so that a mortgage securing a loan of £1,000 required only a £5 stamp.

In the years following the court decision of 1849, the Treasury made a series of attempts to re-impose stamp duties on building society mortgage deeds. The result on each occasion was to bring about a degree of co-operation between societies.

In April 1855 a Bill amending and consolidating the Friendly Societies Acts had passed the Committee stage in the Commons, when the government forced its recommittal to the committee stage in order to add to it a clause, number 13, which would have ended building society exemption from stamp duties. The grounds the government gave for its action were that, "It was at first represented that these societies were of great use to the poor, but they are now converted into larger speculations for builders and capitalists and the indirect effect of this exemption is to defraud the revenue of considerable sums from year to year."[23] Mr. Scholefield of Birmingham divided the House in an effort to remove the clause, but the vote was 37 to 26 against him. The manner in which the clause was introduced helped to create strong feelings against it. As the Earl of Derby put it, "Now when a Bill of such an unobjectionable kind was introduced into the other House of Parliament he thought it a very bad thing that the Secretary of the Treasury should come down to the parties proposing the Bill and say to them that they should not have the support of the Government unless they would consent to introduce into their Bill a provision that had nothing to do with it. Yet it was under that compulsion that the clause was introduced".[24]

Even before the Bill reached the Lords, building societies had been active. The alarm was first sounded in Liverpool, probably by Mr. Horsefall, a local M.P. interested in building societies.[25] On May 7th, little more than a week after the debate in the Commons, the Liverpool Building Societies Protection Association had been formed, and it led, in its own view, the fight against Clause 13. "This association was quite alone in the emergency, but after considerable labour and expense it induced representative gentlemen in London, Manchester, Birmingham, Wolverhampton, Coventry, Derby, Chester, etc., to unite and defeat Mr. Wilson."[26] Such claims are somewhat exaggerated, for it is known that the Birmingham societies were alerted by Mr. Scholefield, once chairman of the Freehold Land Societies Conference, and connected with James Taylor's group of building societies in Birmingham. Some members of the Liverpool Association had been part of the delegation that waited on Spring Rice in 1835, and they naturally turned to him, now Lord Monteagle, again.[27]

Meanwhile, James Higham had called together some London society secretaries, and an association was formed with Scholefield as its president. Before the Lords debate a meeting of delegates, referred to by the Liverpool Association above, agreed on a compromise with the government, in the person of the Hon. H. Fitzroy. When the new clause appeared it was felt that it did not conform to the agreed compromise, so the building societies continued their opposition in the Lords. Lord Ravensworth moved the exclusion of the offending clause and received powerful support from Lord Monteagle, who ". . . expressed his satisfaction at seeing the growth of the societies in question and the benefit they had conferred upon the poorer classes, especially in encouraging habits of providence and foresight . . . it would be exceedingly injurious . . . to discourage them; and with great respect to the provision under consideration, he . . . felt it had no right to be in the Bill at all. It was not mentioned in any of the enacting clauses, or included in the title; so that societies had not had any notice that their interests would be affected by it."[28] The clause was struck out in the Lords.

The government did not give up easily. Ten days later, in a money bill, setting out some minor changes in stamp duties, another attempt was made to extinguish the building societies' privilege. Opposition was again strong and well organised. This was the occasion on which James Higham, leading the London societies, discovered the importance of being in the lobby of the House to bring continuous pressure on sympathetic members during debates, a tactic he was to exploit effectively in later life. "The Bill was read a second time, and on the night of its going into Committee he (Mr. Higham) accompanied a deputation, which had an interview with different members of the Government and also with Mr. Bright [Once a director of the National Society]. Lord Grosvenor (now Lord Ebury) appealed to them to remember that the rejection of the clause would endanger the Bill; but their reply was that such a clause should never have been introduced into such a Bill, and if there was to be any legislation on the question it ought to be open and fair."[29] Again the societies prevailed, the Chancellor of the Exchequer, Sir George Cornwall Lewis, eventually agreeing to withdraw the clause on the understanding that a committee would enquire into the whole subject during the following session. In fact this committee was never appointed.

The Treasury returned to the attack in 1860, when a resolution to abolish the building societies' exemption was one of a group of thirty-six resolutions introduced by Mr. Gladstone. Higham described the outcome thus, "Gentlemen from Liverpool and Birmingham with Mr. Josiah Hosking formed a deputation to wait upon Mr. Gladstone; they were received by Mr. Laing (the Secretary of the Treasury) with the Chairman and Solicitor of the Excise. The deputation argued the matter with them and it was obvious that, although the heads of the departments were the moving parties in the proposition, they knew nothing about the matter. It was declared that a man had actually borrowed £3,000 of a Building Society on mortgage merely to evade the stamp duty. It was well known by those who understood the working of such societies, that borrowers in return for the advantage offered in repayment of sums borrowed by instalments, pay a larger rate of interest than ordinary mortgagors. Mr. Laing was so satisfied with the explanation given by the deputation that he said he would report the result of the interview to Mr. Gladstone, and no more was heard of that resolution."[30]

The Liverpool Association and the London group, now calling itself the Land and Building Societies Protection Association, had been maintained in being following the events of 1855. The London group, following the government's threat of an enquiry, had endeavoured to raise a fighting fund in 1855,[31] and in 1860 had requested a subscription of 10s. 6d. from all its former subscribers to meet the expenses they had incurred.

Things were quiet for a few years until the Treasury raised the matter again in 1866 and in 1867, but it was not seriously pressed until 1868, now as Clause 10 of the Inland Revenue Bill, in the form that only mortgages of less than £200 should be exempt from Stamp Duty. Thomas Hughes, M.P., led a deputation of London building society officials to meet Ward Hunt, the Chancellor of the Exchequer, and a compromise was reached to limit the exemption to mortgages of up to £500. On this occasion there was clearly a breakdown in liaison between societies. T. E. Priest claimed that the clause had passed the Commons before they got to hear of it in Liverpool.[32] Higham was also dissatisfied; the London Association had lapsed after 1860, and he said that ". . . had there been an organisation in July last [1868] he believed that that clause would have been defeated."[33]

The Liverpool Association was soon at work on a petition to effect the repeal of the clause and Higham organised a meeting of London secretaries on February 26, 1869, at Salters Hotel, Kings Arms Yard, Snow Hill; a meeting which was to lay the foundations of a permanent organisation of societies, mainly in London at first, but later nationally. A particular issue that immediately concerned societies was whether an advance of say £300, leading to a mortgage deed securing future payments of principal and interest which would exceed £500, required a stamp. In April 1869, a deputation from Birmingham, Liverpool, London and several other large towns met the Chancellor[34] and appealed for the removal of the duty, or at least for the exemption limit to apply to the actual sum advanced.

However, by 1869 other issues were becoming more important: rulings of both the Registrar and the Courts had created a good deal of uncertainty concerning the precise legal position of the societies. The Court's decision in *Laing v. Reed*[35] concerning borrowing powers was instrumental in leading the agitation from the narrow issue of stamp duty exemption to the wider question of reform of the 1836 Act. The doubts raised by the Courts, concerning the legality of borrowing power, were especially serious for societies in the North East, where there was a heavy dependence on loans. The societies in Sunderland prevailed upon the local member, Mr. Gourley, to introduce a Bill to clarify the question. This he did on August 4, 1869, so late in the session that the Bill was withdrawn after its first reading.[36] The London Association was alarmed that the Sunderland societies had not consulted with other societies and Higham obtained an interview with Gourley, at which the latter agreed to consider any suggestions the London Association cared to make before reintroducing his Bill. Gourley's Bill was considered and amended by the London committee, and the resulting Bill was endorsed at a general meeting of the London Association in October.[37]

The struggle for reform was to prove lengthy. For the next five years this was the main concern of the London group which took the title, Building Societies Protection Association. Led by Higham, that association was the strongest and most continuous force behind the movement for reform. The Association had Higham as chairman from its inception. W. R. Warner was its first secretary, with Higham's son, James Higham, Jnr., taking over that office after the first month.

A mere ten people attended the first meeting. At the second meeting an executive committee of five was elected, though the eventual size of the executive was set at twelve. The Association recruited W. T. McCullagh Torrens, M.P., as president and four other M.P.s, including Thomas Hughes, as vice-presidents. In view of the work to be done, this early move to establish parliamentary connections was both shrewd and important. The Association enjoyed a further advantage, in that a month before its foundation, the *Building Societies Gazette* commenced publication. Given the diversity of societies, without some such means of communication on building society matters, a central organisation would find success much more difficult to achieve. The Association's annual subscription was set at one guinea, unless a society had more than 500 shares issued, in which case it was two guineas. In October 1869 the executive agreed that provincial societies might, for a subscription of 5s., have the advantage of records of legal proceedings to be kept by the Association, and be advised of parliamentary proceedings.

After the endorsement of amendments to Gourley's Bill at the general meeting in October 1869, there were further Court decisions affecting borrowing powers.[38] In the light of these there was a further meeting with Gourley, who agreed to sponsor a more comprehensive bill, if the Association prepared one, and undertook to try and get the co-operation of his Sunderland constituents.[39] A sub-committee was set up to prepare a Bill consolidating and amending existing legislation, consisting of Messrs. Breese, Higham, Stanesby and Warner. Their work proceeded swiftly and the resulting Bill was approved at the Association's first annual general meeting on April 27, 1870.

The Bill was introduced on May 3rd, sponsored by Mr. Gourley, Sir Roundell Palmer, Mr. Stevenson and Mr. McCullagh Torrens. The speed of these proceedings may have been induced by the introduction of a government measure in February, which would have transferred the Registry of Friendly Societies to the Board of Trade. In itself this was an innocent enough matter, though it gave an inkling of the government's later view that building societies were akin to joint stock companies and hence that the Board of Trade was their proper home.

On June 24th a meeting, with Gourley in the chair, was held in London. With fifty people attending, it was certainly the most representative gathering of building societies thus far. While the majority were from London, the following other towns were represented: Sunderland, South Shields, Stockton, Liverpool, Manchester, Newcastle-on-Tyne, Sheffield, Birmingham, West Bromwich, Derby and Norwich. Some northern representatives, led by W. Dodds, M.P., felt the right course was to try and get the Commons to refer the Bill to a Select Committee, so that wide enquiries would be made before the Bill was passed. Higham led the resistance to this, arguing that uncertainty, especially about borrowng powers, created a need for speed. Dodds suggested a compromise; a short bill on borrowing powers followed by a wider enquiry, but the meeting decided to press on with the original Bill slightly amended in the light of the discussion. The provincial representatives commended the London societies for their efforts and the way the conference had been conducted.[40] The London Association had earlier circularised societies to petition Parliament in favour of the Bill. Eighty-four petitions in favour were made and only one against, from John Payne of Moreton-in-Marsh, who was prepared to withdraw his opposition if the Association would offer suitable monetary compensation.[41]

On July 8th a motion was put forward in the Commons to set up a Royal Commission on Friendly Societies. The Association feared this would be extended to building societies, with consequent delay, so that a delegation, introduced again by Tom Hughes, was sent to meet the Home Secretary (H. A. Bruce). Bruce said the government was favourable to the Bill and gave advice on how to get opposition to it withdrawn, so that it might pass unopposed. The promoters strove daily to remove objections but the opposition was too much for them and eventually the Bill was withdrawn.[42] The immediate cause of withdrawal was a threat to pass the Bill to a Select Committee; in the event this rejection of reference to a Select Committee was probably a mistake, for in avoiding the embrace of a Select Committee, the Bill ended up in the even more dilatory arms of a Royal Commission.

The events of the summer were reported to a meeting of the Association on October 14th. The main discussion centred on borrowing powers; while the majority agreed on the need for limitation, there was a wide variety of opinions on how the limit should be set. The executive's view was that, provided an annual statement of assets and liabilities was given, ". . . it may be fairly left to the members and the public to use their own discretion as to the safety of their investments". Such a view showed a lack of appreciation of the degree to which societies were interdependent. As later events were to show, what happened in one society would affect others. The public did not always take only the balance sheet of a particular society into account, in assessing the safety of investment in that society.

The Royal Commission on Friendly Societies was set up on October 29, 1870, and building societies were included in its field of enquiry. Its chairman was Sir Stafford Northcote and building societies were fortunate in that it had as one of its members Sir Roundell Palmer, a barrister (later to be Lord Chancellor) who had been one of the sponsors of the Association's Bill. J. M. Ludlow, later to be Chief Registrar, was appointed secretary of the Commission, more for his knowledge of friendly societies than for his interest in building societies.

The Commission started with its enquiries into the friendly societies, but the Association urged the need for speed in the enquiry into building societies because of legal uncertainties. Sir Stafford Northcote had to leave the country on official business from March to June 1871, and this provided an opportunity to meet the Association's request. M. Hicks Beach took over as chairman for the enquiry into building societies, which took place largely in Northcote's absence. This enquiry began in March 1871, and most of the evidence concerning building societies was taken in London where forty-three witnesses were heard; building societies did not figure largely in the evidence later taken at provincial centres though important evidence was given at hearings in Edinburgh and Belfast.

A first report dealing with building societies, together with minutes of evidence to date, was published in August 1871. Most witnesses were from the large permanent societies and terminating societies were not strongly represented, though Dr. Bowkett gave extensive evidence. An attempt to continue the Commission's enquiries via Assistant Commissioners with quite exceptional powers—those of High Court Judges in respect of summoning witnesses and inspecting documents—was resisted by the Association. A Bill to give effect to these proposals passed the Lords but was defeated in the Commons.[43] The Assistant Commissioners eventually appointed had lesser powers and their reports, together with minutes of evidence taken in Scotland, Ireland and provincial centres, were published with the second report of the Commission in March 1872. The first report was purely formal; the second report gave the Commission's views on matters of substance and its recommendations.

After a description of permanent and terminating societies, this second report set out the need for new legislation very clearly. "The law relating to building societies is undoubtedly in a very unsatisfactory state."[44] The report went on to trace the changes that had taken place in the organisation of societies since the 1836 Act. "Instead of all members being expectant borrowers . . . the two classes of investors and borrowers are now distinct, the former usually outnumbering the latter and monopolising the profits. . . .[45] The most remarkable features, however, by which the present state of things differs from that contemplated by the Act are first the growth of permanent societies; second the growth of the loan or deposit system. . . .[46] It is admitted by even an adverse witness that on the whole permanent societies have been as yet judiciously managed; that failures of building societies which used to be very frequent in the epoch of terminating societies alone, are now rare. It is, however, alleged that the growth of them has altogether changed the character . . . of the building society movement; that it tends to throw . . . [them] more and more . . . into the hands of the middle classes and secure to them its benefits. . . .[47] The Societies which keep closest to the law are almost invariably small in . . . [membership], unimportant in the extent of their transactions and confined . . . to localities where . . . [they appear to] represent only an earlier stage of development in the history of these institutions."[48]

Many complaints were noted: that societies encouraged building speculations, kept defective accounts, charged exorbitant rates of interest, imposed oppressive fines and did not observe their own rules in respect of repayments to members and depositors; but the Commissioners observed that ". . . the mischiefs are not of the essence of this type of association".[49]

The general verdict of the Commission was certainly favourable to the movement. Societies promoted the investment of several million pounds yearly in property with, on the whole, very great safety and they especially encouraged the building of houses to be occupied by the working and lower middle class. "Originating with the working class they must have had a great influence in training that class in business habits. There is no reason *a priori* why the law should look upon them with disfavour."[50]

In questioning witnesses and again in its report, the Commission kept returning to a few central questions. The first was why societies did not solve their problems by incorporating under the Companies Acts.[51] Was it only to protect their privileges that they did not do so? Some companies, especially in Scotland, were carrying on building society business. A tabular comparison of both types of organisation was set out in the second report and the conclusion was that it was not merely their legal privileges which accounted for the existence of building societies; they stood on more substantial ground. The Commissioners were impressed by the non-speculative nature of the activities of building societies. "Its membership always remains open, it knows no share jobbery, fathers no brokers, needs no settling day on the Stock Exchange. . . . Whatever fraud or mismanagement it may be open to, can only be in the actual carrying out of its business and to this the company is equally liable."[52]

They felt the company form was not adapted to an enterprise capable of growing gradually from the smallest beginnings. "The two forms of undertaking we venture therefore to think have an equal right to subsist; the one for those who seek to make capital, the other for those who seek, having made it, to use it."[53]

Concerning stamp duties there was a conflict of evidence between the large permanent societies who felt that, at existing low levels of duty, exemption was unimportant and the small terminating societies, who thought exemption was an important encouragement to working class borrowers. The Commission favoured the reduction of the exemption limit from £500 to £200.[54]

Witnesses also had wide disagreements about the extent of the discretionary powers that should be vested in the Registrar. The Commission's view was that, provided the Registrar was a person of adequate legal ability and experience, and that there was a right of appeal to the Courts, there was no practical danger and much convenience in giving the Registrar discretionary power and in making his certificate conclusive as to the legality of a society's rules. The Registrar's discretion should extend beyond judging whether proposed rules were in conformity with the law. He should have power to strike out rules he held to be inequitable or impracticable, though he should report variations in his practice from time to time. Fines in particular were mentioned in this context.[55] Recommendations were made concerning a number of matters which should be covered in the rules, such as borrowing powers, rights of preference shareholders and investment powers; apart from more obvious matters such as the name of the Society, method of appointing and removing officers, etc.[56]

The Commissioners favoured the inclusion, in any new legislation, of a number of matters not mentioned in the Bills that had been proposed. Societies should be allowed to become bodies corporate, obviating the need to act through trustees. Any Act should include model rules and specimen tables of repayments, showing the true rate of interest, also tables for computing redemption values. Model forms of accounts should be annexed to the Act and societies compelled to use them. Though some witnesses had supported the auditing of accounts by public officials, the Commission did not concur, though they did feel that societies should be required to show all mortgage deeds to the auditors.[57]

There was considerable division of opinion among witnesses on the question of borrowing powers. The Commission were in no doubt that a limit should be set. "The dangers of a system in which . . . money is borrowed at an outside limit of notice of three months and invested for terms of from five to ten years and often double the latter term are obvious." After reviewing various possible limits, they concluded by following the judgement in *Laing v. Reed*, that loans should not exceed two-thirds of mortgage assets in permanent societies. They were aware that such a limit would not be suitable for terminating societies and for these they suggested limiting loans to a certain number of months subscriptions. No specific number of months was recommended, though a term of three was mentioned.[58] The limit of £1 on monthly subscriptions per share laid down in the 1836 Act should be abandoned, and paid up shares, of any denomination, made legal.

Other limits on a society's activities were considered and rejected.[59] First the size of advance, "... Nor do we see why comparatively poor people should be restricted from lending to the comparatively rich, if it is in their interest to do so". Second, limitation of the geographical area of a society's operations. Third, the types of security on which a society might make an advance. At times the Commission seems to have been impressed by the high risk involved in advancing against certain types of security—industrial property, speculative builders and second mortgages —but they concluded, "We think the working classes must be considered the best judges of their own interests in such matters". One might reasonably have asked why, in that case, they should not also be considered the best judges of the amount of loans a society might accept.

Societies had also disagreed in evidence about what powers they should have to invest surplus funds, some favouring no restrictions, others wishing to forbid investment in certain types of assets, such as land. The Commission felt that if societies wished to invest in land they should become companies or provident societies. Apart from this, societies should be free, or at least restricted only by the provisions stated in their rules, which the Registrar would have the opportunity of vetoing.[60] The Commission favoured a limit to the period of liability of members in the event of a society winding up.

Following the first report of the Royal Commission, the Association arranged another conference of building societies, in London, on January 18, 1872. The Association's Bill, further amended as a result of discussions with Sir Roundell Palmer, was considered. The most important amendment concerned borrowing power. A meeting of the Association in November had agreed that in the light of the Commission's views some limitation would have to be accepted, and a limit of two-thirds of mortgage assets was agreed. This agreement shows the extent to which permanent societies dominated the Association, for such a limit in no way met the needs of terminating societies to borrow money in their early years. The proceedings of the January conference were lengthy, each clause of the proposed Bill being taken separately. Borrowing powers were again the principal matter before the meeting, and the two-thirds limit was eventually carried.[61] The Bill was introduced into the Commons in April with many petitions and much lobbying in support of it.

In May a deputation of twenty-five M.P.s and eighteen building society officers met the Home Secretary, still Mr. H. A. Bruce. The government suggested sending the Bill to a Select Committee, but this was resisted. The government's objection was that the Bill did not meet certain recommendations of the Royal Commission: wider powers for the Registrar; deposit of rules with local authorities; reduction of exemptions from stamp duty; the facilitating of the registration of societies under the Companies Acts, and the inclusion of model rules, tables and forms of accounts. The limitation on borrowing powers was also felt to be inadequate.[62] There was little hope of avoiding a Select Committee in view of the government's many objections. Bruce outlined the sort of Bill the government would favour; one that would, in essence, have put the building societies under the Companies Act of 1862.

Another conference was called in June and representatives were informed of the government's views. Feelings were growing strained at the long delay and angry resolutions were proposed. Higham, still directing operations on behalf of the London Association, was losing patience, "He would have nothing to do with any more deputations. He declined as a man of business to be insulted by any man, whoever he might be, in an official position."[63] Eventually calmer counsels prevailed and a firm but temperate resolution condemning the government's attitude was passed. The feeling of the conference was conveyed to the Home Secretary by another delegation on June 24th.

Clearly relations between Bruce and the Association had gravely deteriorated. Bruce was now in no mood for compromise and when the Bill was taken again in the House and his appeal for its withdrawal went unheeded, he attacked it strongly. He attempted to present the Bill as wholly at odds with the Royal Commission Report, though, in fact, it was not. Eventually the government ended discussion with a motion to give government business precedence over private members' time.[64] In the light of such tactics the sponsors of the Bill gave way and withdrew it.

It was not only relations between the government and the Association that were deteriorating; within the movement the strain was also showing. The decision on borrowing powers was symptomatic of a general lack of concern with the interests of terminating societies. A correspondent complained that the Bill did not take account of the needs of non-Londoners. "That the bill has not been specifically fitted to the customs and usages of Lancashire Building Societies is plain and that some of its provisions ignore important principles and practices that we have tried and become attached to."[65] Consultations between Messrs. Robarts and Hosking of Liverpool and the Association led to some attempts to heal the breach by further amending the Bill,[66] but these were not wholly successful and the government were able to make some play with this division among building societies.

When the Bill was next introduced on March 31, 1873 (now in the hands of Messrs. Assheton Cross, Gourley, Spencer Walpole, Gregory,

McGullagh Torrens and Dodds. Sir Roundell Palmer was not among the Sponsors because he had become Lord Chancellor), the Home Office announced a government Bill on the same subject. This was published on April 29th and "... provided practically that all Building Societies should become joint stock companies and be subject to the provisions of the Companies Act, and prohibited the formation of new Societies except under the Companies Act".[67] Building societies could at least unite against this proposal, and so vehement was the reaction from all parts of the country that this Bill was withdrawn on May 7th, though another government measure was to replace it. The Home Office could, perhaps, take some comfort from a letter of Mr. Robarts of Liverpool to Mr. Winterbotham the Under Secretary, warning him against thinking that the London Association "... are in any general sense entitled or qualified to represent the wants or experience of ... [building] societies".[68]

The government's new Bill appeared on June 16th. "This was more elaborate and lengthy than the previous Bill, but as almost every clause and every section was taken from one or other of the Companies Acts, it was clear that the result would be to do away with the system under which Building Societies had developed and prospered. ..."[69] This Bill, too, was successfully opposed and by agreement both it and the Association's Bill were withdrawn on July 7th. Opposition had again been united. At a meeting of the Liverpool Building Societies Association, "the utmost unanimity prevailed . . . [in] condemnation of the Government's Bill".[70]

The government's position appeared to be that if building societies wished to have the privileges and protection granted to such mutual associations as friendly, co-operative and provident societies, they should be prepared to accept the same degree of supervision, and grant the same rights to members. If building societies were not prepared to accept such conditions, then they should become public companies. This view was not without foundation. The Association certainly resisted any detailed measure of public supervision both before the Royal Commission's Report and after. On their side the Association was suspicious of a reforming Liberal Government's intentions. In a letter its President, McCullagh Torrens, expressed these suspicions, saying that if the Government's Bill passed, many societies would fail, "When a sufficient number had failed the Chancellor of the Exchequer ... would bring in a Bill for the establishment of Government Building Societies to be managed by a new tribe of treasury officials; and the additional millions of savings would go to swell the balances with which the Finance Minister is enabled to deal in Consols".[71] Torrens was something less than an ardent admirer of Gladstonian finance!

The Government showed no signs of yielding and many societies grew fearful of the eventual outcome of the battle between the Association and Bruce. The feeling grew, especially in Liverpool, that it would be better to drop the question of reform altogether, on the old principle that a devil, tested in the Courts (if not entirely satisfactorily) is better than a devil you don't know. A Liverpool delegation assured the government that "Liverpool was perfectly content with the existing law".[72] The *Liverpool Courier* remarked, "A section of people interested in building societies as investors and trustees have agitated for a change in the law . . . their conduct is . . . suicidal. There are some few gigantic Societies which might find it worth their while to register under the [proposed] law; and if the facts were probed . . . it would probably appear that the large societies are the authors of the legislation, and seek thereby to legalise their own illegal policy."[73] Liverpool societies took particular offence at the lack of further public discussion before the Association's Bill had been presented the previous March.[74]

A conference of Manchester societies on July 1st set up a committee to watch the parliamentary situation, and after the withdrawal of the Bills its chairman remarked that ". . . those London folks and all the rest of them. . . [needed looking after] . . . they did not look at Manchester affairs in the way he would like at all".[75] There was feeling in Manchester, too, that no legislation was required.

A committee formed at Bristol proposed the creation of a National League to combat the government's ideas. This led to some sharp exchanges between Robarts (Liverpool) and H. J. Brown of the Bristol committee.[76] Robarts also questioned the pretensions of the Association to represent building societies generally. The Association replied with a list of 188 members, of which fifty-four were in the North of England (Liverpool eleven), twenty-six in the Midlands, sixteen in the South and West, six in East Anglia, two each in Scotland and Ireland and seventy-six in London and the South East.[77] T. E. Priest and F. G. Hubbard replied from Liverpool, "Mr. Higham takes it for granted that the eleven Liverpool societies which subscribe to the London Protection Association are in favour of the new legislation; whereas we know that some at least joined it purely as a Protection Association and many of the members are much opposed to their present agitation." In any case, they added, eleven out of the two hundred societies in Liverpool and one hundred and eight-eight out of over three thousand societies in the country [a gross overestimate] represented only a small measure of support. Liverpool was satisfied with the existing legislation and it was not exceptional in this view.[78] Mr. Winterbotham, Bruce's Under Secretary, had apparently informed Priest and Hubbard that if it were not for the Association's proposals the government would not have felt it necessary to bring in legislation. These exchanges led to one substantial change in the Association's proposed Bill. It was to be permissive. If societies wished to ignore it, and remain subject only to existing legislation, they could do so.

Fortunately for the Association its struggle with the Home Secretary did not continue for yet another parliamentary session. In January 1874 Gladstone called for the dissolution of Parliament and his government was defeated at the election in February.

The Home Secretary in Disraeli's administration was Assheton Cross, sponsor of the Association's Bill the previous session. The Lord Chancellor was Stafford Northcote. Hopes that the new government would itself take over the Bill were not fulfilled, but at least the new Home Secretary did not show the hostility of his predecessor, when the Bill was introduced in March 1874. After a second reading in April the Bill was passed to a Select Committee, whose seventeen members included the Bill's six sponsors. After the Select Committee had reported there was a conference between the Bill's sponsors and the Chancellor of the Exchequer at which, in return for some concessions in detail on borrowing power and limitation of liability, the sponsors agreed to give up the exemption from stamp duties on mortgage deeds.[79] In the light of this compromise Gourley, one of the sponsors, wanted to withdraw the Bill and another, Dodds, forced two divisions, in committee (June 16th) and on the third reading (June 19th) in an attempt to retain the exemption. The Chancellor strongly resisted these attempts[80] and Dodds was heavily defeated on both occasions.

With the help of further lobbying by Higham and others the Bill was safely piloted through the Lords where it received its third reading on July 17th and became law with the Royal Assent on July 30th. Only minor verbal amendments were made in the Lords, though one of these had, at least briefly, the serious consequence of bringing all societies under the Act, and reversing the intention of the sponsors to make the provisions of the Bill optional as far as existing societies were concerned. "It may be worth mentioning as one of the curious accidents that occur in the progress of legislation, that an inversion of the words of Section 8 of the Act of 1874 happened (it is believed unintentionally) during the progress of the Bill in the House of Lords. According to the amendment as prepared by the draftsman (who is one of the authors of the present work) [E. W. Brabrook] the clause would have read: 'Every society the rules of which have been certified under the said repealed Act [1836] *may obtain a certificate of incorporation under this Act and thereupon* shall be deemed to be a society under this Act and its rules shall, etc.' As actually passed by their Lordships the clause reads as follows: 'Every society the rules of which have been certified under the said repealed Act *shall be deemed to be a society under this Act* and may obtain a certificate of incorporation under This Act and thereupon its rules shall, etc.' The transposition of words, it will be seen, made a considerable alteration in the sense of this section."[81]

The consequence of this slip went unnoticed for a while. J. T. Stanesby pointed it out in a letter to the *Gazette* in October.[82] McCullagh Torrens held that it did not matter. There was enough in the rest of the Act to show what was intended.[83] The Registrar (A. F. W. K. Stephenson, who had been appointed after Tidd Pratt's death in 1870) took a different view and insisted that all societies were subject to the Act, and thus lost their stamp duty exemption, etc., whether they incorporated or not.[84] However, Assheton Cross quickly gave an undertaking that the mistake would be corrected, and it was, with the passing of the Building Societies Act of April 1875.

Thus the 1874 Act was eventually to apply only to those permanent and terminating societies which incorporated under it. Existing societies continued under the 1836 Act until they incorporated except that they were subject to the new powers conferred on the Registrar. No new societies could be formed except by incorporation (section 7). Existing societies could become bodies corporate, and hence act other than through trustees, by authority of a general meeting and, like new societies, had to obtain a certificate of incorporation from the Registrar (section 9, 10, and 12). Any three or more persons could establish a society to raise a fund to advance on the security of freehold, leasehold or copyhold estate, but any estate foreclosed had to be disposed of as soon as conveniently practicable (section 13). The liability of unadvanced members was limited to the amount they had actually paid or were in arrear; that of advanced members, to the amount payable, under the rules, for their advance (section 14). Permanent societies could borrow up to two-thirds of the sum secured by mortgages; terminating societies the same, or if they preferred, a sum not exceeding twelve months subscriptions (section 15).

Section 16 covered a variety of matters which had to be provided for in the rules if the society was to gain incorporation—the purpose of the society, investment of surplus funds, procedure for altering rules, arbitration procedure, custody of deeds, power of directors, fines and the manner in which the society could be dissolved. The Registrar had no choice but to accept rules as long as these matters were covered and the rules were in conformity with the Act (sections 17 and 18). Officers in receipt of, or having charge of money had to give security to the society (section 23). Surplus funds could be invested only in mortgages and securities the interest on which was guaranteed by Parliament. Securities of existing societies became the property of the new corporate entity upon incorporation, without reconveyance (section 27). Penalties for false representation and for misapplication of funds or securities were laid down in section 31. Dissolution could come about in a number of ways; in terminating societies by the fulfilment of the society's purpose; in all societies as provided in the rules; by three-fourths of the members holding at least two-thirds of the shares signing the instrument of dissolution, which must contain a full statement of the society's assets and liabilities and the mode of division of the society's funds and property; lastly by order of the courts (section 32). Amalgamations and transfers of engagement also required the consent of three-quarters of the members, who must hold two-thirds of the shares (section 33). By agreement between the parties the Registrar could act as arbitrator in disputes (section 34). Where an arbitration order had not been complied with after forty days, or if arbitrators had not taken action after twenty-one days notice, the County Court was allowed to intervene. Findings of arbitrators were to be final (sections 34, 35, and 36). Societies could hold land and buildings only for offices, except under section 13 (section 37). Societies were compelled to make annual audits and statements of funds to members; prospective interest was not to be included as an asset. One copy of the annual statement had to be sent to the Registrar; and another conspicuously displayed in the society's offices (section 40). Section 41 set out in detail the documents which were exempt from stamp duty, mortgage deeds, of course, not being included. The receipt endorsed on a mortgage was to be a sufficient discharge of that mortgage, without reconveyance (section 42). Modest penalties for contravening certain sections of the Act were provided (section 43) and the government were empowered to make certain regulations for carrying the Act into effect (section 44).

The 1874 Act gave building societies the basic framework within which they have operated ever since. This must not be taken to imply that the Act showed great foresight in all its provisions; the experience of the societies in the twenty years during which they operated under the 1874 Act alone is evidence enough to the contrary. It was unfortunate that H. A. Bruce, the Home Secretary, had not accepted the Royal Commission's recommendations and passed a government Bill embodying them. Had he done so, at least some of the financial disasters of the following two decades would probably have been avoided. In the event it was left to the Building Societies Act of 1894 to translate into law some of the wisdom of the Commission which both the Home Secretary and the London Association ignored.

The Commission wished to give the Registrar wide discretion in certifying rules, subject to an appeal to the courts, including power to strike out rules he felt to be inequitable or impractical. If the Registrar had had such power some of the worst excesses of the Starr-Bowkett and similar societies[85] would have been avoided. By the 1874 Act, provided the rules covered certain specified points, the Registrar had no alternative but to certify them.

The Commission favoured the setting out of forms of account in the Act, which societies would be compelled to follow. It also felt that all mortgage deeds should be examined by auditors. Both these points had to wait for attention until 1894 as did the Commission's view that "the penalties clause [of Gourley's Bill as amended by the London Association, introduced in May 1870] should be revised so as to apply to the case of a society exceeding the limits imposed on its borrowing power and *generally so as to render it really effective for the purposes of the Bill.* (Author's italics.) The evidence given before us from the registrar's office as to the inefficiency of the present provisions for enforcing returns from friendly societies has specially drawn our attention to this point."[86]

The 1874 Act in fact gave little consideration as to how its provisions were to be enforced. Officers of societies having charge of monies were to give security to societies, but there was no penalty for not doing so, and there was no guidance as to what was adequate security. A limit was set to borrowing power but there was no penalty for exceeding that limit (although directors became personally liable for any excess). Prospective interest was not to be included in the annual statement of accounts sent to the Registrar but if it was included, indeed if a deliberately false return was made, the penalty was a fine of only £5.

The 1874 Act, while it provided a reasonable legal framework for a well conducted society, gave little protection if a society was conducted otherwise. The passing of that Act gave great satisfaction to its promoters and James Higham was justifiably rewarded for his able leadership in the struggle.[87] This satisfaction would have been smaller had it been realised that already the public were looking at each building society, to some extent, as part of an interdependent movement. Thus what happened to one society was certain to affect public confidence in others. In such circumstances something more was needed than a suitable legal framework for well conducted societies. The movement as a whole had to conduct its affairs well. The obvious person to ensure this was the Registrar but he had to wait until the Building Societies Act of 1894 before he began to receive powers sufficient to fulfil that function.

Chapter Six

STARR-BOWKETT BUILDING SOCIETIES*

T. E. Bowkett, a doctor who began medical practice in London in 1830, was the originator of a special type of building society, variants of which enjoyed an enormous popularity between 1860 and the 1890s. Bowkett was a man of radical opinions, easily moved to anger, with strong sympathies for the working class and a firm believer in co-operation as a means of self-help. These qualities pervade his writing; the following samples are taken from his *Freehold Property for Mechanics* published in 1843. "It has been said if a poor man steal a goose from the common he is transported; if a rich man steal the common from the goose our Commons Houses of Parliament, save the mark! pass laws to enable the common stealers to appropriate to themselves houses which other men have built and paid for. . . . Think you that it is left to landlords, priests and kings whether human happiness and freedom shall progress or not? It depends not on them but on the conduct of the working classes themselves . . . nothing but the disgraceful apathy of the working classes themselves can enforce the continuance of the labourers' degraded position. . . . The proper places for these societies [Bowkett building societies] to hold their meetings are in Mechanics' Institutions; public houses are to be shunned as you would shun pest houses for such purposes. Chapels and churches are abundantly supplied with societies by which misdirected charity works moral and physical degradation on its recipients."

In 1843 Bowkett turned his attention to building societies which were then just beginning to spread in London. The level of subscription and interest rate charged, placed existing societies beyond the reach of the poorer classes and he resolved to try and devise a building society that would be of real utility to working men. He put forward the following scheme. Let 100 people form a society with a subscription of 9½d. per week; at the end of a year the society will have £205 16s. 8d. The members draw lots for an advance of £200 interest free to be secured by a mortgage on house property and the winner, in addition to his subscription, repays about 8s. weekly on his advance, clearing the loan in ten years. Weekly subscriptions, plus repayments on the first advance, enable

* *Notes on this chapter appear on page 295.*

a second draw to take place after a further eleven months. The third, with repayments on two advances flowing in, after a further nine to ten months and so on, until at the end of thirty-one years all members will have had an advance, and after a further ten years the last advance will have been repaid. The total of subscriptions plus any surplus from fines and defaults, less expenses, would then be repaid to the members.

Members lent their subscriptions interest free and, in return, received an interest free loan of £200 for ten years. As between members, clearly those who drew an early advance gained at the expense of those drawing later advances. Bowkett was well aware of this; his feeling was that if people did not join such societies they would not save at all, for he had few illusions about those he was trying to help. "If a man resolve to put say 1s. a week in a savings bank, as there is no fine inflicted on him for not doing so, he will be likely to omit it. Whereas in ours, in addition to having to pay 10d. instead of 9½d. if he pays not on the due day, he will of necessity every time the period of drawing lots arrive be excluded from participation in the draw if his subscription be in arrears."[1] The other advantage that he saw in these societies was that management expenses would be low. He took issue with Scratchley's figure of £400 per year as management expenses. "£400 a year to be paid out of the subscription of men saving 2s. 6d. a week each [many societies had subscriptions of 10s. per month] to be given to one individual for work that a school boy could perform when nineteen out of every twenty members would be glad to devote two evenings a month to the performance of the duty for £10 or even £5 a year! One guinea to be given to a surveyor for looking at a house value of £150!"[2] His distrust of the existing order was general, "Most of these societies are set on foot by lawyers and artful money lenders. Trickery and deception are therefore matters of course to them".[3]

The scheme was first put forward at a series of lectures at the Poplar Literary Institution in June and July 1843. "I could not succeed however in establishing a society by lecturing; what to me was simple, to others appeared wholly incomprehensible. I was compelled to resort to printing a 6d. pamphlet on the subject which in a few months caused 300 people to join the Poplar Societies and led to the establishment of societies in many other places. Many in different localities altered the rules, thinking to improve the society and unconsciously by doing so made a much worse instead of a better society. In 1844 I published the first seventeen tables [of subscriptions, redemptions, etc.] at a low price in order that they might be appended to the rules of societies and serve as a guide to those who were striving to improve or perfect the system."[4] The principles were set forth again in 1844 in a pamphlet extraordinarily entitled "Alchemy or the Art of Converting Base Metals into Gold Familiarly explained, containing also, among much other important information, a Highly Valuable Receipt for the Manufacture of an Accumulating Fund, Investment, Provident or Building Equitable Association". Excellent value at only 2d.!

Exactly how many of these societies were formed in the 1840s is not known. By 1845 they were sufficiently prominent to be commented on by Tompkins in his work on building societies.[5] In 1850 Bowkett wrote: ". . . we have had, in the course of the last four years, the advantage of corresponding with the leading men in some forty or fifty societies established on the same principles as the Poplar societies".[6] The first was formed at the Poplar Institution in 1843 and by 1849 seven had been formed there; accounts for the first three societies are given in *The Bane and the Antidote*. This group, as we have seen, played some part in the agitation against stamp duties in 1846.

Bowkett was given to forthright speaking on the defects of existing societies and those he vilified replied in kind. "It is a trite saying that eggs are eggs and although they differ somewhat in bulk and flavour are generally useful to man, except in such cases as that of our special friend Dr. Bowkett, who, leaving his own roost in the Isle of Dogs, sallies out with the malicious intent of smashing the eggs of all his neighbours, and by his own mismanagement converts his own goose eggs into abortive and immature chickens unfit for nought but the dung hill."[7]

Since the advance in these societies was £200, some people inferred that this meant the nominal value of the share was £200, and the 1836 Act, Section 1, limited the value of any one share to £150. (The total actually payable in subscriptions, 9½d. per week for about thirty years, was about £60.) This went unnoticed by the Registrar until 1846, when his refusal to certify rules with £200 shares, led to minor modifications. Members had to take up more than one share, with the nominal value correspondingly reduced. This setback did not go unnoticed. "We have cited the entire clause at length as it may prevent the Bowkettonians from falling into blunders on other points. . . . no doubt many of the followers of the Poplar theorist will curse the day when his name was heard beyond his native region—the Isle of Dogs, but if they continue their connection with his Ninepenny halfpenny societies, they will soon get used to these sorts of things and after a while will receive them with as much philosophy, as it is said, experienced ells [eels?] do the unpleasant experience of skinning."[8]

Bowkett felt his scheme was making slow progress because it was being misrepresented, so in 1850 he published a much more extensive work than his earlier pamphlets, *The Bane and the Antidote*. This work give a clear exposition of his ideas and a detailed examination of other types of society. Indeed, apart from Scratchley's *Treatise on Benefit Building Societies* published a year earlier, it is the best statement of building society problems in the early literature. Bowkett has suffered in reputation because it is his evidence to the Royal Commission of 1871, not his earlier writings, that is best known. When he was heard by the Commission he was an old man who had seen his ideas exploited for profit by others, and must have been rather disillusioned. The lengthy evidence he gave was something less than crystal clear. Describing his societies he said, "They are based on a principle of arithmetic which scarcely anyone connected with building societies or anyone else seems to comprehend. The principle is this, that by a certain arrangement men uniting together can realise in the first instance the same amount of interest for their own savings as they are accustomed to pay for the use of other people's money, next that they can practically obtain a quarter more than that rate of interest, and next that the rate of interest is compound. The result is that while ordinary investment of their saving can secure very little indeed throughout their whole lifetime, if they are poor, yet if these small savings accumulate at high rates of compound interest, it is sufficient absolutely to emancipate any of them or all of them from poverty[9] . . . all the writers upon it do not perceive the great principle that lies at the bottom of it, namely the accumulation at compound interest of money lent without interest. I used to be exasperated that people would not understand it. I thought they did not want to understand it, but I see now that it springs from the natural intricacy of the thing."[10] All this in societies which lent money interest free!

Bowkett's scheme was a worthwhile attempt to extend the benefits of building societies to the lower paid worker.[11] This could only be done by advancing the full value of property and having low weekly subscriptions, which in turn implied a long period before the society terminated. The weakness was that members disappointed by early lack of success in the draws would withdraw their subscriptions. The non-payment of interest was an attempt to meet this weakness; all the benefit a member could gain was concentrated in the interest free loan; to withdraw early was to forfeit all profit from membership. This was sometimes strengthened by not allowing withdrawals during the first five years of a society's life. Other modifications were introduced to equalise a little the advantages as between those drawing early and late appropriations. For those who had not drawn an appropriation subscriptions ceased after twenty-five years, and as the society ran down after thirty-one years, those who drew the last appropriation were the first to receive the return of their subscriptions. The limited success of such societies in the 1840s no doubt owed something to the gambling element in their make-up, but such evidence as there is suggests that people joined them mainly in order to become home owners. However, the spectacular success, at least in numerical terms, of such societies was to come later and at other hands than Dr. Bowkett's.

The instrument of success was Richard Benjamin Starr, born in 1813, who had followed a variety of trades before becoming a building society promoter. "I have been a hatter, a coffee house keeper, an auctioneer, a coal merchant and an omnibus proprietor. I have an omnibus now. I have a patent to check fares, but for want of means I have not been able to carry it out. I was a partner in the Enpodian Boot Company."[12] Starr first met Dr. Bowkett in 1855, but it was not until the 1860s that he started his promotions. He made some changes in the typical Bowkett Society rules and obtained a copyright for the rules as amended, repeating the process for other occasional amendments over the following twenty-five years. His basic changes were aimed at shortening the life of societies and making conditions more equal between members. The 9½d. a week subscription for a £200 advance (5d., later 6d. per week, entitled the holder to a £100 advance if successful in the draw) was raised to £10 per year after a successful member had repaid his advance, until the total due on the share had been paid. The proportion of the subscription deducted to cover management expenses was lowered for those getting late appropriations; by a later amendment such people were allocated a more than proportionate share of any surplus at the society's termination. The surplus resulted from fines, transfer fees and profits made from the re-sale of appropriations.

As a building society promoter, Starr at last found secure and profitable employment. The first Starr–Bowkett society was formed in London about 1862.[13] At first societies were mainly promoted in London, but by the mid-1870s they were spreading rapidly elsewhere. By 1874 over sixty societies had been started.[14] From the passing of the 1874 Act to 1882 a further 384 started and from 1883 to 1891, 402 more, making a total of 950.[15] Starr's claims went beyond this for the 999th society was started in London in May 1891[16] but some societies were not very long lived. For instance the 77th, founded in London, was incorporated on May 3, 1875, and its instrument of dissolution was registered six weeks later.[17]

At the beginning Starr had at least some help from Dr. Bowkett, for as late as 1869 they both spoke at the inaugural meeting of a new society.[18] Soon after this they must have parted company, for in his evidence to the Commission, Bowkett, after referring to the small salary paid to the secretaries of his societies, £6 10s. p.a., said, ". . . and that was found amply sufficient before the Starrs came and spoilt it all".[19] From the promotion of the first twenty societies Starr claimed he did not profit.[20] Thereafter his enterprise became increasingly profitable. As Starr himself explained, "I will now tell you the *modus operandi* . . . you as secretary for the appointment, instruction, etc., pay me £5 . . . I coach you in all the work. I take all the risks and expenses in books, etc., until we float. You, so agreeing would find three (shopkeepers are best) to act as trustees and four to six to act as directors. Seek out a Solicitor and Surveyor which should be told quite confidentially that I have to agree with such for their appointments and they pay me a fee which I only name to them".[21] The fees were in fact £25 from the Solicitor[22] and three guineas from the Surveyor.[23]

If men were to pay such considerations for offices, they naturally wished for greater security of tenure than the processes of democracy in the society could guarantee. Starr provided it in his rules, which the Registrar described thus, "In not a few instances officers are sought to be fixed and the slender rights of members still further restricted by rules requiring specific majorities, say seven eighths, of the members present at a meeting before a change of particular officers can be made or any serious step taken by a society to secure its own independence. I am sorry to say I have read not one but a good many rules of this description, which I can as little understand to have been framed by honest men as to have been accepted by any but fools".[24]

However, promoters cannot be successful without members and what seems to have increasingly attracted members was the opportunity for quick profits. To win in the ballot the right to a loan of £200 on the security of property, interest free for ten years was to win a valuable right which could be sold for cash. Sales of appropriations had occasionally taken place in Bowkett's societies, but only to other members of the same society.[25]

Thus Starr-Bowkett societies attracted not only those wishing to become owner occupiers but also those wishing, in effect, to take part in a fairly regular ballot for cash prizes. The publicity sometimes given to occasions where a member drew an appropriation after only a few weeks membership suggests that Starr was keen to appeal to the gamblers. The question whether such draws infringed the Lottery Act was raised in the Commons on July 18, 1889, when the Home Secretary replied that ". . . the practice extends far beyond Starr-Bowkett societies, who are not by any means the worst offenders in this respect . . . it is doubtful whether the practice of balloting for appropriations falls within the Lottery Act. It is a practice of very old standing and I should not think it advisable to initiate prosecutions against the societies, especially as no representation has reached me as to the necessity of any such interference of the Government".[26] In fact the courts had dealt with the matter on one occasion in 1882 and had not found such societies illegal.[27]

In 1877 Starr altered his copyright rules to force those members who wished to sell their appropriation to do so to the society itself.[28] The money was then advertised and sold to the highest bidder. About the same time some societies began to borrow money, clearly inappropriate and unnecessary in the original scheme, which could be lent at interest in the open market. Where the society could buy back the appropriation from the successful member, the society could become a simple lottery never in fact advancing money. The society would show annual deficits as the members merely lost their weekly subscriptions in providing the prize—the sum the society paid the member successful in the ballot for giving up his right to an advance. E. W. Brabrook (the Registrar's assistant) referred to such a case in 1887. "A Starr-Bowkett society has completed its third year. Its object, according to the Act, is to make advances to members. It has however not made a single advance. It has received £500 from its members, has declared two appropriations by ballot, paid £130 for them, has spent £120 (on expenses) and has £250 left."[29]

Fees from offices were not Starr's only source of income; he was a partner in the Metropolitan and Provincial Printing Society, from which societies had to buy their rule books, etc.[30] In 1881 the Starr-Bowkett and General Insurance Company was founded and by a rules alteration of 1882, all new Starr-Bowkett societies had to insure their properties with it.[31] A scheme of accident insurance was also organised, which involved an addition to the weekly subscription of from 1d. to 6d. depending on the benefits chosen.[32] However, Starr's main work was promoting societies and by the 1880s this work was going so well that he claimed to be employing fifteen men to assist him in this work.[33]

The creation of Starr-Bowkett societies was not confined to Britain. The first society in Australia was founded at Sydney in 1869.[34] They enjoyed a considerable boom in New South Wales, Victoria and South Australia after the turn of the century.[35] Starr-Bowkett societies are still numerous in Australia and operate on very much the original principles. In 1961 there were 117 societies in New South Wales and in South Australia twenty of the State's twenty-five societies were of this type. "The Starr-Bowkett societies continue to attract a great deal of public support . . . [in New South Wales], with a total membership of 45,000. These societies operate with members supplying the working capital on a contributory basis. Loans, which are interest free, are made available by ballot. Some societies alternate a ballot with an auction as a means of assisting those people whose needs are most urgent. Interest rates charged on monies auctioned are from ½% to 5%. Loan limits range as high as £6,000".[36] An attempt was made to start such societies in the United

States. J. B. McIntyre, a railway engineer, founded the Artisans Savings and Loan Association in Pittsburgh and copyrighted the rules, but his enterprise did not succeed.[37]

In the early 1880s Starr's enterprises received a good deal of public attention; there were a series of actions by Starr to enforce his copyright and fees, in which he was usually successful. Arising from one such successful action, to obtain payment by his Metropolitan and Provincial Printing Society for work in connection with floating a society, a public meeting was called in Shoreham, in December 1880. At this meeting a Mr. Hall spoke in forthright terms calling Starr, among other things, a bully, liar and blackguard. Starr initiated two slander actions arising from the meeting, one against Hall, and another against a Mr. Hardy.

During the hearing much unfavourable light was shed on Starr's methods. Efforts were made by the *Building Societies Gazette* and others to induce the Building Societies Protection Association to lead a campaign against Starr and take up the defence of Hall and Hardy. The Assocation refused, though to take up these causes a private committee was formed on which members of the Association's executive were prominent, including C. Binyon, B. Mitchell and, especially, J. T. Stanesby.[38] Starr won the action against Hall in November 1882 and was awarded £250 damages. Hall appealed, claiming the verdict was against the weight of the evidence, and that the damages were excessive. In December a new trial was ordered. Before that took place the other action, *Starr v. Hardy*, was heard on March 15, 1883. Here the verdict went against Starr and he dropped his action against Hall. Naylor comments on these events, that ". . . the exposures made practically sounded the death knell of the formation of such societies".[39] The extraordinary thing is that they had no effect at all; that the 1880s were the boom years for building society promoters is clear from Table X, p. 113.

The first consequence of the publicity was that Starr started publishing his own journal in 1882 to defend his empire, the *Starr-Bowkett Journal and Building Society News*.[40] In this Starr's opponents got short shift. Mr. F. Creedy, who was prominent in attacking Starr's societies both at public meetings and in the columns of the *Gazette*, was dealt with in a leader headed "Creedy Beware" which began "This brute has been trying by all the dirty means in his power to undermine our societies . . . "[41]

The increase in the gambling element in these societies, while it brought in members of one sort, probably forced out the more stable and serious prospective home owner. A lengthy lack of success in the ballot was anyway likely to cause discontent, even without the society purchasing the appropriations and selling them to outsiders. The quality of officers of societies was likely to decline: they were, in any case, not uniformly efficient, to say nothing of the occasional secretary absconding with the funds. Not that all objections to Starr's societies were well founded; one member complained that ". . . those members whose registered number happens to consist of two or three identical figures such as 22 or 222 are in a much worse position than if all the figures were different as the odds must be very great against three consecutive drawings resulting in the same figure".[42]

Starr and his assistants worked zealously to put down criticism, attending meetings wherever the officers of a society were under attack. One of Starr's postcards reveals the atmosphere quite well. "Urgent—Arrange to attend at——, Tuesday next as the Board has insisted upon a meeting to consider the position of the Society. There must be a row, get a friend or two to join, I will pay. Aid us and you will be rewarded by R. B. Starr."[43] After 1885 there were further legal actions to protect Starr's position, but these were less successful than the earlier ones.[44] In an action against the Surveyor of the 917 Starr-Bowkett Society in 1889 (to enforce Starr's fee, due for the surveyor's appointment) the Judge, finding for the surveyor, said that the agreement between Starr and the surveyor was fraudulent, illegal, and void. Starr appealed only to have the sweeping words of the County Court Judge confirmed by the Lord Chief Justice,[45] who found "the agreement on the face of it was fraudulent and it appeared to him that the learned county court judge was right. . . . The important part of the agreement was that which stipulated that the money was to be paid 'in consideration of the appointment'. The rules were before the Court and afforded abundant confirmation of the corrupt nature of the agreement".

While the publicity did not damage Starr by inhibiting prospective members it did damage him in another way. By revealing the extent of his success, it created competition, much of it from those who had held office in his societies. This no doubt accounts for the appearance of a new rule 4, under which any director or secretary taking office in another society, not a Starr-Bowkett, would cease to hold office in the Starr-Bowkett.[46]

The first of these competitors was Arthur Connor, whose promotions started in 1882. Next to Starr, Connor was the most successful of the building society promoters creating, mainly in Yorkshire, over 260 of his "Model" societies, as well as a few others before that title was adopted.[47] He charged a fee of 65 guineas for his services, usually providing rule books and stationery from his publisher in Leeds. He also frequently held the office of auditor, filling this role in about 150 of his societies. His modification of Bowkett's plan was for appropriations to be made by ballot and sale alternately. This was not a new idea, a number of non-promoter terminating societies used it, and some Starr-Bowketts changed their rules to take advantage of it. A degree of life insurance was also offered. At death a member was treated as having been successful in the ballot, and his estate could sell the appropriation and also withdraw the subscriptions already paid. Anyone who had purchased an appropriation ceased to pay interest when he was later successful in the ballot. At least some "Model" societies appear to have operated as merely gambling institutions; a group of seven had no mortgage assets but a deficiency of £554.[48] Connor told the Select Committee of 1893, "We do not in theory purchase appropriations", but to pass a law forbidding such purchases, "would be a serious obstacle in many instances".

In 1882, Mr. E. Drew, who had experience as a secretary in Starr-Bowkett societies, started business with his "Self Help" societies, fifty-three of which were founded before he went bankrupt in 1889. He attributed his insolvency to a ". . . falling off in business owing to increased competition".[49] Drew's societies excluded balloting. Subscriptions were small and "interest free" loans for ten years were sold to whoever was prepared to pay the highest premium. Drew's income arose under rule 34 of the copyright rules, "Mr. Drew . . . for the trouble and expense of promoting this society and for the use of these rules, which are his property, shall be entitled to receive a commission of £5 per cent on the premium given on every sale by this society of any advance".[50]

In 1884 Edwin Richmond, a member of the Sheffield Town Council, formed the first of eighty-seven "Richmond" societies. Richmond told the Select Committee[51] that his societies were not based on Starr's method, they were something superior. When a man was successful in the ballot he could take an advance at a low fixed premium; the societies were not "designed for a large profit". Purchasing of appropriations by the society was prohibited. Richmond's fees were low, 10 guineas. He continued as secretary of three Sheffield Starr-Bowkett societies and was also secretary of a small permanent society. Richmond seems to have been in a different class from the other promoters, more genuinely interested in promoting owner-occupation among people whose low income would normally make it impossible for them to buy property through an ordinary permanent society.

This view is strengthened by his dealings with the Registrar. The growth of promotional activity after 1882 led the Registrar to attack the rules of these societies in his report for 1884. "It is incredible that persons should be found simple enough to accept rules containing such provisions [e.g. at least seven-eighths of members voting in favour before an officer could be removed] but unfortunately they do, and . . . the good standing of building societies generally must ere long be seriously affected. . . ."[52]

Ludlow returned to this theme in 1886, castigating those ". . . who made use of any temporary prosperity among the working and lower middle classes to flood the country with mushroom societies". Again rules were cited, especially those where it needed the written consent of nine-tenths of the members to alter officers' salaries, to remove officers or to bring or defend actions in the Court. "Without imputing any conscious dishonesty to the promoters of societies governed by such rules, . . . it is difficult to see how the interests of a dishonest officer could be more efficiently guarded."[53] There were further strictures in the 1888 Report. Richmond was alone in taking objection to these blanket censures of promoters. After some correspondence with the Registrar, he at least got some slight retraction. The Report for 1891 notes Richmond's complaints and the Chief Registrar (now E. W. Brabrook) admitted that promoter societies were ". . . not open, without exception, to the justly severe comments made by Mr. Ludlow on the vice of gambling which these societies promote".[54]

One of Starr's own assistants, William Horsley, started in business on his own account in June 1888, promoting in all 137 "Perfect Thrift" societies.[55] In these societies lots were drawn for two-thirds of the money, the interest free loan being repaid over 16⅔ years, the remaining third being sold by tender. Provided the member was between 15 and 50 years old when he joined, an interest free loan was granted in the event of his death. These societies did not borrow money, but they did sometimes purchase their own appropriations. There was a triennial distribution of the profits arising from the sale of appropriations and those still unsuccessful in the ballot after ten years received an extra share in these distributions. As in all the promoter societies, considerable stress was laid on the considerate treatment members would receive, at the discretion of the board of directors, in respect of arrears of subscriptions, in cases of illness or unemployment; no doubt this was a real attraction. Horsley received 10 guineas for his services and was, in addition, auditor of about two-thirds of his societies.

In 1889 the firm of Parker and Sons, accountants of Manchester, started to form the "Popular" group of societies, which were to total fifty in all. These were close to Starr's system with the solicitor paying 20 guineas and the surveyor and secretary 5 guineas each for their appointments. The society itself had to pay 35 guineas for which they received a lecture by Mr. Parker, his advice and 300 rule books.[56]

There were a few other groups of societies with such enticing names as "Easy Payment" and "Hearth and Home" but they were, with two exceptions, small groups of at most twenty societies. The exceptions were the "Economic" societies of which eighty-nine were formed and the "Mutuals", 154.

In spite of this considerable competition, Starr maintained his prominent position as a promoter, though, at the end of his life, as a corporate entity. About eighteen months before his death in January 1892 he formed a company to take over his business interests. When he put forward the idea he suggested that, with adequate resources (the proposed capital for the company was 20,000 £1 shares of which 10s. would be paid up), eighty societies a year could be formed and this should yield, at £38 17s. each, £3,108. After covering expenses there would still be sufficient left to pay a dividend of 10%. He was willing to dispose of his copyright for £3,000 cash and 4,500 fully paid shares in the company, which he was also prepared to serve as managing director.[57] The company was in fact floated, but on what terms is not known.

One of the company's directors, William H. Pearce, gave evidence to the Select Committee.[58] Starr had invited Pearce to become a director at its formation, but he refused because he felt that societies were being formed too rapidly with consequent failures. He joined the board after Starr's death. The slowing down in the rate of formation of societies after 1891 was apparently a matter of policy; only thirteen societies were formed in the period 1892–94. Pearce seems to have given evidence because an early witness, F. Creedy, an old adversary of Starr, had roughly handled Starr-Bowkett societies in his evidence. Pearce was not wholly successful in his efforts to place those societies in a favourable light, as the following exchange with members of the Committee shows. Pearce, who wanted accounts audited by qualified chartered accountants, added, "What that means I do not exactly know." Mr. Jackson, "Did you think so [that they should be C.A.s] because you did not know what that meant?" Pearce, "Very likely so. It sounds very large, Chartered Accountant." Mr. Cremer, "It is calculated to deceive you think?" Pearce, "I think so very much; these letters at the end of these people's names are very deceiving." Mr. Cremer, "Do you think it is desirable that that should be the result?" Pearce, "I do not think it is exactly desirable."

The Chief Registrar gave details, in his Report for 1892, of all the societies registered since the passing of the 1874 Act. Table X is based on these details, and compares the promoter societies with other types. What is most striking about the table is that the rate of dissolution among the promoter societies, especially the Starr-Bowketts, is lower than that of any other type, and the average life of societies dissolved, at least for the larger groups of promoter societies, is as long as that of any other type of society. The table also shows the extent to which a few promoters dominated this particular business, Starr himself being responsible for almost a half of all societies founded. It must be remembered that the 1880s were difficult years for building societies with falling property values eating away margins of security on advances. Much depended on the skill of managements and this varied in the promoter societies as well as elsewhere. Further, societies were the victims of frauds as well as the perpetrators.

TABLE X

Building Societies registered 1874–1891

Type	Number registered 1874–82	1883–88	1889–91	Total	Societies dissolved Number	Average life (years)
Starr-Bowkett	384	355	47	786	186	3
Model[59]	0	84	145	229	31	2
Perfect Thrift	0	12	95	107	3	2
Richmond	0	55	28	83	26	3
Self Help[59]	0	53	0	53	36	3
Economic	0	37	42	79	11	2
Mutual	0	102	25	127	60	3
Popular	0	0	37	37	5	1
Other Promoters	0	74	6	80	65	1–2
TOTAL	384	772	425	1,581	423	
Permanent Societies	421	113	36	570	218	3
Other Terminating Societies[60]	603	281	118	1,002	409	2

Table XI gives a picture of the finances of promoter societies. The data are drawn from those promoter societies which figured in a 10% systematic sample drawn from the annual statements of building societies published in the Registrar's report for the year ending December 31,

TABLE XI

Finances of Promoter Societies (year ending December 31, 1890)

	Number of Societies	Averages: Number of Members*	Receipts in Year £	Due to Shareholders £	Due to Depositors £	Mortgage Assets £	Other Assets £	Balance £
Societies formed before 31/12/1879†	18	117	2,347	7,887	107	8,006	542	554
Societies formed after 31/12/1879								
A—with deficits	34	246	815	2,196	40	1,901	248	−95
B—with surpluses	49	248	1,439	3,353	225	3,677	303	161

* The average number of members is calculated on the basis of only those societies where the return gave the number of members. The vast majority did so.

† All societies in this group showed surpluses.

1890. Societies formed before 1880 (all of them Starr-Bowketts) have been grouped separately in order to show something of the condition of societies which managed to survive the difficulties of the early years. That such difficulties were considerable is shown by the high proportion of dissolutions in Table X, and the short average life of societies dissolved. For each group of societies total receipts have been divided by the number in the group so that the figures show something of the "average" society. It must be remembered that this average conceals considerable variations between individual societies. Grossing up the information from the sample yields an estimate of about £4¼ million as the total assets of the promoter societies, and a total membership of perhaps a quarter of a million. This would mean that these societies had about 8% of the assets of all building societies in 1890, and about a third of all members.[61]

The table shows that societies formed before 1880 and still in being in 1890 were in a healthy position. They had assets of £1,069 for every £1,000 of liabilities compared with £1,039 for the whole building society movement. The weaker position and widespread losses of the post-1880 group again suggest that promoter societies were rather unstable in their early years. The smaller average membership of the pre-1880 group probably reflects a substantial withdrawal of membership in their early years, a withdrawal which many of the post-1880 group had not yet suffered to the same degree. Early withdrawal often carried penalties under the rules, even the loss of all subscriptions, and the strong reserve position of the pre-1880 group no doubt owes something to such forfeitures. Although some promoter societies sanctioned the taking of deposits, deposits clearly played a quite minor role in these societies. This was in fact an element of strength to them; at a time when building societies were much less secure in the public confidence than now, the right to withdraw deposits at short notice was not infrequently a cause of embarrassment.

The passing of the Building Societies Act 1894, which made balloting illegal in all future societies, sharply checked the formation of Starr-Bowkett and like societies. A few attempts were made to circumvent the law. The societies in existence in 1894 were allowed to continue on their uncertain way.

The case for the promoter societies was put by Professor H. S. Foxwell. He believed that Bowkett societies and their successors "... had been the means of encouraging a great deal of thrift ... the least injurious way in which chance could be brought in".[62] Later, replying to those who cited the widespread failures of such societies and their shortcomings, he added, "That faults have occurred in the administration of particular societies may well be true ... this would not affect the general principle".[63]

The opposite view was put by Judge Jordan in the Longton County Court. "These societies have been an unmitigated curse to the working classes of this country. They have done more to destroy the virtue of thrift than anything else."[64] The Chief Registrar, E. W. Brabrook, though opposed to these societies, was less severe. He saw the chief source of trouble in the power to buy back appropriations, it was "in many respects very mischievous indeed".[65] There was a further source of trouble. In many cases unadvanced members could not withdraw their subscriptions directly, but an advanced member could buy the unadvanced members' share and use the subscriptions paid on that share to reduce his own mortgage debt. "Under these provisions members desirous to withdraw have been approached by members who have received advances, with offers to purchase their interest in the society at a heavy discount. . . . Where the borrower has an official position, as a director or secretary of the society, still more if he is also a trustee for the purpose of its dissolution, he is in a position to carry on transactions of this kind to a considerable extent and thus obtain for himself preferential payment in full shares which he has acquired at a much lower price, and to leave the other shareholders only what may remain after he has been satisfied. By astute proceedings of this kind, such a manager or trustee has contrived to secure for himself all the profits of a society and to leave to other members all the losses."[66] J. M. Ludlow, was, as we have seen, more severe in his judgements than Brabrook but Ludlow was at times a severe critic of all building societies, at least as he found them in the 1880s.[67]

Bowkett's idea, for all the weakness inherent in a society with an expected life of over forty years, did open up the chance of home ownership for a class not formerly catered for, a chance which at least some people successfully took. The later variants of his idea were improvements, in so far as they equalised the advantages as between members who drew early advances and the less fortunate who had to wait up to thirty years. However, most of these variants accepted the principle of the society buying its own appropriations for resale to outsiders, shifting the emphasis from home ownership to gambling. The long wait of most members for an advance, by wearing away early optimism, gave an inevitable element of instability to Bowkett societies. The shift in emphasis to gambling greatly increased this instability. Had Bowkett's own principles of organisation been continuously followed, a smaller number of societies would have been formed, but those formed would have been stronger and more uniformly successful.

Chapter Seven

BUILDING SOCIETIES UNDER THE ACT OF 1874*

THE PERIOD BETWEEN the passing of the Building Societies Act of 1874 and that of 1894 was the most troubled in the history of the movement thus far, or indeed, since. The essence of the building society operation is the receipt of money, which, whatever their legal rights, lenders tend to assume to be readily repayable, and that money is loaned to borrowers for long periods on the security of property. The gap between the periods for which societies borrow and lend money might be expected to trouble investors, but if the value of property, mortgaged as security for loans, is well in excess of the money loaned, investors may reasonably feel that their money is safe. If property values are stable or, better still, rising, then the building society manager has a relatively easy task, but if property values are falling, the management of societies becomes a much riskier business. If the value of a property falls faster than the balance outstanding on the loan it secures, the borrower may be tempted to default. In such circumstances the investor may begin to have doubts about the security of his investment. If the general response of investors to such doubts is a move to withdraw money, then, however well run the society, the investors will prove their doubts to have been well founded, for all cannot be repaid immediately—a nice example of self-justifying expectations.

The period from 1874 to 1894 was one of insecure property values. The so-called "long depression" dominates the period and the general trend of prices was downward. Maiwald's index of building costs based on 1930=100, falls almost continuously from a peak of 63·0 in 1873 to a trough of 46·9 in 1896.[1] Business conditions were depressed with a consequent lack of demand for industrial capital. Building societies apparently offering security and a fair rate of return became a more popular haven for savings. The result was an increase of money in the hands of societies, at just the time when it was difficult to find secure mortgages on which to lend the money. In their search for an outlet for funds, building societies were tempted to accept less secure mortgages and, where many were tempted, some were sure to fall.

* *Notes on this chapter appear on page 297.*

It may be objected that the 1930s were just as difficult a period; it is true that money was then flooding into societies and property values, at least in parts of the country, were insecure. However, in the 1880s the borrowing of money to build houses to let was an important source of business to building societies. In addition, industrial property was fairly generally acceptable as security for building society loans. When property values fall people who have borrowed money for speculative ventures are much more likely to default than owner-occupiers, and by the 1930s, building society lending was overwhelmingly to owner-occupiers. This is not to deny the difficulties of the 1930s, except in a relative sense; those difficulties were real enough and while they created their alarms, they did little damage to the movement compared with the events of the period now under review.

The 1874 Act laid certain duties and restrictions on societies incorporating under it; examples are the restriction of borrowing powers and the duty to see that officers having charge of money gave security for the proper discharge of their duties. However, the Act laid down no procedures for enforcing many of its provisions. The annual statement that societies had to send to the Registrar might have been used to give publicity to some at least of the shortcomings of societies not obeying the law, but the Act had given the Registrar no power to publish these annual statements. Fortunately the Building Societies Protection Association used its influence to secure publication. "Details were discussed with the Registrar and at the instigation of the Committee a 'Return of Statistics Relating to Building Societies' was moved for in the House of Commons on the 20th of July [1876]."[2]

Parliament asked for such a return for each year, except 1889, until, with the passing of the 1894 Act, it became the legal duty of the Registrar to publish details of the annual returns of societies. The statements of societies gave the Registrar some indications of whether the provisions of the 1874 Act were being obeyed. From these returns a more accurate picture of the progress, at least of incorporated societies, is available than was previously the case. At the passing of the 1874 Act there were some 1,500 societies still in existence. Table XII shows the extent to which these societies took advantage of incorporation under the 1874 Act over the first five years, as well as the number of new societies formed under that Act.

Table XII shows that only about one-quarter of the societies in existence at the passing of the 1874 Act took advantage of its provision for incorporation. This confirms the earlier suggestion that support for the Bill among existing societies was something less than overwhelming. However, it must be remembered that if a society wished to become a body corporate it usually meant some changes in rules, assuming some new responsibilities and forfeiting exemption from stamp duty on mortgage deeds under £500. As witnesses stressed before the Royal Commission, many members were suspicious of change and if a society was running smoothly, the officers might be loath to risk disturbing the calm. Also,

TABLE XII

Societies Incorporated under the 1874 Act

Date	Societies in existence before the 1874 Act[3]	New formations	Total
England and Wales			
1875[4]	228	70	298
1876	35	195	230
1877	72	136	208
1878	24	146	170
1879	15	150	165
Scotland, 1875–1879	29	25	54
Ireland, 1875–1879	5	23	28
	408	745	1,153

in 1874, terminating societies were still in the majority. Where these terminating societies were early in their life they would be unlikely to incorporate because the 1874 Act severely restricted the traditional pattern of heavy borrowing in the first few years of the life of such societies. Those societies approaching termination, on the other hand, would not be worried by this borrowing restriction, but, having only a few years of life left, might reasonably think the advantages of incorporation not worth the trouble of rule changes, etc.

Another reason, again indicating the conservatism of members, was that incorporation meant the disappearance of trustees. Mr. T. F. Peacock[5] put it thus at a meeting of the Statistical Society of London, "He thought that building societies generally looked with considerable respect on trustees and they believed . . . that so long as they had trustees, those trustees would protect the interests of the members. In consequence of that belief many societies had not enrolled themselves under the Act of 1874". The Chief Registrar, J. M. Ludlow, endorsed this view at the same meeting.

The 1874 Act required building societies not to include prospective interest in surpluses shown in their accounts. The early returns of the Chief Registrar contain complaints that societies were still including prospective interest. With terminating societies, this was a difficult matter; if a society made advances at a premium, then the part of the premium which could reasonably be regarded as being realised as part of the mortgagor's subscriptions during a particular year, depended on the number of years for which subscriptions would be paid. In a terminating society this number of years cannot be known accurately in advance. Since Liverpool was still an important home of terminating societies, one of its leaders, T. E. Priest, pressed the matter in correspondence with the Chief Registrar[6] and the working rule was reached that societies should divide the premium by the number of years of its expected life, in order to decide the amount of premium that should be allocated to each year's accounts. This did not stop societies attempting to give their accounts a healthier look by including the full value of the premium as a present asset. A building society directory of 1885 commented,[7] "The object of including prospective interest in the amount of mortgages is apparent, it is either to conceal an actual deficit or show a fictitious reserve fund. We regret this system is adopted by so many London as well as Provincial Societies, who appear to be able to contravene the . . . Statute with impunity, and we look forward to the official enquiry into this question which sooner or later must be instituted." The Registrar amended the returns of societies whenever his staff detected the inclusion of prospective interest, and noted the fact against the figures for those societies, in the published statistics.

The 1874 Act had made no provision for penalties for those infringing a number of its sections, including some parts of Section 40 which are relevant here. This fact was quickly noted in building society circles.[8] Neither the Registrar, nor the members concerned, took up H. F. A. Davis's suggestion that directors be compelled to observe the Act via writs of mandamus or actions for damages.[9] Under Section 43 of the Act, failing to send a copy of the annual accounts to the Registrar, or sending a "wilfully false" return was punishable on summary conviction by a modest fine, not exceeding £5. Convictions were not easy to secure. In 1889 the Registrar[10] failed to win a case against a secretary for making a wilfully false return, because he could not prove that the secretary had made the return, it being unsigned. This, the Registrar wrote, stressed the need for a set form requiring "certain signatures bringing home responsibility to particular persons". Pressure from the Registrar forced many societies to abandon the inclusion of prospective interest in their annual accounts, but the root of the trouble lay in the weakness of the 1874 Act. It provided little guidance concerning the form of accounts and gave the Registrar no power to enforce his own forms. Before the 1893 Select Committee Brabrook admitted that his eighteen-year battle with societies on this point had not been wholly successful.[11]

The 1874 Act's limit of borrowing powers to two-thirds of the amount secured on mortgage also created problems. Again no penalty was mentioned for those who did not keep within the Statute, though directors were held personally liable for any excess. The intended limit[12] on borrowing was sometimes ignored. In *Cole v. Swansea Co-operative Building Society* it was stated that "The Society started in 1875 and immediately exceeded their borrowing powers, a position in which they have ever since continued.[13] In *Dyson v. Union Bank of Manchester*, the following dialogue took place between Counsel and the Secretary of the Mechanics Mutual Building Society. "Of course as secretary you knew that monies were being obtained in excess of the two-thirds limit?" "I knew nothing at all about it. We never knew until we got into difficulties that we were tied up to that amount." "It came as quite a surprise?" "It did, we had never been used to it. I had had to do with many societies, but we had never been used to any limit whatever." "Did you ever look at the rules of the society?" "No, not particularly."[14]

While the clauses of the Act governing borrowing limits had to be stated in each depositor's book, this provided little safeguard since a small depositor was scarcely likely to inform himself of the position of a society when he made his small deposit. For large borrowers it was a different matter, and the banks in particular viewed building society overdrafts with a more severe eye after the passing of the Act.[15] Some societies sought a way out by depositing some of their mortgage deeds with banks as security. However, where the resulting overdraft meant that a society exceeded its borrowing powers, the courts decided that the security was of no avail to the banks: it had to be returned to the society, the bank's only redress being against the directors personally.[16]

When the two-thirds limit on borrowing was first set in the case of *Laing v. Reed* in 1869, societies avoided its consequences by issuing preference shares. The Woolwich Equitable's decision to issue preference shares in 1875 seems to be a case in point. "During the year . . . as depositors had exceeded the statutory limit, preference shares were first issued."[17] In many cases preferred shareholders provided so large a proportion of total capital that it is difficult to imagine over whom they were enjoying a preference, especially in the case of a Taunton Society where they were the only class of shareholder.[18] Four of eight permanent societies formed in London between 1891 and 1893 had rules allowing the unlimited issue of preference shares. The Registrar attempted to persuade the directors of one society to alter this rule and in an interview asked, "Do you really think you will get members to join, when they understand that by your rules, your directors have power to defeat their claims by issuing preference shares without limit?" and they replied, "Yes". The Registrar commented, ". . . I confess upon reflection that I am afraid they are right. . . [19]."

In his report for 1891, the Chief Registrar advocated placing a limit on the issue of preference shares.[20]

A 10% systematic sample of the 1880 Return showed that of sixty-nine societies with assets of more than £5,000,[21] in eleven cases the total owed to depositors and other creditors exceeded two-thirds of total mortgage assets. Large societies were just as likely to be in this category as small societies. A similar sample for 1890 showed only four societies out of the 117 in the sample were in this category.

The lack of enforcement of the 1874 Act's requirement, that those having charge of money should give adequate security, was to cost many societies dearly as a result of extensive frauds. Frauds were of two types, internal, where some official was defrauding a society; and external, with borrowers defrauding societies, sometimes with the help of officials. From 1874 to 1891 the *Building Society Gazette* reported thirty-one cases of defalcations by officers.

The actual problem was still greater, because where only small sums were concerned, building societies might prefer not to take action. To take action meant publicity, and this might destroy the society as the result of depositors and shareholders rushing to withdraw money. The *Gazette* commented on the ". . . alarming risk of such fraudulent practices being suffered to pass without exposure or punishment, from the fear so commonly entertained by their victims that the exposure of fraud . . . must inevitably lead to further loss". There was also the cost of bringing the suspects to justice.[22] The directors of the Richard Green Society, a large London society, delayed giving information on the extent of a clerk's defalcations for fear of a run on the Society, and hesitated before prosecuting the clerk for the same reason.[23] The clerk's defalcations were discovered in November 1879. The amount involved was first thought about £350. The directors delayed a full enquiry, but an interim enquiry raised the figure to £3,500, and only later did the full investigation show losses to be about £10,000. There was also the temptation to limit losses by coming to some arrangement with defalcators, whereby some of the money stolen would be returned, the society agreeing not to prosecute. The Accrington & District Permanent Building Society, whose accountant had embezzled money, attempted such an arrangement. The money was to be treated as a "loan". Only when the loan was not being repaid did they go to the police. The accountant in fact was found not guilty because of this earlier attempt to treat the money as a loan.[24]

In most of these reported cases the sums involved were fairly large, usually more than £1,000. Ignoring the huge sums involved in the Portsea Island and Liberator Society cases at the end of the period and considered below, some of the most spectacular cases concerned the

Onward Society, Darlington, £45,000;[25] St. Helens Building Societies, Swansea,[26] approaching £35,000 (the opinion of the local press); the Sun,[27] London, about £30,000, and the Union Building Society,[28] Belfast, about £30,000. The frauds concerned both large and small societies, and some of the most prominent societies in the movement were affected. The Sun case concerned W. R. Warner, its secretary, who was a member of the executive of the London Association and had acted as secretary at the Association's inaugural meeting. The Woolwich Equitable's solicitor, T. R. Richardson, son of the Society's chairman, disappeared, leaving the society more than £3,000 the poorer. The threads that run through most of these cases of frauds by officials are inadequate audits and lack of supervision by directors. Defalcations had frequently been taking place over a number of years. In the Union Society, Belfast, the secretary printed his own receipts, similar to those of the society, and thus sent depositors away happy, at least for the time being.

In the Onward Society, when a member increased his borrowing, his earlier mortgage was discharged as part of the transaction. The society advanced the sum mentioned in the new deed; out of this the earlier mortgage was supposed to be redeemed, the borrower receiving the difference. Here the secretary gave the difference to the borrower, but sometimes kept the remainder and did not cancel the earlier mortgage; in one case he himself kept up the repayments on an earlier mortgage for four years. The chairman of the society was one of those who were the victims of this particular fraud.[29] In a Cardiff society "When there was a payment, say a member owed as a balance on his mortgage £54 1s. 0d., after the auditors ticked it as correct, I prefaced a 9 to it, so as to alter it from £54 to £954. Then the auditors would add up the list of mortgages and of course it would be £900 more than it was."[30] The Sun investigating committee found that at the audits "Members' pass books were not compared with the ledger, nor were the journal entries read into the ledger . . . consequently sums of money not accounted for in the cash book could be and actually were, entered in a ledger with impunity."[31]

H. F. A. Davis wrote thus of the requirement of the 1874 Act that officers give security, "This salutary enactment is too frequently disregarded if not in the letter, in the spirit. . . . Often no sum is named either in the rules or by the society or its directors and in consequence no security is given. In other cases the amount of security is fixed at a sum wholly inadequate, so that when losses occur, the money recovered from the sureties is but a drop in the ocean compared with the deficiency".[32] In the case of the Union Society, Belfast, the security yielded less than £15,000 of the £30,000 missing. W. R. Warner had deposited only £500 with the Sun Society. The lack of supervision of the directors of the 239th Starr-Bowkett society was particularly unfortunate in this context.[33] "Wicks [the secretary] could get an open cheque whenever he liked by simply saying, 'I want to pay out a withdrawing member', and in several cases it seems he applied the proceeds of such cheques to his own purposes. There was little fear of detection as the directors seldom, if ever, troubled to see the cancelled books of paid out members. Although the directors saw the bankers' pass book every month they did not enquire into the receipts for the large sums of money being paid out daily . . . one cheque drawn in favour of a guaranteeing society for the premium on a policy [securing the Society against possible misdeeds by its secretary] of £100 was left open and appropriated by the secretary, so that, the premium being unpaid the society lost the benefit of the policy" [when the secretary's misdeeds were discovered].

The most spectacular frauds on societies by outsiders resulted from the forging of deeds, and the most spectacular forger was F. Dimsdale, a solicitor, ably assisted by C. R. Moore, a sometime clerk at Somerset House. At the Central Criminal Court in January 1878 they pleaded guilty to frauds totalling £300,000[34] in the home counties. At least thirty forged leases concerned the same pair of houses. A few weeks later E. Downs, an accountant, was charged with forging conveyances on houses in Dulwich in order to defraud people of nearly £40,000,[35] and pleaded guilty; twenty of his forgeries concerned his own house. By April three other forgers[36] were revealed: Purcell (leases in the City of London), Roupell (in Surrey) and the brothers Arthur and George Newton (in London).

Such activity was not confined entirely to the South East. There were smaller cases in other areas; for example Brecon,[37] Sunderland,[38] Leicester and Norwich.[39] The schemes of forgers were not directed at building societies, but these were involved. Indeed, since private mortgage business so frequently emerges from personal contact between solicitors, the fact that building societies are a more open market in mortgages, meant they probably suffered a considerable share of the losses. At this period, given a surplus of funds, there was considerable pressure on societies to find mortgages, and securities were not always examined very carefully. "No Building Society should make an advance on a leasehold property unless the leasor's title has been previously investigated. This is supposed now in theory to be done, but in practice it is, alas, too frequently omitted altogether."[40] A bankrupt explaining at his examination why he had liabilities of £76,000 and assets of 18s. 1d., said he had borrowed heavily from building societies and had been caught by the fall in property values. Asked whether he needed special influence to borrow so heavily, he replied, "Oh no, it was very easy; they tried to push money on you almost in those days."[41]

Building societies, in common with others, worked under difficulties in checking the adequacy of property deeds, for there was no system of registration outside Scotland, Ireland, Yorkshire and Middlesex at this time. It is notable that in spite of the concentration of forged deeds relating to land around London, land in Middlesex was not involved. But this protection from forging was expensively purchased; the Yorkshire and Middlesex registries were continually criticised for both the expense and delay in their operations.

Outsiders also defrauded building societies by foisting on them inadequate securities, though here the responsibility was mainly that of the societies. Losses occurred mostly, but not entirely, because societies were lax in their valuations, or because directors were corrupt. A frequent practice was for the landlord, in obtaining a loan, to over-state, sometimes with the collusion of the tenant, the rent of the property. The Municipal Society made an advance on the assumption that a property was let at £30 p.a., in fact it was £25, "the tenants stating that though they had signed agreements to pay £30, they were only charged the latter amount [£25]".[42] The *Gazette* commented editorially ". . . so extensively do such arrangements prevail that it is incumbent upon Building Societies . . . to investigate . . . not only the conditions of tenancy of the properties actually offered to them, but also other properties of the like kind in the same neighbourhood".[43]

Some frauds were more elaborate, involving builders and dummy purchasers. An inflated price would be agreed after much haggling between the builder and purchaser, and the money paid over before the building society solicitor. The purchaser then got an advance related to this price. The borrower soon disappeared, and when the society entered the house it found the building incomplete. "Pipes have been put up and not connected with cisterns, baths and domestic offices. Drains are there but have no opening into the sewer. Brass taps, locks, everything in short that can be taken away has been removed. . . ."[44] To rely on a house being built in conformity with the local by-laws was also dangerous: it was not unknown for inspectors to be bribed by builders.[45] In 1883 a builder used garden mould instead of mortar in building a pair of houses, but fortunately he was caught.[46]

Collusion between directors, or valuers, and borrowers was also a source of trouble. The eighth largest society in the 1880s, the Municipal, was gravely weakened by such practices, and never regained its former strength.[47] The weak state of the mortgage market led some societies, the Municipal among them, to offer commissions to directors on business they brought in. In 1887 that society had half its capital under notice of withdrawal, and, while the Chairman refused to reveal the extent of properties in possession, it can be deduced from the rental income in the accounts, that it must have been about three-quarters of the society's mortgage assets—£46,000 was owed by one developer, all of whose properties were in possession.

This situation was taken to reveal the results of "pernicious commissions and bonuses which warp the judgement and throw dust in the eyes of reason when dealing with applications for advances".[48] In 1889 the *Gazette* noted that it was becoming customary at the Official Receiver's examination of bankrupt builders to ask whether they had paid bonuses to building society officials. W. J. Parry, who had wide experience in winding up building societies, spoke to the Select Committee of 1893 of several cases "in which sums were so taken [as bribes] by officials for advancing moneys which they should have known could never be repaid or never recovered from the properties".[49]

At the extremes it is not difficult to distinguish between a valuer receiving a gift in return for placing a fictitious value on a property, and a director, having spent a great deal of time and effort securing a particular mortgage for his society, being given an increased fee by his fellow directors. But, in practice, the one situation gradually merges into the other; there is an extensive twilight zone, bordered by whole hordes of directors allowing their collective judgement to be clouded by a desperate need to find any mortgage on which the society's accumulating cash balances can be advanced. Pressure of money can warp judgement as surely as bribes. The fact that mortgages normally included the personal bond of the borrower may actually be harmful, for men are more difficult to value than property. There is a temptation to lend because one trusts the man, even if one thinks he is misjudging the value of his investment project. This danger is particularly great when a fellow director is applying for the loan. The personal covenant of the borrower may be very valuable, when the advance is a small one to finance owner-occupation, but of little value if the advance is a large one for property development.

The pressure of money in the 1880s led many societies to make advances on doubtful security, apart altogether from cases where there was at least the suspicion of fraud. One solution was to restrict the inflow of funds. Certainly interest rates on both shares and deposits tended downwards. Sometimes the issue of shares was stopped altogether; both the Temperance and West London Societies did so in 1877;[50] sometimes new issues of shares carried a lower rate, or did not participate in profits, while old shares remained unchanged.[51] Rates on advances fell, and at particular times a society might hope by charging lower rates to be more selective in its advance policy, though the *Gazette* issued a warning against these cut-throat policies.[52] Differential rates on advances were seen as one solution. "If Building Societies were to adopt two or three scales of repayment, it would put them in a fairer position to secure their share of the *best* mortgage business, because if only one scale be employed, it can scarcely be fixed *low* enough to attract the best business, such as would be suitable for employing the reserve fund; nor, on the other hand, could it be fixed *high* enough to meet the ordinary risks of advances with very moderate margins of value."[53]

The more usual response was to strenuously seek any business, and competition took the form of more generous advances and a less careful selection of securities. In the Registrar's view permanent societies were the worst offenders, no doubt because they had more surplus funds. He told the Select Committee of 1893, "The permanent societies run the greater risk in regard to the tendency to speculation, the ignoring of the risk of loss and the entering on extraneous business such as banking."[54] H. F. A. Davis commented in 1884, "Of late years the rule as to margins has been gradually relaxed until often it is possible for a borrower to obtain a loan of the full sum he has given for a security."[55]

Lack of care in selecting securities was particularly dangerous where advances were made on industrial property. The value of industrial property is a reflection of the profitability of these undertakings, and profits are likely to fluctuate, as a number of building societies found to their cost. The Patriotic Societies, a series of terminating societies in Sheffield, lent money to one of their directors to build an iron works and, after his bankruptcy, was left with the property. The property could be disposed of only by lending money to others to buy it; among them, another director of the Patriotic Societies. This director took further advances to finance the operation of the ironworks and in all the societies lost over £60,000 on the venture. The history of this series of societies was also marred by actions of a more criminal kind.[56]

Sheffield provides a second noteworthy example. In 1878 the Sheffield and South Yorkshire B.S. made an advance of £25,000 to Thomas Joseph on the security, among other properties, of a second mortgage on the Dunraven Colliery in South Wales. In 1881, Joseph being unable to meet his commitments on the first mortgage, the society made a second advance of £40,000 to prevent the holder of the first mortgage from taking possession. The colliery did not prosper and Joseph was again unable to meet his commitments with the result that the building society had to take over the colliery and manage it. Not surprisingly the colliery was no more prosperous in its hands than it had been in Joseph's and further sums had to be advanced to pay mining royalties due and to cover losses.[57]

The building society failed in 1886 and the liquidator's report showed that against £193,000 due to depositors and shareholders the main asset of the Society was the loan, ultimately standing at £117,885, to the Dunraven Colliery. One can understand the emotions of a Mr. Caunt, who spoke thus of the directors at a later meeting of the society, " 'I hope the curse of Heaven will fall on them and I ask you all here to say Amen to that' (Loud cries of Amen, Amen)".[58] The colliery was eventually disposed of in 1890 for £26,000.[59]

There were occasions on which societies got into difficulties in circumstances which were largely beyond their control. Heavy withdrawals of funds might have their origin in the revelation of defalcations in a neighbouring society or in events altogether outside the building society world. To give two interlocked examples. The City of Glasgow Bank failed in October 1878. In Manchester there were rumours, which had no foundation in fact, that the Queen's Society (the fourth largest society in the country) had balances at the City of Glasgow Bank. In consequence there was a run on the Queen's (and some smaller Manchester societies) and £50,000 was withdrawn in four days, equal to about 5% of its total assets. The Society was compelled to enforce its rules regarding notice of withdrawal. Civic leaders intervened to restore confidence; a letter from the Bishop of Manchester, to the press, seems to have been influential.[60]

At the same time there was a run on the Burnley Society. The society was known to have made loans to the owners of local weaving sheds, some of them directors of the society, and, as a result of a strike of weavers, it was felt that the owners would be unable to meet mortgage payments. No doubt strikers withdrawing their savings to meet current expenses, and the news of events in Manchester, helped to speed withdrawals. The result was that the Burnley Society's cash balance of £15,000 quickly disappeared. Notices of withdrawal in the last two weeks of October rose to nearly £50,000 and by December they had climbed to nearly £75,000 compared to a normal figure of £10,000. The directors reacted sharply, pointing out that unless notices were withdrawn the Society would have to go into liquidation; this would be a huge expense and in any case assets could be only slowly realised. The outcome was an investigating committee which issued a mainly reassuring report, although it considered "that the practice of lending large amounts in one hand had been carried to an indiscreet extent". It recommended revising the rules so that a director would be compelled to retire if he borrowed more than a certain sum from the Society.[61]

The combination of a large amount of property in possession and falling property values is clearly a dangerous one for any building society. J. M. Ludlow wrote[62] of the dangers, "When this [a fall in property values] takes place the directors or committee of management are too often tempted to conceal the fact. They know that any loss incurred in this manner, though it may have arisen from causes quite beyond their control, is sure to be attributed to their own incapacity. Moreover, every admission of pecuniary loss on the one hand tends to provoke a run on deposits, if they are taken, and on the other, a pouring in of notices of withdrawal. What wonder if the policy of concealment is thus pursued as far as possible and as long as possible." A queue for withdrawals leads at best to stagnation,[63] at worst to liquidation.

Societies adopted a variety of responses to such situations. Most societies were agreed that the extent of properties in possession should not be revealed, because it was likely to lead to withdrawals. Questions on the subject were likely to be met with "The Chairman thought it would not be wise nor was it usual to answer that question",[64] or "The Chairman did not think it would be wise to publish abroad the amount [of property] on hand".[65]

Such an attitude was generally accepted; on one occasion where the information was given, a member responded ". . . that these figures . . . should be made public . . . appears to me to be an act of insane folly, by which the directors have incurred the risk of wrecking an institution . . ."[66] When the Select Committee of 1893 was taking evidence on the proposal that properties in possession should be revealed in the annual return, the proposal was generally strongly resisted. Edward Wood stated that, "To lay open to the inspection of the world the very worst transactions that a banker or other commercial undertaking has carried through, would be most perilous to many strong institutions and would result in disaster to some that are perfectly sound".[67] The Chairman of the Building Society Association, C. Binyon, justified his objections to the proposal by saying, "that those [advances] most in arrear were generally the soundest securities which the society who possessed them ever had". But after further questioning he withdrew this remarkable assertion. A few societies did regularly state in their annual report the extent of properties in possession. The South Wales and Monmouth Society was one such. Clearly it would not help to start revealing these figures in bad times, but their regular publication would encourage the directors to ensure that possessions did not increase rapidly.

The 1874 Act, section 13, laid down that properties in possession should be sold or converted into money, as soon after coming into possession as might be conveniently practicable. No penalty was stated for failure to do so and no guidance was given as to how "conveniently practicable" was to be defined. The societies therefore had complete freedom of action here. The result all too frequently was inaction, if to sell a property meant realising a loss, which would show up on the balance sheet and lead to criticism, or worse still, to a general lack of confidence. It was easier not to sell and hope for better times. In the 1880s better times did not appear, and with the position worsening the arguments for inaction became all the stronger. Where rents did not cover outgoings on the property, it was not unknown to write up the difference as an increase in mortgage assets.[68]

The classic case here was the Liberator Society. A sea wall was being built as part of a development scheme on which it had advanced money. "The sea wall was washed away several times and each time the value of the property increased, because the expenditure on the sea wall was added every time to the value."[69] Vice-Chancellor Bristowe, commenting on building societies in this context, said, "They went on holding properties thinking times would mend and the market become better, until they were just worth nothing at all".[70]

In September 1893, after the Liberator crash, W. L. Jackson, M.P., persuaded the House of Commons to call for a return from building societies of all their properties in possession at the end of 1892. The Home Office published these returns in April 1894. Unfortunately it covered only the various aspects of properties in possession, giving no information about the total assets of societies. However, this return can be set beside the annual statements that societies sent to the Registrar, published in his Report for 1892, to discover the extent of properties in possession compared with a society's total mortgage assets. Of the 2,370 societies on the register, 218 made no return, 1,436 returned no properties in possession and 716 had properties in possession. For the movement as a whole properties in possession were security for £3,714,000 outstanding on mortgages in respect of them; this amounted to 12% of all mortgage assets. Given that nearly two-thirds of societies had no possessions, the remaining third of societies, or some of them, were in a serious position. Table XIII gives the results of matching the return of properties in possession with the figure of total mortgage assets in the Registrar's Report for 1892 for a 10% systematic sample of societies returning properties in possession. Nearly two-thirds of the societies in the sample had more than 10% of their mortgage assets "in possession" and nearly a quarter had over 25% of their mortgage assets "in possession".

When building societies were being started and rules were being framed, there was an understandable reluctance to contemplate the unwelcome possibility of losses. Consequently the rules of many societies provided no means for allocating losses among members. This was a problem confined to permanent societies. In terminating societies losses implied a longer life; this affected all members, thus all shared the losses. The Registrar commented on "the unwillingness that they [permanent societies] show to provide in their rules for what is to happen when losses occur".[71] Thus when losses were made, disputes were likely to arise concerning their allocation.

TABLE XIII

Properties in possession as a percentage of total mortgage assets

Size of Society Total Mortage Assets	Percentage −5	−10	−25	−50	−75	−100	Total
Under £5,000	0	1	8	1	0	4	14
£25,000	10	4	12	3	1	4	34
£50,000	3	1	4	0	0	1	9
£100,000	1	0	0	0	0	0	1
Over £100,000	2	2	1	0	0	0	5
TOTAL	16	8	25	4	1	9	63[72]

In the case *Auld v. Glasgow Working Men's Society*[73] the Society had made losses, and there was no rule governing their allocation. Before any method of meeting the loss was decided, Auld gave notice to withdraw and, before he was paid, the Society passed a rule reducing the credit of each shareholder by 7s. 6d. in the pound to meet the losses. Auld claimed the alteration left his position unaffected. The Court upheld this view, finding that an investing member was entitled to receive the full amount standing to his credit according to the rules at the time he gave notice of withdrawal. This added a grave instability to those societies which had no rule governing the allocation of losses. Commenting on the decision C. J. Lowe wrote, "Thus, in the event of some rumour adversely affecting the credit of a Society being circulated, a premium in the shape of a preference is offered to every member who hastens to wreck the Society by giving notice to withdraw and so precipitating a panic".[74] As Brabrook put it, "It is one of the most iniquitous results of the present state of the law, that a number of members, by taking advantage of an imaginary contract with the other members, have escaped without any contribution to the losses of the society, leaving an increased contribution to be borne by the whole of the other members."[75]

Efforts were also made to make advanced members bear a proportionate amount of losses, but the decision in *Brownlie v. Russell*[76] made it clear that, where the rules of the society, and hence the mortgage deed, made no provision for the allocation of losses, advanced members were not liable. The rules of some societies did make such provision. Mr. C. B.

Catnach of the Northern Counties Society took the view that "With regard to losses someone had to take the risk and it was felt in the North that it should not fall upon investors but upon the borrowers."[77]

The present method of meeting losses by building up reserves was not everywhere looked on with favour. T. Fatkin, secretary of the Leeds Permanent, the fifth largest society in 1880, said, "I look myself rather with suspicion on large reserve funds".[78] He saw the reserve as being in the value of the property over the advance; if losses seemed likely on properties taken over, they should be met out of profits. The total of unappropriated profit of societies making returns in 1880 was £1,105,000 (and this included an unknown element of anticipated profit) when total assets were £36,950,000, 3·0%. By 1890 the figure had risen to 3·7%. The general view was that reserves should be invested in mortgages.

For once, Jabez Balfour of the Liberator Society can be allowed to speak for the movement:[79] "It would add very much to the strength of the Society if the reserve fund could be invested in Consols or an equally valuable security; but it would be a serious loss of interest to do so. If the investments in mortgages were good enough for the principal it appeared to him that they were good enough for the reserve fund which was to secure that principal." Some societies had invested reserves in more liquid securities and abandoned that practice. The Chairman of the Temperance Society said in 1877, ". . . the directors found that bricks and mortar were the most profitable mode to adopt. They had formerly invested £20,000 in Consols at about half the rate of interest obtained on house property and that made nearly a ½% difference in the annual dividend".[80]

The capital structure of societies had a good deal of influence on a society's ability to withstand any loss of confidence on the part of investors. In this respect the development of deposit banks in connection with building societies was viewed with suspicion by a large part of the movement. Deposit bank facilities had been developed by a number of societies, as a means of attracting extra funds at low rates of interest. However, the right of customers to withdraw funds without any notice from banking departments was a source of considerable weakness in times of stress, especially where directors yielded to the temptation to invest the bank's funds heavily in the ordinary business of the building society. If the banking department was not to be a liability in times of stress, then its funds had to be invested in easily realisable securities, and if this was done, the normal activities of the building society would not benefit much from the creation of banking departments. This was the orthodox view of societies. The view would have carried greater conviction if societies generally had paid more attention to the terms on which ordinary deposits were taken. Such deposits were frequently withdrawn on demand[81] and the societies had created what were, in effect, banking departments without that detailed consideration of the consequences, which the formal creation of a banking department was likely to imply. The 1874 Act required that a society's rules should set out the terms on which shareholders could withdraw, and in most cases only very short notice was required. It is clearly a great convenience for a shareholder to withdraw at short notice, and as a matter of grace it does the society no harm, provided funds are available. But if depositors can demand repayment immediately, and shareholders at short notice, any modest shock to confidence is going to bring a sufficient demand for repayment to absorb all available funds. The fact that a society cannot then meet its obligations, is likely to give such a secondary shock to public confidence, as to severely restrict a society's future development, even if it does not bring its downfall.

In general too little attention was given, both to capital structure and to preserving an adequate proportion of readily realisable assets. In 1880, claims of Depositors and Shareholders were about £34,900,000 and non-mortgage assets £2,100,000. The extent to which these non-mortgage assets were liquid is unknown, but in 1900, by which time, as a result of the Liberator crisis of 1892, societies were much more aware of the importance of liquidity, freehold and leasehold securities were still rather more than 20% of non-mortgage assets. To assume that in the 1880s 75% of "other assets" were in cash and fairly easily realisable securities, is probably still to exaggerate the degree of liquidity. On that assumption liquid assets were only 4·4% of the total of shares and deposits in 1880, and 5·5% ten years later. For particular societies the situation was much worse. Discussing liquidity ratios in 1881, the *Gazette* gave details of four societies in which the total of cash and securities was below £500 against a total of shares and deposits of £112,000 (Hull Permanent), £83,000 (Leicester Permanent), £33,000 (Borough of Finsbury Permanent) and £57,000 (Modern Permanent).

A number of societies attempted to improve their position by limiting the terms on which part of their capital could be withdrawn. The Bristol and West of England Society probably went further than any other society in this direction. Deposits were taken at one month's call at 2½% interest, three months 3%, six months, 3½%, and for terms of three, five or seven years at 4%.[82] There were two issues of shares at 5%, the principal not withdrawable for twenty-one years, but transferable.[83] The Bristol and Clifton Society had 4½% three-year debentures.[84] The Cork and General had two types of share, one requiring the longer term of six months notice of withdrawal.[85] Something of the same purpose was achieved by new issues of shares at lower rates,[86] which would make holders of earlier issues reluctant to withdraw, and by allowing participation in profits only to shares which had been invested for a period of years: five in the case of the Leeds Permanent.[87] The Leeds Permanent is also an example of a simpler restriction on withdrawal of deposits; to withdraw over £100, six months notice was required, over £50, three months, over £5, one month though ". . . if we have plenty of money we meet them on short notice if they require it".[88]

In addition to the various ways in which societies adjusted their internal organisation to meet the changing environment, some societies, as members of the Building Societies Protection Association (referred to as the London Association above) took joint action. Two matters received continual attention from this Association: leaseholds and registration of titles to real property.

The Association was concerned with the wide variety of restrictive covenants appearing in leases, some of which adversely affected the position of building societies as mortgagees. For examples: a lease might be forfeit if a man went bankrupt, thus leaving the society without security for an advance made on the property; all future legal matters concerned with the property were to be handled by a particular solicitor; fire insurance to be with a particular firm; annual painting to be done to the exterior of a property, etc.; and even that no enquiry should be made into the title of the lease. Bills were drafted to alleviate these grievances in 1876 and 1880, though only the second was presented and that did not pass.[89]

The question of such covenants concerned a wider field than the building societies. The Association's efforts via conferences and petitions helped the general agitation which, in 1881, achieved partial success with the passing of the Conveyancing and Law of Property Act. Section 14 (1) opened up possibilities of avoiding forfeiture, by offering reasonable compensation for failure to observe covenants and Section 14 (2) enabled the courts to grant relief "having regard to the proceedings and conduct of the parties . . .". This relief was not complete and the Association lent its support to the efforts of the Leasehold Enfranchisement Association. A conference of the Building Societies Protection Association in 1887 called for petitions from building societies in support of a Bill introduced by Colonel Hughes.[90] The Association drafted another Bill itself in 1889, and after consultations, steps were taken to introduce the Bill in 1892.[91] This Bill did not pass and the Association took no further steps in the matter. The issue of enfranchisement had become increasingly a party political matter, not regarded as a suitable subject for a non-political organisation; moreover, the fall of some prominent societies in

1892 gave the Association other preoccupations. However, the Conveyancing Act of 1891 did slightly improve the position of leaseholders.

The registration of titles became a prominent issue with the discovery of the Dimsdale forgeries in 1877 and was to occupy the Association for many years. A meeting on April 9, 1878, "was called . . . to consider the advisability of urging the Government to introduce a general system of registration of all dealing with houses and land throughout the country . . .".[92] In May a deputation discussed the matter with the Home Secretary and members of parliament were lobbied to gain support for reform. In 1880 the Association had a Bill introduced to set up a Metropolitan Registry of Deeds, but its progress was cut short by a dissolution. The Bill was introduced again without success in 1881 and in 1882. After a gap to deal with more urgent business, the Association returned to the question in 1885, when a prize essay on the subject of registration of title was sponsored.

The winning essay by R. Burnet Morris was published; it helped to create interest in a somewhat unexciting subject. More important, Morris's ideas on possessory titles were "considered so important that the Solicitor General expressed the intent of drafting a Bill on these lines".[93]

Certainly a government Bill on the subject was introduced in 1887. Strong exception was taken to this Bill when it was discussed at a conference in December 1887; it was not the complete reform desired, it was likely to be expensive and to introduce considerable delays in transfers of title. A deputation saw the Lord Chancellor, who did not placate the opposition and the Bill was ultimately withdrawn.

In November 1889 a further conference on the subject was held and resolutions were passed favouring compulsory registration of title. The first registration would be a possessory title, with power to register an absolute title if desired, and in any case, the possessory title would become absolute if unchallenged for twenty years.[94]

The Association did not again introduce a Bill of its own, but Bills were introduced in 1891 and 1895. Neither became law. The main obstacle to reform came from the Law Society, whose members naturally saw in any simplification of land transfer a diminution in one of their most profitable activities. In July 1897 the legal profession agreed to allow passage of a Bill provided the reform was treated as experimental, applying only to one county for an initial period of three years, all work concerning transfer of land to be carried out by the legal profession.[95] As a result a Bill was passed in September 1897. London was the county chosen, although the local authority could still block the implementation of the Act. If the experiment proved successful, other local authorities could apply to have their areas included under the Act. The hope that in this way, in time, registration of transfers of land would be compulsorily extended over the whole country has not been fulfilled, only a handful of areas having been brought under the Act in its first fifty years. The number of areas wishing to be brought under the Act has increased sharply in recent years.

The Association had a more complete and swifter parliamentary success with the Building Societies Act, 1884. The Building Societies Act of 1877, which had not been sponsored by the Association, arose from the Registrar's insistence that a society's rules must state the address of its office;[96] thus any change of address involved the somewhat time-consuming and expensive business of altering the rules. It was suggested, at the annual general meeting of 1876, that the Association should endeavour to get the Registrar to alter his procedure on this point, but James Higham, as chairman, replied, "No doubt the expense of obtaining an alteration in the rules, in the case of removal of offices, was a very serious thing to a struggling society but as there were only a few of that class in the country, he did not think the Association could take that as a ground for objecting to the Registrar's opinion."[97] Mr. Waddy, an M.P. connected with the Planet Society, sponsored a Bill which passed in September 1877. This allowed changes of offices without changing the rules, and also took care of two small omissions in the 1874 Act, the more important being that where a transfer of engagements took place, under the 1874 Act, the property of the transferring society became the property of the continuing society without reconveyance.

The Building Society Act of 1884 arose from the decision in the case of the *Municipal B.S. v. Kent.*[98] Kent had borrowed money from the Municipal Society and had fallen into arrears. The Society commenced an action to recover the money due. Kent took out a summons to stay proceedings on the grounds that one of the Society's rules required all disputes between itself and members to be settled by arbitration. Kent got his stay of proceedings in the Queen's Bench Division, and successfully resisted the Society's appeal against that decision, in the Appeal Court in April 1883 and in the House of Lords in March 1884.

The implications of these decisions for building societies were serious. "As there might not be any 'dispute' as to the money being due, there might not be any ground for the Society submittting the matter to arbitration and, as the doors of the Law Courts were closed against the Society, there were no means of compelling payment".[99] "It was stated that between 200 and 300 cases were dependent upon it [the decision of the House of Lords] and the position was one of extreme gravity as 'from all quarters reports were received from societies expressing the extreme difficulty felt in recovering their payments under mortgages and that difficulty was such as to jeopardise the societies themselves."[100] The committee of the Association considered the matter and called a meeting of societies in June 1884, at which it was decided to draft and introduce a Bill to rectify the situation.

Fortunately the Lord Chancellor, the Earl of Selbourne (formerly Sir Roundell Palmer), had dissented from the judgement in the Lords, and in his personal capacity the Earl introduced the Association's Bill as a matter of urgency on July 11th. The Bill passed the Lords and Commons with extraordinary swiftness, having its third reading in the latter House on July 29th. The Bill had only one operative section: where a society's rules provided that disputes be referred to arbitration, that rule "shall not apply to any dispute between any such society and any member thereof . . . as to the construction or effect of any mortgage deed".[101]

The quick passage of the Building Societies Act, 1884 was achieved under the direction of Mr. Charles Binyon, who had succeeded James Higham as Chairman of the Association in 1883. The Association's parliamentary activity was not restricted to promoting bills. Higham had already established a tradition of careful examination of all proposed legislation which could conceivably affect building societies, and of sustained pressure to protect the interests of societies. Here the practice of appointing a number of M.P.s interested in building society matters as Vice-Presidents gave the Association considerable power and influence.

While the Association's main influence came from its interest in legislation, there were two occasions when it attempted to give a lead in more domestic matters. Mention has already been made of the public concern about the heavy fines levied by some societies.[102] The Association called a conference in April 1877, following the decision in the case *Lovejoy v. Mulkern*, "to consider the recent decision and the advisability of reducing the fines charged by Building Societies".[103] Conditions varied too much among societies for a single scale of fines to be recommended by the conference and the matter was passed to the committee. The committee recommended a maximum fine of 6d. per £1 per month for the first six months and 3d. thereafter. A recommendation, that where rules levied fines exceeding this they should be changed, was adopted at a conference in July.[104]

In 1886 an effort was made to protect societies from fraudulent practices by some applicants for advances, by creating a "black list" of borrowers. Out of 109 members, only 22 gave names; naming 277 persons in all. The scheme was not a success. James Higham said that "Some directors had not fallen in with the spirit of the application and did not make any return at all . . . if certain societies did not take sufficient interest to give information, they could not expect to receive any information themselves."[105] Many societies did not take part because they feared that if the list was published, legal action might be taken against them.

During the agitation preceding the passing of the 1874 Act the Association claimed a membership of 188 societies.[106] After that important success membership fell rapidly to only about seventy in 1877. Membership rose with a second legislative victory, the Act of 1884, to 109 in 1885 and 112 in 1888.

The Association had a fairly rapid succession of secretaries in its early years, James Higham, Jnr. (1870), F. M. Whittingham (1874), G. W. Phillipson (1880) and E. F. Brabrook (1883) before the appointment of R. H. Marsh (1888), who was to hold that position for forty-eight years.

With the falling off in membership after 1874, an attempt was made to expand the Association, especially outside London, and provincial members from Bradford, Barnsley and Sheffield joined the executive. The experiment did not succeed; as the Chairman Mr. Higham put it in 1880, "It was useless to retain the names of some of their county friends [on the committee] as they did not attend any of the meetings." Binyon's comment revealed perhaps more of the nature of the Association than he intended when he said that "... at the time they [the provincial members] were appointed there were special reasons why they should appear to be working with representatives from the country, but these reasons had now expired".[107] Certainly the Association's committee came entirely from the South East. A situation seems to have been reached in which provincial societies, feeling the Association was not widely representative, did not join, and the committee was resentful at their refusal. Regarding some information about income tax Higham said, "It would hardly be fair to make the matter generally public, so that the societies which did not subscribe would have the benefit of the expenditure of the Association's funds."[108] Efforts to involve the Association, as such, in the Starr-Bowkett controversy were resisted.[109]

In 1886, when the 1884 Act was challenged in the case of the *Western Notting Hill and Suburban B.S. v. Martin*[110] efforts to get the Association to help with the legal costs of an appeal failed, the society having ceased its membership a few years earlier. Voices were raised from time to time in the *Gazette*, editorially and in letters, in favour of the Association showing a more general concern for the wellbeing of the movement as a whole.[111] Reformers made themselves heard at the annual general meeting in 1885, when J. T. Stanesby suggested the Association should find a home of its own,[112] drop the word "Protection" from its title and build up a library.[113] At the annual general meeting in 1886 there was a call for more frequent general meetings, and a proposal that no more than one member of any society should sit on the executive committee. Neither point was carried.[114] The reformers did gain something, perhaps symbolic, at that meeting: the dropping of the word "Protection" from the Association's title, so that it became the Building Societies Association. It was not until 1896 that serious attention was given to making the Association more representative; the agitation started then produced major reforms in 1898. These reforms were made necessary by a rapid increase in membership after the passing of the Building Societies Act, 1894. That Act had resulted from the disastrous events of 1892, symbolised in the failure of the Liberator Society, to which we now turn.

Chapter Eight

THE LIBERATOR CRASH AND THE 1894 ACT*

WHILE IT IS TRUE that "The Liberator failure forcibly directed attention to the weaknesses of existing building society legislation, and it was generally agreed that some amendment was a matter of urgency",[1] it would be quite wrong to conclude that there was no awareness of weakness or desire for amendment until the Liberator Society fell. Inadequate auditing, so frequently exposed as providing the opportunity for fraud, had much earlier convinced many people of the need for stronger government control. By 1884 government supervision of auditing was being advocated,[2] and the *Gazette*, usually opposed to the idea of official audits, commented in 1887, "It has sometimes occurred to us that Building and Friendly Society accounts might well be audited by officials appointed in the same manner as the District Auditors of the Local Government Board."[3]

In 1885, E. W. Brabrook, then assistant registrar, drew attention to the inadequacies of existing legislation in a paper to the Statistical Society of London.[4] He gave more detailed suggestions for reform in an address in 1886.[5] These included publication of details of properties in possession, revaluation of properties when they came into possession, the right of members to inspect a society's books and call for an official enquiry, and stricter auditing. J. W. Campbell (Sunderland Workingmen's Societies) reported in 1889 that he had been approached, as one of those prominent in the events leading to the 1874 Act, to draft a reform bill and he invited suggestions.[6] The Chairman of the Building Societies Association discussed the need for new legislation in the *Oracle* in 1890.[7] The theme was taken up again by Brabrook, now Chief Registrar, in his first report for 1891. He stressed the need for limits on preference shares, supervision of dissolutions, heavier penalties for false returns to the Registrar, a prescribed form of return, and powers for the Registrar, at the request of members, to investigate a society. Thus there was, by 1892, a considerable opinion in favour of changes in legislation.

However, the events of 1892 were the immediate cause of the 1894 Act. The year opened in the shadow of the failure of the Portsea Island Society.

* *Notes on this chapter appear on page 300.*

In September 1891 the secretary of that society, T. P. Wills, admitted to the directors "that the accounts of the Society had been falsified by him to a large extent for many years. . . ".[8] The directors required Wills to correct the accounts of the Society published in its monthly magazine, and corrections of sorts were made in succeeding months. Such sudden changes in the Society's accounts naturally gave rise to doubts about its stability, and there was a consequent withdrawal of funds. The Society suspended payments on December 14th. In all, Wills himself borrowed over £90,000, the value of securities held by the Society in respect of these loans being under £24,000, a deficiency of over £66,000.[9] Wills was similarly accommodating to his friends, fellow property speculators or builders, so that a number of other accounts were unsatisfactory. "Another debt to the Society from one man, a builder, wholly unsecured, amounted to £32,324, which had steadily accumulated from 1883 to 1891 and on which no interest at all had ever been charged. . . . In addition to this amount the same man was indebted to the Society on thirteen different mortgage accounts, amounting altogether to nearly £50,000."[10] Another debt of £6,450 "included as good up to September 1891, for which there was no shadow of security"[11] was due from a man who was a bankrupt eight years earlier.

The Society had been started in 1846 with the same T. P. Wills as secretary. The Society grew to one of the country's largest, with assets (or at least liabilities!) of over £600,000. The methods of the Society took no account of its changing size; one of the two auditors at its demise was a government clerk, who had held the office for the whole forty-five years of the Society's existence, the other was a schoolmaster. The yearly audit of the huge Society occupied these two men for a mere three evenings and a Saturday afternoon. "The directors for many years past had been in the habit of signing thirty or forty blank cheques at each meeting, leaving the same with the secretary to fill up as and when he required, and taking no steps to see how the cheques so signed in blank, were applied."[12] No proper record was kept of advances sanctioned at the monthly directors' meeting. In such circumstances Wills' method was simplicity itself. "The difficulty of balancing the accounts to the entire satisfaction of the auditors was got over by the . . . suppression of any undesirable liability or the elimination of an undesirable asset. The Secretary explained that this method . . . was intended to show the public that the deposits received were within the borrowing power of the Society."[13] The liquidator found that, at the date of its suspension of payments, the true position of the Society showed assets of £435,464 against liabilities of £624,721, a deficiency of £189,257. The assets included advances of £168,792 made on properties then in the Society's possession.

The failure of the Portsea Island was spectacular only in the size of the deficiency. The essential causes of the failure, lack of supervision by directors and auditors, were something less than novel; none the less the deficiency was spectacular and other societies experienced the usual difficulties that result from any shock to public confidence. The damage was to some degree limited by the fact that the Portsea Island Society, in spite of its size, was still relatively local. This partially explains the difference in the impact of its failure compared with that of the Liberator later in 1892.

In May, Mr. Gerald Balfour, M.P., took up the cause of reform. He called for a return of societies which had gone into liquidation in recent years; and wanted accounts audited by certified accountants, a limit to the advance on any single security, both in absolute size and as a percentage of the value of the property mortgaged, and an annual certified return of the value of each property in possession.[14] Balfour was later joint author of one of the reform bills introduced in 1892.

The Liberator Society[15] was founded in June 1868. J. S. Balfour was at first Vice-Chairman, then, successively, Secretary, Managing Director and Vice-President. He was, whatever position he happened incidentally to occupy, the main force behind the Society. After he had ceased to be a director he attended board meetings and practically controlled affairs.[16] Balfour's parents were both well known in nonconformist and temperance circles, and his father was a director of the Temperance Society from 1854 to 1878. Balfour surrounded himself, on the board of the Society and among the arbitrators, with prominent leaders of the Congregational and Baptist churches and the temperance movement. These connections were the main asset which enabled the Liberator to grow rapidly and become, by 1890, much the largest building society in the country, about twice the size of its nearest rival.

The Society's respectable connections gave investors immediate confidence, so that it did not have, in its early years, the problem of proving to the investing public that it was a safe repository for their funds. Even more important, Balfour used his religious and temperance connections more directly by creating among nonconformist ministers and laymen a vast agency organisation, paying commission to those who brought in money or found borrowers. By 1878 these commissions totalled nearly £7,000[17] and, in all, the Society paid over £140,000 in commissions during its twenty-four years existence.[18] Publicity was used extensively and ingeniously. The agents were well armed with persuasive literature and, in comparison with most societies, press advertising was considerable.[19]

In its early years the Society carried on its affairs according to normal practice. After only two years investors' credits stood at nearly £24,000 and by 1880 they were £1,264,510.[20] Balfour had become manager in 1872. The character of the Liberator began to change about 1880. Balfour controlled two other enterprises, the Lands Allotment Company (formed 1867), of which he became managing director in 1872, and the House and Land Investment Trust (formed 1875). These were essentially property development companies, at first concerned largely with house building, drawing on the Liberator as well as on the public for funds. Later the type of developments became more speculative, with hotels and blocks of luxury flats. In 1880, about 20% of the Liberator's assets were mortgages for advances to these two companies. Other companies which Balfour managed and which had financial dealings with the Liberator were the London and General Bank (1882), the Building Securities Company (1884), George Newman & Company (Surveyors, 1886) and the Real Estates Company (1888). Most important of all was J. W. Hobbs & Company. Hobbs was a builder who had had considerable dealings with the Liberator, and in 1885 his business became a public company with Balfour dominant, and it was through this company that Balfour's larger developments were carried out. At its winding up the Official Receiver found that of the Liberator's nominal mortgage assets of £3,423,000, £2,099,000 represented advances to J. W. Hobbs & Company, £457,800 to the Real Estates Company and £636,800 to the House and Land Investment Trust.[21]

Normal building society advances declined rapidly after 1880. By 1885 they represented only £328,705 of total mortgages of £2,164,000 and at the close they were only £62,672, 1·9% of the total.[22] This change in the Liberator's character was not revealed to shareholders, indeed speculative building was a frequent subject for condemnation by Balfour at meetings of the society. In 1885 Balfour quoted a Mr. Robins as saying, "Probably the rock on which most building societies foundered was the speculative builder" and commented, "With that I entirely agree . . . the speculative solicitor has generally gone on advancing to builders as long as it was safe, and then he has started a Building Society to carry on."[23]

Balfour's method of operation was simple. "A favourite enterprise was for Balfour, Hobbs or Newman to obtain an option on an estate, or even purchase it outright, then to sell the option or estate to one of the four property companies at an excessive price, the full purchase money being borrowed from the Liberator." That, at these inflated values, the property company could not produce an income sufficient to pay a dividend to shareholders, and pay interest to the Liberator on its mortgages, created no difficulty. The interest could always be paid with a further loan from the Liberator, no additional security being given; the book value of the original security being written up to include the new advance.[24] The result was that security given for advances started life as inadequate and became increasingly so as time went on. Interest to Liberator shareholders, to put it another way, was being paid out of current subscriptions and deposits. So long as the Society continued to grow rapidly, the nature of the enterprise might not be revealed. One can understand the urgency with which Balfour resisted moves, at a general meeting in 1888, to cut interest rates, fearing that to do so would restrict the inflow of funds.[25]

About 1887 the auditors called the attention of directors to the fact that interest was being paid out of new advances, but made no move to inform the shareholders, merely issuing a certificate stating that the balance sheet agreed with the books.[26] The auditing was admittedly meticulous. In 1886 Balfour said, "The audit was continuous throughout the year and no Society could have a more thorough audit".[27] In 1892 reference was made to the fact that two of the auditors were chartered accountants, a thing rare among building societies.[28] The previous year one of the auditors, on re-election, declared that "Everything is kept in the best possible style and every paper, voucher and deed that we ask for has been at once produced . . . we go through the deeds every year and I can assure you that it is a very long and dirty job."[29] Just how "dirty" was soon to be revealed.

Eventually, the inflow of funds was not sufficient and in the search for further money, the Liberator was greatly weakened. This society accepted the position of second and third mortgagee, so that Balfour could raise money elsewhere on the first and second mortgages, originally held by the Liberator. Something of the desperate position is shown by the fact that Balfour was eventually borrowing at rates as high as $17\frac{1}{2}\%$.[30]

Doubts about the Liberator seem to have existed among some shareholders at the Annual General Meeting in February 1892. The directors were closely questioned about the true value of securities and were pressed on the subject of getting independent valuations.[31] The Board presented a picture of steady progress and stressed the dangers of looking on the dark side of the picture. However it was not the Liberator that cracked first, but Balfour's London and General Bank, which suspended payments on September 2, 1892.

As a result the Liberator could not provide funds for immediate withdrawals; depositors and shareholders giving notice were told they would be paid in rotation. The queue naturally began to grow and on October 4th a compulsory winding-up order was made with liabilities to shareholders and depositors standing at a total of £3,300,000. The Society's assets, in the view of the liquidator, "consisted almost entirely of second and third mortgages. The prior mortgagees had, in a number of cases, gone in and . . . were in a position to sell". If they had sold, the

Liberator's assets would have amounted to about £50,000. In fact moves were quietly afoot to make good the claims of prior mortgagees, though the unscrambling of the claims of the various Balfour companies and the realisation of their assets proved a lengthy business.

Even though the extent of losses was not immediately known, the failure of the country's largest society was a great shock to public confidence in building societies generally. Many were under extreme pressure and a few failed, notably the London Provident Society. The Birkbeck Society provided the most dramatic evidence of public concern. That society had developed a banking department, which eventually overshadowed its ordinary building society business, and was now one of the ten largest banks in the country. In 1892 the Birkbeck had only £469,000 due on mortgage loans while deposits alone were £5,131,000.[32] Unlike the Liberator, the Birkbeck had accommodated itself to the changed nature of its activities, keeping a third of its assets in Consols and the remainder in liquid securities and freehold ground rents.[33]

The run on the Birkbeck started on Saturday, September 10th.[34] A vast queue, with many police on duty, formed and though the bank remained open late, anxiety continued. To cope with an even larger queue the Bank opened early on the following Monday and remained open for thirteen hours, during which half a million pounds were repaid. This did much to restore public confidence, although business continued very heavy until Wednesday. Immediate cash was found by a loan of £500,000 from the Bank of England. It was fortunate for societies generally that the Birkbeck was able to withstand the run; the public do not make nice distinctions between building societies that operate largely as banks or property development companies, and the normal variety. Had both the Birkbeck and Liberator gone down in less than a fortnight, the shock to confidence might have brought down many others.

At James Higham's invitation leaders of a number of London societies met on September 19th, but proposals for joint action to allay public fears were resisted on the grounds that any statement would do harm, by keeping building societies in the news; least said, soonest mended. Individual societies did take action. The Temperance Society, drawing many of its members from the same religious and temperance groups as the Liberator, was particularly vulnerable. Edward Wood, who had become its manager only five years previously, took vigorous action, with a circular to members giving the background to the Liberator crash and, in contrast, a complete analysis of the mortgages of his own Society. This showed that 43% of its mortgage assets had less than £300 due, while cases where over £1,000 was due accounted for only 17%. Even for these larger mortgages, the average amount due was less than £2,000.

The general attitude of societies was that "The business transacted by the Liberator . . . was not in the ordinary sense Building Society business. Although the Building Society system had to some extent to bear the discredit, the mischief which was here done, was in ignoring the Building Society system and acting illegally, as proceedings in the Law Courts subsequently made clear."[35] A number of Liberator directors were tried and sentenced, not on any count that arose out of their activities as directors of the Liberator, but only for actions taken as directors of associated companies. To many people, the main cause for anxiety was that nearly everything leading to the Liberator crash was legal under the 1874 Act.

With the reassembly of Parliament, three Bills were introduced (one by the Government) to regulate societies; to which a fourth, originating with the Building Societies Association was added in 1893. In October the executive of the Association discussed, with the Chief Registrar, what measures would be necessary to prevent a recurrence of the Liberator disaster.[36] In the light of this discussion an executive meeting in December put forward proposals which were carried at a general meeting in January 1893.

These proposals called for a uniform system of accounts; advances only on first mortgages; the prohibition of banking; efficient auditing; official inspection provided members requisitioned it; penalties for false returns; compulsory incorporation and a right for depositors to claim against a society, where it had exceeded its borrowing powers.[37]

Not all these points were relevant to the immediate situation, and indeed the last could reasonably be regarded as retrogressive. Many of them had been put forward by the Chief Registrar when he addressed a meeting of building society representatives in London in November 1892.[38] The Registrar also wanted members to have some rights of inspection of a society's books. This was resisted strongly by Edward Wood, who also opposed a suggestion by Ravenscroft (Birkbeck) that a half of total deposits should be invested in liquid securities. Wood appears to have been the dominant personality in these reform discussions. There were differences between the Association's Bill, drafted in the light of the resolutions carried at the general meeting, and the other Bills. These tended to give extensive powers to the Registrar, offered members the right in varying degrees to examine a society's books, and called for publication of details both of properties in possession and mortgages.[39] All four Bills were given a second reading and referred to a Select Committee, which worked rapidly; holding twelve sessions with witnesses, and reporting on June 29, 1893, only three months after its nomination.

In its examination of witnesses the Select Committee concentrated on a fairly small number of topics: methods of keeping and auditing accounts; publication of details of mortgages and properties in possession; the desirability of advancing only on first mortgages; whether tables were necessary for a society to conduct its business; whether the Registrar's powers should be extended; limitation of borrowing powers and banking activities; the right of members to inspect a society's books; and the activities of promoter societies. Binyon represented the Association's views, although Higham and Wood of the executive also gave evidence in their individual capacities. The Select Committee used the Government's Bill as the basis for its deliberations and reported it with certain amendments. The three other Bills were reported unamended. In the main the suggested amendments to the Government Bill tended to strengthen the degree of public regulation and the Registrar's powers: balloting for advances, and advances on second mortgages were to be prohibited; at least one auditor was to be a professional accountant; registrations of societies could be cancelled or suspended; the Registrar could dissolve a society after investigation; commissions and gifts to society officials in connection with their work were to be illegal.

The Association's special meeting, called to discuss the published report, disclosed a split between those who followed Higham, with his "strong objections to the whole of the proposed legislation"; and those, led by Wood, who were more discriminating. The Select Committee's proposal to publish details of mortgages and properties in possession was violently attacked, the meeting voting to publish only the aggregate figure of mortgages where the current debt exceeded £5,000. The conference totally opposed the proposal to give members the power to call for an enquiry by the Registrar, and also voted against the exclusion of properties in possession from the total of mortgage assets used to determine borrowing powers. Attempts to weaken the sections of the amended Bill dealing with auditing and the prohibition of balloting failed.[40] Thus vigorous opposition was manifested, and M.P.s sympathetic to the Association's views put down such a battery of amendments that, with time short at the end of the session, the Government Bill was withdrawn on September 12th.

In 1894 the Government's and the Association's Bills were introduced again. Both were given a second reading and referred to a standing committee. At a conference of societies in May, discussion centred on the schedules in the Government's Bill concerning properties in possession and large mortgages, and on a member's right to call in the Registrar.[41] A resolution in favour of the Association's Bill and of amendments to the Government's Bill was carried. The Committee again canvassed support in the House, but this time the Government was adamant. Sir John

Lubbock, M.P., the Association's President, "conveyed to the executive the information that the Government preferred its own more drastic Bill and was determined to pass it".[42] Efforts were concentrated on amending the Government Bill, but in this the Association fell "far short of what was aimed at",[43] and the Bill became law on August 25, 1894.

The new Act was to be construed with the 1874 and subsequent Acts. The following were the main changes called for by the various sections of the new Act. Section 1 required that a society's rules should specify the terms on which all types of shares were issued, and the way in which losses were to be met. Sections 2 and 3 laid down that one of the auditors must be a person "who publicly carries on the business of an accountant"; strengthened the auditors' certificate; and required a return of amounts due on mortgages, in aggregate for certain groups up to £5,000 and individually for mortgages in excess of that. Sections 4 and 5 gave the Registrar power to allow members to inspect a society's books or to appoint an inspector himself, subject to certain conditions. By Sections 6 and 7 registrations could be suspended or cancelled, or societies dissolved by the Registrar in certain circumstances; including violation of any of the provisions of the Building Societies Acts, or where investigation showed that a society could not meet the claims of its members. Section 11 tidied up the law as regards dissolutions. Balloting for advances was prohibited in new societies by Section 12, and Section 13 prohibited advances on second mortgages, except where the same society held the first mortgage, in England and Wales; and, except for existing societies, in Scotland and Ireland. By Section 14 mortgages on properties a year in arrears or a year in possession were excluded from mortgage assets in calculating borrowing powers under the 1874 Act. Section 17 extended investment powers to include any investments in which trustees might invest. Section 20 relieved building society arbitrators from that provision of the Arbitration Act, 1889 under which arbitrators might be compelled to state a special case on any matter of law.[44] Section 23 prohibited the taking of gifts and commissions, not authorised in the rules, by building society officers. Section 25 effectively brought all unincorporated societies, founded since 1856, under the same provisions as incorporated societies. Societies founded before 1857 were left under the 1836 Act, mainly to safeguard the Birkbeck Society; since that society was essentially a bank, it would have been impossible for it to continue if it had to comply with the requirements of the later Building Societies Acts. The date was set at 1857 to accommodate a Scots society founded in 1856.[45] Section 27 provided for an annual report and an abstract of the annual returns of societies, to be made by the Registrar; parliamentary authority would no longer have to be sought each year for publication.

The Association was clearly disappointed that the government had been prepared to compromise so little; its main achievement had been to ensure a slightly longer period of transition, before certain sections of the Act became operative, than the government originally planned. Section 2 was not to operate for the first year and Section 14 for three years. For the most part the Act was accepted with reasonable grace, ". . . your Committee cordially welcome the Act so far as it further safeguards the interests alike of members and depositors".[46] The welcome was not universal, one member describing the Act thus: "Most of its clauses have been drafted by those with little knowledge of and no friendship for Building Societies."[47]

Section 2 of the Act empowered the Registrar to lay down the form of the annual return, and some of the irritation of the movement found expression in criticising the precise form laid down by the Registrar. In this, building societies were joined by many accountants. Strong criticisms were expressed by the Chairman and others at the annual meeting of the Association in March 1896. But again Wood dissociated himself; he felt that too much fuss was being made by members about the forms. Wood's view prevailed and no resolution condemning the Registrar's form of accounts was passed.[48]

The sections of the Act having most immediate impact were those requiring publication of the extent of mortgage assets on which payments were a year in arrear or the properties were in possession. The societies' objections were threefold: publication would needlessly damage a society's credit; to keep the figure low societies would foreclose quickly with consequent hardship to the borrower;[49] and for the same reason, societies would dispose of properties immediately they came into possession and resulting prices would be low, to the disadvantage of both the borrower and the society.[50] The government's view had been that a knowledge of these matters was essential if the public were to correctly assess the strength of a society; that the threat of publication would ensure more care in making advances; and that if a sale resulted in a loss, the earlier it was faced the better.

The first publication of scheduled mortgages was in the Registrar's Report for 1896. He made no direct comparison with the situation revealed in 1893 by the parliamentary return made in that year, of properties in possession at the end of 1892, because not all societies completed that return. The threat of publication was clearly salutary in some cases. Ten societies which together returned £863,276 as the mortgage debt on properties in possession in 1892 had reduced the figure to £503,321 by 1897.[51] Not all societies showed such improvement; the Clarence St. Society properties in possession represented 92% of mortgage assets in 1896, and the figure could scarcely have been much higher in 1892. In 1892 properties in possession of those societies making returns in England and Wales were 11·9% of the mortgage assets of all societies. Allowing for the facts that the 9·0% of societies making no return for 1892 had, in the Registrar's view, higher than average possessions, and that the crisis of 1892 probably led societies to try and increase liquid assets at the expense of mortgage assets, the true percentage of mortgage assets in possession was probably not much different in 1892 from the 14·3% for 1896.

There was certainly no sharp reduction in properties in possession between 1892 and 1896; but as Table XIV shows, the situation improved fairly rapidly thereafter. Possessions fell almost continuously, with only a slight check in 1899. The measure of the achievement is even greater when it is recalled that mortgage assets rose by less than 50% over the period. There was an absolute as well as a relative decline in properties in possession.

Mortgages in arrear were a much smaller problem; clearly most societies foreclosed before payments fell into twelve months' arrear. Nevertheless, properties in arrear were reduced in the years following the Act, though not as fast as possessions. Evidently societies were not achieving the decline in possessions by delaying foreclosures. The Act had no immediate impact on large mortgages, though there was a fairly rapid decline in such mortgages after 1900.

TABLE XIV

Scheduled Properties and Mortgages as a percentage of Mortgage Assets
(England and Wales)

	Date							
	1896	1897	1898	1899	1900	1905	1910	1913
Properties in possession for more than one year	14·3	12·4	10·3	10·3	7·2	4·7	4·4	4·1
Properties more than one year in arrears	1·3	0·9	0·6	0·5	0·5	0·4	0·6	0·7
Mortgages, current debt over £5,000	5·2	5·2	5·2	5·3	5·1	4·2	3·7	3·4

The exclusion of properties in arrear or possession for more than a year, from mortgage assets in calculating borrowing power, had some immediate effect. The object of clause 14 was to prevent societies going too near the limit of borrowing power, and to give greater security to depositors. Deposits were 29% of total liabilities for the United Kingdom in 1890, falling to 25% in 1900 and remaining at 25% in 1910.[52] This is in line with Table XIV which shows that the excluded categories fell more sharply, from 16·6% to 7·7% of mortgage assets, in the decade before

1900 than in the decade after, when they fell from 7·7% to 4·8%. Here there were in fact two contrary tendencies at work. Societies near the limit of borrowing power in the 1890s, were forced to reduce deposits to avoid breaking the law. On the other hand, given the lowered public confidence, it would be surprising if some investors had not shown an increased preference for deposits as compared with shares, in view of the smaller risk involved.

The changes shown in Table XIV are strong evidence of the success of the Building Societies Act, 1894, in dealing with certain weaknesses among societies. Other consequences of that Act are not measurable directly, and especially is this true of the extensions to the power vested in the Registrar. However, the twenty years that followed the 1894 Act show a marked contrast in their relative tranquillity, with the twenty years that preceded it, which is very strong evidence of the efficacy of that Act generally. In time, of course other weaknesses were to emerge, against which the 1894 Act provided no defence. Even so, the 1894 Act became important in setting the trend for future legislation; it worked through two channels, giving publicity to the details of building society finances and giving the Registrar increased power to intervene in their affairs. Subsequent legislation has followed the 1894 Act, meeting abuses in the movement by further increases in the Registrar's powers, and insisting that still more details of building society accounts be made public knowledge.

Chapter Nine

RECOVERY AND ANOTHER FAILURE, 1895–1913*

PUBLIC CONFIDENCE in building societies was considerably reduced by the disasters of 1892 and recovery was slow; events conspired to keep the Liberator headline news for some years. While the investigation of the affairs of the Balfour group of companies was proceeding Balfour himself disappeared, living incognito in Argentina, where he was eventually recognised and arrested in January 1894. Extradition proceedings were protracted and he was not returned to Britain until the September. In the meantime, public interest had been maintained by the trial and conviction of three of his fellow directors in 1893. Balfour's own trial did not begin until September 1895, when he, in the company of three more of his fellow directors, faced a jury. Balfour and two of the others were found guilty, Balfour being sentenced to seven years imprisonment on each of two counts, to run consecutively.

Not only the criminals kept the Liberator in the public eye; there was also the plight of the victims. The shareholders of the Liberator were drawn from all parts of the country. The assets of the Society were so small as to leave nothing whatever for them; this created a good deal of hardship, especially among many old people who had made the Liberator the sole repository of their savings. A relief fund was started and the secretary of the fund, the Rev. J. Stockwell Watts, backed the appeal with a series of pamphlets between 1892 and 1897 which served to remind the public of the disaster.[1]

This adverse publicity was reflected in the decline in the total assets of incorporated building societies, from £52 million in 1890 to £42 million in 1894. As a result of the 1894 Act, later totals given by the Registrar are not strictly comparable, since they include unincorporated societies. In 1895 total assets were £52 million, unincorporated societies accounting for £5½ million. Thereafter total assets rose slowly but continuously to £76 million in 1910. In the following year the failure of the Birkbeck "Bank" again sapped public confidence and assets fell sharply to £58 million. In 1912 a recovery started which raised the total to £66 million by 1914. Allowing for the fact that at its failure the assets of the Birkbeck were £12 million, this represented a new peak.

* *Notes on this chapter appear on page 301.*

At the same time, the number of societies in existence was falling rapidly. With balloting for advances illegal for new societies, the activities of building society promoters quickly declined. Between 1883 and 1891, 1,745 societies were incorporated, an average of 194 per year. Between 1898 and 1914, 370 societies were incorporated, an average of only twenty-two per year. As the old terminating societies wound up, and with few new societies being formed, the total number of societies fell from 3,642 in 1895 to 2,286 in 1900 and only 1,506 in 1914.

The failure of the Liberator Society had its effect on the extent to whch the assets of the movement were concentrated in a few societies. In 1880 the ten largest societies had between them 28% of the total assets of incorporated societies. During the next decade there were two contrary influences on the course of this 'concentration percentage'; the rapid increase in the number of small promoter societies was tending to reduce it, while the rapid growth of the Liberator Society tended to increase it. The former influence predominated: the 'concentration percentage' by 1890 had fallen to 25, and if the Liberator figures are excluded, to 20. The inclusion of unincorporated societies in the Registrar's reports following the 1894 Act affects the comparability of later data. But after 1900, when the percentage was 22 the large societies became more important, raising the percentage to 26 for 1910[2].

By the end of the century building societies were beginning to realise that they were part of a wider capital market, not mere specialised institutions competing only with private mortgagees. In part this was a consequence of increasing competition from other institutions for mortgage business, and in part the result of the growth of the societies themselves. A small society may ignore what is going on elsewhere in the capital market for some time; depending on its strong local connections and good will, built up over the years, to prevent an outflow of funds and ensure a reasonable share of the mortgage business available. A large and growing society will become more impersonal and will have, for example, a smaller proportion of members whose fathers opened a share account on their behalf at birth; such societies will depend much more for their business on their ability to meet the requirements of the "informed" investor and borrower better than any alternative institution.

The competitive position of the Post Office Savings Bank had been improved in 1893 when the limit on a person's total investment was raised from £150 to £200 and later (1905) when sums up to £1 were withdrawable on demand at any Post Office. Both the P.O.S.B. and the Trustee Savings Banks continued to pay interest at 2½% although their funds were invested in government securities whose yield was falling. For the period 1896-99 the average yield on Consols was under 2·6%, leaving a quite inadequate margin to cover the considerable expenses of operating a savings bank. The Trustee Savings Banks, as a group, had deficits, which were met by the government, for every year from 1892 to 1908.[3] In these circumstances such banks were seen by building societies as unfair competitors, and were frequently the subject of criticism.[4]

The increasing attention paid to mortgages by other institutions presented a greater threat. The *Gazette* commented, in 1898, that life assurance offices "have in many instances been successfully competing for building society mortgage business, as some societies know to their cost".[5] The Building Societies Association conference of 1909 considered such competition and some members favoured the Association's starting its own life office as a reply.[6] Private mortgagees were increasingly allowing mortgagors to repay the sum borrowed by instalments.[7] Sometimes banks also were keen competitors.[8]

Not all relationships between life offices and building societies were competitive; the period before 1914 saw the development of assurance policies to cover mortgage loans in the event of death. Such policies were not new, indeed Scratchley's Western Life Assurance Society had offered them in the 1840s and he had commended them in his writings. Such policies did not gain great popularity and seem not to have been much publicised, either by building societies or life offices.[9] In 1898 the Planet Society, for a monthly payment of 22s. 8d. per £100 advanced, against the normal 21s. 6d. offered free[!] life assurance, for the balance outstanding on mortgage advances. The subject was of sufficient interest by 1905, to warrant a paper at the Association's conference by J. H. Watling (Bristol Economic). Current attitudes were perhaps represented by the contributions to the discussion of Mr. Warren, who felt that if a man wanted life cover he should arrange it himself; and Mr. Holland who arranged such a scheme for his society with an assurance company. The scheme was a failure: the public did not want it.[10]

The most urgent cause for concern was the activities of bond companies. These companies offered bonds which, in return for weekly or monthly subscriptions, would yield a capital sum after a term of up to thirty years. What particularly affected building societies was the offer, after say a year's subscriptions, of a loan of a proportion of the face value of the bond; the loan to be secured by a mortgage. These companies relied on intensive door to door selling campaigns, offering the prospect of loans at low interest rates. Frequently when the subscriber wished to take up the loan offered, no loan was available. If, as a result, the subscriber decided to stop his subscriptions, so much the better for the bond company, for to default on subscriptions meant, at worst, forfeiting all claim to ultimate benefit, or at best the return of only a modest proportion of the subscriptions already paid. Building societies suffered in two ways, first from the direct competition of these companies, but more seriously because the inequitable dealings of bond companies led to hostility, the public tending to confuse the two types of institution, especially where the company called itself the "—— Building Society Limited".[11]

The activities of the bond companies were severely criticised by a departmental committee of enquiry in 1906; and in 1909 the Board of Trade issued a memorandum on "Bond Investment and House Purchase Companies", designed to inform the public about the activities of such companies and to serve as a warning. The memorandum caused a considerable number of enquiries to be made to building societies, under the impression that a warning therein given was intended to apply to them.[12] A letter from the Board of Trade correcting this false impression was given wide publicity.

Increasing competition caused building societies to change their methods of business in a number of ways. They became more conscious of the power of advertising.[13] Many of the larger societies had been founded around 1850 and the turn of the century saw a number of elaborate brochures celebrating golden jubilees. In 1907 the Woolwich Equitable first used railway poster sites to proclaim its wares.[14] Before 1900, in the Halifax Building Society, ". . . advertising in the newspapers was looked upon as an unnecessary expense, and was confined to a small weekly announcement in a few local papers".[15] This attitude began to change with the appointment of Enoch Hill as secretary in 1903.

Instead of thinking in terms of the three categories: shareholders, depositors and borrowers, some societies began to cultivate particular groups within each category. The Halifax Permanent, progressing rapidly under Hill's management, is the most striking example; by 1915 it had six types of shares with interest rates designed to reflect the low cost of dealing with large accounts and also to attract the small regular saver. In 1903 a penny savings department, planned to attract children among others, was opened and after ten years showed balances totalling £90,000. In 1905 a special reserve fund was started so that the society's diamond jubilee, in 1913, could be celebrated with a "jubilee bonus" to shareholders, and the prospect of receiving this attracted many new people.[16] "Home Safes" were introduced in 1910 and the number in use eventually reached 10,000.[17]

The importance of owner-occupiers was greatly stressed by Hill, who felt that entrance fees and premiums should be abolished for this class of borrower. A higher percentage of the value of the property was advanced to owner-occupiers, up to 90% for houses valued at less than £200.

Repayment terms were kept flexible to meet borrowers' circumstances and they could redeem their mortgages without penalty.[18] These policies produced a dramatic change in the pattern of mortgages held by the Halifax Permanent. In 1903 it had £207,000 advanced on mortgages of under £500 and £516,000 on mortgages over £5,000. Only eight years later the figures were £947,000 (under £500) and £288,000 (over £5,000). Small mortgages had increased from 15% to 38% of the total of balances owing to the society and large mortgages had declined from 39% to 11%. The proportion of large and small mortgages held varied widely between societies. The Registrar's report for 1911 gave details of mortgages for a few societies; Table XV gives these details for three societies, the Westbourne Park Society showing a great concentration on small mortgages, the Burnley Society a concentration on large ones, with the Northern Counties Society (Newcastle-on-Tyne) in an intermediate position.

TABLE XV

Mortgages of various sizes as a percentage of Total Mortgage Assets

Society	Amount of outstanding mortgage balance under £500	–£1,000	–£5,000	over £5,000
Westbourne Park	84·5	11·6	3·7	—
Burnley	26·2	16·6	36·0	21·0
Northern Counties	31·4	22·3	41·1	5·0

Increased competition meant that those who were in a position to influence a borrower's choice of mortgagee, or an investor's choice of investment, were able to secure a consideration for using that influence. As a result some societies began to pay commission for the introduction of business, an arrangement which was to become a serious problem in the 1930s. Extra payments to directors in connection with particular mortgage investments had earlier been a feature,[19] and a problem, in some societies[20] and commission was sometimes paid to outsiders. In 1884 the Woolwich Equitable paid a commission of ¼% for the introduction of a £10,000 mortgage.[21] After 1900 the system began to spread with builders, bankers, solicitors and accountants all seeking commission for introductions; some of them advertising to find which society would offer them the best terms.[22]

The growth of societies, especially where the bulk of the members lived away from a society's home town, created problems. The possibility of making the annual general meeting a social occasion was rapidly dying for the larger societies, though some of them maintained that tradition into this century.[23] Size and a dispersed membership meant that the election of officers at general meetings could be unrepresentative. As early as 1877 the Bradford Third Equitable had sent out ballot papers to all members with the annual statement of accounts;[24] this was exceptional, in most societies only those present at a meeting could vote. In 1904 the Woolwich Equitable altered its rules to allow voting by proxy.[25] Other societies, while still insisting on voting in person, kept the ballot boxes open, at the Society's office, for up to a month.[26] Size was also having its effect on office organisation, a subject first dealt with at the Association's conference in 1913, when E. Naylor read a paper which discussed, among other things, punched card systems.

The increase in the funds withdrawn from building societies by investors, following the collapse of the Liberator Society, demonstrated the importance of liquid assets. Societies generally took the demonstration to heart. While, as stated above, not all non-mortgage assets were liquid, the relation of non-mortgage assets to total assets does reveal something of the potential liquidity of the movement. In 1880 non-mortgage assets were 5·7% of total assets and in 1890 7·2%. Following the Liberator failure there was a rise to 9·1%[27] in 1900. Thereafter there is a fall to 7·9%[27] in 1909 and to 6·5%[27] in 1910. The fall in 1910 shows the effect on the movement generally of the spectacular run on the Birkbeck Society described below. The failure of that society in 1911 resulted in a further fall to 6·0%, from which low point non-mortgage assets were built up again to reach 7·8% of the movement's total assets for 1914.

As noted above the Birkbeck[28] had adjusted to the changed nature of its business from building society to bank, by changing its assets from mortgages to more liquid securities, investing heavily in government stocks. When the yield on government securities was rising, the consequent fall in the capital value of these securities created problems, though the Birkbeck had been able to weather a number of such shifts in yields before 1911. The annual average yield on Consols rose from 2·56% for 1898 to 2·68% for 1899. The press noted that in these circumstances the Birkbeck published a balance sheet valuing its securities at cost and not at market prices. The Birkbeck board moved swiftly to safeguard public confidence. A prominent firm of accountants was called in and a new balance sheet was issued, with securities valued at market prices.[29]

In 1910 the failure of a large loan company, the Charing Cross Bank, led to another run on the Birkbeck. The trouble was caused by an anonymous circular addressed to members of the Birkbeck which said, "Dear Sir or Madam, For your personal information I beg you to withdraw your deposit from the Birkbeck Bank, as I have heard on sound authority the Company are in very low water, and there may be a run on the bank any day. This has occurred through the failure of the Charing Cross Bank. There may be no cause for anxiety but it is as well to be on the safe side. Yours, A. Friend".[30]

The result was a run on the Birkbeck starting on November 11th. The circular's inference was denied and notices posted stating that the Bank of England, as in 1892, was offering substantial help. With this assistance the Birkbeck survived the run, but the defence had necessitated heavy sales of Consols at a considerable loss,[31] and left the society in a weakened condition. There were further heavy withdrawals in May 1911 that appear to have resulted from no specific cause, and on June 8th the Birkbeck suspended payments. In subsequent legal proceedings to determine the rights of shareholders and depositors, the judge commented, "It was an admirably conducted business and the misfortunes that have befallen it are rather the result of overcare than undercare because it was the best securities that suffered most".[32] The judge, perhaps wisely, did not commit himself on the question of "best for what?" The view of the Official Receiver, estimating the society's deficiency at nearly £1 million, was that the failure was caused by the decline in gilt edged prices and the inexperience of the directors and officers in banking business.[33] The Birkbeck eventually paid 16s. 9½d. in the £ to its depositors and shareholders.[34]

On the occasion of the Birkbeck failure the Building Societies Association issued a press statement pointing out the difference between most building societies and the Birkbeck, where mortgages formed only about 7% of total assets. The Association must have regretted that its efforts, at the time of the 1894 Act, to require all building societies to incorporate, were of no avail. Had those efforts been successful, the Birkbeck, faced with the prospect of limiting the deposits it accepted to two-thirds of the mortgage assets it held, would have had to change either its name or its business. In the public's view another large building society had failed, and all societies paid something of the penalty; the total assets of the movement, even excluding the Birkbeck, suffered a sharp fall.

The ingenuity of some societies in their efforts to meet the need for liquidity is illustrated by the case of the Woolwich Equitable. That society had suffered heavy withdrawals, for local reasons, in 1869 and 1886, but it was the withdrawals that followed the Liberator failure that stirred the board to action.[35] They decided in October 1892 that at least 5% of the amount due to depositors should be held in Consols or other readily convertible securities. This could not be achieved at once because of a considerable net withdrawal of deposits. By 1900 it was accepted that 5% was too low and the figure was raised to 10%. It was realised that a liquid reserve of at least a third would be necessary to meet a panic situation, but to provide such a reserve would be too costly—the rate of return on Consols was less than the rate paid to depositors. The Society's manager, G. Bishop, tried to get an agreement with the London and County Bank that the bank would advance up to £100,000 to repay depositors if needed. The sum advanced would be secured by a prior charge on the society's mortgages and in addition an annual premium would be paid. Clearly a bank was scarcely the right institution for such a transaction. The bank advance would be required only in a situation of some stringency, when the bank might well have liquidity problems of its own. The London and County Bank refused the agreement.

Next Bishop approached the Law Guarantee and Trust Society and they agreed to guarantee the repayment by the Woolwich Society of a bank loan, provided the Woolwich took deposits of not more than 50% of its mortgage assets (against the legal limit of two-thirds) and made no advance of over £10,000 without first getting the approval of the guarantee company. With this guarantee Bishop returned to the London and County Bank, but it was still not interested. A second bank, after showing some early interest also refused the offer. Bishop needed some institution with large funds that would not itself be suffering from liquidity problems in a situation where building societies might encounter them.

The answer lay in the life assurance offices with their steady inflow of cash on a contractual basis. Eventually Bishop managed to get a policy written assuring the loan of £100,000 if and when required even without the guarantee of the Law Guarantee and Trust Society. The annual premium was £525, a rate of 10s. 6d. per cent. Bishop contrasted these terms with the Woolwich's previous experience. For four years £33,000 had been invested in government securities with professional advice, and this had yielded 2½% interest and a capital depreciation of £3,000. The difference between the yield on government securities and the yield on mortgages was still more than enough to cover the ½% premium on the policy. In addition there was no question of depreciation: in case of need the Society could be sure of £100,000 from the assurance society, not a doubtful £30,000 from its government securities.

The last years of the nineteenth century saw the end of the dispute between the tax authorities and societies concerning liability to income tax. There were two questions at issue. First, could societies be compelled, by the tax authorities, to deduct income tax from the dividends paid to investors, leaving the investor, if not liable to tax, to reclaim the tax paid from the revenue? This question was already a cause of friction in the 1840s and arose from the presumption by societies that all their members had incomes of less than £150 a year. Incomes below £150 a year were exempt from tax and at that time £3 a week would have represented a good income. The second question concerned borrowers. Should they be allowed, where they were subject to tax, to deduct the tax element from their interest payments to building societies? This issue did not assume prominence until much later, partly because it was not easy, in terminating societies, to identify the interest element in the monthly subscription; and even in permanent societies, especially in their early years, part of the interest was payable as a premium when the loan was made.

In 1849, in reply to an enquiry as to whether societies were liable to income tax on the mortgage interest paid by borrowers, the *Reporter* replied, "No; according to our reading of the Friendly Societies Act all Friendly Societies (and Building Societies are of that class) are free from the impost, though it is right to state that in some quarters doubts exist upon the subject."[36]

The exemption of Friendly Societies derived from section 88 of the 1842 Friendly Societies Act, but that Act did not mention building societies, and indeed the tax authorities successfully claimed that "such associations are liable to the payment of 7d. on every 20s. of interest paid to the societies by the respective members who have purchased out their shares [i.e. borrowers] notwithstanding any rule or agreement made to the contrary by such society. (*Caigell v. Durham Building Society*)".[37] In 1848 the Leeds district tax surveyor, presumably believing that shareholders were not declaring dividends received from building societies in their tax returns, declared that he would not grant borrowers tax relief, on their interest payments to a particular society, unless all that society's 600 members would go into court and prove that their income was less than £150 a year.[38] The Friendly Societies Act of 1853, while confirming income tax exemptions, again did not mention building societies. The building society view was that income tax was an individual matter for investors and borrowers: the tax surveyors should claim tax and grant relief via the individual tax returns. Not all tax surveyors agreed with this view. In 1863 the board of the Halifax Permanent received a demand for £56 for income tax and they reported that "Although the tax has been paid, the Directors cannot understand on what principle the charge has been made".[39] The society grew and the next year the tax demand rose to £114. The directors "feeling strongly the injustice of such demands determined to resist it". A delegation, joined by the Member of Parliament for Halifax, saw the chairman and solicitor of the Board of Inland Revenue. The result was the "receipt of a communication entirely exempting the board [of the society] from income tax". This exemption was confirmed in 1866 when J. W. Campbell, Secretary of the Sunderland Workingmen's Societies, raised the matter.[40]

Unfortunately, the nineteenth-century tax surveyors were not as much part of a centralised bureaucracy as their present counterparts. The fact that the Inland Revenue Board had disclaimed any right to tax the

Halifax, did not prevent surveyors in various parts of the country claiming tax. At the second meeting of the London Association in March 1869, the tax question was raised and both James Higham and H. J. Phillips (Temperance Society) reported that non-liability had been conceded by the authorities to their societies.[41] In November a Greenwich society asking what should be done with a tax demand made to it, was advised by the Association to ignore it.[42] The point was raised again in 1877 and the same reply given.[43] The authorities clearly felt that the recipients of interest were not declaring it in their tax returns, and with the growing importance of building societies, it was believed that the resulting loss to the revenue was becoming substantial. Some surveyors tried to find a simple way out by asking building societies for a list of members receiving interest, but such requests were resisted by societies, as being *ultra vires*. Here an element of confusion had been introduced by the Industrial and Provident Societies Act of 1867, under which surveyors had power to seek information about persons receiving interest from these societies. It must be remembered that some societies established under that Act conducted mortgage business and were in most respects exactly like building societies; this no doubt added to the confusion. The general position apparently was that societies taking a stand in the matter would not be held liable to pay tax on the interest paid to shareholders and depositors.

Regarding the position of borrowers, in 1874 the claim of a borrower, for relief of tax on the interest he paid to a building society, was rejected by the income tax authorities. He was told that a borrower's payments to a building society were regarded in the same way as cash paid into a savings bank.[44] This was manifestly unjust. As H. F. A. Davis pointed out,[45] if a tax were levied on the dividends paid to shareholders, and borrowers were not allowed to deduct tax from their interest payments, while paying property tax, there would be an element of double taxation. With tax in the 1870s at 4d. per £1, a man borrowing £1,000 at 7% would pay £1 3s. 4d. per year more if he borrowed from a building society than if he borrowed privately and, as was his right, deducted the tax from the interest paid. Such a differential must have been some disadvantage to societies seeking large mortgages.

The movement was clearly in a difficulty. If tax were allowed to borrowers, then either rates of dividend to shareholders would have to be reduced, or the tax deducted from interest payments; leaving those shareholders who were not liable to tax, to reclaim the tax deducted, from the revenue. Most such claims would be small. Many shareholders would not bother to reclaim because of the form-filling necessary, and some of those who did probably felt this a considerable imposition, bearing in mind the standard of literacy at that time. Either way building societies would become a less attractive investment. Societies varied in their treatment of borrowers; in 1881 Charles Binyon stated that "very many of the Liverpool societies for many years had allowed borrowing members income tax on repayments".[46] The more general view was given by Davies,[47] "For many years the societies with one accord insisted upon no deduction being made [by borrowers]; and though this sometimes caused friction between the borrowers and the directors, the point did not come before the Courts until quite recently."

In 1883 the tax authorities changed their position somewhat, when they stated that it would be possible for a building society borrower to establish a claim for relief of tax, only if part of the repayment was clearly identifiable as interest. The *Gazette*'s comment on this shows something of the movement's lack of regard for the borrower's position, ". . . it would appear that it only rests with societies themselves, to so arrange their accounts with their borrowers, that no sum shall be specifically applicable to interest, in order that they may successfully resist such claims".[48] This reflected a short-sighted viewpoint; societies then had plenty of money to lend and should have considered the borrowers' interests. A public meeting was held in Battersea in January 1884 to discuss, or rather condemn, the building societies' treatment of borrowers. Mr. Mellor "was afraid the directors of building societies would try to evade the decision [of the authorities mentioned above] by making the borrowers' repayments take the form of a lump sum". Mr. Millard reported an eighteen-month fight he had had with the Temperance Society, to get a refund of the 9s. 7d. tax element in his repayments.[49] In March Mr. Millard, while retailing his grievance to another public meeting, this time at Clapham, referred to a government circular of 1855 exempting societies from income tax; but he felt this was no longer applicable because societies were now much larger bodies.[50]

The position of borrowers was raised in the Commons in 1884, when Mr. McLaren invited the Chancellor to enforce, against building societies, the £50 penalty prescribed for refusals to allow rebates of interest to cover income tax. The Chancellor said this was a subject of frequent complaint, referred to the difficulty of separating principal and interest and promised to look into the question further.[51] In 1886[52] the matter was raised on April 1st and again on April 19th, when the Chancellor refused Mr. O. V. Morgan's suggestion that he should take legal action against societies: the Chancellor felt that cases were being satisfactorily handled, without such action. It would appear that many societies were yielding on this matter. At the Association's meeting in May 1886 it was stated that the liability to income tax of societies was not defined in law;

the *Gazette* reported that the Association's committee felt that the less said about it the better.[53] In October the *Gazette*, probably reflecting changing opinion among societies, took a more positive line: ". . . for a long time the consideration that societies gave this matter, was rather with a view to evading a somewhat troublesome duty, than with a desire to meet the just demand of the borrowers."[54]

The Association reflected the changed view when in March 1887 they agreed to petition Parliament, praying that allowing borrowers to deduct income tax from interest payments should not lead to a disproportionate burden on investors, and that income tax should be levied on the net value of a house (i.e. allowing for costs of maintenance) and not gross value.[55] In July 1887 the tax authorities published a memorandum to clarify the position.[56] The gist of this was that interest from borrowers with incomes below £150 was exempt from tax, and tax relief on their interest payments was to be allowed to other borrowers by the building society. The society was entitled to offset this shortfall in interest received by deducting tax from the interest payments to shareholders and depositors with incomes in excess of £150 per annum. Where the total interest paid by borrowers, on which a tax relief had been allowed by the society, exceeded the total interest paid to shareholders, on which the society had the right to deduct tax, the society could reclaim the tax on this difference from the revenue. The society was to submit annually a list of members to whom interest was paid, whose incomes exceeded £150 per year. Properties in the possession of societies were to be exempt from tax, an unlooked-for concession.[57]

The Association held a conference in February 1888, to discuss this memorandum and strong resolutions were passed condemning it. The general feeling was that the interest paid to shareholders and depositors was a confidential matter and to reveal it would damage a society's relations with its members. A request to the Chancellor to receive a deputation was refused, it being pointed out that the memorandum had no legal force and would only be applied to a society at its own request—this had not been clear in the memorandum itself. One of the Association's leaders, T. Y. Strachan, commented, "When the matter comes to be fully understood no society will seek to evade it. . . . But if societies persist in repudiating their legitimate liabilities, they need not wonder if any account they may have to redeem is received with suspicion by the tax authorities, and strict legal proof enforced whatever the cost and annoyance may be."[58] Although the memorandum was said to be optional, some tax surveyors tried to enforce it upon societies. Pressure was put upon the West Middlesex Society to make a return of interest paid, and when it was not forthcoming, the surveyor attempted to assess the society on its "profit"—taken as the total of interest paid to shareholders and depositors. In November 1890, the society appealed the case to the Special Commissioners who found against the society, but limited the claim, somewhat irrationally, to the interest paid to depositors. The society asked the Commissioners to state a case on the legal issues involved, so that the question could be taken into the Courts, at which the surveyor withdrew the assessment saying the tax authorities would not contest the case in the Courts.[59] A Barnet society was concerned in a similar case in 1892.

Collecting tax directly from societies was not a very satisfactory way of stopping the tax evasion that resulted from people not declaring the interest they had received. James Higham had earlier pointed out that if the authorities "were foolish enough to charge the societies it would put the Government to more expense than they would get in return, because they would have to refund more than half the money, for the greater number of members were not liable to tax at all".[60]

In 1894 the authorities offered societies two alternatives, neither of which had the force of law; they were attempts to find a mutually satisfactory way of meeting the problem. Societies were free to reject both, and continue in the existing uncertain position. Arrangement A was essentially a repetition of the memorandum of 1887. Arrangement B provided that the society pay tax on half the sum distributed to shareholders and depositors in the previous year. In return shareholders and depositors would not be taxed on the interest received. Borrowers were to have no claim on the society for a rebate of tax on mortgage interest, but if the borrower's income was below (now) £160 per annum, he would not be charged property tax, and if above £160, the authorities would allow against his property tax an amount equal to the mortgage interest he paid. Arrangement B was certainly a great convenience, but in practice most societies probably had a majority of shareholders with incomes below the limit and so the tax paid by such societies would be greater than their members' liability to tax. However, rates of tax were low and the arrangement saved both societies and members much paper work, so that an increasing number of societies adopted arrangement B.

Some societies attempted to exploit arrangement B in the interest of shareholders. Clause 5 of that arrangement stated, "Investors and depositors [were] not to be charged for the dividends or interest they received; if charged, on proof thereof, they were to be entitled to relief". It is difficult to see any point to this clause; it would seem to apply only if neither arrangement were adopted.[61] Some societies adopting arrangement B exploited it in the following manner: Tax was paid on half the total interest paid to shareholders and depositors. The society then deducted tax from the interest paid to depositors (not shareholders) and these deductions would go some way to meeting the society's tax bill, reducing the tax burden on shareholders. If depositors were not liable to tax they claimed a repayment from the revenue. In spite of clause 5 the authorities soon refused to give relief, setting out their position thus: All exemptions were covered by taxing only half the total interest paid out by societies; the Board of Inland Revenue "... would not therefore be able to allow claims, on the ground of exemption, for repayment of any tax deducted. If, none the less, a society which has accepted arrangement B chooses to deduct income tax from payments of interest, it is not a matter which concerns this department and no objection would therefore be raised by the Board".[62] However, no society which deducted tax from people whose incomes were below £160 would retain the deposits of such people for long, in the face of this ruling; there might still be scope for deducting tax from the interest paid to depositors with incomes of over £160, who would not in any case have a claim for a repayment from the Board. If this was done, the effective rate of interest on deposits for people with incomes over £160 would be lower in such a society than in one in which arrangement B was operated equitably, and competition between societies could be relied on, given the position taken by the Board, to ensure that all societies in fact accepted the spirit of the arrangement.

Arrangement B was clearly a good bargain from the Treasury's point of view, and was attractive to many societies. Not least it enabled societies to advertise the dividends and interest they offered as being "free of tax"; or if they wished to be accurate "tax paid by the society". The terms of the arrangement continued virtually unchanged, until the sharp increases in tax rates during the first World War led to modifications in 1916.

There were considerable changes after 1894 in the central organisation of the movement. The activities of the Building Societies Association in connection with the 1894 Act led to a sharp increase in membership to 134 in 1896, after being steady at around 110 for some years. At the annual general meeting in that year, W. H. Walbank (Bingley) suggested "that the Annual Meetings should be held in various parts of the country during the summer months with a view to increasing the interest in the work of the Association".[63] The Committee of the Association went some way to meet the suggestion; the meeting of 1897 was held in May, instead of the usual February, but still in London. At that meeting Walbank pressed again, suggesting that a provincial centre be chosen every third year. Other members felt that provincial members should be represented on the Committee.[64] The result was that the annual general meeting of 1898, a meeting that had important consequences for the Association's future, was held at Bradford. A committee representing eleven Yorkshire societies, feeling that something more than a purely business meeting was called for, arranged for a series of papers on building society topics to be read and also an excursion and a dinner, the whole programme covering three days and setting the pattern for the future. These arrangements expressed the growing strength of the professional element in building society management, which wished to discuss common problems and interests in a wider context than the legal framework imposed by Parliament.

At the Bradford meeting there was further criticism of the unrepresentative character of the Committee. Eventually nine provincial members were appointed to meet the Committee, as Edward Wood put it, "to prepare a complete scheme and practically reorganise the association".[65] The outcome was that instead of the Committee consisting of twelve London members, it was increased to eighteen, nine to be drawn from London and nine from the provinces. The London members were to form the Parliamentary and Finance Committee, thus advantage was taken of their wider experience in Parliamentary matters. The full Committee was to meet three times a year and the Parliamentary Committee monthly. The resulting committee was not only more representative geographically but also in terms of the size of societies, for most of the largest societies were provincial. The annual general meeting was to be held alternately in London and the provinces. A further break with the past was made in 1903 when Edward Wood succeeded Charles Binyon as chairman; Binyon resigned after holding that office for twenty years.

On the Parliamentary front the Association was very concerned about the Small Houses (Acquisition of Ownership) Bill. This was a permissive bill that would allow local authorities to lend money to finance the purchase of small houses for owner-occupation, the local authority in turn borrowing the money from the government. Such a measure was first proposed by Thomas Wrightson in 1895,[66] but it did not become a real threat until Joseph Chamberlain, although Colonial Secretary, took it up in 1899. Societies saw the bill as a direct threat to their activities; at a conference in April 1899 strong resolutions were passed condemning the bill and a delegation was appointed to wait on Chamberlain. At the subsequent meeting Wood made a forceful attack, disconcerting a badly briefed Colonial Secretary, and securing some concessions, although Chamberlain stood firm on the principle of the bill. A limit was to be placed not only on the size of the loan, £240, but also on the value of the house, £300, to prevent building society borrowers transferring to local authority mortgages when they had reduced their debt on large houses to £240.[67]

In the event loans under the resulting act presented little threat to building societies, for little use was made of the powers it conferred. In its first two years, ninety-nine loans, totalling £21,423, were made by twenty-four local authorities. Had they wished to do so building societies could probably have played a part in the administration of the Act, but this suggestion was resisted. A similar point arose in connection with the Housing of the Working Classes Amendment Bill in 1906. This Bill would have given societies power to borrow money from the government to build houses, but they resisted the proposal.[68]

The question of registration of title deeds, which was an important theme in the 1880s, continued to interest the Association and dominated its annual conference in 1902.[69] Again little came of the agitation, though some changes in the procedure of the Middlesex Registry to overcome delays, were secured. The Association's Chairman, Mr. Wood, was a member of a royal commission appointed to look into registration in 1908, but no action was taken on the commission's report.

The Association had a number of brushes with the reforming Liberal administration which took office in 1906, and some of the positions taken by the Association did little to improve its public image. The Town Tenants (Ireland) Bill, which would have given dispossessed tenants of houses the right to compensation for improvements, was opposed. Wood agreed it might be just to compensate those who improved business premises but not those "who occupied a private house, who could get another one like it in the same or the next street without sustaining serious harm".[70]

In 1909 the Housing and Town Planning Bill was opposed. The Bill (later Act) gave local authorities power to close houses in certain circumstances and prohibited the building of any new back-to-back houses. The latter point, which particularly affected building societies in Yorkshire, where this form of construction was fairly common, rather divided the Association. Arthur Webb (Co-operative) was vigorously opposed to the Association going on record as approving back-to-back houses. Eventually a resolution was carried at the conference, that such houses could still be built, provided the local authority sanctioned them.[71]

Clause 51 of Lloyd George's National Insurance Bill was another point of friction. This would have given tenants receiving sickness benefit six months protection from distraint upon their goods, in cases of rent arrears. Wood led the Association in opposition to the clause saying it would be used by the shiftless to avoid paying rent.[72] Pressure secured the amendment of the clause so that only those certified by a doctor as being in danger of death were protected. None the less, said the *Gazette*, people might see it as "an attack on house property and will not care to own any, or advance money upon mortgage of it".

Some of the views expressed by the Association through its committee were too extreme for some members and warning voices were raised. One of the Vice-Presidents, F. Maddison, M.P., advised the Association in 1907 "... not to give any sort of impression that it took the mere property owners' point of view".[73] Enoch Hill, commenting on the defensive attitude of the Association, said in 1909, "... something ought to be done to make it felt that building societies are in existence for the benefit of the working class."[74]

The Committee could claim a number of substantial victories. Pressure was successfully brought to bear against an increase in the duty on cheques in 1902; mortgages on loans of under £500 were exempt from an increase in stamp duty in 1909; the position of mortgagees was safeguarded against a bankrupt's creditors during the passage of the Bankruptcy Act, 1913.

The most significant clash with the Government came as a result of the 1909 budget which proposed to tax increments in land value. That budget did much to inflame political passions generally; the Association did not escape unruffled. Wood's leadership did much to prevent the Association showing extreme opposition, which would certainly have endangered its unity—Liberals and Nonconformists had played, and were still playing, a very prominent part in the movement. Wood stressed the non-party nature of the Association and advised concentrating on a few issues of central importance. Where concessions could not be obtained, Wood firmly held that there was no point in passing resolutions that merely denounced the budget, however roundly; it was better to concentrate on the possible cases of hardship. A delegation to Lloyd George in 1911, after the budget passed, obtained a promise that any cases of hardship raised by societies, resulting from the land tax, would be investigated.[75] Wood's firm line was not everywhere welcomed and he talked of the harsh criticisms "not always in the most courteous language", which the Committee had endured;[76] "as he valued his self-respect more than the chairmanship of the Association", he had asked the secretary to strike his name from the list of those seeking re-election to the Committee. However, he had received such letters of support that he could not press his resignation.[77]

The discord in the Association starting over the Finance Act of 1909 did not quickly subside; it became a general call for reform. The Committee erred in that their circular calling societies to put pressure on Members of Parliament, following a conference on the Finance Act in March 1911, gave the substance of only the Committee's resolutions. In particular, the substance of motions proposed by Hill (Halifax Permanent) and Modger (Bath) was omitted, it being stated merely that they would be "dealt with when opportunity offers".[78] Hill, since 1903 secretary of the Halifax Permanent, by this time the largest society in the country, was not a man to accept even minor slights quietly. In a paper to the Association's conference in 1911, he said that any criticism of the committee was their own responsibility: they failed to keep the members informed of their activities. Hill put forward a number of suggestions that the Committee, he felt, should examine. These included proposals for obtaining greater publicity for the movement, and Parliamentary representation for the Association, and for the Association to organise a scheme for providing emergency help to any member society in difficulties.[79]

The Committee did not take up many of Hill's suggestions—they would certainly not have had the resources to examine or act on them all—and he returned to the attack at the conference of 1912. "There is room for some constructive and positive work on the part of the executive . . . we do not sufficiently exert ourselves. . . ."[80] Incidental events further estranged Hill and the Committee. In 1912 Hill had been invited to address the conference of United States building societies, but illness prevented his attendance. At that conference the Americans decided to organise an international conference to meet in London in 1914 and Hill was, not unnaturally, asked to undertake the local work of organisation. Since Hill was not yet a member of the Committee of the Association, this caused some embarrassment. The affair was smoothed over in 1914 when Ezra Naylor (Bradford 3 Equitable) who had become Chairman of the Association on Wood's resignation in 1913, visited the United States. As a result, the Committee of the Association took over responsibility for some of the arrangements for the international conference, which met in London in August 1914, despite the declaration of war.

There was some dissatisfaction with the unchanging composition of the Committee. Retiring members were always re-elected; if a member could not finish his term the Committee itself filled the vacancy; only at the end of the unexpired term did the Association have a voice in the matter. As is not unusual where re-elections have become traditional, an impasse is reached. Strong men may emerge who have no committee place, and there is no way of giving them a place without a contested election, which, tradition dictates, must be avoided at all costs.

Criticism became strong in 1913, and as in 1896, the Bingley Society, now in the person of H. N. Dawson, gave it voice. "Unfortunately, owing to the way in which the Executive was elected at the annual meeting, no delegate had an opportunity of moving any amendment or any addition, or even of voting on the members proposed."[81] Dawson wished to propose Hill, but had not given due notice. Wood, in the Chair, said he had no doubt that in the near future Hill would probably be a member. T. Whitely (Halifax Permanent) added "That not only Mr. Hill's society but others should have consideration shown to them as regards representation".

By 1914 there was no change and Dawson was moved to further criticism. He suggested the nine London Committee members should be taken as representing the whole of the home counties, thus releasing one or two places for the north. In addition to the retiring members, T. Ellsworth (Bradford 2 Equitable) and Hill were nominated for the Committee. While the tradition of no contested election was maintained, by Hill and Ellsworth withdrawing before a ballot was taken, Ellsworth in withdrawing said his society wished to see a more democratic representation of the whole country with representatives of districts or counties. Whitely commented acidly on the proceedings: "I do hope the Executive will not on every occasion think it imperative to re-elect those who have been on the board, but will consider the claims of those outside."[82] A further important reform was suggested by J. B. Annan (South Staffs). He proposed the formation of area organisations and committees.[83] The proposal was met with little enthusiasm by Wood, in the Chair owing to Naylor's being ill, but the Committee was unanimously asked to investigate the possibility.

With the retirement of C. J. Lowe (Bristol and West) in November 1914, Hill was at last given a place on the Committee. The argument about representation however continued at the annual general meeting in 1915. An election was again avoided by nominees withdrawing, but criticism was sharp. D. Bottomley (Bradford 3 Equitable) said, ". . . members of the Executive are out of all proportion . . . our societies in the North have grown immensely and we want a redistribution . . . united we stand and divided we might fall, and we certainly shall be divided if the Executive do not take a broader view."[84] A special general meeting was called, to follow the annual general meeting, to amend the rules. Instead of the Committee consisting of nine Metropolitan and nine Provincial members, it would in future consist of not more than nine or less than six Metropolitan and not less than nine or more than twelve Provincial members.[85] Although no immediate change was made in the composition of the Committee, when Metropolitan members retired replacements would not necessarily come from the same locality.

Chapter Ten

WAR AND POST-WAR RECONSTRUCTION, 1914–1922

The First World War, with its high interest rates and restrictions on the rights of property owners and mortgagees, faced building societies with substantial problems of adjustment. The declaration of war itself, followed as it was by a bank rate of 10%, naturally gave rise to fears of a sharp increase in withdrawals of funds from societies by shareholders and depositors. It was a tribute to the public's confidence in the stability of societies that these fears were not realised to any great extent. Many societies decided to require the notice which their rules provided, for withdrawals of sums over £5, but even this restriction was not usually maintained for very long. The Woolwich Equitable required one month's notice of withdrawals from August 7, 1914, except where the money was needed to meet such obligations as the payment of rates. The restriction lasted only seven weeks, being lifted on September 25th.[1]

The proclamation by the government on August 3rd of a moratorium on payments of one month, later extended for a further two months, may have added some restraining influence, but clearly the movement survived the immediate shock of war without difficulty. The total assets of the movement having risen a little from £65·3 million to £66·2 million between 1913 and 1914 fell back only slightly to £64·8 million in 1915. However, by 1915 societies were suffering competition from the high rates of interest the government was offering on its war loans, 4½% and 5% against about 4% on building society shares. "The effect upon building societies", said Edward Wood, "was immediate and far reaching. Four large societies paid withdrawing shareholders and depositors over £500,000, while demands made upon many other societies were on much the same scale. . . . The societies acted splendidly . . . they borrowed from their bankers at substantially higher rates than they were paying on the shares and deposits withdrawn, and in some cases realised securities at depreciated prices, thus incurring considerable loss."[2] Gross withdrawals from the Halifax Permanent rose from £573,000 in 1914 to £1,103,000 in 1915.

* *Notes on this chapter appear on page 303.*

High interest rates and patriotism ensured that the savings of the public went mostly to the government throughout the war. The result was that although the incomes of members of building societies rose substantially, the total assets of societies increased only marginally, to £68·5 million by 1918. Allowing for the rise in prices this meant that the movement ended the period with a much smaller command over resources than it had when war started. This did not affect the business of societies during the war. On the outbreak of war most societies ceased making advances, except those which were in process of negotiation on August 4th, and though these complete prohibitions were soon lifted (on October 16, 1914, by the Woolwich Equitable) government controls on building, and the general uncertainty of the times, greatly decreased the demand for advances. Advances fell from £9·1 million in 1913 to £8·8 million in 1914 and a low point of £4·5 million in 1917. Even without much inflow of new funds, repayments of existing mortgages were more than enough to finance this modest scale of new business.

Societies in fact found themselves with considerable surplus funds which, in accordance with the spirit of the times, were largely invested in government securities. The Halifax Permanent's holding of government securities of less than £15,000 in 1914 had risen to £1,302,000 by 1919.[3] Not all societies took up government securities on this scale, but for the movement as a whole non-mortgage assets increased from £4·6 million in 1914 to £15·3 million in 1918, that is from less than 7% to more than 22% of total assets. This change in asset structure had worrying implications for those societies which entered the war with deposits at or near the legal maximum of two-thirds of mortgage assets. As mortgage assets fell, with old mortgages being repaid and little new mortgage business, if such societies were not to exceed their borrowing limits, borrowing on deposit would have to be curtailed and in extreme cases depositors would have to be repaid. This situation led to moves in 1917, to relate borrowing power to holdings of government securities as well as mortgage assets, but requests to amend the 1894 Act in this direction were refused.[4]

The rights of societies as mortgagees were restricted by two measures. The Courts (Emergency Powers) Act, passed in August 1914, suspended, among other things, the legal remedies of mortgagees against defaulting mortgagors, where the default was attributable to causes resulting from the war. As a result societies could take possession and dispose of properties only with the consent of the Courts. This Act provides an excellent example of the keen way in which the Parliamentary committee kept a watch on legislation. Although the bill passed through all its stages in the Commons between August 26th and 31st, the committee, or rather three of its members—events moved too swiftly for meetings of even a body of nine members—managed to secure an amendment which at least excluded from the provisions of the Act those properties where societies were already in possession at the time the Act was passed.[5]

Late in 1915 came the Increase of Rent and Mortgage Interest (War Restrictions) Act. The relatively large movements in population resulting from the war, together with the lack of house building, created severe shortages of accommodation in certain towns. Some landlords availed themselves of the opportunity to make large increases in rents; Glasgow figured prominently in the parliamentary discussion of this matter. Originally, the Act was intended to deal with sharp increases in rents in limited areas. In the event it applied nationally, to all rented houses with a rateable value not exceeding £35 in London, £30 in Scotland and £26 elsewhere. At the time the limits were regarded as very high, as indeed they were if rateable values were any accurate reflection of rents; a rent of 10s. per week in a country town could have been afforded by only a small proportion of the population. Worse still, from the societies' viewpoint, the Act was "back dated", increases in rent or mortgage interest above the levels prevailing on August 3, 1914, were forbidden, and any such contract entered into in the meantime was void. Further, the right of mortgagees (where they possessed it) to demand that the loan be repaid, was extinguished for the above mentioned classes of houses. The Act was to continue in force for not longer than six months after the end of the war.

Building societies, and especially the Association, which had felt themselves snubbed by the failure of the government to consult them early in the war about such measures as the extension of the moratorium on payments,[6] were fully consulted about rent restriction; but the results were not happy. A delegation from the Association met the government, in the person of Walter Long, Secretary of the Local Government Board, at Long's request, on November 15, 1915, while the Rent Restriction Act was being prepared. Edward Wood reported that, "We left feeling that the legislation to be proposed was such as need not cause us any apprehension". Long had informed the delegation that the powers sought "would only be applicable in districts where there was clear evidence that trouble existed" and that the Government "would be careful to avoid anything which would affect great interests like yours, or above all react on the general credit of the country". Not surprisingly, the terms of the Act when passed were seen as a betrayal of these assurances. Wood felt Long had given way too easily to his Cabinet colleagues; he should have stood firm and prevented "the perpetration of the gravest act of injustice that had ever been inflicted by the British Parliament".[7] It should be added that Wood's anger did not arise only from his position as manager of the Temperance Building Society; he was also a director of one of the country's largest property companies, which owned over 7,000 houses.[8]

During the passage of the Bill, "Members of the Executive Committee [of the Association] had been in attendance at the House of Commons with a view to arranging for the moving of amendments excluding Building Societies or giving them a limited power to raise the rate of interest [on existing mortgages] and such amendments had been moved, but were not accepted by the Government."[9] During the debate the Minister yielded so far as to agree to consult with the Association again, before the Bill was read a third time. The Association's reaction was that since its amendments were not acceptable, there was nothing that could usefully be done; it would not attempt to force any minor amendments. The Minister responded with the following pledge, "It will be our duty, if building societies find that special difficulties are created . . . to do what we can to assist them."[10]

The government had been led to place restrictions on increases in the rate of interest charged on existing mortgages, partly as a result of pressure from property owners; and this in turn was the result of the pre-1914 pattern of financing rented houses. In many instances landlords had borrowed on mortgage the money to finance the purchase of houses to let. If no increase in rents was allowed and interest rates were raised on mortgages, the landlord would be placed in an impossible position. Building society men wished to carry the logic of this argument a stage further. If building societies could not increase interest rates to existing borrowers, when interest rates generally were rising, shareholders and depositors would tend to withdraw their money, placing building societies in great difficulty; this situation should be eased by legislation restricting the right of withdrawal.[11]

The Association's parliamentary committee did secure some amendments to the Bill. The most important of these was the exclusion from its provisions of mortgages, repayable by monthly instalments, over a period of more than ten years. This meant that at least a portion of building society mortgages were excluded. Fears that with the limited guarantee given by the Act to mortgagors, against foreclosure, people might let property fall into disrepair, and leaseholders not observe covenants, were met by allowing an appeal to the Courts in such cases.

Many societies were keen to raise interest rates to mortgagors, in order to obtain sufficient funds to raise rates paid to investors and prevent withdrawals of shares and deposits. But in addition to the legal restrictions, many societies had no power, in their mortgage deeds, to raise interest rates. The widespread lack of such power was a reflection of the extreme stability, by modern standards, of building society interest rates in the period before 1914. Societies rarely had to change their rates, and such changes as occurred, were mainly downwards, as in the 1880s as a result of surplus funds, when the only question was at what point the reduction should be passed on to existing borrowers. Hobson[12] gives the interest rate charged to borrowers of the Halifax Permanent as 4½–5% continuously from 1859 to 1915 except for a wider spread of 4–5% for the period 1885–1912. The Co-operative Society "For the first time since its second year [1885] . . . found it necessary to alter its rate of interest to investors in 1914".[13] In these circumstances it is not surprising that many societies found themselves without power, in 1914, to raise interest rates to existing borrowers.

On this subject there was a difference of practice between North and South. In a paper to the Association's conference at Cardiff in 1912,[14] Ezra Naylor had mentioned that in the north many societies had a clause in their mortgage deeds empowering them to demand repayment of their loans at six months' notice. This surprised the representatives of many southern societies, ". . . in the south it had not been the practice to reserve such power except in the case of special mortgages in which surplus funds had been invested".[15] Thus some societies were in a position to raise mortgage rates by calling in existing mortgages and relending at higher rates. Even where societies did not have this power, rates could be raised by voluntary consent. In 1915 the Halifax Permanent had asked existing borrowers to accept an increase of ½% in the rate paid, and "nearly all of them gave their consent within a few weeks".[16] It is not revealed whether these consents were obtained under the implicit threat of calling in the loans.

The Association's advice to members was that they should take power in their rules, to be recited in mortgage deeds, to call in mortgages and alter interest rates. Such alterations would not affect existing mortgages, but at least the future would be safeguarded.[17] The Association's report for 1915 stated that if societies did not currently have power to raise interest rates, the Rent Restriction Act did not provide it. This suggests that the matter may have been raised by the delegation to the Secretary of the Local Government Board, and it was interest rates that Long had in mind in making his pledge to help, if societies got into difficulties.

Fortunately, in spite of heavy withdrawals to subscribe to government issues, societies did not become unstable and Long did not have to make good his pledge of help. The increasingly liquid position of societies, as the war continued, alleviated the situation: the repayments on mortgages yielding only 4% could be reinvested in government securities with higher yields. Further, while the power to raise mortgage interest rates was rare in the south, the need to do so was frequently less pressing; interest rates to both investors and borrowers tended to be higher, and thus the competition from high government interest rates was less keenly felt.[18]

Not everyone favoured using the power to raise rates, even where it existed. The offer of advances at fixed interest rates for a definite period of time had traditionally been an important advantage of building societies,[19] especially in competition with private mortgagors, and some people wished to safeguard this tradition. "What a choice of evils is the mortgagor's—interest to be raised or the mortgage to be called in . . . others will get to learn . . . how they, if they join building societies as borrowers, are likely to be similarly treated."[20] None the less many building society men felt that justice here was asymmetrical. Borrowers normally had the right to redeem their mortgages, and when societies in the past had reduced interest rates to new borrowers, they had been forced rapidly to extend the reduction to existing borrowers, by the threat to redeem mortgages and borrow again elsewhere at the new lower rate. Now the boot looked as though it should go on the other foot, but it could not be made to fit.

War created difficulties also for mortgagors, especially for those joining the forces, and suffering a severe fall in income. For the many owner-occupiers among these, the Rent Restriction Act offered no protection. In general, building societies gained in public reputation, by meeting the difficulties of such borrowers in a sympathetic spirit and granting relief without the imposition of any fines or penalties. In his statement to the annual meeting of the Woolwich Equitable Society in 1914, the chairman said, "While we resolved [at the outbreak of war] not to make any fresh advances, we also agreed that any member applying to us for assistance to pay ground rent, repairs or taxes, or anyone requiring some alleviation in regard to his monthly repayments, should receive prompt and sympathetic consideration".

Concern was expressed that societies, by meeting the difficulties of mortgagors in the forces might suffer in their credit standing, by showing an increase in the number of mortgages where repayments were more than twelve months in arrear, on their annual return to the Chief Registrar.[21] The usual method adopted was to lengthen the term of the loan, the mortgagor paying only the interest element in his monthly repayment. With such a solution the mortgage did not officially fall into arrears if the mortgage deed was suitably amended. The situation was helped, as the war progressed, by the creation of the Statutory Pensions Committees, which had power to make monetary grants to members of the forces to meet certain civil liabilities, including mortgage interest.

In 1914 properties in possession constituted 3·2% of total mortgage assets and this percentage dropped continuously through the war years to 2·3% in 1918. Mortgages in twelve months' arrear did increase but only from 0·5% of the total in 1914 to a maximum, in 1917, of 0·8%. Experience on both counts was surprisingly favourable to building societies, but it must be remembered that before 1914 building societies depended much more than in recent years on advances to those investing in property to let. Many such borrowers were elderly people who would not have suffered the sharp fall in income that military service so often entailed. Further, war conditions brought in special legal obstacles, mentioned above, to societies seeking possession of the properties of defaulting mortgagors.

War created other problems, among them the threat of physical damage to property as a result of enemy action; a threat which considerably increased with the coming of the Zeppelin raids. A few societies acted swiftly to insure their properties against war risks. In the Co-operative Society, "At an early stage [1914] in the war . . . steps were taken to protect all properties mortgaged to the society against loss or damage likely to be occasioned by aircraft, bombardment or contingent risks."[22] Some societies insured only their more exposed properties: the Leeds Permanent "covered all the amounts secured on properties within ten miles of the east coast against risks of war. . . . This insurance covers the large sum of £130,000".[23] Zeppelin raids in 1915 led more societies to insure and also created a demand for a national scheme of war damage insurance, partly because many large insurance companies were refusing to write policies covering war risks.

The government responded quickly. A committee was appointed to consider the question on June 21, 1915; it reported on July 9th and its proposed scheme of war damage insurance came into operation ten days later. This speed contrasts strongly with the extended prevarications of the government when faced with the same problem in the 1930s.

The government scheme was a voluntary one. The policies written under it would cover all losses "directly and indirectly caused by aerial craft; hostile or otherwise, or shots, shells, bombs or missiles from or used against aerial craft or by bombardment by hostile guns not landed on British territory".[24] The premium was 2s. per £100 to cover damage resulting from "aerial craft" risks and 3s. per £100 if bombardment risks were included as well. The scheme was criticised because it was voluntary; clearly properties in inland towns would not be insured against bombardment, and would probably not be insured against damage by aircraft either. In setting up the committee the government made it a condition that any scheme must make provision for a reasonable contribution from property owners. Critics claimed that the committee, in making its recommendations about premiums, had naturally borne in mind that only high risk properties would be insured, and thus the rates set were unreasonably high. Criticism was also levelled against the ruling that proposals were only to be accepted where the full value of a property was insured. Many societies had narrowly drawn rules about what insurance cover mortgagors could be compelled to take out, and were thus powerless to reclaim, from mortgagors, the premiums the society paid for war damage insurance. In these circumstances they wanted to be allowed to insure only the society's interest in a property, not its full value.[25]

Efforts to persuade the government to make war damage insurance compulsory continued and the Association sent a delegation to the Board of Trade, without result, in June 1916.[26] Other organisations were pressing the matter, the local authorities in the exposed areas being particularly concerned. Eventually the government partially gave way in 1917, by itself accepting responsibility to compensate owners, in the cases of properties valued at up to £500, even though no premiums had been paid under the insurance scheme.[27]

By 1916 thoughts were being turned to the post-war housing situation. The first building society leader to take up the matter was Arthur Webb, moved by the lack of attention paid to the part building societies could play. At a London conference on post-war housing it was suggested that the government set aside £20 million to aid local authorities and other agencies in building houses. Webb felt building societies should be among these "other agencies". He was dissatisfied with a situation in which societies "have had no part or influence in the character of building other than the very wise discretion of refusing to lend upon houses unsatisfactorily built". Societies hesitated to make innovations for fear of competition and with some prescience he added, "Some form of uniformity is desirable. This question might well provide matter for a conference of representative building societies." His idea was that societies should take the lead in planning housing developments, putting up 80% of the finance themselves, with the builders finding the remainder. He stressed the need "of requiring larger cash payments from the purchasers of property, rather than affording any encouragement to the system of second mortgages by the builder, whereby the purchaser not infrequently has merely a few pounds at stake".[28]

The general question was taken up at the Association's conference in 1917. J. D. McPhail (Liverpool Investment) reiterated some of Webb's points and put forward a variety of ways in which the government could help. Solicitors' charges could be subsidised and the government itself could become a mortgagee, with building societies acting as their agents.

Alternatively the government could advance money to societies at $\frac{1}{2}$% below the rate charged by societies to their mortgagors. At the same time the Small Dwellings Act should be amended so that local authorities would be lending on terms comparable with building societies, i.e. with only monthly repayments, for terms not exceeding fourteen years, and at rates not necessarily related to the rates at which local authorities borrowed. Mr. F. W. Pinch (Bath) felt the post-war situation would be abnormal and in meeting it nothing should be done to interfere with normal building society business. There was wide sympathy with the view that building societies would do well to keep out of the argument about ways of meeting the immediate post-war shortage of accommodation. As Ezra Naylor, in the chair, put it, the problem of housing for the lower paid workers would require special solutions ". . . but whether or not building societies should mix themselves up in it, required very careful consideration. They must not take risks; they must not prejudice the high position in which they stood among the financial institutions of the country".[29]

The general expectation was that in the immediate post-war years building costs would be very high, both through pressure of demand and the difficulties of recreating the building industry which had been allowed to run down during the war. The high cost of meeting the immediate shortage of accommodation would require some help from the government. With that shortage met, the Rent Restriction Act could disappear and the housing market revert to its pre-war normality; building costs would have fallen and private investors would again be able to finance the building of houses which could be let at rents which the bulk of the population could afford.

The confidence with which such a view could be held, depended greatly on estimates of the extent of the post-war housing shortage. The level of new house building had been low in the years before the war, in part as a result of the 1910 budget with its additional taxes on property; and during the war very few houses had been built. If the same proportion of houses to population as in 1911 is taken as a measure of a normal balance between supply and demand in the housing market, then there was a shortage of about 600,000 houses in 1918.[30] Clearly this shortage would not be met in two or three years, since in the period of "normality", 1901-1911, rather less than 100,000 houses were being built annually.

The considered view of the Association was presented in the report of a special sub-committee on post-war housing in November 1917. The central proposition was that because building costs would fall, after being very high in the immediate post-war years, house prices and rents would in turn fall and hence no one would be prepared to invest in houses to let.

None the less private enterprise was the most efficient means of providing such houses; this led to the conclusion that some encouragement would be needed in the form of a subsidy. Subsidy proposals included rate and tax holidays for a period of years; relief for builders over road charges; and direct payment of the difference between high post-war cost and long run economic cost of houses.[31]

The Association's ideas were put to the Secretary of the Local Government Board in February 1918 but these did nothing to alter the government view, announced later in February, that the local authorities should be responsible for meeting immediate post-war needs. Unfortunately, the government was a long time transforming ideas into policy; it was not until August 1919 that the Housing and Town Planning Act was passed. In the meantime, the hopes of the less conservative building society officials were raised by the report of the Housing Financial Assistance Committee, which made many favourable references to building societies and recommended that the government should encourage societies by depositing government funds with them. The suggestion was that in suitable cases advances be made on the basis of £1 from the societies' funds and £2 from government deposits with building societies. Another recommendation was that local authorities be empowered to guarantee a portion of a building society advance (the difference between two-thirds and three-quarters of the value of houses up to £500). It should also be made legal for a building society with surplus funds to invest them in another building society: this would enable the surpluses of societies in areas where the demand for advances was low, to be used to meet the heavy demand in other areas.

The committee's recommendations found no place in the Housing and Town Planning Act. Local authorities were given the responsibility of providing houses to let, and all losses beyond the contribution of a 1d. rate were to be borne by the Treasury, providing the local authorities' plans had been approved by the Ministry of Health. Subsidies were also to be available to other non-profit making housing agencies. This Act was a severe blow to building societies, which were thinking in terms of a return to a pre-war situation, in which substantial business was done in advancing money to finance private investment in houses to let. At a meeting with the government in July 1919, Webb and Hill, representing the Association, were told that building societies did not fall within the government's definition of non-profit-making bodies under the Act. At further meetings in September and November, Webb and Hill supported the opinion that subsidies would need to be more widely available if the required houses were to be built. The government soon came round to this view and gave it expression in the Housing (Additional Powers) Act at the end of the year. That Act offered subsidies on small houses built by private enterprise up to a maximum of £160 on a house of 920 feet super. In 1920 the limits were raised to a maximum of £260 and 1,400 feet super. The tax on increases in land values, first introduced in 1910, was abandoned in the 1920 budget, a further measure of encouragement to private enterprise; but these measures had no sooner been adopted than a depressant was delivered in the shape of the continuation of the Rent Restriction Act to 1923, though modest increases in rents were allowed. Private enterprise was slow to respond. Fears of a coming fall in housing prices were too great. The subsidies offered were viewed by many as insufficient to cover the probable fall in costs of construction and there was an understandable reluctance to invest in houses.

With local authorities responsible for financing most of the new houses built there was not much business for building societies in this sphere. However, a demand for their services quickly emerged in another quarter. The high cost of repairs and the low level of controlled rents meant that the return to those who owned houses and let them was small. Thus whenever a rent-controlled house became vacant, the landlord had a strong incentive to sell it, an incentive all the stronger as the pressure of demand on the few houses that were for sale forced up prices. Further, many investors in house property were willing to cut their losses by offering to sell their rent-controlled houses to the occupying tenants. Both these types of sale provided building societies with mortgage business.

The existence of two sets of values for houses, one with and one without vacant possession, created opportunities for profitable speculation. Rent-controlled houses could be bought at low prices and the sitting tenants persuaded to buy their houses at higher prices (especially when, as in 1918, the continuance of rent control was uncertain). In these circumstances a group in control of a building society could use that control to finance such speculations for their own profit, and when that profit, rather than the quality of the resulting building society mortgages, is the governing consideration in making loans, the shareholders of the society may be left with very inadequate security for their money. The actions of some societies brought the following comment from the *Gazette* in 1921, "The competitive seeking for mortgage outlets tends to lead into business outside the legitimate operations of the Building Society movement. Far better lend on loan to Corporations than to finance dealings and speculations, in connection with houses which are a disgrace to our civilisation."[32]

Such questionable dealing concerned only the fringes of the movement. For the most part societies took the legitimate opportunities offered of financing owner-occupiers, which they were well placed to do. At the end of the war, though the total assets of the movement were only slightly higher than in 1913, £68·5 million against £65·3 million, societies were, as we have seen, in a very liquid position, with large holdings of government securities. The amount advanced on mortgage rose rapidly from under £7 million in 1918 to £15·8 million in 1919 and £25·1 million in 1920. The slump in economic activity then led to a decline to £19·7 million in 1921 and £22·7 million in 1922. The inflow of new investment money was strong and societies could have financed still larger advances without endangering their stability. Non-mortgage assets remained high for some years after the war; as late as 1922 they were still 22·1% of total assets.

In the early post-war years there was an increased risk in advancing a high percentage of the purchase price of a house, for if the expected sharp fall in house prices took place, its value might fall below the borrowers outstanding mortgage debt. Here societies such as the Halifax Permanent, which had concentrated on advances to owner-occupiers before the war, were at an advantage; their greater experience enabled them to assess the value of an owner-occupier's personal covenant more accurately.

The existence of this increased risk centred attention on the question of taking collateral security; if it held such security a society would have a greater chance of always holding assets greater than the mortgage debt outstanding. The legal position regarding the taking of collateral was not clear. The leading case on this issue was *Sheffield and S. Yorks B.S. v. Aizlewood*[33] in 1889, where the judgement implied that the legality of an advance on mortgage by a building society must be judged as if no collateral were taken, but if a society wanted the extra security of collateral, then it could take it. Some lawyers felt that if a society, in view of a possible fall in values, was only prepared to advance 70% of the value of a house without collateral and, say, 80% with it, it was in effect advancing the difference (10%) against the collateral security, and under the 1874 Act advances could only be legally made on freehold and leasehold property. E. W. Brabrook, after his retirement as Chief Registrar wrote,[34] "In its ordinary business, therefore, as distinct from the investment of surplus funds, the building society is absolutely restricted to investments on first mortgage of real or leasehold estate. . . . Even collateral security is not admissible. This is rather an important point. We have known cases where the directors, granting an advance to a member, have been tempted to accept, in addition to a mortgage, some other security such as a policy of assurance or even personal security, as a sort of extra guarantee. This is clearly not allowed by the Act. Their answer—we have got our mortgage and there can surely be no harm in taking collateral security in addition—is quite a fallacy. It is obvious that the collateral security would not have been offered or taken if the mortgagor and mortgagee were not both conscious that the mortgage by itself was not a sufficient security for the advance made".

In fact societies regarded the risk of being left with inadequate security as greater than the risk of breaking the law, as interpreted by Brabrook. They tended to cover themselves against a possible fall in values by taking collateral security. Describing the experience of the Burnley Society, Walter Harvey, its secretary, said, "For a long time our solicitors ruled against our accepting collateral, even special personal covenants, and we acted on their advice; until rising prices of property occasionally compelled us to lend larger proportions than we should have felt safe, unless extra cover were provided".[35]

The post-war boom broke in the summer of 1920 and this had important consequences for the housing programme. The success of the local authorities in building houses meant that the bill for subsidies would be larger than some had anticipated, and there was anxiety about the scale of this form of government expenditure. A departmental committee on the high cost of working-class housing was set up and reported in 1921[36] on ways in which the subsidies could be more effectively administered and ways in which local authorities could bear a greater share of the cost. While this committee was sitting, the government's more widespread concern with the level of expenditure found expression in the appointment of the Geddes Committee. The outcome was that the report on working-class housing was ignored in favour of a swift blow from the "Geddes axe". "It was decided that building houses with the subsidy was too expensive and that the total number to be completed under the Housing and Town Planning Act, 1919, should be limited to 170,000. The number was only a little in excess of that of the houses for which contracts had already been agreed."[37] Approvals of plans for subsidised building ceased in 1921, though schemes already approved were not finally completed until 1923. Between January 1919 and March 1923, 252,000 houses were built, 198,200 with subsidies and 53,800 without. Of the subsidised houses, 154,500 were built by local authorities.[38]

The end of the boom led to a fall in building costs. Taking the level of wholesale prices of building materials in 1913 as 100, these prices increased to a peak of 311 in the autumn of 1920, then fell to 242 a year later. Bricklayers' weekly wage rates (1914=100) rose to nearly 240 by 1920 and fell to 168 by the summer of 1922.[39] Bellman estimated that building costs per foot super fell from a peak of 20s. 2¼d. in 1920 to 9s. 4d. by 1922.[40]

Thus by 1922 at least part of the "return to normality" had been realised. Local authorities had been forced by government economy measures to abandon, at least temporarily, the housing field to private enterprise; subsidies were gone and there had been a substantial fall in building costs, though they were still well above pre-war levels. Unfortunately one element of anticipated "normality" was missing. If the country was 600,000 houses short in 1918, with 250,000 houses built to 1923, there was still a shortage of 350,000, to say nothing of the needs of an increased population and especially the increased number of married couples as a result of the falling age of marriage during the war years. In consequence rent control had, in the government's view, to remain and this had important consequences for building societies during the inter-war years. However, the basic pattern of building society operations for the future, the financing of house purchases by owner-occupiers, had already been set.

Chapter Eleven

WAYS AND MEANS OF EXPANSION

IN 1922 BUILDING SOCIETIES advanced £22·7 million to mortgagors and had total mortgage assets of £83·7 million. Only fourteen years later, in 1936, advances were £140·3 million and mortgage assets, £586·6 million. The rate of expansion varied but 1932 was the only year in which the amount advanced on mortgages was less than the previous year. After 1936, although total mortgage assets continued to increase, with new advances exceeding repayments, the total of new advances itself ceased to grow and eventually fell off sharply in 1939 with the onset of the Second World War. Over the fifty years from 1870 to 1920 the total assets of the movement grew to about three and a half times the 1870 figure. In less than twenty years after 1920 they increased to more than ten times the 1920 total. Two general aspects of this fantastic rate of growth require examination; the sources of the huge increase in the demand for mortgages and the sources of the vast flow of funds into building societies that enabled that increased demand to be met.

There are no precise statistics of the extent of owner-occupation of houses before 1914, though the general view is that it was very limited at least among wage and salary earners. Some light can be obtained from the findings of the Ministry of Health Departmental Committee on Valuation for Rates, 1939.[1] The Committee found, when it collected data in 1938 of the total dwelling houses built before 1914 and still in use, that 1,436,715 were owner-occupied. The definition of a dwelling house used, excluded separately rated flats, houses let wholly in tenements, agricultural houses let with a farm at an inclusive rent and buildings partly occupied for purposes other than those of a dwelling house. Most of the accommodation in these excluded categories would be rented and not owner-occupied. The census returns for 1911 showed 7,753,000 dwellings of all types. Assume for the moment that all these 7,753,000 dwellings were still in use in 1938[2] and that no owner-occupier of a pre-1914 dwelling was excluded from the total of 1,436,715 owner-occupiers mentioned above. Then the Committee's figures would show that 19% of pre-1914 dwellings were owner-occupied in 1938. We know that many of these

* *Notes on this chapter appear on page 304.*

dwellings became owner-occupied after 1914, so that the percentage of owner-occupiers in 1914 would in fact be a good deal less than 19%. The figure would be still further reduced if, as seems likely, a less than due proportion of owner-occupied pre-1914 houses did not survive (e.g. as a result of slum clearance) until 1938. On the other hand some properties excluded by the Committee's definition of a dwelling house were owner-occupied before 1914 (e.g. shops with living accommodation attached) and this would tend to raise the percentage of dwellings that were owner-occupied in 1914. Taking all these factors into account, it seems very unlikely that more than 15% of all dwellings were owner-occupied in 1914 and the figure could easily be 10% or less. *The Economist* has suggested that only 10% of house building before 1914 was for owner-occupation.[3]

Building societies played a more important part in the financing of houses for owner-occupation than they did in financing building houses to let. Thus the rising importance of building societies is a reflection of the declining importance of the private landlord. There are a number of factors which help to explain the decline, almost the cessation, of private investment in houses to let after 1918. The Rent Restriction Acts are usually regarded as the villains of this particular piece, but it must be remembered that the restrictions did not apply to new houses, and in the immediate post-war years there was some expectation that restrictions would in fact cease, as they were due to, in 1923. In the early post-war years, high interest rates, the high cost of house building, the general, and correct, expectation that such costs would fall and the government's apparent determination to rely largely on local authorities to meet the housing shortage, were convincing deterrents to private investment in housing even without the Rent Restriction Acts.

This is not to deny that the original act and its subsequent extension to more expensive houses in 1919 and 1920, was a severe shock to the confidence of investors. Further, investors were to be reminded of the losses they had suffered when, from time to time, the expiration of the restrictions on rents was postponed. The Rent Restriction Acts probably influenced thinking in another way. Behind each decision to delay the termination date, there was an implicit assumption that by the new termination date the market for small houses to let would be in balance, at rents somewhere near those laid down in the Act; "... the maintenance of control was based on the assumption that the controlled rents represented the proper rents for working-class houses".[4] This might reasonably lead potential investors to feel that, unless they could show a reasonable profit on new houses let at rents not much above the restricted levels, there would be no point in building them.

Changes of policy by successive governments about the part local authorities were to play in the housing market, did nothing to restore confidence among private investors; this question became something of a political football. In 1923 the Conservatives offered local authorities a subsidy of £6 per house for twenty years, without any contribution from the rates, for houses built by October 1925; this subsidy was also available to private enterprise, in the form of a lump sum of £75. Local authorities were not allowed to build houses themselves, unless they could convince the Minister of Health that private enterprise could not be relied on to do so. This condition was dropped by the Labour Government in 1924 and the subsidy to local authorities increased to £9 per house for forty years (£12 10s. in rural areas) for houses built before October 1939, provided local authorities were prepared to pay an additional subsidy themselves, from the rates, up to £4 10s. per year for forty years. Where these conditions were not met, the 1923 subsidy of £6 per house was to be available for all houses completed before October 1939. The 1924 Act, while it was soon revised, did have one important consequence. On the basis of the long-term encouragement it gave to the building industry, the government were able to secure a gentlemen's agreement with the trade unions to relax their apprenticeship rules, so as to increase the supply of skilled labour available, thus removing one of the important obstacles to an expanded programme of house building.

The return of the Conservatives led to further changes. The level of subsidy on houses built under the 1923 and 1924 Acts was reduced in 1927; in 1928 subsidies under the 1923 Act were restricted to houses completed by 1929 (instead of 1939) and there was a further reduction in the subsidy on houses built under the 1924 Act. The return of the Labour Government in 1929 meant that the proposed reduction of subsidies under the 1924 Act did not take place. That government also started to direct attention to slum clearance, with special subsidies for the purpose. This was the beginning of a stable policy, for in 1933 the Conservatives confirmed this approach in their Housing Act. The job of local authorities was to clear the slums and henceforth subsidies would only be available for that purpose. Thus, until 1933, potential private investors in housing were faced with the possibility of increased competition from subsidised local authority housing. In their efforts to keep down deficiencies in housing accounts, and hence restrict the subsidy that would have to come from the rates, local authorities tended to build houses to let to the better paid workers: those who could afford to pay rents which, with the help of the government subsidy, approximately met the cost of providing the houses. Dr. Bowley discussing the results of housing policy up to 1933 concludes that, "In effect the working-class families who benefited most directly from the subsidies were the relatively small group of about half a million families who were the best off."[5] And if private investors were to build to let, it would be for just this group that they would first be building.

If there was to be much private investment in houses to let, it would presumably come from those who had made such investments before 1914, for this group had most experience of this particular market. Here the Rent Restriction Acts had a direct effect, for by restricting the incomes of these potential investors, they limited the funds available for investment. The increased level of taxation, even on these restricted incomes, did nothing to improve matters. Gone was the nineteenth-century dream of building one or two houses, then another one or two from the rents of the first, and so on to a comfortable retirement on the rents of a whole street, perhaps named after the owner.

Housing is, by most standards, a very long term investment and thus future expectations, over a long period, concerning building costs and interest rates are important. If both building costs and interest rates are low and are expected to be stable, or better still to rise, then housing becomes an attractive investment. Neither of these conditions was met in the 1920s. Although building costs had fallen from their post-war peak by 1922, they were still well above pre-war levels, and were continuing to fall. *The Economist* Index of Building Costs fell from 109·6 in 1924 to 100 in 1930, on down to 90·7 in 1934. The average contract price of local authority houses fell by nearly a third in the same period.[6] It is significant that when in 1935 building costs ceased to fall and interest rates were very low, there was a revival of private investment in houses to let. From 1935 to 1939, of the 1,317,000 houses provided by unsubsidised private enterprise, 330,000—almost exactly a quarter—were houses to let with rateable values of under £26, and of these 189,000 had rateable values of under £14.[7] When conditions were right, there appeared to be no great hesitancy on the part of private investors, to invest, at least on a modest level, in houses to let.

The main source of the increased demand for building society mortgages came from people forced to become owner-occupiers because there were no houses to let. The gap left by the withdrawal of the private investor was only partially filled by local authorities. The owner-occupier is not deterred by the expectation of future changes in building costs in the same way as other investors. Death apart, his house will be sold only in order to buy another house, and if building costs are falling, while he loses on the sale of his present house, he gains by being able to purchase his next house more cheaply. He has suffered a capital loss, but given that he needs a house as long as he lives, it is a capital loss that will only be realised by his heirs.

The new owner-occupiers were so by necessity rather than choice. "Home buying since the war," wrote Walter Harvey,[8] "has not been a voluntary gesture." But lack of rented accommodation is not the whole story. To quote Dr. Bowley:[9] "Obviously the system has a lot of advantages and it has always been common among the well-to-do. An owner-occupier can decide within fairly wide limits when and where he will have his house built. He is free of interference from landlords and the risk of his rent being raised against him at the expiry of his lease. All these are specially attractive characteristics if there is a shortage of houses. The solution of the housing problem is complete for those who can afford it. Nor must the pleasing sensation of property ownership be overlooked; a house, after all, is a very tangible form of property."

An increasing number of people could afford to buy modern houses. The inter-war years tend to be remembered through the eyes of the 10% to 20% of the population who were unemployed at any one time. For those in work the picture was rather different; prices were falling more rapidly than wages and salaries, so that many people experienced a distinct increase in real income, some of which was devoted to improving their standard of housing. Table XVI traces the course of money incomes and real incomes for wage earners in the United Kingdom between 1920 and 1938.

TABLE XVI[10]

Money Incomes and Real Incomes of Wage Earners, 1920-38

1924=100

	1920	1923	1926	1929	1932	1935	1938
Money Incomes	142	99	98	99	95	97	106
Real Incomes	100	99	100	106	115	118	118

This increase in the real income of a substantial part of the population also provides part of the explanation of the increased flow of funds into building societies, to meet the increased demand for mortgages. There was no obligation on such people to save, but the intense savings drives of the First World War no doubt did something to spread the savings habit, and once acquired it was likely to continue. Widespread unemployment, creating uncertainty about the future of those still employed, reinforced the normal feeling that prudence implies saving. For those taking this view, investment in building societies would be attractive because of its fixed capital value and high liquidity.

The number of shareholders of building societies in 1938 was about 3·7 times as great as that for 1922.[11] The size of the average shareholding increased by 1·8 times over the same period. This increase could have arisen as a result of a few huge investments while the bulk of new investors were investing only modest amounts. The possibility that such was the case is strengthened by the rule that exists in many societies that mortgagors have to invest a small amount, usually not more than £1, in order to qualify as members of the society making the advance. Thus the huge inter-war increase in the number of mortgagors would tend to inflate the number of shareholders and depress the average size of shareholding. Details are available for one society that had such a rule, the Abbey Road, which throw further light on the matter.[12] Table XVII shows the percentage of total share capital in that society invested by members having shareholdings of various sizes, for the years 1913 and 1932. Thus in 1913 shareholders with less than £100 invested, accounted

TABLE XVII

Relative Importance of Small and Large Shareholders

Size of Shareholding (£)	Percentage of Total Share Capital	
	1913	1932
Up to 100	21·8	6·8
,, 250	30·2	13·6
,, 500	25·0	21·4
,, 1,000	15·3	25·9
,, 3,000	6·0	25·6
,, 5,000	1·0	7·7

for 21·8% of the total share capital. The average holding in 1913 was £78 and in 1932, £169. Clearly the increase in the average size of shareholdings was not just the result of the accession of a few massive shareholders. In 1913, 55% of shares were held by people with between £100 and £500; in 1932, 47% were held by people with between £250 and £1,000. However, the sharp increase in the importance of large shareholders, especially those with more than £3,000, is equally clear. A new type of shareholder was growing in importance; building societies were becoming, in Mr. Bellman's words, "... the preserve of more substantial investors".

The fact that income tax rates were higher after the war than before, made building society shares and deposits more attractive to those liable to this tax. Income tax is paid by building societies under special arrangements with the Inland Revenue Board, so that recipients of this interest do not pay tax on it. Thus a given rate of building society interest represents a higher gross (of tax) rate when there is an increase in income tax rates, and it is this gross rate which is relevant when an income tax payer is comparing the yields of alternative investments. This fact helps to account for the increased attraction of building societies for Bellman's "more substantial investors". Some of these were people who before 1914 had invested in houses to let and who had now to find an alternative.

Building societies provided one. The collapse of the stock market in 1929, so soon after the new issue boom of 1928, must have disillusioned many, especially new investors and persuaded them that building societies provided more security.

After 1931 investment in societies had a further attraction. Table XVIII compares the yield on Consols with that of building society shares.

TABLE XVIII[13]

Yield of Consols and Building Society Interest Rates

Date	Yield on Consols	Building Society Interest Rates	
		Shares	Mortgage Loans
1922	4·4	4·4	5·7
1925	4·4	4·4	5·5
1928	4·5	4·5	5·7
1931	4·4	4·6	5·9
1932	3·7	4·5	5·9
1933	3·4	4·0	5·6
1934	3·1	3·4	5·4
1935	2·9	3·6	5·2
1936	2·9	3·5	5·0
1937	3·3	3·4	4·9
1938	3·4	3·3	4·8

Through the 1920s the two run very much together. After 1931 there is a sharp divergence; building societies become more attractive. In 1932 societies were reluctant to cut mortgage rates because they were uncertain about the permanence of the lower structure of interest rates that began to emerge in 1931. They were thus able to continue to pay 4½% to shareholders. The resulting increase in the inflow of investment money, so great that many societies placed limits on the amount they would accept, led to growing competition between societies for mortgages, and interest rates began to fall. In turn rates paid to shareholders had to be cut. Continued keen competition for mortgages made it difficult to raise interest rates to mortgagors, when the yield on government securities began to rise after 1936, consequently the rate paid on building society shares could not be raised and the gap between the two rates of return closed. Interest rates on building society deposits moved fairly closely in line with shares, being usually about 0·6% lower. "The circumstances of the times [the early 1930s] threw into bright relief the virtues of investment in building societies. There is no variation in the capital value of a building society share, while the rate of interest is consistently above that of gilt-edged securities. The movement offered an ideal form of investment in a stormy world, and the response was at times embarrassing."[14]

The other source of funds is deposits. For the whole movement, in 1922, deposits were 20·7% of the total of shares plus deposits.[15] This percentage fell during the 1920s reaching 12·7 in 1930. Thereafter it recovered, as societies placed severe restrictions on new share investments, to 22·1 in 1938. Between 1928[16] and 1938 the number of depositors increased 2·3 times and the number of shareholders 1·9 times. Over the same period the size of the average deposit balance rose from £101 to £194, an increase of 93% which compares with an increase of 35% in the size of the average shareholding.

The main increase in the size of the average deposit took place after 1932; at that date it had only increased to £113. As in the case of shares favourable interest rates were attracting investors. Many holders of government securities preferred to deposit money with societies when stocks matured, rather than take up the new government securities at lower interest rates; while with the depression in trade some companies had idle balances which were placed on deposit with societies. The increase in deposits would have been still greater, if societies had not taken active steps to discourage them by limiting new deposit accounts to a maximum of £500 in many cases.

At the Association's 1932 conference Bellman said, "We should not allow the movement to be exploited and flooded with funds, which by no stretch of the imagination can be described as normal building society money. . .".[17] Some of the increase in deposits was the result of diverting money which would have gone into shares, if societies, as mentioned above, had not placed restrictions on share investments. In 1932 some societies ceased to accept investments in fully-paid shares.[18]

Altogether the inter-war years offered a very favourable environment for the growth of the building society movement. The demand for mortgages was based on rising incomes and a continuing shortage of houses to let. At the same time changes in taxation, together with low interest rates and general uncertainty elsewhere in the capital market, ensured that there was a strong flow of funds into building societies.

This must not be taken to imply that expansion, at least on the remarkable scale achieved, was automatic. A good deal depended on the skill and initiative that societies showed in exploiting opportunities. This point can be illustrated by examining the fortunes of one society, that adopted a fairly passive policy. The Temperance Society had been the largest in the land in 1908, and just before the war, in 1913, its total assets were 3·10% of the total assets of the movement. By 1933 this percentage had fallen to 0·98 and thereafter fell more slowly to 0·78% in 1939. Contrast this with the progress of the Abbey Road Society. While the assets of the Temperance Society roughly trebled during the inter-war years, those of the Abbey Road Society, during the same period, increased by nearly seventy times—clearly success depended on something more than a favourable environment.

No product will sell unless the public is made aware of its existence, and this was accomplished by some societies with great skill. Harold Bellman, who led the Abbey Road's spectacular advance, said in 1923, "Of our external operations perhaps the most important is advertising . . . My impression is that [that] advertising is weak. . . . Many Building Society advertisements are crude in design and overcrowded with matter".[19] Enoch Hill at the Halifax Permanent had already taken this point and used the skill he had once developed, as a printer, to good effect; the pre-1914 rise of the Halifax was partly a result of more imaginative advertising.[20]

Apart from their importance in other connections, branch offices can provide a substantial reminder to the public of a society's existence and the expanding societies often built branch offices a good deal larger than the foreseeable flow of business required. The opening of such offices was usually turned into something of a local occasion, by finding some prominent figure to perform the ceremony. The Lord Mayor of London, complete with coach and postillions and outriders in traditional costumes, opened the Halifax's London City Office in 1931. In the nine years following the war, the Halifax Permanent doubled the number of its agencies and branches, opening about 100 new ones.[21]

Advertising is one activity that offers considerable economies of scale. A society which is not represented nationally, or regionally, gets less than full value for its money, when it advertises in the national or regional press. Equally such a society does not get full benefit from the "free" publicity that results from creating a news story about itself. The Abbey Road Society gained wide publicity by ensuring that ". . . there was no annual meeting that was not graced by someone distinguished in the national life".[22] The same society always had an elaborate and effective display at the Ideal Homes Exhibition. Something of the scale of the change can be seen from the expenditures of the Co-operative Permanent Society.[23] In 1913 that society spent, on printing, stationery and advertising, £410; for 1931 the figure was £28,405; a rise from £0·73 to £1·91 per £1,000 of assets, and the relative increase for advertising alone was probably greater still.

Nor was there a lack of attention to the product sold. Other societies followed the Halifax in creating a wide variety of share and deposit investments to suit all tastes; catering for large and small sums, regular savers and those making a single substantial investment. It was, however, on the side of advances that the greatest changes were to be found. The shift to owner-occupation highlighted the importance of the borrower's initial down payment on his house. The proportion of the value of a house that a society would lend had always varied; the personal circumstances of the borrower, the type of property and the relation between the flow of funds into societies and the demand for mortgages, being important considerations. Advances beyond 75% or 80% of the value of a property were rare; leaving the borrower to find the remaining 20% or 25%, or even more if the building society's valuation fell short of the market price. This was a substantial barrier to prospective home owners and various ways of reducing it were found.

Unstable property values after 1918 had accustomed many societies, which had not previously done so, to taking collateral security.[24] Collateral security was made still more respectable by the 1923 Housing Act, which gave local authorities permissive power to guarantee societies against a portion of the loss that resulted from the default of certain borrowers. The Act, which is discussed below, did not itself create much business as a result of such guarantees, but it had other consequences. "Following the grant of powers to local authorities to give guarantees in respect of new houses, certain leading insurance companies opened enquiries into the prospect of business for them, as guarantors of building society advances."[25] The resulting arrangements varied in detail, but basically they applied only to owner-occupiers of houses valued at up to £1,500, where not more than 90% of the valuation was advanced, over a term not exceeding twenty-one years. The insurance company guaranteed the building society against any loss (resulting from the default of the mortgagor and subsequent sale of his property) greater than would have occurred if the society had advanced only 70% or 75% of the valuation, instead of 90%. Such policies were available in return for a single premium, which varied, depending on the precise form of guarantee and the term of the advance, from 6% to 10% of the sum guaranteed.

Other forms of collateral were acceptable; life assurance policies, trustee securities and even preference shares. Guarantees were arranged with some employers to cover advances to their employees.[26] Mortgages were made attractive to some borrowers by offering, in combination with life offices, an arrangement whereby only the interest on the mortgage was paid, the principal eventually being cleared by the product of an endowment assurance policy. Arrangements which, through life assurance policies, cleared a borrower's debt to the society in the event of his death, were given greater publicity. One variant of this scheme was particularly convenient: mortgage cover in the event of death was provided, in return for the payment of a single premium, which the society would advance in addition to the mortgage advance. The society held the policy, and its surrender value was adequate security for the additional advance in the case of an early default. This variant had been originated by the ingenious George Bishop (Woolwich Equitable) in 1909.[27]

The local authorities helped to provide some new business. The 1923 Housing Act afforded the first opening here. Authorities could guarantee societies, in certain cases, against part of the loss resulting from advances above the normal percentage of their valuation of a property. The fact that the Act did not specify at all precisely the form of these guarantees, was an important reason for its relative failure. Soon after its passing the Cumberland Co-operative Society negotiated a guarantee, with the Carlisle Council, which building society opinion held to be much too favourable to that Council. Among other points, the guarantee ceased altogether when the outstanding mortgage debt fell to 65% of the valuation of the property.[28] This did not help the Association in its attempts to negotiate a generally acceptable form of guarantee with the Ministry of Health and local authorities. The Association erred in not informing societies that a standard form of guarantee was being sought, and other societies negotiated separate agreements.[29]

These negotiations were inconclusive and the Ministry eventually circularised authorities on the matter. Although the Act set no limit to the guarantee, the Ministry said that it should only cover the difference between a normal advance and a 90% advance, and was to cease when the outstanding debt was reduced to the level of a normal advance. The Ministry did not consult the Association about the circular and this caused great dissatisfaction. Hill said that time and again the Ministry had been asked either to accept the Association's proposed form of guarantee or suggest revisions, but without result. "I think," he said, "there is some socialistic influence in the Civil Service, which does not want any private enterprise."[30] The Ministry got a number of societies to accept its recommended form of guarantee, apparently playing one society off against another.

On the other hand many local authorities were annoyed at the decreased role in housing matters allocated to them by the 1923 Act and were unco-operative. Agreement between the parties was eventually reached late in 1924. Local authorities were to make good any deficiency that arose, from the societies granting 90% loans, in excess of what the deficiency would have been had the society made only a $66\frac{2}{3}$% loan. The guarantee was to cease when the outstanding mortgage debt had been reduced to 45% of the original valuation of the property. Many local authorities did not take advantage of their powers under the Act, claiming that lack of experience made it impossible to make accurate provision for their liabilities, whereas with subsidies they knew precisely their future commitments.[31]

The 1925 Housing Act was more specific concerning the extent of local authority powers to guarantee building society advances. This time agreement between the Ministry and the Association was more quickly reached, in the light of the 1924 agreement, "... but unfortunately a number of local authorities refuse to accept it".[32] Altogether local authority guarantees were not a conspicuous success; in all, loans on only 26,775 houses were guaranteed.[33]

Local authorities also provided some business, by transferring to building societies the mortgages they held as security for loans made under the Small Dwellings Act. The fall in interest rates in 1932 gave an impetus to this activity. Local authorities, having borrowed the money to make these advances for long terms at fixed interest rates, were unable to lower interest rates on their mortgages in line with falling rates elsewhere. The Association had hopes of persuading the government to end the powers of local authorities to make advances, and of securing the transfer of all mortgages under the Small Dwellings Act to societies.[34] While these hopes were not realised, some progress was made. The Ministry of Health, in its circulars, tried to persuade local authorities to guarantee loans made by societies rather than make advances themselves, thereby reducing their capital expenditure,[35] and the 1935 Housing Act, section 92, reduced the value of houses on which advances under the Small Dwellings Act could be made, from £1,200 to £800.

The 1933 Housing Act made possible further business for societies, in association with the local authorities, and represented a serious attempt by societies to resuscitate private investment in houses to let at low rents—about 10s. per week. Societies were to make advances to investors of 90% of the value of such houses for the very long term of thirty years, at interest rates 1% below prevailing rates. Losses that resulted from advancing 90% instead of the now usual 70%, were to be met in equal portions by the local authority, the central government and the society.

Walter Harvey was the leading spirit, on the building society side, in the negotiations leading to this Act. Harvey had long held that home ownership could not be a complete solution to the existing housing problem: "Housing service to the country calls for dwellings to let in fair proportion to all others."[36] In 1933 the inflow of funds into societies was having to be restrained; it was outrunning the demand for mortgages and this, in part, explains the acceptance by societies of weaker guarantees from local authorities, than had previously been the case. This excess inflow did not continue for very long; with improving trade the demand for loans from owner-occupiers increased and this affected the enthusiam for the new Act in certain quarters. Some societies stated that they were not interested in the scheme at all,[37] and those that welcomed it, as did the Halifax, which set aside £10 million for such advances, did not in fact do much business under it. The Halifax Society provided the advances for 60% of the 17,000 houses built under the Act up to September 1937 and the £10 million it set aside proved well in excess of the demand.[38] *The Economist* concluded that "The guarantee scheme has not achieved any great success and would appear to be in danger of neglect by those societies who dislike advances on rented houses and by Local Authorities who prefer to use the Small Dwellings Acquisition Act to assist purchasers of small dwellings."[39] Taking all the various schemes of co-operation between societies and local authorities, they scarcely repaid, in terms of business done, the considerable expenditure of time and effort expended in creating them. However, they did provide some extra mortgage business.

A more substantial flow of business resulted from sections 1 and 2 of the 1923 Act. These provided a subsidy of £6 per year for twenty years for houses built by both local authorities and private enterprise.[40] Originally this subsidy was only available on houses built before the end of October 1925; it was extended by subsequent Acts, though the amount of subsidy was later reduced. One attractive aspect of the subsidy, from the viewpoint of the private builder and prospective owner-occupier, was that the subsidy could be received as a lump sum; the local authority recovering it from the Treasury in annual instalments over the twenty years. At a rate of discount of 5%, the subsidy yielded a lump sum of £75. This went a considerable way to meeting the initial stake required of borrowers by building societies before they would make an advance. Of the 878,000 houses built by private enterprise between 1924 and 1930, when this subsidy was available, 362,700 were built with its aid. Clearly subsidies under the 1923 Act played an important part in the expansion of the movement in the 1920s.

The most effective stimulus to new business was found in a more direct attack on the obstacle presented by the large personal stake demanded by societies from borrowers. The method chosen was the "builder's pool". Mortgages under this arrangement started in the mid-1920s, but did not reach a peak until the 1930s, when subsidies under the 1923 Act were no longer available.

In 1924 Walter Harvey discussed a builder's proposal, that societies should advance the whole purchase price of new houses, receiving a cash deposit of 25% from the builder and the buyer—presumably contributed in proportions negotiated between the two of them. The building society was to hold this deposit until the mortgage debt was reduced to a given amount, when the builder's portion of the deposit would be returned to him. He commented, "I do not like the business and I would not willingly be associated with any such scheme . . . a question of legality is whispered —Is a building society justified in lending the full cost of a house under any conditions whatsoever, even with cash or anything else as collateral? I have some doubt."[41] Experience overcame these doubts, on the part of building societies generally, and produced much more sophisticated pool rrangements.

In 1939 *The Economist* described the system: "The builder's pool has the dual object of enabling a house purchaser to acquire property on a modest initial payment (as low as $7\frac{1}{2}$ or even 5% of its valuation) and also of covering the building society for the excess of its advance over the normal proportion of 75 or 80% of valuation. The builder usually makes a cash deposit with the society equivalent to the excess advance (i.e. 15 or 20% of the valuation) on the first batch of houses built. On the basis of its initial experience with the builder and the new estate, the society may subsequently accept cash deposits in respect of only part of the excess advances, but it protects itself for the remainder by obtaining the builder's personal guarantee and also retains the right to draw upon the pool in the event of default. When an estate scheme is in full operation this cash proportion may vary between one-quarter and one-third of the excess advances. Finally as the loan on a given property is reduced and the excess advance is recovered, the due proportion of the builder's cash deposit is released. . . . It is thought that for some of the larger societies pool business may account for as much as a half of the total."[42]

The inter-war years were a period of rapid change, with building societies showing a good deal of initiative and enterprise in exploiting the opportunities that faced them. Not all the innovations made were equally sound, and the builder's pools in particular were eventually to threaten the legal and financial standing of the movement.

The 1920s brought considerable changes in the central organisation of the movement, the Building Societies Association. After 1911 a reform party had been active at the Association's conferences. Among other suggestions was a proposal by J. B. Annan for the creation of district bodies within the central organisation. The war was not long over when a meeting in Barnstaple, on September 22, 1919, led to the formation of the South Western Counties Association.[43] Annan continued in his efforts to persuade the Association's Executive to take the initiative in forming district associations, stressing the importance of mapping out areas so that no unfortunate rivalries might develop.[44] Fears were expressed that district associations would take away strength from the central body. The Executive continued to be reluctant to take the initiative and it was not until March 1922, by which time additional district associations had been formed for the Midlands, North-East, Sussex and Yorkshire, that the

Executive allowed the districts to affiliate to the Association and approved a set of rules for them.

Harold Bellman, in his first conference speech, took the Executive to task for the half-hearted welcome that had been given to district associations and suggested, with Annan, that these associations might take part directly in the election of the Executive.[45] In 1923 Annan outlined a scheme that would have made these associations district committees of the central body.

The Executive felt that it was too soon after their formation, to decide the way in which the district associations should be fitted into the structure of the Association. The rules regarding the districts were not revised until 1926, by which time the Metropolitan and the Western Counties Associations had been added to the list. Such associations were now to consist of not less than six members; were to be subject to the approval of the Executive and were, for an annual subscription of one guinea, affiliated to the central Association and given the right to send two representatives to its meetings. District Associations were to be formed for mutual assistance and to forward the interests of building societies locally. Further district associations were formed in Lancashire and Cheshire (1927), Scotland (1928) and Somerset and Wiltshire (1929).

Wartime inflation had taken its toll on the finances of the Association and in 1922 an increase in membership fees was agreed. More important for the future, the basis on which fees were assessed was changed, from the number of members in a society, to its total assets.[46] Since its inception, the Association had not related voting power to the size of societies at all closely. Subscriptions had varied a little with the size of societies, but the maximum was reached at the modest figure of 1,000 members. With the change in the basis of subscriptions, from members to assets, came differential voting power. A society with assets up to £100,000 was allowed two representatives; up to £500,000 assets, three representatives; up to £900,000 assets, four; up to £1,600,000 assets, five, with a further representative for every £800,000 of assets thereafter. Voting strength was still greatly biased in favour of small societies; in 1926 the largest society had only thirteen times the voting strength of the smallest, although its assets were several thousand times larger. In fact in the past, except occasionally for elections to the Executive, votes had very rarely been taken.

Other rules were revised in 1922 when again there was criticism of the geographical spread of the composition of the Executive. Three vacancies were created which enabled provincial societies further to increase their strength relative to London. The London members still made up the Parliamentary Committee, an arrangement that survived another revision of rules in 1926. Of the Executive's increased membership of twenty-one not more than seven, or less than six, were to be from London.

The Executive was now given modest disciplinary powers; the Executive could, after investigation, expel a society by a two-thirds majority vote, "If any circumstances connected with the conduct, status or financial operations or condition of a Society in the National Association, considered likely to be detrimental to the reputation, welfare or good government of the Association, or of the Building Society Movement, be brought to the notice of the Executive Committee. . .".[47] In 1925 another move to protect the good name of the movement had been taken with the setting up of a Publicity Committee to defend the movement against misrepresentation in the press or elsewhere.

The rules revisions in 1926 included a change in the title of the Association; henceforth it was to be the National Association of Building Societies. The membership of the Association increased rapidly from 216 at the end of the war to 280 in 1923 and 310 in 1928.

A further revision of rules in 1932[48] set the maximum representation of a society at twenty-six irrespective of its assets. The Executive Committee, whose title was now changed to the Council, was increased from twenty-one to twenty-four members, and given power to co-opt a further six members, with eight of the elected and all co-opted members retiring annually. Concern was expressed from time to time that the Executive was almost entirely in the hands of managing directors and other full-time officials of societies; other directors rarely being elected. A proposal to amend the rules so that six members of the Executive would always be directors, other than managing-directors, was defeated. The Council was given power to delegate its responsibilities to an executive committee of up to twelve members. This provision was to prove useful later, in wartime, but its adoption in 1932 was related to the then current controversy about co-operation between societies. The council was also given the power, which had been refused it the previous year, to support societies in legal actions and even power to initiate such actions itself.

An organisational landmark of the 1930s was the creation of the Building Society Institute, a professional body formed to direct the education of the staffs of building societies; and, in the process of granting various degrees of membership, to set and maintain professional standards by its examinations. The Institute was another product of the growth of the movement. While building societies were small, it was reasonable to depend largely on outside recruitment to fill responsible posts. Employees were understandably reluctant to commit themselves to qualifying for membership of a specialised professional body, when the number of positions requiring such qualifications was small. Able recruits to building society employment preferred qualifications in such institutes as the Chartered Secretaries, which would be acceptable over a wider range of employment. Now the expansion of societies brought a stream of vacancies in responsible positions and recruits were willing and anxious for courses of education specifically designed for building society needs.

In the 1870s there had been a venture, probably short-lived, by A. R. Wormald, a building society actuary, to provide an institute for building society students.[49] A more serious attempt to form a professional institute took place in April 1920, when the Building Society Officers Guild was started in London.[50] This Guild aimed at raising the status and education of staffs and at assisting boards of directors to decide minimum salary scales.[51] The Guild's committee anticipated opposition on this last matter and it was probably the main reason for the Guild's downfall.

At first, under its secretary, J. W. Smith, the Guild made rapid progress in London, claiming support from all the leading London societies with the exceptions of the Temperance and the Westbourne Park societies.[52] Arthur Webb, who had long been an advocate of specifically building society education and A. W. Cope (Planet) were two of the three Vice-Presidents, and J. B. Knight, managing-director of the Abbey Road agreed to take the chair at a meeting in October 1920. Outside London enthusiasm was less marked, and in particular the influential Halifax and Leeds Permanent Societies stood aside. The Building Societies Association was asked for its support but declined to give it, replying that, while it was in sympathy with any "efforts to promote the educational and professional efficiency of building society officials . . . such objects were already provided through the Chartered Institute of Secretaries".[53] The fact that the Guild disavowed any intention of using force to increase salaries, suggests that part at least of the opposition sprang from a fear that it would do so. Loyalty to existing professional institutes, through which many leading officials had qualified, was no doubt another source of opposition. J. W. Smith resigned as secretary in January 1921, because of ill-health. In April 1921 there was a change of name to the Institute of Building Society Officials and hopes were expressed that at some future date the Association would give support.[54] The *Gazette*, which had been generous in the space devoted to the Guild's affairs during its short life, reported nothing after the April meeting, so it may be presumed that the new Institute was stillborn.

During the 1920s the need for such an institute was increasingly felt. Individual societies organised lectures and weekend schools and some technical colleges started courses for building society employees. The district associations took the lead in organising week-end schools; these not only helped to meet an educational need, but also served to advertise the existing lack of provision and to provide a forum at which ways of filling this gap could be discussed.[55] There were attempts to make the examinations of the Chartered Institute of Secretaries and the Incorporated Secretaries Association more relevant to building society work and in 1930, as a result of the efforts of the Education sub-committee which had been set up by the Association's Executive, papers in building society law and practice were included in them.[56]

Eventually, under pressure from the district associations,[57] the Association's Council agreed to take the initiative in forming an institute, providing sufficient support was forthcoming from staffs. The suggestions of a committee, appointed to draft a constitution, were approved by the Council on May 4, 1934. W. G. Boys of the Burnley Society was the Institute's first secretary and the first meeting was held in September 1934.[58]

The fact that the new body was sponsored by the Association's Council might be seen as compromising its independence, but basically the Institute was the result of pressure from below. Further, it must be remembered that the Council itself was almost wholly composed of building society managing officials. The Institute gained in strength in its early years, as a result of the Council's sponsorship. Harold Bellman, then the Association's Chairman and the first President of the Institute, said at its inauguration, "One method . . . would have been to ask the staffs to outline and draft a constitution for the Institute . . . from the outset we wanted to work in close co-operation with the National Association of Building Societies, and in order to have something concrete to put before you, we had to outline our own constitution."[59] Of course, once formed the Institute could change its constitution and alter the membership of its Council, whose thirty-five original members were nominated by the Association and its district bodies.

From its inception the Institute had local groups as its active elements. By the end of the first year a scheme of examinations had been constructed, an employment register started, 596 associate, and 597 student members enrolled. In addition there were 246 honorary members, mainly building society directors, who gave important financial support. The early strength of the Institute is reflected in the fact that when the Association split, in 1936, over the issue of the "Code of Ethics", into two bodies, the Institute continued intact.

Chapter Twelve

THE CONSEQUENCES OF EXPANSION*

EXPANSION HAD ITS EFFECTS on the structure of the building society movement. The inter-war years in Britain brought heavy unemployment in the coal, iron and steel, shipbuilding and cotton industries. These were heavily concentrated in the North of England, Scotland and Wales. On the other hand the Midlands and especially the South East of England benefited from the rise of new industries, producing motor cars, electrical appliances and a host of other new consumer goods. Thus the Midlands and South East grew in prosperity, and some of the increasing wealth was spent on improved housing. At the same time these better employment prospects attracted migrants from the depressed areas; this again increased the demand for houses.

Before 1914 the main strength of the building society movement had been in the northern industrial towns and thus its location was at variance with the new pattern of housing demand. In 1922 the six largest building societies were all in the North and possessed between them 29% of the total assets of the movement. As long as the pre-war structure of the movement was maintained, when the activities of even the largest societies were essentially confined to their own region, there would be societies in the North with funds exceeding the demand for mortgages and societies in the South with a great demand for mortgages but insufficient funds to meet it. One way of meeting this disequilibrium would have been to create some new institution to equalise the supply of funds and demand for mortgages between societies. In 1921 Walter Harvey, recently recruited as secretary of the Burnley Society from the banking world, put forward the idea of a central building society bank. Societies with surplus funds would deposit them with such a bank, to be borrowed by societies with an excess demand for mortgages.[1] To set up such an institution would have necessitated changes in the law, but in fact discussion did not proceed very far, the movement showing no great sympathy for the scheme.[2]

Something of the same idea appeared in 1925, as a solution to the increasing competition that was developing in London. It was suggested

* *Notes on this chapter appear on page 306.*

that the Metropolitan Association should become a limited company to organise such a bank, and all London societies would carry on business on standard terms as its agents, adopting common titles, e.g. the Metropolitan (Temperance, etc.) Housing Society.[3] Again the scheme made no progress.

Societies were left to adjust individually to the changed circumstances, and they did so. Thus London societies began to advertise more extensively for funds in the North and Northern societies found some outlets for their funds in the South. If no independent central organisation was to be created, then it was open to individual societies to become, in effect, central organisations themselves. A society with branches all over the country would be likely to have branches in the North doing largely investment business, and branches in the South advancing more money than had been invested locally. Of course not all societies could become national societies, even if they wished to, and most had no such wish. There was room for only a modest number of these giants.

Clearly societies that were already large and were already established regionally had an advantage in the race, but enterprise counted as well. The London societies were, of course, favoured by having a strong demand for mortgages on their doorstep and some Northern societies were favoured by their initial large size. Between 1913 and 1930 Northern societies increased their percentage of the movement's total assets from 44·5 to 47·5 and London societies from 27·3 to 31·7; all other areas showed a decline in this percentage, the sharpest falls being in Scotland and Wales.[4] In 1922, of the ten largest societies, seven were in the North, two in London and one in the Midlands; by 1930, the respective figures were four, five and one (one of the Northern giants had disappeared as a result of amalgamation). Even more significant, the three London newcomers to the top ten occupied the second (Abbey Road), fifth (Co-operative) and ninth (Westbourne Park) positions in the list. The emergence of these national societies implied a measure of concentration within the movement. The ten largest societies had 37% of all building society assets in 1922 and only eight years later, in 1930, this percentage had risen to 53.[5] In a way the opening, by the Halifax Permanent Society, of an impressive office in London in 1924 symbolised the new trend. By 1930 there were basically three types of society: the new nationals; the old regional societies, which contented themselves with limited expansion, opening new branches without moving from their home territory, societies like the Cheltenham and Gloucester and the Temperance;[6] and lastly, the small local societies operating in a single town usually without branches.

The emergence of national societies equalising the flow of investment and mortgage business had important implications for the other societies.

As long as there was no national market either for investment funds or mortgages, the Northern societies, with an assured inflow of investments, could try to encourage borrowers by offering low rates on mortgages; and Southern societies, with a strong demand for mortgages, could afford to charge high rates and consequently offer high rates to investors in an effort to attract more investment funds. There was thus a good deal of bitterness among the small, and indeed larger, Northern societies when the equilibrium of their local markets was upset by the invasion of Southern societies offering higher interest rates on investments. James Brace (Eastbourne Mutual Society) analysed the accounts for 1929 of a random sample of 110 societies, about 11% of all societies. The unweighted average rate of return on mortgage advances for the London and Northern societies in the sample were 6·4% and 5·3% respectively; the respective rates paid on share investments were 4·8% and 4·4%.[7]

However, the combined forces of inertia, habit and local loyalty were strong enough to ensure that there was no dramatic switching of the modest holding of the average building society investor.

Table XIX compares the relative dependence of Northern and London societies on share and deposit investments and the average size of these investments.

TABLE XIX

Liabilities of Northern and London Societies 1930

	Average holding of— Shares	Deposits	Total deposits as a percentage of total shares plus deposits
Northern	£274	£ 87	16·6
London and Home Counties	£191	£240	15·6

The average shareholding is substantially lower in London. This may be explained by the fact that it was more common in London than in the North to require borrowers to have at least a nominal shareholding, as a condition of receiving an advance; thus the average figure would be lowered by the inclusion of a large number of small shareholders. There is a very strong contrast between London and Northern societies in respect of deposits.

The explanation is partly historical. The greater strength of northern societies in the nineteenth century and the fact that many of them, such as the Halifax Permanent and the Leeds Provincial societies, quickly opened a number of branches in and around their home towns,[8] meant that they could be used as savings banks by small depositors in a way in which their London counterparts, such as the Temperance Society with its single office, could not. "Generally speaking, Northern depositors and shareholders appear to regard their society more as a savings bank than their Southern counterparts. . . ."[9] This is reflected in the much higher rate of withdrawals in Northern societies. In 1930 withdrawals as a percentage of new share and deposit investments for five large societies were: Burnley, 79; Halifax, 64; Leeds Permanent, 61; Abbey Road, London, 19; and Woolwich Equitable, 21.[10] The contrast between London and the North, is strong.

The small average deposit in the North, and paradoxically the high rate of withdrawals, made for stability. These Northern investors were placing their money with building societies not only to obtain interest; the ability of the society to provide a saving bank service was also important; the convenience of this service was lost if the money was transferred to a London society, with no local branch. On a small deposit the rate of interest was unimportant and even among shareholders, the urge to take advantage of an interest rate differential of $\frac{1}{2}$% or even 1%, is not great when the sum involved, as was frequently the case, is only £100 to £200. With new and larger investors turning to building societies in the early 1930s, interest rates took on greater importance.

It was not only higher interest rates that disturbed Northern societies; the invasion from the South affected other practices. Southern societies sometimes paid commission to procure both investment and mortgage business and this was rarely done in the North. Advertising budgets had to be stepped up in the North as a defensive measure. In 1930 J. Rolinson (Padiham Society) said, "Instead of reducing these extraneous costs [such as advertising, commissions and outside representatives] we are increasing them . . . stealing business by the aid of commissions and alluring terms, every one of which is a further cost on the house . . . The easy access to building society funds for mortgage purposes, has given a tremendous impetus to profiteering in land and houses".[11]

Worse still, the sharp rivalry that developed worked to the advantage of outsiders, especially the builders, and the precise terms of pool arrangements with builders became an area of especially intense competition. To a society the attraction of the builder's pool was that it tended to tie a builder to that society, for the amount of money a builder had to deposit per house declined as the number of houses mortgaged to a particular society increased. In the early 1930s with the inflow of funds outrunning the demand for mortgages, builders were in a strong position. The Association's 1930 conference was told, "The greatest menace which the movement has to face today . . . [is the] building syndicates, which . . . [hold] a pistol to our heads in reciting to one society the terms which they say they can get from another".[12] Three years later Harvey said, "The profits of house builders and landowners are in many instances unconscionable and responsibility attaches to societies which make them possible. There is a growing danger to our movement, as well as possibility of injury to present home owners, in the reckless extensions of lending . . . obviously because of the large funds, in the hands of societies, for which there is no demand. . . . As for builder's pool agreements they must always be suspect from the point of view of the borrower and it would be a courageous and proper step to put an end to this system of lending."[13]

In their anxiety to attach themselves to the estate builders, many societies did little to safeguard the interests of borrowers. Under pool agreements, because of the builder's cash deposit, a very large percentage of the value of a house could be advanced. Where the borrower was unaware of that cash deposit, the builder could play on this ignorance. The fact that a society was prepared to make so large an advance was presented as clear proof of the value of the house. As early as 1930 Harvey was protesting that it was "unfair to the borrower who became the purchaser in ignorance of the collateral . . . It is not difficult to conceive of circumstances in which, by giving £50 collateral, a builder can afford to lose it because of the increased price at which he sells the house".[14] Some societies did inform borrowers when collateral was taken, "But this is I believe exceptional rather than the rule".[15]

The scramble for business led societies to value badly built houses as though no defects existed. H. W. L. Lester commented that societies, in their own interests, should protect buyers from inferior building and design. "If we must have breeze block let us at any rate see that the builders do not forget to put in the cement."[16] Similar complaints were made by S. J. Walter, a prominent member of the Council in 1933, and again in 1935, when, in commending the proposed code of ethics, he said that the knowledge that building societies were co-operating would enable the societies to insist upon better standards of materials and construction.[17]

With the personal stake of borrowers reduced in some instances to as low as 2% or 3% of the purchase price of the house, it is not surprising that, if a house showed serious defects, the purchaser might prefer to disappear, leaving the society with the defective property, rather than continue with his obligations. The willingness of societies to lend also made them the victims, on occasion, of collusion between builders and purchasers. Fictitious purchase prices were stated, in the confident expectation that, in its desire to get business, a society would make its valuations agree with these inflated purchase prices.[18] The payment of commission for the introduction of business increased these possibilities of collusion, and was "a temptation to agents and others to submit and support securities not wholly desirable".[19]

Competition also affected advances backed by indemnity policies. "The scheme was extended greatly beyond its original intentions and a number of features were introduced which could only be regarded as unsound practice. Most of these changes resulted from representations made to insurance companies by building societies . . . influenced very largely by intensive competition for business especially in the seven or eight years before the war."[20] Advances were made at valuations that equalled the purchase price and additions were made to cover legal and incidental charges and the premium on the indemnity policy. The scheme originated in connection with advances over sixteen years, but this period was rapidly extended to eighteen, twenty-five and even thirty years.

The danger that intense competition might threaten the stability of the movement was heightened by the fear that the deepening depression of the British economy after 1930 would lead to falling property values. "It was mutually agreed," said Bellman in 1931, "that the long anticipated fall in property values is probably approaching. It was recognised that the competition of recent years had led to the granting of terms [on which advances were made] which, however justified under boom conditions, might be a source of danger on a falling market . . . the small deposit system had had the effect of depriving purchasers of negotiating power, since they paid what they were asked and were unconcerned with the question of value."[21]

Efforts were made to restrain competition, by agreement between societies on the terms on which they would do business. The attempt to get societies to subscribe to such a "Code of Ethics" dominated the activities of the Association in the 1930s. Voices in favour of co-operation were raised in many quarters, but it was in the Metropolitan District Association that the first active steps were taken. In the Spring of 1930 a group of large London societies began meetings to investigate the question[22] and they seem to have quickly reached an informal agreement not to lend at less than 6% interest. At the Association's 1930 conference W. McKinell suggested that the wise course would be to seek agreement locally before seeking it nationally, but this suggestion was not taken up. At the 1931 conference it was claimed that "The District Associations have already asked the National Association for a lead with regard to pooling agreements and it is time we had a lead on rates of interest".[23] Certainly the Yorkshire Association had approached the Executive in April 1931 and had been informed that "a group of societies is meeting to explore the possibility of co-operative action and hopes in due course to report to the executive".[24] This was the group of London societies mentioned above. It would probably have been wise for the Executive either to have constituted this group formally as a committee, perhaps with some additional members, or to have set up a committee of its own. There were enough hard feelings about the success of some London societies, to make any report emanating from that source suspect.

In due course the group's report was received and endorsed by the Executive and a confidential circular was sent to societies in November 1931. Though not yet known as the "Code of Ethics", this circular covered much the same ground as the later code. It set out the Executive's views on the limits of safe lending in regard to the borrower's personal stake; maximum percentage advances; maximum terms for loans; builder's pool deposits; rates of interest on deposits and the payment of commissions.[25] There was no mention of interest rates on shares; perhaps in deference to the views of Enoch Hill, the Association's chairman, who had declared himself against attempts to fix interest rates.[26]

Harold Bellman, Chairman of the Metropolitan District and the leader of the struggle to secure co-operation, was due to address the Midland Association in December, and naturally he would talk about the progress of co-operation. A digest of his address was given to the press some time in advance of the meeting. At the same time the contents of the confidential circular were leaked to the press and the two items were treated as one. It was assumed, in some building society quarters, that Bellman was the source of both items and that a serious breach of confidence had been made. Bellman repudiated any responsibility for the leak, but none the less the cause of co-operation was off to a bad start.[27]

The recommendations of the Executive were not everywhere welcomed, H. E. Spells (Chelsea P.B.S.) complained that small societies, which paid high rates to investors because they had more good applications for mortgages than they could meet, were being asked to cut their rates, so that they would have to turn down still more applicants for loans. "The example of the larger societies is likely to lead to policies which suit them but which would not be good for small societies." The dominant position of large societies on the Executive was also noted.[28] In April 1932 the Executive enquired of members how far their recommendations were being followed. While societies generally accepted them in principle, there were many objections to particular points, especially the 90% maximum suggested for advances.[29] A special advisory committee, consisting of the manager and a director of each of the six largest metropolitan and the six largest provincial societies, was set up to review the situation.[30] In the light of the earlier reaction of small societies, the composition of this committee was something less than diplomatic. The advisory committee submitted modified proposals to the Executive and these were circulated to societies in December 1932, with a strong plea that they be considered "in an atmosphere free from any prejudice and with the realisation that the approach to common problems on co-operative lines, is usual in movements which have attained the economic significance of building societies".[31] This circular seems to have been received with little enthusiasm. H. Preston (Northampton) reported to the Midland Association that only seventy replies were received from the over 300 members.[32]

Co-operation faced a severe test during the second half of 1932 and in 1933, with a fall in the general level of interest rates and a flood of money into societies. Some societies soon took the view that the new lower level of interest rates would be permanent, and pursued an active lending policy; others, including the large London societies, took firmer steps to stem the inflow of funds and invested the mounting excess in trustee securities. *The Economist* commented that the existence of two such policies, side by side, was bad for the movement. Further, the fact that societies had not moved in step in cutting mortgage interest rates to existing borrowers suggested ". . . the absence of co-operation between leading London and Provincial societies on a major matter of policy".[33] Attempts to secure greater co-operation on the basis of the Executive's new proposals were pursued through the district associations, with Bellman, and T. R. Chandler (Woolwich Equitable) prominent as visiting speakers.

With the great inflow of money, competition became more fierce. Hill told the 1933 conference, "In my long experience, I have not seen previously anything approaching the degree of competition, often regardless of courtesy as between one society and another, which has been experienced during the past year . . . if this continues there will be no alternative but that every society should be free to adopt measures . . . to guard against a deflection of long associated business by undercutting terms," and Chandler added, "We were hopeful of securing agreement, at least in principle; but the apathy of a considerable number of societies, and the definite hostility of a small but important section, rendered all our efforts vain."[34] The small societies found a champion to speak for them. "The big societies of this country have been wanting to rule the movement with an iron hand and too little attention has been paid to the smaller societies," said H. J. Brown[35] (Leeds Permanent; scarcely a small society!). The following year W. S. Heatley (Coventry Economic) told the Midland Association, "The blame for the present state of affairs is mainly at the door of the large societies and therefore I feel that if any co-operation is to be obtained, the big societies must make the essential move."[36]

Discussion now shifted to the district associations and late in 1933 separate proposals were received by the Executive, now called the

Council, from five districts. These were passed to a special advisory committee, which included representatives of the district associations as well as Council. This committee recommended a series of district meetings to discuss the proposals, the discussions to be introduced by the chairman of the Association, Harold Bellman.[37] These discussions "showed an encouraging unanimity in the recognition of the need for co-operation and in the readiness to secure it. It will be for the Association to prove its statesmanship in laying down equitable and practical conditions . . . [and to] give careful consideration to the suggestion that continued membership [of the Association] be made dependent upon the observance of regulations, when made by the Association in General Meeting."[38]

The practical outcome of these discussions was the formulation of a "Code of Ethics": a set of rules that would govern building society practice. While this code was amended in detail from time to time, the main areas of policy it dealt with remained unchanged; compare the contents of the Executive circular, above p. 208, with the final version of the code, below p. 212. The code was presented to the 1934 conference of the Association, which overwhelmingly endorsed the proposals and decided that in the event of a postal ballot showing a two-thirds majority in favour, the acceptance of the code should become a condition of membership of the Association.[39] In the resulting ballot, the code received less overwhelming support than at the conference and negotiations continued. The payment of commission was now an important source of discord and representatives of the districts were again co-opted on to the advisory committee to deal with this and other matters.[40] In response to requests from the smaller societies, the Council decided that societies with assets of less than £500,000 should have five of the ten seats on the committee that was to be set up, to supervise the implementation of the code and advise on all questions, such as dispensations, that might arise in the course of administering it.[41]

During the summer of 1934 the code was further amended. Small societies felt that the proposed interest rates were too low for them to secure adequate funds, so that the proposals on rates reverted to the status of recommendations and were not binding. The amended code was circulated with voting papers in October; in the event of acceptance it was to become binding on March 31, 1935. The resulting vote favoured the code, but negotiations continued in a search for unanimity. A special meeting of the Association in January 1935 made further alterations, agreeing that, "In view of changing conditions, the control of interest rates be left in abeyance, until the position with regard to interest levels generally was clarified."[42] The further revised code, to become operative on April 15, was circulated and societies were asked to sign their acceptance by February 28th. In a covering letter the Council stated that "While the present proposals may not, in every detail, recommend themselves to your Directors, they represent the outcome of protracted negotiations and the most careful consideration. They have received the all but unanimous approval of a thoroughly representative Special General Meeting of delegates of societies from all parts of the country and the Council therefore looks with confidence for your support."[43] Hope was expressed that interest rates might yet be brought within the code, and to further this hope, societies were specifically requested to make no changes in interest rates at this juncture. This last request was to be of some importance.

Just before the code was due to become operative in April, warfare broke out again. In March a large builder advertised that purchasers of his houses would be able to obtain mortgages, via a provincial society, at 4½% interest against the prevailing 5%. Some other provincial societies followed this rate cut. In April the large London societies followed (including the Abbey Road, whose manager, Bellman, was still chairman of the Association) without informing the Council of their intention of so doing. The majority of societies (and especially the largest, the Halifax) left their rates unchanged, respecting the wishes of the Council as expressed in its February letter. These societies were understandably annoyed. "The recent action seemed to them a breach of faith and to be as far removed as possible from the spirit and letter of co-operation. Boards of Directors had tried to be loyal to the Association, but the action of the London societies might have a serious effect on the co-operation proposals."[44] The best reply that Bellman could make, was that the paragraph urging no change in interest rates had been overlooked; and that if the London societies had not made the cut, which they had not initiated, they would have lost business. Bellman tendered his resignation as chairman of the Association but after a vote of confidence at the next Council meeting, May 1935, he re-occupied the chair. Feelings in the Halifax were bitter, and that society announced that it would match anyone else's cuts in interest rates to borrowers.[45] The Council offered to send a deputation to meet the Halifax board and requested that society to agree to the code becoming operative from December 1935. That the coming into effect of the code could be switched so easily, to help in solving disputes between large societies, was scarcely calculated to inspire trust amongst their smaller brethren.

The resulting delay meant a further opportunity to revise the code in view of changing circumstances. Once re-opened, discussion proved lengthy and it was not until January 1936 that the Council approved a new draft on which societies were to vote by February 29. This final code consisted of six articles, of which the last was the most crucial. Societies had to agree: (1) to conduct their affairs in such a way as to preserve public confidence, especially with regard to the safety of funds; (2) to refrain from any statement injurious to other societies; (3) to submit differences of opinion with other societies to the Council before taking legal action; (4) to inform the Council if a society was in difficulties so that the Council might have an opportunity to organise help; (5) to refrain from soliciting business in respect of housing estates where the terms of another society had been accepted; (6) to adhere, in conducting their business, to standard conditions in regard to interest rates, maximum duration of mortgages, maximum percentage of normal advances, minimum personal stakes for borrowers, acceptance of collateral security, and the payment of commission.[46]

Of the Association's 374 member societies, 282 replied in February; 198 voted for the code, 40 against, 37 were doubtful and 7 postponed their vote asking for clarification of some point. In terms of voting strength under the constitution, 667 votes were for the code, 136 against, 112 doubtful and 37 postponed a decision.[47] There were some large societies among the opposition. Later some of the doubtful declared in favour of the code so that eventually 77% of the movement's strength voted in favour and 11% against. The number of societies in favour of it rose to 228.

Three identifiable groups formed the opposition to making the signing of the code a condition of continued membership of the Association. First, those societies (the Temperance was the clearest example) which had pursued conservative policies in regard to advances and had suffered a relative decline in consequence. The Temperance Society ". . . had not been engaged in methods which might be inimical to the standing and good name of building societies and in most respects their terms were stricter than those proposed in the code. Surely they [the directors of the Temperance Society] contended, it was for any society whose methods had been brought into question to put its house in order."[48] The opposition of the Temperance Society was based on righteous indignation. It is bad enough, when inviting a man of transparent honesty to dine with you, to ask him not to steal the spoons, but to go further and demand that he signs a formal undertaking not to steal them, is pretty certain to leave you a guest short.

Second came a group of substantial societies, who had adjusted more slowly than some others, to the aggressive expansionist atmosphere of the 1920s, which had created some of the new giant societies. These societies felt that the code was denying them the opportunity to re-establish their relative position in the movement, by outlawing the very means which some of the code's sponsors had used, to achieve their spectacular growth. Northern Societies were making up lost ground quite rapidly during the 1930s. In 1925, societies with head offices in the North advanced 55·5% of the total amount advanced by all building societies and those in London (and the Home Counties) 21·7%. Thereafter the Northern societies declined relatively, so that for 1930 the respective figures were North 40·2% and London 42·2%. After 1930 Northern societies began to re-establish their position and by 1934 the respective figures were 46·5 for the North and 31·6 for London.[49]

The third group consisted of small local societies who did no business in connection with the building of estates and whose business was conducted in a rather different fashion from that which the code envisaged. For example, a society in a small country town might feel understandably aggrieved at being compelled to require a 10% personal stake, from the son of one of its investors, who having built up a substantial shareholding over the years, was prepared to guarantee the advance to his son. As T. W. Tanfield (Dudley and District Society) had put it much earlier, when challenged about the low interest rate his society charged, ". . . if they are willing to accept 4% while saving, to build up the fund from which advances are made, they are entitled to borrow at a low rate such money as they require to complete their purchases".[50] Some societies had nothing to do with builder's pools, commissions and extensive advertising, preferring to offer lower interest rates; why, asked Alderman Creighton (Cumberland Co-operative), should they be stopped?[51]

There was a further objection, common to all three groups, and indeed held by many societies which signed the code: that it was too detailed to be enforceable. David Smith (Halifax Society) put it thus in 1935, "I would stress the importance of all societies abiding by such a scheme in spirit . . . rather than attempting to . . . quibble over the meanings of words in the body of the text. . . . The scheme is too ambitious and too conservative . . . whilst the framework is sound, its detailed application, for use under all conditions, is likely to make the general scheme of co-operation difficult to work".[52] Time was to prove Smith abundantly right.

If signing the code was to be made a condition of membership of the Association, there would have to be changes in its rules and even then some members of the opposition might not leave quietly. "The Temperance Society," said Bellman, "has flourished a shillelagh at the Council. Its manager has stated that he has the authority of his board, to say they would not retire from the Association; 'they would be kicked out' . . . if its continued membership was refused, the board would commence litigation. . . . The legal advice submitted to the Council made it clear that no partial, or even complete revision of the Rules of the . . . Association could adequately protect the Council from an attack, by a society bent on litigation."[53]

At the conference of the Association at Llandudno, June 3, 1936, the rules were amended to provide for the possibility of winding up the Association. Last-minute efforts at compromise failed and just over three weeks later, on June 26th, a special meeting was held in London for that purpose. There was some surprise that the winding-up rule was invoked so speedily. Some delegates claimed that the Chairman (Bellman) had given the impression at Llandudno that it would not be immediately invoked. Bellman's reply, "I was very careful to refrain from stating that the provisions of the new rule would not be put into force,"[54] suggests that he was equally careful to avoid stating that the new rule *would* be put into force.

The same afternoon those societies that had assented to the code were summoned to a meeting to form a new Association. This was to be the Building Societies Association, almost identical with the old Association, but having acceptance of the code written into its constitution. (By June of the following year, 210 of the old Association's 374 members had joined the new Association.)

The majority of the opposition also met in the afternoon, when a committee was established to guard the interests of "non-assenting societies" and in October these societies formed a new organisation, the National Federation of Building Societies, which eventually had a membership of about seventy. Some large societies, such as the Temperance, the Bradford 3 Equitable and, after a very brief period of membership of the new Association, the Leeds Permanent, held aloof from both the new central organisations. The district associations for the most part remained loyal to the Association, though the North Staffordshire District Association affiliated to the Federation,[55] and the South Eastern Counties Association was dissolved.

The fact that some large societies were outside the ambit of the code and were prepared to compete aggressively for business, considerably increased the difficulties of administering the code. Dispensations had to be allowed to societies facing such competition and this created ill feeling among societies not so favoured. The Association had little in the way of a secretariat to administer the code, indeed the realisation of the inadequacy of the secretariat may have been a factor in creating opposition. R. H. Marsh, who had served the old Association faithfully for nearly fifty years, was the whole secretariat, and he held only a part time appointment and had his own professional practice, as an accountant, to attend to as well. It was only with the retirement of Marsh in 1936, at the ripe age of

80, that a start was made in organising a permanent staff for the Association.

The code itself proved difficult to implement. "The weakness of the code, it is now generally acknowledged, was its early tendency to proliferation. In the course of its passage through all sorts of deliberative assemblies, conciliation has too often been won at the cost of additional detail, which in action has proved to be a great agent of obstruction rather than a lubricant."[56] Harvey, the newly elected chairman, told the new Association at its first conference in June 1937 that it had attempted to make conditions of membership too rigid. The conference called for a simplification of the code. This revised version was approved by the Council in December 1937 and it ". . . sought to concentrate on the standardisation of essential terms of business, eliminating much of the over-elaboration. . . . It may be that expediency has dictated the sacrifice of certain provisions which would have been of value . . ."[57] This new version was circularised and what proved to be an inconclusive special general meeting to consider it, was held in March 1938.[58] Discussion continued at the Association's annual conference in June, but again agreement proved unattainable and the code was virtually abandoned.

Relations between the Association and Federation were indirectly established in March 1938, when representatives of the two associations met, with representatives of two large societies affiliated to neither body, to discuss the implications of the Borders case (see below). This meeting led, in June, to the setting up of a joint committee to co-ordinate activities of general interest. During 1939 this committee was fully occupied in guarding building society interests during the passage of the 1939 Building Societies Act through Parliament. Personal relationships between the leaders of the two bodies had not suffered from their professional disagreements, and this was to prove important in re-establishing unity. Harvey, elected chairman of the Association in 1937, was a personal friend of Alderman Creighton, chairman of the Federation. At the opening of the new offices of the Leek and Moorlands Society in November 1937, in the presence of Harvey and Enoch Hill of the Association, H. Preston, vice-chairman of the Federation, quoted Falstaff to good effect, "A plague upon it when thieves cannot agree".[59]

During 1939 the Leeds Permanent and Bradford 3 Equitable Societies rejoined the Association; formal negotiations for union opened between the Association and Federation and terms were agreed on September 20.[60] All reference to the code was to be dropped from the Association's rules, though power to make and enforce regulations about the conduct of business was retained. Council was deprived of its power to enforce such regulations: only a general meeting could now do so. Provision was made for some of the Federation's vice-presidents to have the same office in the Association and four of the Federation's committee were to be co-opted on to the Association's Council, when 90% of the Federation's members had rejoined the Association.

At a late stage the Federation objected to the preponderant voting power of large societies and requested that the Association's rules be amended to reduce the relative strength of these societies. Wartime conditions delayed the completion of formalities and the Association's rules were not altered until May 1940.

There was some feeling in the Association against the terms for reunion; some members objected to the deletion of all reference to the code; D. W. Smith (Halifax), elected chairman of the Association in 1940, replied, "a code that is more honoured in the breach than the observance is . . . worse than useless".[61] A few days later a meeting of the Federation expressed itself satisfied with the changes in the Association's rules and while the final meeting of the Federation did not take place until February 1941, most of its members had by that time already rejoined the Association. Effectively the final episode in the drama was reached on August 27, 1940, when the directors of the Temperance Society accepted an invitation from the Council to re-join the Association.[62]

Prior to the efforts to secure the establishment of the code of ethics, societies had moved to protect themselves from the sharp practices of some builders and borrowers by setting up a Status Enquiry Bureau to exchange information about unsatisfactory clients. This had been suggested by Harvey in 1924,[63] but it was not until 1932 that, through the initiative of the Association, such an organisation was established. The Bureau was in fact a special section of an outside trade protection body, the International Association for the Promotion and Protection of Trade Ltd.[64] Large societies had particular need of such a bureau and in 1934, fifty-four societies were supporting it. The Council calling for wider support, stated that, "The statistics of the Bureau indicate most strikingly that troublesome borrowers do in fact go from one society to another in larger numbers than might be supposed."[65]

In 1936 the Registrar sought to safeguard the public by making certain alterations in the form of the annual return made by societies of their operations, so that the true position of societies might be more clearly revealed.[66] When a society took possession from a defaulting mortgagor and sold the property for less than the balance outstanding on the loan, the extent of the loss had to be stated, even though the loss was written off via the societies reserves. Previously the fact of such losses might not be revealed; true, the reserves would fall as the loss was absorbed, but the change in the reserves from year to year was affected by many factors and could not be traced to any particular item. There were other changes of a more general nature which would help an investor to judge a society. All reserves had to be revealed, likewise details of all investments made and realised. These last items aroused strong opposition from the Association.[67]

The Registrar further performed a useful service in drawing attention in his annual reports to certain doubtful practices. Some societies were concealing the extent of mortgages in arrear, by not including them in the schedules of the annual return provided the interest element in the repayments was being met, even though the mortgage called for capital repayments as well.[68] Also properties effectively in the possession of societies were sometimes excluded from the return, by passing the properties to a property company before the date of the return. Such companies were likely to be financed, directed and even staffed by the building society, and the property could fall back into the possession of the society again after the date of the return.[69] This matter was also the subject of attention in Parliament; a questioner, wanting the societies to give more explanatory data about scheduled properties, was told that this would be impossible without changes in the law.[70]

The 1930s saw the formation of new societies, or the taking over of existing societies for the purpose of financing property speculation.[71] In some instances high rates were offered by societies whose main business was to advance money to property companies; these companies and societies could have common boards of directors. The passing of the Prevention of Fraud (Investments) Act in 1939 provided a remedy. The original Bill did not include building societies, being concerned only with companies, but societies were added during the Bill's progress through Parliament. By giving the Registrar power to forbid such societies to invite the public by advertisement, etc., to invest money with them, their chief source of funds could be cut off. The Act also empowered the Registrar to require a society to furnish him with information and produce its records for inspection.

At quite an early stage in the struggle to secure the code, some of its supporters began to feel that a more effective method of achieving their purpose would be to seek changes in the law. In 1933 Harvey wrote, "Everybody who is in close association with building society practice will agree that the Building Societies Acts need consolidation and drastic amendment; and I hope that when someone with vision, knowledge and courage offers a lead in this important task he will have full support, with suggestions for the consolidation of the law and the sanctioning of new practice which is good while definitely disallowing much that is doubtful or bad."[72] Arthur Webb took up the challenge and presented suggestions to the conference of the Association in 1935; but little support for the project was forthcoming on that occasion and the matter was dropped.[73] However, in 1939 as a consequence of the action *Bradford 3 Equitable B.S. v. Borders*,[74] some at least of the matters with which the code had sought to deal were settled by changes in the law, with the passing of the Building Societies Act, 1939.

The Borders case started in the Chancery Court in January 1938 and lasted, with the subsequent appeals, until May 1941, when a judgement was given in the House of Lords.

The case raised two issues that were of critical importance to building societies. Mrs. Borders had borrowed money from the Bradford 3 Equitable Society to purchase a house, which all parties later agreed was badly built. When Mrs. Borders failed to make the payments due under the mortgage deed the Society brought an action to secure possession of the property. In making the loan the Society had, without telling Mrs. Borders, taken collateral security under a builder's pool arrangement. The action raised a variety of issues of which two affected the movement generally.

First, Mrs. Borders resisted the Society's action, claiming that the mortgage deed was unenforceable because the Society had taken collateral security in making the advance and this was illegal under the Building Societies Acts. Second, Mrs. Borders in a counterclaim sought damages from the Society because, allegedly, it had fraudulently misrepresented the house in question as being well built. She claimed she was persuaded to purchase the house, which proved to be less than perfectly constructed, by statements in a brochure issued by a builder. The brochure made a number of claims but the crucial ones were the following: "... the fact that a leading building society makes a more generous advance over a longer period than for any other estate in Britain speaks volumes for the construction of the houses" and "Morrell (Builders) Ltd. are the only builders in Great Britain who can offer, by a special arrangement with a leading building society, a 95% mortgage advance over a period of 24 years at 5% interest. This proves without a shadow of doubt the amazing value of Morrell houses."

In the Chancery Court judgement was not given until thirteen months after the action commenced, and in the meantime building societies suffered a good deal of uncertainty and indeed adverse publicity. If the Court held that the taking of builder's pool deposits was *ultra vires*, it was believed in some quarters that all such deposits would promptly revert to the builder, leaving societies very ill-secured in respect of many of the advances they had made. Further, builders might successfully reclaim from societies the amounts previously deducted from pool deposits to meet deficiencies on the realisation of properties, following defaults of borrowers.[75] And if pool deposits were illegal, what of the other forms of collateral that had become widely acceptable?

Inspired by Mrs. Borders' example, a number of purchasers of properties that proved defective, refused to continue their mortgage repayments until the defects were made good, and formed Tenants' and Residents' Associations to sustain them in their action.[76] This movement was mainly centred on a few estates in the Home Counties, though a National Federation of such Associations was formed.

The Chancery Judge found that the Borders mortgage was enforceable,[77] without having to pronounce on the validity of the builder's pool arrangement that lay behind it. However, the admission that "... although the society considered the house good value for money, they would not have lent so much without collateral security", clearly ran counter to the view of legality earlier expressed by E. W. Brabrook, the late Chief Registrar.[78]

Mrs. Borders also lost her counter claim for damages because she had failed, in the Court's view, to show that the society was responsible for the misrepresentations quoted above. In fact, just before the house was sold to Mrs. Borders, Morrells had changed the building society with which they were doing business. The brochure had been produced while Morrells had a pool arrangement with another society, and thus, since the brochure existed before the arrangement between Morrells and the Bradford Society, it was difficult to prove that that Society was in any way responsible for it. Mrs. Borders might well have been on stronger ground, had Morrells not changed their building society.

Mrs. Borders, who added to the drama by conducting her own case, appealed against the judgement. In the Appeal Court the issue concerning the enforceability was again decided in favour of the Society,[79] but Mrs. Borders succeeded in her claim for damages, though she seems to have done no more than prove that the Bradford Society were aware of the existence of the brochure. The Society now appealed on this point to the House of Lords and that tribunal decided the issue unanimously in favour of the Society. While it was agreed that "The statements in the brochure, to the effect that the house was well built were no doubt untrue", the building society was in no way responsible either for the statements, or for Mrs. Borders' belief in their veracity. Building society officials no doubt saw "puffing" statements, like those made by Morrells, as the common currency of their trade in the 1930s: a Mr. Clough in this case, "... did not feel concerned about the brochure or attach any importance to its statements". Lord Wright noted in his judgement, that "... such an attitude is not incomprehensible, though it is to be regretted".

It is a measure of the serious consequences that would have flowed from a judgement adverse to societies in the original hearing, that before judgement was given a government measure concerning societies was in preparation. This disclosure was forced on February 21, 1939, by the imminence of the introduction of a private members' Bill by Miss Ellen Wilkinson. This latter Bill would have been a severe one for building societies, but it made no progress in the face of the government measure, introduced on March 28th.

The Chancellor of the Exchequer, Sir John Simon, defined the Bill's five objects as:[80] (1) to define the types of collateral security that could legally be taken by societies and specifically to secure the inclusion of builder's pool deposits among these types; (2) to keep the roles of a builder with a house to sell and the building society with money to lend quite separate; (3) to ensure that societies made adequate arrangements for the valuation of properties; (4) to ensure that borrowers were in no doubt as to whether a society's willingness to lend did, or did not, give a guarantee as to the value of the house; (5) to ensure that when a society sold a property as mortgagee it secured the best price available.

Section 1 of the Building Societies Act 1939 reflects current uncertainties regarding the legality of collateral. For advances made before the Act came into effect in November 1939, societies were "deemed always to have had power" to take into account additional security. Thus whatever the eventual outcome of the Borders case, the position of societies was safeguarded. But for the future, something less than this blanket legality was to prevail; limits were placed on both the types and amount of collateral that could be taken (Section 2).

Acceptable types of collateral were life assurance policies, up to their surrender value; guarantees by insurance companies and local authorities; a charge upon money or trustee securities deposited with the society, and certain guarantees from third parties, including guarantees under continuing arrangements (as builder's pools were called). These latter were very strictly controlled by a schedule to the Act. The guarantee had to cover the amount by which the advance exceeded two-thirds of the purchase price and no money was to be released until the debt had been reduced to that level. The whole of the excess had to be deposited by the builder in respect of the first five guarantees and at least one-third of that amount for subsequent guarantees. These conditions were a good deal more stringent than those applied under many existing pool agreements, as were the rules governing the return of these deposits to the builder as the purchaser reduced his mortgage debt.

The term of mortgages under continuing arrangements was set (Section 6) at a maximum of twenty years, after July 1940. So severe were these conditions that the Act effectively killed the builder's pools. Section 3 permitted additional advances to cover the single premium payable under certain assurance policies to cover the mortgage debt in the event of the mortgagor's death. Section 4 prohibited the taking of additional security by societies in connection with advances to non-members.

Both in the Commons and the Press there was a good deal of discussion of the willingness of societies to lend, in some instances, on poorly built houses and their lack of concern with standards of construction. There were efforts to lay upon societies the duty of guaranteeing that the purchase price of houses on which they lent money, was reasonable, at least for houses purchased with the help of builder's deposits. Societies strongly resisted these efforts, and in this they were supported by the Government; "I do not see," said the Chancellor, "that you could possibly establish as between borrower and lender a warranty which may be appropriate as between buyer and seller."[81] The strength of feeling on this matter can be judged from the fact that in spite of the government's very large majority in that parliament, an amendment requiring societies to give such a guarantee was defeated in the standing committee, to which the Bill was referred, only by the casting vote of the chairman. A clause that required societies to inform borrowers three days before the execution of the mortgage, whether or not the house was in good and tenantable repair, was carried against the government in the standing committee, though it was deleted later.

Eventually under Section 9 societies were deemed to warrant the reasonableness of the purchase price of properties mortgaged, unless the borrower was specifically informed that no such warranty was given. Further, anyone with a financial interest in selling a house, who represented that the making of an advance by a society implied that the property was sufficient security for the advance, and who could not prove that he had reasonable grounds for making such a statement, was made liable to a fine of up to £100 or three months imprisonment or both.

Section 5 was an attempt to encourage better standards of building. Where houses were certified by an officially recognised body, as being of an adequate standard of construction, builder's pools were allowed to operate on slightly less stringent requirements; for example loans could be made over a period of twenty-three years instead of twenty.

Where any security was taken from third parties, Section 7 required that societies inform borrowers of the fact and state the maximum advance that would have been made if such security had not been taken. If societies did not so inform borrowers, "no sums shall be recoverable . . . in respect of the advance . . . except by leave of the court". If the security arose under a continuing arrangement, then, under Section 8, the borrower had to be given notice in writing of this fact and if he had previously entered into a contract with the builder and paid a deposit, he could now rescind the contract without penalty and recover his deposit.

Where societies exercised their power of sale as mortgagees, Section 10 required them to take reasonable care to secure the best price for the property sold, and agreements to act otherwise were void. Some societies had agreements with builders, as part of pool agreements, that if a mortgagor defaulted on his obligations the builder would purchase the property at a price sufficient to cover the mortgagor's debt to the society. Such agreements could be highly prejudicial to the mortgagor's interests.[82] Further, Section 13, the details of the sale of his property had to be sent to the mortgagor within twenty-eight days, and the Registrar was given power to require societies to include details of properties sold in their annual return to him.

Section 11 made it unlawful ". . . for any person having a financial interest in the disposal of freehold or leasehold estate . . . to receive . . . any commission from a society . . . in consideration of the introduction of mortgage business [in connection with such estate]". Likewise it was illegal for a society to offer such a commission. Solicitors, surveyors, etc., receiving commissions as agents of societies were excluded from this prohibition.

Section 12 was an effort to secure adequate provision for the valuation of properties on which advances were made, as a separate matter from decisions about the adequacy of the security for the advance. As many building society directors, especially in small societies, carried out both functions (the first usually for an additional fee), this section was closely fought. Eventually it was agreed that the same person would be allowed to have a part in both functions, but a separate record of the valuations had to be kept by societies, and the name of the person making the valuation included. These records were to be available to auditors and to inspectors, appointed by the Registrar under the 1894 Act.

Section 14 declared void any agreement or rule of a society exempting any director or officer from any liability "which by rule of law might otherwise attach to him" in respect of any negligence or breach of trust he committed. This section brought building society personnel into line with that of companies. Section 15 set out penalties for breaches of certain sections of the Act and Section 16 dealt with matters of interpretation.

The 1939 Act contrasts to a considerable degree with previous building society legislation. For the first time the legislature was concerning itself in some detail with the day to day practice of societies, instead of, as previously, confining itself to laying out a general framework within which building societies were free to act as they pleased. This changed attitude of the legislature was to be continued in its subsequent ventures into building society legislation. The 1939 Act did more than merely embody "... a number of essential protective measures that formed part of the code".[83] The code was only concerned with protecting societies from the consequences of intense competition; the Act, as well as protecting societies, included some sections (7, 8, 9, 10 and 13) aimed at protecting the borrower; this had not been prominent among the objectives of the code.

In 1942, when thoughts were turning to problems of post-war reconstruction, Walter Harvey reviewed the inter-war years, to see what lessons they taught. He felt that the societies had not taken their due part in the provision of houses to let. "... they were drawn off financing the building of houses to let by the ... much more profitable business of financing house purchase at scarcity prices, mainly for the benefit of the builder-seller. Several types of collateral security were devised to back up the lending of an unduly high proportion of purchase prices ... all excellent in their own way and now legalised. But the use of collateral was much abused and shouted for regulation in the public interest. ... The mistake made by building societies (speaking widely and generally) had been that they had a greater regard for the builder-vendor than the buyer-borrower, who in many cases has been induced, by the difficulty of renting a home, to take on mortgage obligations too onerous for his means".[84] Expansion had a dark as well as a bright side.

Chapter Thirteen

THE SECOND WORLD WAR*

THE THREAT OF WAR raised the question of whether the new investors, some with substantial holdings, attracted to building societies during the period of rapid expansion, would prove as stable as the small share and deposit holders had been in 1914. If there was a rush to withdraw money, some sections of the movement were not too well placed to meet it. During the late 1930s the liquidity position of the movement had deteriorated; non-mortgage assets as a percentage of total assets declining from 14·3 in 1934 to 10·6 in 1936 and 9·5 in 1938. There were considerable variations between societies and some of the larger ones had only 3% or 4% of their resources in cash and securities. With the rate of return on building society shares less attractive compared with other investments after 1936, some societies had come to depend on bank loans to provide part of the money for advances. The possibility of banks recalling such loans in a crisis made this a dangerous practice. In an effort to attract investors another risky procedure had developed in some quarters, "... of making an unqualified promise of repayment on demand of either depositors' or shareholders' money".[1]

Had there been a sudden declaration of war, as in 1914, some societies would have been in great difficulties. In the event, the dress rehearsal provided by the Munich crisis in 1938 averted that danger. The movement then survived the moderate strains placed on it, which helped to sustain the confidence of investors when the actual declaration of war came in 1939. The Munich crisis led to an increase in withdrawals, but for the year 1938 as a whole the withdrawals were exceeded by receipts from both shareholders and depositors; see Table XX. There was a modest increase in bank loans to help meet withdrawals at the time[2] and the crisis had the salutary effect of emphasising the importance of liquidity, thus giving societies, in the interval of a year before the actual declaration of war, the opportunity to improve their position. "At the end of November 1938 the Woolwich Equitable Society's bank loan stood at £300,000; by the end of February 1939 the Society had on deposit with the bank £300,000."[3]

* *Notes on this chapter appear on page 308.*

On the declaration of war the Association recommended that societies should enforce the requirements, set out in their rules, regarding notice to be given by those wishing to withdraw funds. Societies generally adopted this policy, though small withdrawals were usually granted on demand.[4] The increase in withdrawals was sharp, so that for the year 1939 withdrawals of shares, and especially deposits, exceeded new investments. This is shown in Table XX, which sets out some aspects of building society finances during the war years. The result was a further increase in the borrowing from banks and a deterioration in the liquidity position of societies.

TABLE XX

Some Aspects of Building Society Finances 1937-44

	A	B	C	D	E	F
1937	74	74	13·7	100	710	636
1938	83	82	12·6	97	759	687
1939	111	122	10·6	91	773	706
1940	163	163	7·3	106	756	678
1941	166	142	6·9	142	749	644
1942	143	111	8·5	195	753	608
1943	98	99	10·5	261	769	576
1944	83	88	12·1	316	795	562

A. Withdrawals of Shares as a percentage of receipts.
B. Withdrawals of Deposits as a percentage of receipts.
C. Mortgagors' repayments of advances and interest minus interest charged, as a percentage of the Balance due on Mortgages.
D. Non-Mortgage Assets compared with 1937 = 100.
E. Total Assets £ million.
F. Mortgage Assets £ million.

Just as societies were beginning to recover, the military defeats of 1940, culminating in the fall of France and the threat of invasion, led to further pressure for withdrawals. On this occasion the Government intervened. Defence Regulation 1137 of July 2, 1940, enabled societies to require six months notice of withdrawals. "This afforded relief to those societies whose rules included no such provision. The order was perhaps a concession to the principle of the weakest link in the chain."[5] Many societies were in no difficulty; some decided not to take advantage of the concession and most would have survived the pressure without its help. However, there were societies to which the regulation was of real help, and there were cases where some shareholders found they had a further wait in the queue for withdrawals even after the six months notice had expired. *The Economist* commented,[6] "Societies that have been compelled to resort to this rota scheme have frequently been those whose liquidity margin was allowed to run unduly low before the war, or whose ambition to expand was accompanied by relaxed financial standards".

For most societies the crisis was over by the end of 1940, though as Table XX shows, withdrawals were still heavy in 1941, and it was 1943 before there was a net inflow of funds from investors for the movement as a whole. Those societies best prepared for the trials of war were by 1941 already having to take measures to restrain the inflow of funds, while the worst prepared were still embarrassed by an outflow.

The stresses of 1939 and 1940 had been aggravated by a decline in the return flow of money from mortgagors repaying their loans. This was partly the result of legislation. Even before the outbreak of war, those called up for compulsory military training, members of the territorial forces, and reservists recalled, were protected; where necessary their mortgage repayments were suspended. The disruption created by the war itself, necessitated more widespread protection of mortgagors. This was provided by the swift passage of such emergency legislation as the Courts (Emergency Powers) Act and the Rent and Mortgage Interest Restrictions Act.[7] Protection was granted to those whose financial position was seriously affected as a result of the war.

At first it was widely believed that no mortgagor need pay anything beyond the interest due on his mortgage, and the Association had to issue a press statement disabusing mortgagors of this fallacy. Nevertheless societies, as during the First World War, were ready to consider all hardship cases on their merits and many mortgage payments were re-arranged. Eventually the rising incomes of the war years gave many borrowers the opportunity to increase their repayments on their mortgages; after 1941 the increase in the inflow of funds from this source helped those societies which were still in difficulty.

There was inevitably a rapid decline in advances. In 1938 societies had advanced £137 million, by 1940 this had fallen to £21 million and the low point was reached in 1941 when only £10 million was advanced. On the other side of the account high incomes and a lack of consumer goods meant a high level of saving in the country generally, much of which was invested in building societies. Rising war time income tax rates made such investment increasingly attractive. By 1942 the inflow of funds was proving embarrassing to an increasing number of societies, and steps were taken to restrain it. For example, in the summer of 1942 the Abbey Road refused to open any new share or deposit accounts.[8]

The embarrassment arose because the only outlet for such funds was investment in Government Securities. Here the Second World War was very different from the first, being fought at very low interest rates. Early in the war "... the Chancellor of the Exchequer had secured from insurance companies, building societies and other investing bodies undertakings that they would invest all their available funds in Government bonds".[9] Societies building up large holdings of these low yielding securities risked substantial capital losses if interest rates later rose. A concession was made to societies to help them with this problem. They were allowed to invest up to £250,000 in the Post Office Savings Bank in any calendar year instead of, as previously, only £10,000.[10]

At the end of the war this limit was reduced and in 1946 very severe restrictions imposed; no society could deposit any money in the P.O.S.B. which would increase its deposit beyond £5,000, although societies whose existing deposit was above that figure were not required to withdraw the excess.[11] In March 1942 societies were given the opportunity to become agents for the sale of such securities as National Savings Certificates.[12] Those societies taking advantage of this opportunity were able to deflect some of the money, offered to them by investors, directly into National Savings.

With their investments in Government securities yielding so little, societies had no alternative but to discourage the inflow of funds by reducing interest rates to investors. Other forces added to the need for such reductions; rising income tax rates meant higher tax bills for societies; they also had to pay contributions under the war damage compensation scheme. In order to slow down the reduction in its relatively high yielding mortgage assets, one large society in 1941, ". . . actually invited borrowing members, irrespective of their circumstances or the amount of the balance outstanding, to withhold repayments of capital",[13] and some other societies followed suit.

During the First World War high interest rates on government loans coupled with the restrictions on raising mortgage interest rates had created severe problems for societies. In this respect at least the situation was easier in the second war. The low yield on government borrowing meant that there was no call to raise mortgage interest rates. This aspect of the Rent and Mortgage Interest Restriction Act had no force.

Other Acts limiting the rights of mortgagees did create problems. The Courts (Emergency Powers) Act gave the Courts power to suspend a mortgagee's rights, where a mortgagor's default resulted from circumstances attributable to the war. The working of this Act, and the suspension, with the consent of societies, of capital repayments by some mortgagors, led to a considerable increase in mortgages where repayments were more than a year in arrears. The balance due on such mortgages grew rapidly from £1·1 million in 1939 to £9·7 million in 1941, reaching a peak of £11·0 million in 1942. The balance due on mortgages where the society took absolute possession also rose though less significantly from £1·4 million in 1939 to a maximum of £3·3 million in 1941. In general mortgagors met their obligations and the balance due on the two types of mortgage mentioned above, in the worst year, 1942, were only 2·3% of the total mortgage assets of the movement.

One of the major problems of societies during the Second World War was bomb damage to properties mortgaged to them. By 1936 insurance companies were refusing to insure properties against the risks of damage as a result of war. The Association's Council began negotiations with the Government in search of a solution. At first these negotiations went smoothly,[14] but in May 1937 when the Government was questioned on the subject, Mr. Oliver Stanley replied, "Any scheme of compensation would be for the government of the day [when the emergency arose] to decide."[15] The issue was to continue in this uncertain state for a long time.

In March 1938 the Chairman of the Insurance Association (Sir William Elderton) gave it as his view that the government could not sponsor an insurance scheme, because there was no possible basis on which premiums could be calculated; if war came, they could only wait until it ended, see what damage had been done and pay such compensation as was possible. The Government was ultimately to accept this view, but for the time being, even during the Munich crisis, the silence continued. "It is obvious," said the *Gazette* in January 1939, "that no scheme could be worked out independently of the Government and equally obvious that the Government could not, in the public interest, decline to recognise its responsibilities in the matter. Unfortunately the Government could not be induced to reveal its hand."

On January 31, 1939, the silence was broken.[16] Sir John Simon announced that "The general principle which the Government think should be applied is that such loss or injury ought not to be treated as merely the concern of those who suffer it, but must be regarded as falling upon the community as a whole and consequently as constituting a proper subject for compensation from public funds . . . the insuperable difficulty is that no possible basis for an actuarial calculation exists." Consequently, no compensation would be paid until the total of losses was known, when the government would make a "reasonable" contribution. While helpful, this statement did not do much to dispel uncertainty. The Association decided to take no further action until more details were given. The Government later stated that legislation would only be introduced in the event of war, and thus no further details would be revealed.[17]

In spite of this, in July 1939, the Government set up an expert committee to examine possible schemes. This committee, with Viscount Weir as its chairman, reported in October, soon after the declaration of war. It endorsed the Government's view that no insurance scheme was possible and compulsory insurance was thus ruled out. To have to wait until the end of the war, not only to receive the actual compensation, but even to know what compensation would be given, was not a very happy prospect for building societies.

Early in 1940 at least part of the uncertainty was relieved by the report of a committee, chaired by Mr. A. A. Uthwatt, which put forward recommendations about the extent of compensation. It held that compensation should be based on the cost of reasonable reinstatement of the damaged property, less the cost of salvaged materials; it was, rightly, assumed that most damage would be less than total. Compensation for reinstatement should be based on the level of costs prevailing in March 1939. The diminution in market value was suggested as an alternative basis for compensation.

After the experience of bomb damage in the summer of 1940, the Government agreed to reopen the question, and as a result a War Damage Compensation Bill was introduced in December 1940 and passed through all its stages by March 1941. Where damaged property could be reinstated, compensation would be on a "cost of works" basis. Where property was totally destroyed a "value payment" would be made; the 1939 value of the property plus interest at 2½% per annum from the date of the damage to the date of payment, which would be after the war. The effect of rising costs would clearly be to make compensation less than equitable to those receiving "value payments". Provision was made for immediate payments of up to £800 in cases of hardship; such payments would of course be taken into account when the damage claim was ultimately settled. The Act required a compulsory contribution from all property owners; this was set at 10% of the net annual value of the property, to be paid for five years, irrespective of the actual duration of the war. Where property was mortgaged and its net annual value was less than £150, the mortgagee had to pay a proportion of the contribution. This proportion started at one-sixth, where the balance outstanding on the mortgage was over one-third of the purchase price of the house and rose to a maximum of two-thirds, where the outstanding balance exceeded three-quarters of the purchase price. The original Bill had called for more modest contributions from mortgagees. Building societies as the main mortgagees affected made representations when the Bill was being prepared and accepted the principle that mortgagees should bear part of the contribution. "These representations had the desired effect on the terms of the Bill as originally issued. At a later stage, however, the indemnities payable by mortgagees were unexpectedly and, as it seemed to the Association, unjustifiably raised."[18]

Building societies contributed a great deal to the success and smooth working of the Act. The Association set up a War Damage Committee to deal with general questions and a Technical Sub-Committee, which instructed societies on the detailed working of the Act in a series of pamphlets and circulars. These were especially valuable to small societies, which suffered severely from the conscription of specialist staff. Where a borrower's property was damaged, while societies were certainly interested parties, it was the responsibility of the owner of the property to initiate and substantiate the claim for compensation. In the event, however, many building societies in effect took over this responsibility and dealt with claims. This must have been a very welcome relief to bomb damage victims, faced, as they saw it, with a complicated legal tangle and its attendant forms. The operations of the Woolwich Equitable, as described by Collin Brooks,[19] will serve as an example of the service given by societies.

This had three aspects. First, "As part of this service it was able to issue forms, take particulars, notify claims and the like work on behalf of borrowers whose property was more or less seriously damaged." Second, where the damage was repairable, "The Society would inspect the property and would then assist in the drawing up of a specification for repair and in securing from local builders, estimates for carrying out the work. These estimates would be expertly examined and the best selected . . . when the work was completed . . . the bill was paid and the claim on the War Damage Commission lodged on behalf of the borrower. The reputation of the Society, with the Commission, was so good and its skilled technical service so well appreciated, that very early a relationship was reached which caused prompt payment of claims and broadly speaking, payment without question. . . . Over the whole period of operations less than one per cent of the total amount claimed was disallowed." Third, with totally destroyed properties, restoration had to wait until after the war, but again the Society offered its services to ensure that properties were restored as quickly as possible. Borrowers were not charged any fees for this service, which was quite expensive to provide.

Borrowers who suffered the complete destruction of their property were in a particularly difficult position. Eventually they would receive compensation equal to the 1939 value of their property, plus interest at $2\frac{1}{2}\%$ from the date of destruction. In the meantime they were legally liable to continue their repayments to the building society, including interest at 4% or 5%, depending on the terms. Even if capital repayments were suspended the differential between the interest rate paid, and the rate at which their compensation payment was accumulating, constituted a considerable hardship. The position of some of these unfortunate borrowers was eased by building societies accepting lower rates of interest than was their legal due. Early in 1944 the Halifax Society reduced the rate of interest to be paid on loans, where a property was demolished or rendered uninhabitable, to the same rate as was allowed by the War Damage Commission, $2\frac{1}{2}\%$. This reduction was made retrospective to the date of the damage.[20]

The Halifax's action, later followed by other societies, was not universally welcomed. The North Western District Association protested[21] at the unilateral action of the Halifax Society; all societies, it was claimed, should have been given the opportunity of announcing the concession at the same time. The gesture was seen in some quarters as a publicity move in the battle for post-war business. This was not an isolated disagreement, for by 1944 the harmonious relations between societies that characterised the early war years, following the healing of the rift between the Association and the Federation, had given way to a measure of discord.

Trouble arose from two sources: the question of the desirability of amalgamations between societies and the inflow of funds in excess of present requirements. Attention had first turned to amalgamations as a solution to the movement's problems in the 1920s. At that time enthusiasm for rationalisation was a common feature of the discussions of industrial problems. It bore fruit in such widely differing re-organisation schemes as the creation of Imperial Chemical Industries and the London Passenger Transport Board; and in the Coal Mines Act, 1930. Among building societies, enthusiasm for amalgamations was stronger among the larger societies than among the smaller ones, which would be taken over. Indeed aggressive talk of the urgent need for amalgamations probably contributed, in some measure, to the bitterness that accompanied the discussion of the "Code of Ethics". There had been a modest number of mergers in the 1930s, some of which, in the view of the Chief Registrar, had had undesirable features. Where small societies with strong reserves were taken over, there were instances of an undue part of these reserves being paid to directors as compensation for loss of office.[22] Such compensation was a substantial temptation to directors and was likely to improperly influence them, in deciding whether a merger was in the best interests of the members of their society.

The Building Societies Acts of 1874 and 1894 set stringent conditions[23] which had to be met if a society was to transfer its mortgages to, or amalgamate with, another society. These conditions were eased by the Societies (Miscellaneous Provisions) Act, 1940. The circumstances of war created difficulties in meeting legal requirements concerning such matters as the appointment of officers and holding meetings, for a variety of organisations, including building societies. The primary purpose of the Act was to alleviate these difficulties, but it also amended the statutary requirement that when building societies amalgamated, or transferred their engagements, the concurrence in writing of those holding at least two-thirds of the whole number of shares needed to be obtained. The Registrar could, if he felt that the change was not prejudicial to the interests of members, dispense with this requirement. In the case of a transfer of engagements, he could authorise either or both of the Societies concerned to proceed by way of a resolution of a general meeting or of the board of directors.[24]

In July 1941, with thoughts already turning to the post-war situation, the Co-operative Permanent Society began to examine the possibilities of other societies merging with itself, appointing special staff for the purpose.[25] In February 1942 a letter was sent by the Co-operative Society to a number of smaller societies, suggesting that the Co-operative take over their engagements; this initial letter was followed up. The result was considerable and widespread resentment. In April the Midland District Association whose chairman, Mr. Hubert Newton, had been the vice-chairman of the Federation, resolved "That this Association very strongly deprecates any attempt to force amalgamation on any society not desiring it; it deprecates also, and particularly at the present time, any tendency to take advantage of the manpower problem [the smaller societies were very vulnerable to the call-up of one or two key men] to force such amalgamations."[26]

The *Gazette* commented, "A persistent and systematic method of following up an unsolicited first approach, has given great offence in many quarters. Feeling . . . has been grievously provoked by the launching of the attack when the future policy of the movement was . . . *sub judice*".[27] The Council endorsed the Midland Association's resolution and circularised all members on the subject. The Co-operative Society felt aggrieved at the criticism and explained that no further letters were sent to any society, after the Council's circular, unless that society showed interest.[28]

There were also suggestions that if societies did not form a more compact organisation as a result of voluntary mergers, the Government would be forced to pass measures involving stricter control.[29] In December 1942 the Association's chairman, W. McKinnell, deprecated attempts to achieve mergers by dangling compensation for loss of office, before the eyes of directors of small societies, and by threats of increased local competition if mergers were not accepted.[30]

Some amalgamations and transfers of engagements were arranged between large and small societies, but the major proposals involved large societies in particular. In July 1943, the Abbey Road and the National Societies (then the second and sixth largest societies) proposed an amalgamation, which was successfully completed, to form the Abbey National Society. In 1944 there was a proposal to amalgamate the Leeds Permanent and Woolwich Equitable Societies. This amalgamation had much to recommend it since the Leeds Society was strongly represented in the North and the Woolwich in the South. The Woolwich shareholders sanctioned the move, as did a majority at Leeds, but that majority was insufficient to meet the legal requirements.[31] In 1945 the Bradford 3 Equitable and the Leeds Provincial Societies amalgamated to form the Provincial Society.

The controversy about amalgamations became involved with a further area of disagreement. It had proved difficult for the Association's Council to meet regularly in wartime, and so, in May 1940, it had appointed a small Emergency Committee to carry on its business in the intervals between the now infrequent Council meetings. At the Association's conference in June 1942, fears were expressed that this small body—composed, quite naturally, of the managers of a few large societies—would commit the movement to a policy of amalgamations. More important, the Council's report referred to the screening of new applicants for membership of the Association, to ensure that they met appropriate standards in regard to such matters as reserves, liquidity, etc., adding, "It is possible also that the Reconstruction Committee will concern itself with this problem [i.e. of standards] as it applies to members as a whole." Some societies feared that the Emergency Committee wanted to re-write the "Code of Ethics". A proposal that the Emergency Committee be superseded by the Council returning to its pre-war pattern of meetings was carried,[32] but it proved impossible to implement the proposal. While the full Council met more frequently during 1943 and 1944, the Emergency Committee remained in being.

The growing surplus of funds in societies generally, after 1942, led to severe competition for the limited but growing amount of mortgage business available. Given the low rate of return on their investments in Government securities, societies were naturally anxious to get as large a share as possible of this mortgage business, with its higher yield. This increased competition probably lay behind the Council's concern about standards of conduct mentioned above. Property values had risen considerably compared with 1939 and societies were divided about how much of this increase should be taken into account when making advances. In February 1943 the Council recommended that societies should take little account of such "temporary" increases in value. At the same time it made suggestions concerning appropriate rates of interest and the payment of commission, and stressed the importance of societies preserving adequate liquidity. These suggestions were criticised at the Association's 1943 conference in terms that referred back to the disagreements of the 1930s. However, efforts to secure co-operation continued and in November 1943 a committee was established to frame regulations concerning standards of business conduct. This body decided to defer recommendations until the subject had been discussed with the District Associations.

Early in 1944 some large societies forced the competitive pace with cuts in mortgage interest rates; offers of loans for periods up to thirty years; and offers to relate advances to current valuations, not those of 1939. Against such a background, the committee's discussions with the District Associations did not prosper and the outcome was reported thus: "The Committee is of the view that no good purpose would be served at the present time by framing regulations which could not be enforced on all societies, whether in membership or not; but that the suggestions regarding control over societies through regulations as to liquidity and reserves are desirable."[33] In 1944 the Midland Association was told by its chairman, Hubert Newton, "We agreed to disagree on domestic matters concerning rates of interest to shareholders and borrowers, payment of commission to agents, solicitors and others and the basis of lending, having regard to wartime values. . . . We have had occasion during the last twelve months to frown on the actions of certain societies in this country and to view with grim concern the wide publicity given to their manoeuvres".[34]

These manoeuvres were to continue into the post-war period, but in the meantime the war created many domestic problems for individual societies. The threat of bomb damage to records of transactions was met by making photocopies for storage in safety. Some London societies evacuated their head office administrations early in the war, as a precautionary measure, and others were forced to do so later when bombing had resulted in the wreck of offices. The expansion of the inter-war years entailed a rapid growth in building society staffs, recruited to a considerable extent from school-leavers. As a result societies entered the war with predominantly young employees and were thus very vulnerable to the claims of conscription. Continuous efforts to improve this situation, by getting more generous exemptions from service for building society employees, were not very successful. Cases were considered individually and the loss of an employee had almost to threaten a society's continued existence before exemption was granted. As in the First World War, many women were recruited and others promoted to enable societies to sustain the increased burden of administration that wartime conditions brought.

In December 1941 the Council of the Association decided to appoint a committee to consider the post-war situation of societies and in March 1942 this Committee on Post-War Reconstruction was established.[35] The terms of reference included consideration of building society procedure and practice as well as more general questions of policy; these two areas were investigated separately, through *ad hoc* sub-committees. The Committee was a strong one, with Viscount Sankey as its chairman and some members drawn from outside the ranks of societies. The work of the policy group was inevitably hampered, in its consideration of post-war housing, by the Government's lack of energy, proceeding no doubt from political disagreements, in developing its ideas about how to meet the housing problem that would certainly face the country at the end of the war. This problem would clearly have similarities with the situation in 1918, with the added complication of extensive war damage. The War Damage Commission was eventually to report that over three million private houses had suffered damage. As during the First World War, there had been little new construction of houses, and normal repair work was neglected in an effort to make good bomb damage, where this was not too extensive. Again there had been population growth and the partners to war-time marriages would be seeking accommodation.

While inter-war building had added considerably to the nation's stock of houses, the proportions of these additions that were houses with low rateable values was much too small. The Report of the Inter-Departmental Committee on Valuation for Rating set up in 1938, for England and Wales, gave details of the rateable values of the then (1938) existing stock of pre-1914 dwelling houses[36] and of the dwelling houses built after 1918. These results are given in Table XXI which also expresses the inter-war additions as a percentage of the 1938 stock of pre-1914 houses. The contrast between the additions to low and to medium rated houses is striking. It must be remembered that the greater age of pre-1914 houses tends to give them lower rateable values. Further, with rising incomes people demand better houses. On the other hand, there is more than a suspicion that houses built between the wars were undervalued for rating purposes. Taking all these factors into account it seems clear that inter-war building did not go a very long way to meet the need for houses at

TABLE XXI

Rateable Value of the 1938 Stock of Dwelling Houses

Rateable Value	Houses built pre-1914 still occupied in 1938 '000	Houses built 1918–38 '000	Inter-war additions as a percentage of the 1938 stock of pre-1914 houses
Up to £20 10s.	3,227	1,126	32
£20 10s.–£40	1,293	1,527	118
Over £40	486	292	60

the bottom end of the scale. In addition owner-occupation was rare among the houses of low rateable value; 19% compared with 56% in the middle group. It is reasonable to conclude that the overwhelming need was for houses, with low rateable values, to let.

The Reconstruction Committee made admirable, if not novel, recommendations concerning the improvement of building standards, but on the central problem of building society participation in the provision of houses to let, it could make no compelling suggestions. In 1944 the *Gazette* stated, "The building societies are prepared to make the fullest contribution in their power to a solution of the houses for letting problem. . . . If no practical scheme for implementing this offer has yet been forthcoming it is due to the absence of guidance on how they might . . . fit into the general attack".[37] As in 1918, there were doubts about how long the expected high post-war cost of building would last. Indeed the efforts of the Council to get societies to disregard much of the war-time price increase, when valuing houses for advances, helped to form a general expectation that house prices would fall after the immediate post-war period. In such circumstances private investors would be unlikely to put much money into houses to let. In addition there was the further shock to confidence that had resulted from the wide extension of rent control in 1939.

In some quarters there was hope that a combination of subsidies and guarantees, such as those initiated in the 1933 Housing Act, would provide a basis for building societies to finance private investors.[38] In 1944 the report of the Private Enterprise Sub-Committee of the Central Housing Advisory Committee recommended such an approach, but with the Government providing the whole of the guarantee, not sharing it with the local authorities and the societies. Apart from authorising local authorities to recommence building subsidised houses for general need, not just for slum clearance; and making provision for the financing of a programme of temporary pre-fabricated houses, the wartime Government made little progress with post-war housing plans.

It was agreed that the overwhelming need was for houses to let, and statements suggested that, at least for the first two years, local authorities would play the most important part. Private enterprise would assist, with the aid of guarantees and subsidies. This would still have left some risk to be taken by the private investor. If building societies were to play a part, since they could not build themselves they needed some intermediary to assume this residual risk. The Co-operative Permanent Society had plans to meet the need by creating a chain of housing societies under the Industrial and Provident Societies Acts, which would organise the building; borrowing money from the Co-operative Society to finance their operations.[39] Whether such a scheme would have been successful, and whether many potential risk bearers existed, who would borrow money from societies to build houses to let, became academic questions. The 1945 general election returned a Labour Government with rather different ideas on housing policy.

The new Government relied almost entirely on the local authorities to provide the needed houses. Substantial subsidies were offered to offset the high cost of building, so that the resulting houses could be let at low rents. The wartime system of building licences was retained, with the local authorities as the licensing agents. Licences could be granted to individuals to build privately for their own occupation, but the number of such licences was severely restricted. At times as many as one in five licences could be granted to prospective owner-occupiers, but whenever unfavourable economic circumstances forced cuts to be made in the housing programme, this proportion was reduced and at times no private licences at all were granted. A severe limit was placed on the total cost of such private houses, to ensure that only small houses were built. Licences were granted only on condition that the house built was not resold for four years, and even then the house was subject to price control. In this limited area of building for owner-occupation, local authorities were encouraged to provide the finance, as they were for the purchase of existing houses changing hands. The maximum for loans by local authorities to house purchasers was raised to £1,500 in 1945 and to £5,000 in 1949.

In spite of the lack of new houses being built for owner-occupation, building society advances grew rapidly. The amount advanced had reached its lowest point, £10 million, in 1941 and thereafter rose steadily each year, reaching £97·6 million in 1945. There was a huge increase in 1946, when £188 million was advanced to borrowers. This was higher, at least in money terms, than the pre-war maximum of £140 million in 1936. The total advanced rose further to £264 million in 1948 and then fluctuated narrowly about £270 million until 1953.

There was no shortage of funds to finance this high level of lending. While the national total of small savings dropped rapidly from the high levels of wartime, the proportion of this total going to building societies increased dramatically.[40] Thus there was a sharp rise in the total of both shares and deposits; indeed societies had to retain restrictions on the amount of money they would accept.

In December 1948 F. Bentley (Halifax) could still talk of ". . . the inability of many societies to accept the amount of money the public would be willing to place".[41] Restrictions on deposits by limited companies were very stringent in many societies, ". . . if the societies had not strictly limited the amount of such refugee money which they were willing to accept, they would soon have found themselves flooded".[42]

In 1949 the Council made formal recommendations to societies concerning the terms on which such deposits should be accepted.[43] Some money was also made available to meet the increase in lending, by societies reducing the highly liquid position that had been built up during the war years. Non-mortgage assets as a percentage of total assets, which had reached a maximum of 30·4% in 1945, fell by about 3 points each year, to reach 16·5% in 1949. Investments held by societies fell from £216 million to £146 million over this period. There was a considerable divergence between the willingness of various societies to run down their liquid resources; some, the Halifax Society in particular, still had percentages well above 20 in 1949.

With few new houses being built for owner-occupation, a pattern of building society activity emerged that was very different from that of the 1930s, but similar to that of the years immediately following the First World War. With the huge overall shortage of housing accommodation in the country as a whole, and with local authority waiting lists for houses lengthening, a strong market soon developed in the sale of existing houses with vacant possession. In addition the extension of rent control (and in the light of past history no very immediate prospect of its removal) and the rising cost of repairs meant a low return to landlords. This gave landlords a strong incentive to cut their losses and sell their houses to sitting tenants at prices which were attractive when compared with vacant possession values. Building societies provided the finance for both these types of transaction. Indeed the attractions of both types were enhanced for the purchaser, by the keen competition between societies to provide this finance on favourable terms.

Societies competed in a variety of ways. Some canvassed solicitors and estate agents, offering commission for the introduction of investment and especially mortgage business.[44] Numerous new agency connections were established, and after the lull of the war years, some societies began a rapid expansion of their network of branches. Advances were related to valuations that included an increasing proportion of the wartime rise in house prices.[45] In the summer of 1945 the large societies began another unco-ordinated round of cuts in mortgage interest rates and there were extensions of the period for which loans were made.[46] Sitting tenants were encouraged to borrow the whole of the purchase money required to become owner-occupiers, indeed in some cases more was advanced than was needed to complete the purchase.[47] The cheap money policy of the Labour Government, with its reliance on physical controls rather than high interest rates to restrict the level of investment, meant that societies could afford to reduce the interest rates offered to investors without fear of cutting down the inflow of money.

There was a perceptible increase in substantial loans to limited companies, a return to a form of business that had considerably declined since its heyday in the nineteenth century. This form of business was not everywhere viewed with favour, because it could involve higher risks than loans to owner-occupiers. In 1945 all mortgages on which the outstanding balance exceeded £5,000 were 7·2% of total mortgage assets. This figure rose to 9·4% in 1948 before dropping back again. These figures almost certainly understate the extent of these large mortgages because of the practice, in some quarters, of splitting a loan of, say, £30,000, into six transactions each of £5,000. This avoided revealing the transaction in the annual return made to the Registrar.

Another activity that did not gain universal approval was the increase of loans to existing borrowers. Suppose a person had borrowed £400 to purchase a house before the war: with the rise in house prices and the reduction of his mortgage debt, the house could now be regarded as adequate security for an advance of, say £600. Part of this sum would be used to extinguish the original mortgage. The effect of such transactions was to enable owner-occupiers to turn part of the appreciation in the value of their houses into cash. In as far as this was done to enable house owners to make good the lack of maintenance on their properties during the war, or to enable them to make improvements, building societies were fulfilling a traditional function. However, not all these loans had such objectives. In some cases the cash was required to purchase other items, such as cars or furniture.[48]

Since part of such a new loan was used to repay the outstanding debt on the original mortgage, the increase of such loans should be reflected in a rise in the percentage of total mortgage assets repaid each year. Table XX (above p. 225) shows that such repayments fell during the early war years, but began to rise again after 1941, reaching 12·1% of the total mortgage assets in 1944. After the war there was a rise to 15·3% in 1945, then a steep rise to 20·0% in 1946; a peak of 21·7% was reached in 1947, after which there was a continuous reduction to 15·3% in 1951. While higher earnings of borrowers would account for some of the increase in repayments, this factor had already been operative during the later war years. Further the total of mortgage debt, to which repayments are related above, was increasing sharply after 1945. The increase in repayments in 1946 was quite exceptional, especially as this was the period of post-war resettlement with many people facing the uncertainties of changing from wartime to peacetime employment.

A further type of transaction accorded little with traditional building society practice and standards. The gap that emerged, as a result of rent control, between the vacant possession value of a house and its value with a sitting tenant, provided opportunities for profit which some people exploited with the help of building society funds. Persons in control of a society could form a limited company to buy a block of rent-controlled property at a low price, based on the low net return of such property regarded as a permanent investment. Because of its access to the funds of its companion building society, the company could then sell the houses to the sitting tenants at prices well above those paid by the company. The access to the building society's funds enabled the company to offer these purchasers generous mortgage terms; high advances, even over 100% of the purchase price; with long periods of repayments; and the society might not look very closely at the borrower's ability to repay the loan.[49]

To the operators of such schemes, their profit as shareholders in the company, not the security of the funds that the general public had invested in the building society, determined the terms on which mortgages were granted. As early as 1946, W. H. Scanlan told the Association's Conference, "Many speculators, with the co-operation of building societies, have been quick to seize the opportunity to profit from present conditions. They either sell pre-war holdings of property or purchase a block as an investment, based on the controlled rents, for resale to tenants at prices that bear no economic relationship to the net rent being paid by those tenants. Frequently the houses are of a type that would not sell before the war and are often of poor construction . . . we should combine to ensure some limit to the value of this class of property."[50]

The profitability of such operations made it possible for the building societies concerned to offer higher interest rates than societies conducting more normal activities; the nature of their operations was concealed from their investors. Given the high profits that such activities could produce, it is to the movement's credit that only a small minority of societies made such operations a major part of their business. This minority was, however, sowing the seeds of government intervention which eventually flowered as the Building Societies Act 1960.

There were more sophisticated and dangerous techniques for using building society funds for speculative purposes: these involved the taking over of companies rather than modest blocks of rent-controlled property. These techniques did not emerge fully until the 1950s and were the immediate cause of the 1960 Act. Some of these abuses would have been checked, or at least more clearly revealed to potential investors, if action had been taken on Walter Harvey's suggestion in 1942, "that any loans to directors, either personally or to any business or concern in which they hold executive office or where they are guarantors, should be disclosed in the balance sheet."[51]

The period of war and post-war reconstruction had its effect on the organisation and activities of the Association. During the war the Chief Registrar ceased publishing his reports and statistics of the movements activities, leaving a gap that needed to be filled. Indeed even when these reports were available they were necessarily somewhat behind the facts. At publication they reflected a year's activity already about nine months past, and thus before the next report the latest data would be nearly two years old. Annual statements of societies came more rapidly to hand, but something more frequent than an annual picture of individual societies was needed. A start was made in meeting this need in 1941, when the Association began to collect statistical information itself, with, of course, the co-operation of societies. At first the resulting information was circulated only to those participating in the scheme.[52] Eventually statistics of certain important aspects of building society activity, such as amount of advances, flows of investment funds, etc., were made generally available at quarterly, and from 1965 at monthly intervals.

Another wartime innovation was that "every year since 1940, the accounts of all member societies have been carefully and impartially scrutinised by the accountancy committee [of the Council] and reports thereon submitted to Council".[53] From this scrutiny it was possible to offer many societies valued advice on matters of financial policy and accountancy practice.

One outcome of the unco-ordinated cuts in interest rates at the end of the war was the agreement that societies would inform the Council in advance, of any intended changes in interest rate policy. During the brief reign of the "Code of Ethics", the Council had the duty of setting the interest rates that societies should pay investors and charge borrowers. After recommending societies to reduce their rates late in 1939, the Council took no further action in this field[54] until March 1952. The general reductions that took place in rates during the war years took place without the Council offering much guidance.

As the end of the war approached and travelling became easier, the Council met more frequently, but the Emergency Committee remained in being until November 1945.[55] One of its last tasks was to consider the way in which the Council could best conduct its business during the post-war period. Its recommendation was that the Council should not return to the pre-war system of working through a series of standing committees.[56] Instead there should be only one standing committee, the General Purposes Committee, to oversee the affairs of the Council between its meetings; special panels might be created as circumstances dictated, to study particular subjects. These recommendations might be viewed as the continuance of something not unlike the Emergency

Committee. In the light of the criticisms of that body earlier in the war, the Council was probably wise not to act on these recommendations, though some of the committees that had been created in response to particular wartime needs, were dissolved at the same time as the Emergency Committee.

Proposals for the reform of the Council itself were put forward at the Association's conference in 1946. These proposals emanated from the South-Eastern District Association. They aimed at giving the districts direct representation on the Council, in order to achieve closer liaison between the Council and the individual societies. Since the district associations met frequently, sometimes monthly, district representatives would be able to keep their constituencies informed about the proceedings of the Council, and could bring back to the Council the reactions of the individual societies.[57] After being referred to a joint committee of members of Council and the district associations, a measure of district representation on the Council was agreed to. The Council was enlarged, so that it would in future consist of twenty-four "elected" members, plus one member "appointed" by each of the district associations, and up to a maximum of six co-opted members. The "appointed" and co-opted members were to retire annually and the "elected" members served for a period of three years.[58] So large a Council would inevitably have to rely on committees for the effective discharge of its business; arrangements were made so that committees would deal with their respective business at regular monthly meetings, held before the monthly Council meeting, which then received the committees' reports.

Wartime inflation took its toll of the Association's finances. Deficits after 1942 were met by special levies on societies. In 1945 there was a revision of rules, which increased subscriptions for societies with assets above £1 million, by 50%; this increase did not affect the relative voting power of societies.[59] A further deficit in 1948 necessitated a further levy and led to a more realistic (in the light of continuing inflation) change of rules in 1949. This gave the Council power to increase subscriptions by up to 25% as circumstances required.[60] While this provision did not eliminate rules changes regarding subscriptions, at least it made them less frequent. When the basic scale of subscriptions had again to be raised in 1956, the Council was given the same power to make increases. There was a significant new departure when, in 1949, provision was made to enable societies in overseas countries to become associate members of the Association.[61] The provision only extended to societies "carrying out the functions of a building society" in countries that were members of the British Commonwealth or territories under the Crown. Membership was also opened to societies in the Republic of Ireland.

The severe restrictions placed upon building for owner-occupation, and the encouragement given to local authorities to meet the mortgage needs of house purchasers, made relations between the Labour Government and the Association less than cordial, and Mr. Aneurin Bevan, the Health Minister, scarcely improved matters by his public comments characterising societies as mere moneylenders. The Council was reluctant to reveal the nature of the representations it made to the Government from time to time. When strongly pressed on the subject at the Association's conference in 1949, the Chairman, Sir Charles Davies, replied thus: "It is not advisable that some of the representations should be divulged. The Council was proud to think that in some quarters there was fairly ready acceptance of their views and many things were said which were not recorded in any public document."[62] The change of government in 1951, in so far as it meant a change in housing policies, was clearly not unwelcome to the Association. With greater emphasis on building for owner-occupation, a new period of expansion of building society activity began, with societies resuming the role that they had played during the pre-war period.

Chapter Fourteen

EXPANSION AGAIN, 1951–63*

THE CONSERVATIVE GOVERNMENT which was returned to power in 1951 was committed to an expansion of the housing programme, having set itself an eventual target of 300,000 houses per year. It was also committed to an increase in the volume of building for owner-occupation. Instead of four out of every five houses being for letting by local authorities and one for sale, the level of building for local authorities was to be kept at the then current level of about 150,000 houses, the remainder being for sale. This implied that when the eventual target was reached, equal numbers of houses would be built for local authorities and private owners. The volume of building continued to be controlled via a licensing system; there was a limit to the size of houses that could be built and also to the price at which a house could be resold. The increase in the total housing programme was to be met partly by a reduction in the average size of the houses built and partly by increasing the resources devoted to the building industry.

The immediate response to this greater degree of freedom to build for sale was cautious. In 1952 the total of houses built for private owners increased compared with 1951, by 11,000 to 36,000, while the number of houses built for local authorities increased by 36,000 to 199,000. There was a further easing of restrictions in December 1952, which gave almost complete freedom to build houses for sale, although price controls and controls on the use of some materials remained. The licensing system was finally abandoned in November 1954.

The position of prospective owner-occupiers was further improved in 1953, by the partial repeal of the Town and Country Planning Act, 1947. That Act, in addition to setting up a system to control the location, extent and type of new buildings, attempted to divert to the public purse a part of the increase in land values that such new building created. This was done by levying a development charge on those to whom permission was given to erect new buildings. In 1953 development charges were abolished.

Building societies were eventually to expand rapidly in this new environment, but the expansion was not immediate, indeed the total

* *Notes on this chapter appear on page 310.*

amount they advanced fell marginally in 1952 compared with 1951. While the policies of the new Government were generally welcomed by the Association, there was some restlessness; its Chairman, Mr. Hubert Newton, commented, in 1953, "The general situation has improved so little that we have some cause for impatience."[1]

There were some hopes that the Government might follow the lead of its predecessor in 1923 and give the same subsidy to private enterprise as that given to local authority building, but no such subsidy was forthcoming. With the existing high level of house prices, the high initial payment required of borrowers before a building society could make an advance was restraining the demand for mortgages. Attention turned to the possibility of the building societies advancing a higher percentage of the purchase price of houses, the resulting increased risk being underwritten by the Government and the local authorities. Legal provision had been made for local authorities to provide such guarantees in the 1949 Housing Act, Section 5.

Negotiations between the parties were started in 1953, and agreement was reached in 1954. As a result two schemes were started to aid prospective owner-occupiers: (a) for houses valued at up to £2,500 advances of up to 90% could be made by societies, and (b) for houses built after 1918, valued at up to £2,000, advances of up to 95% could be made. Any loss resulting from the fact that the advances made were in excess of normal building society practice, defined as advances of 70% for scheme (a) and 66⅔% for scheme (b), would be shared equally between the Treasury, the local authority and the building society. The guarantee continued until the outstanding mortgage debt was reduced to 60% of the valuation for scheme (a) and 50% for scheme (b).

The Economist commented that the Association had driven a hard bargain, because it felt that current building society practice would in fact have sanctioned advances of 80% for scheme (a) and 85% for scheme (b).[2] The hardness of the bargain did even more credit to the Association's negotiators, since the Government threatened to increase the powers of local authorities to finance mortgages, if agreement was not reached.[3] In 1955 the two schemes were amalgamated. On houses valued at up to £2,500, 95% would be advanced if they were built after 1918, 90% if built before; the normal advance being defined as 66⅔% for both types. Although participation in these schemes by local authorities was voluntary, over two-thirds of them in fact took part; this was a much higher proportion than had co-operated in any of the inter-war guarantee schemes. Within a year of the inauguration of these schemes advances of nearly £12 million had been made under them, with about the same amount approved and awaiting completion.[4] This total of £24 million was equal to about 8% of all building society advances for 1954. The tighter monetary policy of 1957 resulted in this initial success being short lived.[5]

There were other developments in the housing policy of successive Conservative Ministries which stimulated the demand for owner-occupied houses and thus were helpful to the growth of building societies. In 1954 subsidies to local authorities, on houses built for general needs, were reduced. The Housing Subsidies Act 1956 concentrated subsidies on houses built to replace slums; this, rather than building for general needs, was seen as the main future function of the local authorities. The Rent Act of 1957 began the process of dismantling rent controls. Although the process was halted after less than 10% of the controlled properties had been freed from rent restrictions,[6] the wide publicity given to the resulting rent increases, especially in London, must have enhanced the attractions of owner-occupation for many people. In 1958 stamp duties on the transfer of houses, selling at up to £3,000, were reduced.

Official encouragement of owner-occupation was taken a stage further with the announcement of new government proposals in November 1958. With the demand for loans usually outrunning the supply of available building society funds, societies were able to be selective in the choice of houses on which they were willing to make advances. This situation naturally worked to the disadvantage of those people who wished to buy houses built before 1919; some societies did reserve a portion of their funds for advances on such houses, but this was by no means universal.

To remedy the situation the Government agreed to make loans, up to a total of £100 million, to building societies, repayable over twenty years, to reimburse them for advances made on houses built before 1919.[7] Building societies agreed to make advances of up to 95% of the valuation of these properties, with the margin above 75% covered by some collateral security, for terms of up to twenty years. The rate of interest charged on these advances was to be not greater than the recommended rate of the Association. Any society taking part in this voluntary scheme had to agree to make advances on post-1918 houses on terms no less favourable than those set out above for pre-1919 houses. The government loans to societies would rank with deposits in the event of a society being wound up, and interest was to be paid on them at a rate ½% below the Association's recommended rate. This last provision was the subject of some criticism, for it meant in effect, that any society charging its borrowers a lower rate than that the Association recommended, was excluded from the scheme. There were also complaints that the margin left to societies to meet their management expenses, ½% was too low.

To be eligible to take part in this scheme, a society had to have assets of at least £5 million and meet certain conditions with regard to liquid assets, reserves, etc. These conditions were bound up with the eligibility of societies for trustee status.[8] The granting of trustee status to certain societies was one of the concessions the Association secured from the Government during the discussions.[9]

These arrangements were given legal effect in the Housing and House Purchase Act, 1959. Government loans to societies rose rapidly; £8 million was lent in 1959, £37 million in 1960 and £47 million in 1961. Thus almost the whole of the proposed £100 million had been loaned when the government gave notice of the termination of the scheme in July 1961; three months' notice was required under the Act if either party wished to suspend the scheme.

The incentive to become an owner-occupier was further strengthened by the promise given in Mr. Selwyn Lloyd's budget speech of 1962, to exempt owner-occupiers from liability to income tax under Schedule A; a promise that was fulfilled a year later.

In equity there is no reason why the return on an investment in property for owner-occupation should be treated differently from the return on any other form of investment. True, it is not an income that arises in money terms, it has to be imputed, but it is not the only imputed income. Indeed if the point was that imputed incomes should not be taxed, there would be a widespread movement for all incomes to be paid in kind so as to make them non-taxable. Owner-occupiers had long received favourable treatment in respect of their liability to income tax; the imputed return on their investment in their houses was considerably below the net return they would have received, had they let their houses (though less so, if their houses were let at controlled rents!). Indeed it was the imminence of the increase in these imputed net returns to realistic values, as a result of a revaluation of properties for rating purposes, that Mr. Lloyd gave as one of the reasons for promising exemption. "It is obvious that we could not charge owner-occupiers of residential property with Schedule A income tax on the new rating valuations effective in 1963."[10] Earlier efforts to secure the abolition of the tax had been resisted by the Government. Among other reasons, it was felt that such abolition would have to be matched, in equity, by allowing occupiers of rented accommodation a rent allowance, in assessing them for income tax.[11]

The cost to the Exchequer of this relief to owner-occupiers was put by the Chancellor at about £50 million at the old valuations; at the new valuations it would have been about £125 million. With tenants of local authorities being subsidised to the extent of £137 million in 1963 and a further substantial group enjoying the benefits of controlled rents, it might be held that rough justice was being done; though this verdict would scarcely commend itself to people renting uncontrolled property, who have to meet their housing costs without relief from any source.

Government initiatives since 1961, to encourage housing societies, have also provided the possibility of further business for building societies. The Government's aim was to encourage the building of houses to let at rents high enough to cover all costs, and the housing society was its chosen instrument. Housing societies are non-profit-making voluntary bodies, and in the past have often been formed to build houses to meet some special need, such as housing retired people, or the disabled. The society organises and finances the building operation and administers the letting of the houses when completed. Their success depends on the existence of nuclei of able and enthusiastic people capable of organising a moderately complicated venture.

The Housing Act of 1961 provided for loans from public funds of up to £25 million to housing societies, but apart from a modest increase in the annual government grant to the National Federation of Housing Societies (which provides advice and information to societies) nothing was done in respect of the main problem: the creation of new societies.[12] In 1963 the Government sought to remedy this by the creation of a new organisation, the Housing Corporation, to take the initiative in forming new societies to meet the general need for houses to let. "The aim will be to secure the formation of strongly organised societies operating (with paid staff) in the main centres of population, each capable of undertaking a series of building schemes and managing a substantial number of dwellings."[13]

After discussion with the Government it was stated that "The Building Societies Association believe that many of their members would be ready to lend two-thirds of the money needed by a housing society for a building scheme, if the remaining one-third can be found; and agree that forty-year loans would be reasonable to housing societies."[14] The Government proposed that the remaining one-third of the necessary finance could come from the £100 million with which the Housing Corporation would be endowed.

These proposals formed part of the 1964 Housing Act. As a safeguard against the risk of any building society becoming too enthusiastic in its embrace of housing societies, a clause in that Act limited the advances that could be made to housing societies, to 15% of the total advances made by a building society in any year. The Registrar was given power to raise this limit in any case he thought desirable.

When the Housing Corporation was set up in August 1964, two of its seven members were directors of building societies. It will no doubt be a year or more before the Corporation becomes fully operative, with a consequent increase in building society loans to housing societies. No period has been specified over which the Corporation is expected to dispense its £100 million, but if it did so over a five-year period, this would imply that building societies would be making some 5% of their advances to housing societies.

Against a background of government encouragement of owner-occupation, and probably more important, a rising level of incomes amongst those seeking housing accommodation, the period since 1951 has seen building societies making very rapid, if uneven, progress. Total assets rose from £1,357 million in 1951 to £4,331 million in 1963, an increase of 319%. Mortgage advances totalling £268 million were made in 1951 and £849 million in 1963, an increase of 311%. The rate of expansion was not steady.[15] There was a rapid rise in advances after 1952, to £373 million in 1954; then followed four years of relative stability until a sharp increase to £517 million in 1959. Three years later the total had climbed to £612 million and then, in 1963, there was a dramatic rise to £849 million.

This large increase in the amount of money advanced by building societies does not signify a similar increase in the number of properties whose purchase was financed by societies; house prices were rising almost continuously during these years. The number of mortgage advances made rose from 302,000 in 1951 to 352,000 in 1954, a figure that was not reached again until 1959, when there were 370,000 advances. After four years at about that level there was a second sharp increase to 477,000 in 1963. All these figures include further advances made on properties already mortgaged to societies; no figures of the extent of such further advances are available before 1959, when they were slightly less than 5% of all advances.

Table XXII compares the course of the average size of advance made by societies with the course of house prices for the post-war years; 1946=100 for both series.[16] The size of the average advance increases roughly in proportion to the rise in house prices for the period as a whole. However, there is a strong contrast between the slow rise in the average advance up to 1953 (even a fall after 1948) and the rapid increase there-

TABLE XXII

The Average Size of Advances and House Prices, 1946-63

Date	1946	1948	1951	1953	1955	1958	1961	1963
Average Advance	100	112	99	107	127	143	165	196
Price of Existing Houses	100	120	147	138	141	149	184	207

after. The rise to 1948 represents the adjustment to post-war values; it is also partly accounted for by the increase in the number of large advances, over £5,000. The relative scarcity of mortgages to owner-occupiers made the lending of larger amounts to companies more attractive. Before 1954 a good deal of business was done in financing the purchase of rent controlled properties by their occupiers, and the low prices of such properties helped to hold down the size of the average advance. After 1953 new houses become increasingly important, and their higher prices required larger advances.

It is natural to suspect that, while other factors, such as the increase in building costs, are relevant, the ability of societies to lend is an important influence on the rate of increase in house prices. Table XXIII compares the percentage change, from year to year, in the amount advanced by societies, and the percentage change in the price of houses, measured as in Table XXII. The fit between the two sets of figures is not close. However, it is considerably improved if the data for the change in house prices is lagged one year (i.e. 1949 house price change compared with the 1948 change in advances and so on). There is a positive correlation between the two series in this form, the value for the coefficient being +0·64. This suggests that when societies are able to increase the total

TABLE XXIII

Yearly Changes in Total Advances by Societies and in House Prices

Date	1948	1949	1950	1951	1952	1953	1954	1955	
Total Advanced, % change	+9	+5	−2	−1	−1	+12	+23	+6	
House Prices, % change	−2	+9	+3	+9	−6	−1	−2	+4	
Date	1956	1957	1958	1959	1960	1961	1962	1963	1964*
Total Advanced, % change	−15	+12	0	+38	+8	−9	+12	+38	+31
House Prices, % change	+4	0	+2	+4	+10	+8	+4	+8	+8

* The figures for 1964 are for the first nine months of that year. The increase in house prices for 1964 is taken from the Ministry of Housing index of prices.

amount advanced, as in 1953 and 1959, there is a substantial interval before house prices respond. Similarly, when the amount advanced falls, as in 1956, it is some time before the rise in house prices is checked. It would be unwise to press this relationship too far; sometimes there are excellent *ad hoc* reasons for changes in the course of house prices. For example the sharp rise in prices in 1960 may have owed more to the Government's scheme to assist the purchase of pre-1919 houses than to the easier availability of building society loans in 1959.

The money needed to finance the rising level of advances was mainly derived from share subscriptions, with deposits becoming decreasingly important. Table XXIV traces the changes in the importance of these two sources of funds.

The increase in the total of shares was the result of an increase in both the number of shareholders and the average size of shareholding. Both factors were of roughly equal importance until 1960, but the rapid rise in the total share holding after that date was largely the result of the increase in the number of shareholders. The modest increase in the total

TABLE XXIV

Shares and Deposits,* 1951–1963

	1951	1954	1957	1960	1963
Total Shares £ million	1,057	1,535	2,085	2,721	3,732
Total Deposits £ million	208	222	189	222	271
Deposits as % of total Shares + Deposits	16·5	12·6	8·3	7·5	6·8
Average Shareholding £	448	548	609	696	763
Average Shareholding compared with 1951	100	122	136	155	170
Number of Shareholders compared with 1951	100	119	145	166	207
Average Deposit £	333	376	331	389	458
Average Deposit compared with 1951	100	113	99	117	138
Number of Depositors compared with 1951	100	95	92	92	95

Source: C.R.R.

* Excluding Government Loans.

of deposits is entirely the result of the increasing average size of deposit holdings, for the number of depositors shows a slight decline over the period as a whole. Towards the end of the period there were signs of a change; the number of depositors began to recover and there was a sharp increase in the average deposit balance. As a result the decline in the importance of deposits relative to shares, is slowed down after 1957, but not halted.

The preference of investors for shares rather than deposits is strong evidence of public confidence in building societies. Having seen societies withstand the shocks of war without any serious damage to them, the public was generally unwilling to sacrifice a ½% in the rate of interest received, in order to obtain the greater security that deposits give. The decline in deposits would have been still greater if personal deposits alone were being considered. There is a general consensus of opinion that, in the post-war years, large deposits by limited companies and others became increasingly important as a source of funds. No figures of these deposits are available before 1957, in which year deposit holdings in excess of £5,000 were 23% of total deposits; by 1963, perhaps as a result of societies having to disclose the amount of these rather transient funds, the percentage had fallen to 15%.

The post-war expansion brought about some modest changes in the structure of the movement. Table XXV gives the percentage of the total assets held by societies, ranked according to size. The table shows that between 1945 and 1950 there was a decline in the degree of concentration.

TABLE XXV

Percentage of the Movement's Total Assets, held by Societies, ranked according to size

	Rank 1-5	6-10	11-20	21-40	41-60	Remainder	Total Number of Societies
1945	41·2	11·4	10·9	11·1	6·8	18·6	890
1950	37·4	11·6	13·6	11·9	6·7	18·8	819
1963	46·7	12·1	11·9	9·9	4·8	14·6	662

Source: Building Societies' Yearbooks.

During these years societies had little difficulty in attracting funds, so that the advantage that the very large societies have in this respect (as a result of the popular belief that size means strength; and of large advertising expenditures over many years) was of little importance. Also some of the very large societies, but not all, followed a cautious policy in their lending; in particular some were reluctant to adjust valuations to the high level of post-war housing prices.[17]

With the greater competition for the public's savings in the 1950s the appeal of the "giants" was more influential. While the group of the five largest societies in Table XXV consists of the same five societies at all three dates, this is not true elsewhere in the table; and even among the top five there were slight changes of rank. Overall the ten largest societies have increased their importance in the movement since 1950, and there has been a fall in the importance of all the other segments separately identified in the table. However, the smallest societies, the remainder in the table, have declined remarkably little, bearing in mind that the fall in the total number of societies has mainly been at the expense of this residual group. It is perhaps significant that the individual societies among the top sixty, with the highest rates of growth since 1945, were the Alliance, the Co-operative and the Leek and Moorlands; all three have figured prominently in amalgamations with and transfers of engagements from, other societies. The total number of societies declined quite rapidly during the eighteen years, one society in every four disappearing.

The post-war expansion of the movement took place without the high degree of innovation in building society technique that characterised the expansion of the 1920s. With ample funds available to societies in the late 1940s, and hence no concern about the return flow of funds from borrowers, there was an increase in the number of advances made in combination with endowment assurance policies. In order to reduce the initial payment required of borrowers, wide use was made of indemnity policies to secure societies against the risk of default, by those to whom societies had advanced more than the normal percentage of the value of properties. Later the same purpose was met, in some cases, by local authority guarantees.

In an effort to keep down the monthly repayments on advances and so meet the needs of those with moderate incomes, advances over periods of thirty and thirty-five years were introduced by some societies. This innovation did not meet with general approval; the Association recommended twenty-five years as the maximum term for advances. With the average age at marriage falling, many people seeking loans had low present incomes, but a high probability that their incomes would rise substantially as they progressed in their business or profession. In order to match mortgage repayments to this rising income stream, mortgages were introduced with low monthly payments in the early years and higher payments later. The Government's active monetary policy after 1951, meant that interest rates had to be raised to borrowers from time to time, and societies almost universally gave existing borrowers the option of leaving their monthly payments unchanged; the only effect of the higher interest rate was thus to lengthen the term of the mortgage.

Both investment and mortgage business were stimulated by expanding the network of branch offices, increasing advertising budgets, and paying commission for the introduction of both investment and mortgage business; the effectiveness of all these techniques had been well established during the inter-war years. The development of the branch networks was particularly important in attracting funds from investors at a time when unit trusts, hire purchase finance companies and other such institutions were developing as substantial competitors for the public's savings. There was a considerable extension of the payment of commission to solicitors, accountants and others who were in a position to influence the destination of the funds of prospective investors. In 1957 Mr. J. M. Hannam, Vice-Chairman of the Yorkshire District Association, noted that "The phenomenal demand for mortgages in the last few years has encouraged certain societies to attract investment funds by offering to all and sundry commissions for their introduction".[18] The Association made an effort to reduce the payment of such commissions in 1957. "The proposal divided the Association and was withdrawn, but not before the Provincial Society . . . had resigned from the Association."[19] The Provincial Society, the sixth largest in the country, rejoined the Association in 1960.

There were some innovations in technique, as societies increased their efforts to attract regular small savers. Some societies organised savings schemes in factories and offices; and in 1961 the Association, in co-operation with the Service Ministries, sponsored a scheme to enable members of the Forces to have part of their pay transferred directly to building society savings accounts. As part of this arrangement, special consideration was to be given to such savers if, at a later date, they applied for a mortgage advance.

To the same end, there was a considerable increase in the number of societies offering subscription shares[20] which carried a higher rate of interest than other shares, provided the saver made the requisite payments regularly over a period of years. Subscription shares were not new, indeed they were the original type of share, but the loading of interest rates in their favour was more widespread than had been the case earlier. Another old device, shares and deposits for a fixed term of years at special interest rates, was resurrected as a response to the instability of shares and deposits, at a time when frequent changes of interest rates made it profitable for an investor to move his money to some competing institution. Unfavourable opinions were passed on this latter type of share,[21] which ran counter to the Association's recommendations concerning the interest rate structure that best served the movement's needs. As these recommendations were not binding on members, the offending societies were not inhibited from continuing their offers.

The need to adjust building society interest rates, as the rates offered by other institutions varied, was one of the major problems of the movement after 1951; when, after long disuse, interest rates replaced physical controls as the Government's main weapon in regulating the level of investment. The long tradition of keeping interest rates as stable as possible for building society borrowers made societies reluctant to respond quickly to changes in interest rates elsewhere. Given the other tradition, that irrespective of shareholders' precise rights, they could withdraw at least part of their savings from building societies at short notice, it was increasingly important that societies kept a proportion of their assets in a form that could readily be turned into cash when the need arose. In the early post-war years the problem of adequate liquidity was solved by the considerable holdings of government securities built up during the war years. As these holdings were run down, the Association, which had for some years had a recommendation that societies hold at least $7\frac{1}{2}\%$ of their assets in something more liquid than mortgage securities, decided, in 1951, to make that recommendation a condition of continued membership. Societies were given three years in which to reach the target figure. The vast majority of members had always kept a much higher ratio of liquid assets than the $7\frac{1}{2}\%$ required, but eventually thirty-two members left the Association as a result of their inability to meet this requirement.[22]

The need to keep a reasonable proportion of liquid assets posed other problems. When the general level of interest rates was high, funds could be invested in readily convertible securities without any great loss of interest compared with using the funds for mortgage advances. If interest rates were high, and likely to move downwards, societies had no problem; any delay in responding to a fall in interest rates elsewhere would lead to an inflow of funds; further the fall in rates would mean a capital gain on such quoted securities as were held.

At the other end of the scale, when interest rates were low, and the next move likely to be upwards, the need for liquidity was great, but so was the cost. The choice lay between short-dated stocks, which insure against large capital losses but usually involve a considerable sacrifice of interest, or longer-dated stocks, yielding a higher return but involving some substantial risks of capital losses. The desire is for liquidity, security and a rate of return comparable with that on mortgage advances.

Unfortunately, while investments can have any two of these qualities, they cannot have all three. It would always be possible for the Government to rid societies of this triple-horned dilemma. An appropriate form of investment could be created, having all the three desired qualities; for example the Government could undertake to discount some of a society's mortgage securities at a purely nominal rate, whenever a society needed cash. However, to do so would be to insulate societies from the consequences of changes in the Government's own monetary policy, and the desirability of this would depend on wider considerations than the need to solve the investment problems of building societies.

This was not entirely a new problem for the societies, though the rapid changes in interest rates in the 1950s after twenty years of comparative peace on that front, gave it a new significance. Some societies chose to insure themselves against capital losses by lending money on mortgage to local authorities; this often meant that much of the money lent was not really liquid; and when withdrawals were high such societies had, for a period, almost to suspend mortgage advances. Others chose the simple expedient of investing in quoted securities and valuing them at book values in successive balance sheets. Again where the quoted values fell, if the society was reluctant to realise the capital loss, such securities were scarcely liquid and the consequences for mortgage advances were the same as in the first case. If liquidity was really to be preserved, there had to be a sacrifice of interest or a good deal of time, thought and experience had to go into the management of the society's investments. This latter course was not one which building society boards and officials were necessarily qualified to undertake.

Many societies had, and no doubt will continue to have, troubles as a result of capital losses on their liquid assets; these assets have become the risk assets of the movement. Two societies came to grief as a result of being unable to handle these problems, the Exeter Benefit Society in 1956 and the much larger Scottish Amicable Society in 1958. In both societies a situation arose, where, valuing their investments at market prices, they showed capital losses greater than their respective reserve funds. Fortunately in each instance another society took over the engagements, and shareholders suffered little loss or inconvenience; though they had a period of anxiety.

What liquidity and reserve ratios should be regarded as adequate, became questions of official concern in 1959. As part of the arrangement for channelling public money into building societies to finance loans on pre-1919 houses, deposits in certain building societies were given trustee status. The Registrar was given the task of deciding what conditions a society had to meet, if it was to attain that status, and he was given wide discretion in the exercise of his powers.[23] The conditions set included total assets of at least £5 million and liquid assets of not less than 7½% of total assets; liquid assets being defined as cash, plus investments valued at the lower of book and market values, less bank overdrafts and loans and other liabilities such as income tax and the money needed to pay interest to shareholders, etc. Liquid assets were examined by the Registrar to ensure that the apparent liquidity existed also in reality.[24]

Further, free reserves plus reserve funds set aside to meet capital losses on investments, had to be at least 2½% of total assets. These were not exacting requirements. The Association for example had long had a recommendation that reserves should be 5% (though its definition of what constituted reserves was less strict than that of the Registrar),[25] and a liquidity ratio of 7½% was a condition of membership. In practice, for the movement as a whole, cash and investments (valued in many cases at book values) had not been less than 14% of total assets since the war.

The figure of 2½% as the minimum for reserves was greatly at odds with the Association's recommended 5%, a figure which it still regarded as appropriate in 1958.[26] Sir Oscar Hobson commented that the Association had never had second thoughts about its recommendation of 5%. ". . . now, with the prospect of . . . trustee status for its members' deposits dangled before it, the Association has hastily concluded that after all 2½% of reserves is quite good enough. I think it is an unjustifiable depreciation of standards."[27] The answer was probably that the 5% figure was picked in the early post-war years, when after the stagnation of the war reserves were generally high, and in any case the figure accorded well with pre-war practice. Since then, with the rapid expansion of the movement, its reserve ratio had fallen almost continuously from 6·03% in 1948 to 4·51% in 1959 and 4·48% in 1963.[28] Medium-sized societies tended to have stronger reserve positions than very large societies; thus in 1963, the reserve percentage for societies with assets exceeding £100 million, was 3·99%; for societies with assets between £5 million and £10 million it was 5·40%.

If reserves are viewed only as a provision against possible losses when the properties of defaulting mortgagors are sold, then in recent years no such reserve has really been necessary. In the worst year, 1958, losses on mortgages were less than 0·02% of total assets. These have, however, been years of rising property values and full employment. Also the demand for mortgages has generally outstripped the ability of societies to attract funds, with the result that societies have been fairly selective in choosing the borrowers to whom and the properties on which they have made loans.

In the 1930s, known losses did not exceed 0·1% of total assets, though with some societies partially concealing the extent of their losses the true figure was probably somewhat higher. It is safe to presume that unemployment will not return to the level of the 1930s, with its corresponding increase in risks of losses to societies. However, if societies are to continue to grow, owner-occupation must increasingly spread to people with lower incomes, bringing an increase in the risk of losses, especially where a high percentage advance is made and where the loan is for a long period, with negligible repayment of capital for some years. Reserves of 0·2% might be regarded here as reasonable. Given that a society is making a margin of more profitable advances on other than owner-occupied property, where the risk is still higher, the reserve against losses on property needs to be increased to say 0·25% or 0·3% of total assets.

A reserve is also necessary to cover a possible fall in the value of investments. In 1963 investments were about 13% of total assets. An average fall in the market price of these investments of 7% would yield a loss of about 1% of total assets; this may be an unlikely contingency, but is certainly a conceivable one. It suggests that a reserve of something less than 1·5% of total assets would be the lowest any society could possibly contemplate. Looking to a future in which the country's housing stock more closely approximates the demand for accommodation, with a consequent brake on the rise in house prices, and the "built-in" reserve this represents for mortgagees, a rather larger reserve would suggest itself to the prudent.

The continued growth of the movement since 1959, when the Registrar decided that reserves of 2½% were necessary for the grant of trustee status, further reduced reserves so that by 1963, some societies were precariously near the point at which trustee status would be lost. It seemed that some societies might be forced to make a choice between slowing their growth rate and losing trustee status. They were saved, at least for the moment, from having to make this invidious choice, when the Treasury, in September 1964, approved a change in the reserve requirements for trustee status. Reserves of 2½% were still required for the first £100 million of total assets, thereafter the reserve requirement was cut to 2%.[29] In the light of the argument above, these new reserve requirements are not unreasonable, but they clearly do not leave much room for a further reduction, if the continued growth of some societies should again endanger their trustee status.

The Registrar's power to influence the liquidity position of societies was greatly increased by Section 11 of the Building Societies Act 1960, which reads, in part, "The manner in which a building society may invest any part of the funds of the building society which are not immediately required for its purposes shall be such as may be prescribed by the Chief Registrar by an order made with the consent of the Treasury. . . ".

The Registrar has exercised his powers under this section in two ways. First, by restricting the types of security in which a society may invest; the permitted list for example ". . . excludes altogether local authority loans maturing in more than five years and other permitted securities in more than twenty-five years".[30] Second, the permitted list is divided so that a society may not invest in securities maturing in more than five years, until it has 7½% of its assets in securities of shorter duration. Similarly it cannot invest in securities with more than fifteen years to run until it has 15% of its assets in securities of shorter duration. The impact that the Registrar's control has had, on the choice of securities made by societies, is shown in Table XXVI. This table shows, for societies with assets over £½ million,[31] the percentage of their total investment portfolio held in unquoted securities and quoted securities divided according to their date of maturity. The proportion of unquoted

TABLE XXVI

Investment Portfolios of Societies with Assets exceeding £½ million

	Quoted, years to maturity		Unquoted
	Up to 5	Over 5	
1959	9·5%	41·2%	49·4%
1963	21·2%	26·9%	51·8%

Source: C.R.R.

to quoted securities held has not changed significantly. However, the proportion of shorter dated quoted stocks held has increased very much at the expense of longer dated stocks. Further, for unquoted securities, the percentage of the total holding maturing in less than six months, increased from 72·8% for 1961[32] to 86·8% for 1963.

The changed financial climate after 1951 affected not only the individual societies and the Registrar, but also the Council of the Association. One of the Council's duties is to make recommendations about the interest rate structure societies should adopt, in response to the changing interest rates offered by other institutions. The needs of small societies are best met by a rapid response, at least when interest rates are rising, to avoid withdrawals of money by investors. Indeed some of the smaller societies, especially in London, where competition for funds is particularly strong, always pay investors a little more than the recommended rate; this practice, while never officially sanctioned, seems in recent years to have been tacitly accepted by the Association.[33]

In the same circumstances, the largest societies have shown themselves able to survive, at least for a time, without increasing their rates; the need for a rapid response is not so urgent. The Association's recommended rates have tended to be a compromise between these two positions. Since these recommendations are not binding, some members, at times quite a substantial minority, have adopted other rates. The Halifax Society in particular, in the mid-1950s adopted an independent policy, which because of the size of that society and its high reputation, created considerable difficulties for the rest of the movement. When the Halifax offered to advance on mortgage at lower than recommended rates, it was a formidable competitor, and when it later offered higher rates to investors, it was a very substantial magnet drawing in funds which would otherwise have gone elsewhere.[34]

At the Association's conference in 1955, some strong attacks, made on societies which did not abide by the Association's recommendations, were supported by the generality of members. Alderman Dean (Portman Society) having rejected his original idea of moving a vote of censure, said, "It ought to go on record that this annual meeting takes a very poor view of the behaviour of what is evidently a strong group on the Council, who seek to tie our hands in matters of policy, leaving themselves free to indulge in undesirable competition".[35] This discord provided at least the background to the departure of the Halifax Society from the Association in 1956.

Events conspired to place the Halifax Society in something of an embarrassing position, for its General Manager, Mr. F. Bentley, was a member of the Council and was due to become the Chairman of the Association in 1956. The Chairman of the Halifax Society, the vigorous and independent-minded Alderman A. Denham, was unlikely to relish the prospect of his General Manager, in the latter's capacity as Chairman of the Association, possibly defending the Association's policies, which might be running counter to those of the Halifax Society. This prospect was not in fact realised, for later the Halifax resigned from the Association and Mr. Bentley resigned his appointment with that society.

In the autumn of 1955 the Halifax Society pressed the Council to make regulations limiting the amount that any member society might accept in large deposits from limited companies, threatening (in Mr. Bentley's view)[36] to resign if the Council did not act. There was also a demand that every member of the Council give a personal undertaking that his society would not accept any investment of over £5,000 from any source. No immediate action was taken,[37] indeed the only possible action was to make a recommendation, specifically controlling deposits from companies, which members might well ignore. Anything more drastic would have required a motion passed at a general meeting with the requisite majority. In April 1956 the Council ". . . after a good deal of thought could not see its way to make any recommendation".[38] There were further exchanges[39] but the outcome was the resignation of the Halifax Society, which remained outside the Association for eight years, before rejoining in December 1964.

These events did have some useful results. First, the publicity given to the affair and the immediate public point of contention, probably made it easier for the Registrar to require societies to give details, in their annual return, of the amount of share and deposit balances in excess of £5,000. The first year for which this information became available was 1957 and it showed that the bulk of societies depended very little on these large balances. However, there were a few societies, among them large ones, where such balances approached 10% of total liabilities.

Second, the publicity which attended the general meeting of the Halifax Society, at which Mr. Bentley successfully stood for election to that Society's board of directors, drew attention to the inadequate legal rights of shareholders, not only in the Halifax society but in very many others. All this helped to ensure that when building society law was next reformed, the legal rights of shareholders would be substantially increased.

As it happened, this reform was imminent. Existing legislation was proving itself incapable of curbing the activities of certain societies. These societies presented themselves to potential investors as normal building societies, but used the money invested with them to finance property transactions far removed from the bulk of normal building society lending.

As the law stood there was nothing illegal in the following types of activity. A group of people form both a limited company and a building society. The limited company raises sufficient funds, perhaps by way of a very short-term loan as bridging finance, to purchase a property and immediately repays the loan, from the money obtained by mortgaging the property to the companion building society. Indeed as long as the building society takes care to ensure that the property is reasonable security for the loan, and perhaps does not invest too much of its funds in loans to these companies, especially a single company, such activities would not be far removed from an acceptable pattern of building society practice. If such considerations are not kept in mind by the building society, then there are dangers. The possible abuses of such combinations of companies and societies, in the purchase and re-sale of blocks of rent-controlled property were discussed above.[40]

The technique was capable of other uses. Hotels, farms and industrial properties might be purchased at prices that included a considerable element of goodwill; and provided the building society was sufficiently liberal in its valuation, a not unlikely eventuality if the valuer was a director of both the company and the society, then the society could legally advance the whole of the purchase price, and indeed more than that. Investors in such building societies, who thought that their money was secured by mortgages on mainly owner-occupied property, were a good deal more vulnerable than they imagined.

Those sections of the 1894 Act which sought to reveal such transactions by requiring details of all advances in excess of £5,000 were frustrated by making a series of small advances each backed by a separate mortgage deed. The most difficult problem the law presented was the need for bridging finance, for the assets had to be the property of the company before the building society could make a loan to that company. In some cases these transactions became so formalised that cheques for advances to be made were sent by the building society before the property had been purchased; the society in effect providing the bridging finance.

It was one such transaction that, because of its size and potentially disastrous consequences, ensured that changes in the law would not be long delayed. This transaction involved the State Building Society whose mode of operation was described thus, "Before a bid was made for control of a property company, Mr. Murray would inspect the properties concerned and assess the amount which the Society would be prepared to advance on mortgage. 'Bridging finance' was then obtained, partly from banks and partly from clients of Harewood & Co. [the State Society's solicitors]. Frequently, however, part of the 'bridging finance' was provided by the Society, which having agreed to mortgage advances, sent the money to Harewood & Co. before the date for completion of the purchase of control of the company, and therefore before the date when Harewood & Co. were in a position to arrange for the corresponding mortgages."[41]

In July 1959 the State Society sent one such cheque, for £3,255,000, to Harewood & Co., in connection with its associated property company's efforts to acquire control of the Lintang Company, another property company. To complete the deal over £13 million was required, and when the operation fell through for lack of bridging finance, the State society was left without any mortgage security for the £3,255,000 it had advanced.

The profitability of such property speculations meant that those societies which indulged in them were able to advertise extensively and offer high interest rates to prospective investors. Despite warnings from time to time by the Registrar that high interest rates implied risky advances, investors were attracted on a large scale, and these societies grew rapidly. In 1952 the State Society's assets were £560,000; they rose to over £14 million by 1959. Shareholders of several old established societies were repaid, ". . . by persons who wished to obtain control of the society for the purpose of using its name and date of establishment to encourage investment by the public on a much wider scale. . . . The new directors of these societies authorise advances on mortgage to themselves. In one such society comparatively large sums were spent on advertising and within a period of three years the figure of the assets of the society was increased by over 400 times".[42]

The Registrar made strenuous efforts to curb the activities of these "rogue" societies, by investigations,[43] by orders forbidding them to advertise for funds and by publicising the dangers they presented to the investing public. In his Report for 1954, he wrote, "A disturbing feature . . . in recent years has been the tendency on the part of certain societies to advance substantial sums of money to companies or groups of companies".[44] Consequently in 1956 he altered his requirement regarding the information to be given in the annual return societies made to him; particulars had now to be given ". . . of mortgages where, in respect of any one borrower, there was more than one mortgage and the total indebtedness at the end of the society's financial year exceeded £25,000"[45].

The resulting figures showed that such substantial loans were made by very many societies. While they did not play a significant part in the operations of most ordinary societies, there were a number of cases, including three of the twenty largest societies, where they exceeded $7\frac{1}{2}\%$ of total assets. The response of the "rogue" societies to this attempt to force them to disclose their large loans, was to create chains of subsidiary companies, making only one advance to each. In 1956 one society made, at the same time, twenty-six advances, to a series of companies, each of £9,860.[46]

In 1959 the Registrar moved again, the phrase "one borrower" in the quotation above was now defined to include ". . . companies or subsidiary companies under common control and borrowers acting as nominees for one nominator—an indication is also required in respect of such mortgages where any director of the society or nominee of a director is a borrower or is a partner or shareholder of a borrower".[47]

By this time it was clear that the Registrar needed greater powers if he was to act effectively in curbing these excesses. In February 1959 it was revealed that the Government was considering fresh legislation. However, it took the revelations concerning the State Society, later in the year, to add a sense of urgency to this consideration. The Association had long been preparing for possible changes in the law. In 1954, the Council requested one of its committees to examine the existing laws. By late 1958 the terms of a short Bill had been agreed, which it was hoped would form the basis of legislation for which the Government had promised time during the parliamentary session 1959-60.[48] This hope was overtaken by events.

While a number of individual building society leaders, notably Sir Bruce Wycherly, gave public warnings of the dangers of the activities of certain societies, the Association itself did little, at least openly. It would certainly have been good for the public image and reputation of the Association had it pressed more urgently and publicly for legislation, but it was inhibited by certain fears. The Association's Secretary later commented, ". . . the risk involved in asking for legislation was threefold: the movement might not obtain the legislation which was desired; it might get what was not desired; and a request for legislation might stimulate unfair criticism".[49]

The Government's Bill was introduced in the Lords in March 1960. The resulting Act, the Building Societies Act 1960, covers many matters other than those which were the immediate cause of its introduction. The activities of the "rogue" societies are controlled by the first two sections of the Act. "Special advances" must not exceed 10% of the total advances made by a society in any one year. A "special advance" is defined as any advance of over £5,000,[50] or an additional advance which raises a mortgagor's total debt above £5,000,[50] or any advance to a limited company. Where more than 10% of a society's funds are already advanced in these ways, the Act limits its ability to make special advances still more closely, so that eventually no society will have more than 10% of its assets so applied. The Registrar has power to relax the limits in certain circumstances, such as to encourage the financing of houses to let.

The creation of new societies is made more expensive; at least ten people are required to invest £500 in the society and not withdraw it for at least five years. No new society can advertise without first getting the permission of the Registrar. No application for such permission may be made until the Registrar has had at least one annual return from the society, to enable him to judge the nature of its business (Sections 3, 4 and 5). Where the Registrar feels that the character of the business of a small society is being changed he can insist that its directors have £5,000 of their own money at risk in the society (Section 9). The Registrar's powers over existing societies are considerably increased. Not only can he stop a society inviting the public to subscribe funds, he can prevent a society from accepting any money offered to it. Further he has power to effectively censor the content of advertisements, and can require a society, against which a stop order has been issued, to use a proportion of its return flow of money to repay investors (Sections 6, 7 and 10).

Section 11 gives the Registrar powers to make regulations concerning the way in which societies must invest surplus funds;[51] an attempt to prevent a recurrence of situations such as that of the Scottish Amicable Society in 1958. Where a society is in difficulties, for instance has insufficient funds to meet a sudden increase in applications for the withdrawal of money by investors, another society may now lend money to it, with the consent of the Registrar (Section 12). Societies may now use part of their funds to make contributions to mutual guarantee funds or other insurance schemes to protect investors (Section 21).

As in the case of the 1939 Act, the section dealing with valuations was hotly contested by societies. As originally drafted this section (Section 14) would have made it illegal for directors to undertake valuations. Eventually existing directors were allowed to continue making valuations, with the annual consent of general meetings of the society concerned, for up to ten years. The section makes other provisions in an effort to separate the function of valuing a property from the function of judging what advance should be made on that property. A register must be kept of the value placed on each property and the name of the person making the valuation.

Sections 14–20 make minor alterations in the types of security on which advances can be made and in the method of discharging mortgages. More important, the Registrar is given power to amend the types of collateral security which societies are permitted to accept. This section probably raises hopes that, with suitable amendments, the pool deposit system may be resurrected.

Sections 22–37 are concerned with various aspects of the relations between members and societies. At some points the effect is to make mandatory, on all societies, patterns of members' rights that already exist in certain societies; at other points quite new rights are established. A copy of the accounts of a society must be given to all new shareholders and depositors; annually to shareholders with £25 or more invested and to any other shareholder or depositor on request. The rules of all societies must contain provisions concerning the calling and holding of meetings and voting rights of members; and state how members may requisition a meeting. Meetings must not be called with less than twenty-one days notice or more than fifty-six, and notices must be sent to all holders of £25 or more in shares. In the case of special resolutions, i.e. those requiring a three-quarters majority to be effective, all members must receive a notice of the meeting at which such resolutions will be moved and the text of the special resolutions. All members have the right to vote by proxy when a poll is taken and also the right to demand a poll, provided they have the support of nine others. Each society must keep a register of the names and addresses of members, which members may inspect, by right in certain circumstances, such as the society being in arrears with interest payments; and otherwise, providing they can convince the Registrar that allowing them to do so will serve the interests of the society as a whole.

Sections 38-49 deal with the duties of directors in supervising the management of a society; the auditing of accounts and their presentation to the annual general meeting and the qualifications, appointment and retirement of auditors. The auditors' certificate is strengthened (Section 51) by extending the matters on which auditors are required to report. The Registrar is given power (Section 40) to make regulations concerning the form and content of the revenue and appropriation account and the balance sheet, both of which must be presented to the annual general meeting. Provisions relating to the annual return societies must make to the Registrar are made in Sections 50, 51 and 54. This return must show details of all advances to directors and officers and to companies in which they have an interest. Directors must also declare to their fellow directors any interest they have in any contract or proposed contract with the society (Section 52). Where a society nominates the company with which a mortgagor must insure, in respect of an indemnity, fire, etc., insurance policy, it is unlawful for a director or officer to receive any commission on that insurance (Section 55).

Unions and transfers of engagements are dealt with in Sections 56 and 57. Directors must send to all members of the societies concerned a statement, approved by the Registrar, of the financial position of those societies and details of any compensation that directors will receive, as a result of the union or transfer. The Registrar has power to exempt a society from these requirements. The remaining sections deal with penalties for certain offences—penalties under this Act are a good deal more severe, in general, than is the case under earlier Acts—definitions and some miscellaneous matters.

The Act[52] attempted to close the various avenues, which had been used in certain cases, to operate building societies in the interests of directors and their associates rather than in the interests of members.

The Act uses three means to achieve this end. First, by legislating in some detail about the way in which societies should be managed, certain types of conduct (such as advancing most of a society's funds to a property company, as the State and other societies had done) were made illegal. Second, the rights of members were extended to ensure that if they were concerned about the way in which a society's affairs were being conducted, they could effectively intervene. The rules of societies could no longer be silent on such matters as the right of members to call meetings. Further, the necessity for a society now to keep a register of members at last made it possible for a member to contact his fellow members, with a view to getting their support to change the course of a society's business. To the same end various sections of the Act attempt to see that members have sufficient information about the nature of a society's business, to judge whether it is in accord with their wishes.

While it is certainly important to give members such rights of intervention, it would be as optimistic to hope that members would generally take a close interest in a society's affairs, as it would be pessimistic to fear in general the consequences of their not doing so. Most building society assets are held by societies with huge memberships, over 100,000 in some cases, not many of whom have more than a few hundred pounds invested. In such circumstances few people will have sufficient interest to examine the policy of the board closely; if they disagree with that policy, the difficulties of organising an opposition party among so diffuse a membership, are so immense that such interested members are likely to withdraw their shares, rather than attempt it.

Building society boards are for all practical purposes self perpetuating groups.[53] Because it is so difficult for shareholders to exercise control, the Registrar has to assume the role of shareholders' representative.

Thus the third approach of the 1960 Act was to greatly extend the powers of the Registrar. Efforts were made during the parliamentary proceedings to give societies a right of appeal against certain of his decisions. While these efforts failed in general, they did succeed, in so far as the Registrar was required to inform a society in writing of the reasons why he is taking certain actions: e.g. forbidding a society to advertise for funds. This makes it easier for a society to judge whether the Registrar has good grounds for the proposed action, and also easier to raise in the Courts the question of whether the Registrar has acted in accordance with the precepts of natural justice.[54]

Section 21 of the Act was an invitation to the Association to create a mutual guarantee fund for the further protection of investors, but no action has yet been taken under it. The wide disparity in the size of member societies means that more than half of the income of such a fund would probably be contributed by a handful of members. The creation of such a fund would be unlikely to increase the confidence of investors in these very large societies; it is the smaller societies that would be the main beneficiaries. In these circumstances it is unlikely that the Association will take any initiative in setting up a guarantee fund. However, if a large group of the smaller societies were to establish a fund, it might considerably increase the attractiveness of their shares. Given that many small societies have more than average reserve ratios, they could afford to subscribe to a guarantee fund, without weakening their individual balance sheets very much.

The Association has taken action under Section 12 of the Act, which allows one society to come to the aid of another society in difficulties. "The Council has set up a plan to enable this section to be implemented in the unlikely event of any member society being under pressure due to exceptional withdrawals. This will result in financial assistance being quickly forthcoming from other member societies to tide it over its difficulties."[55] To further such action, in 1964 it was made a condition of membership of the Association, that any society receiving written notice from the Registrar that he intended to revoke its trustee status or contemplated an investigation of its affairs, must inform the Association within forty-eight hours.[56]

The course of building society affairs over the last hundred years has followed an oddly repetitive pattern. Ignoring the decade of the First World War, there has been a major crisis every twenty years, and four of these five crises have resulted in legislation. The basic cause of the 1874 Act was that a building society practice (borrowing on deposit) which everyone had assumed to be within the law, was challenged in the Courts. The second major Act, in 1894, was the result of the speculative activities of certain building society directors, especially those of the Liberator. The third Act, in 1939, was again the outcome of a practice (pool deposits) which was generally and rightly thought to be legal, being made the subject of a Court action. With the latest Act, the cause was again the speculative activities of a few societies.

According to this pattern the next legislation is thus due in about 1980, when some practice—at present widely acceptable—is challenged. The frivolous might well point to the possibility, by that date, of a society owning a whole shopping precinct and of the Courts being asked to decide, whether the fact that the society has opened a branch office in one corner of the precinct, makes the whole operation legal under section 37 of the 1874 Act.[57]

The Building Societies Association was, of course, consulted during the framing of the 1960 Act and many of the Act's provisions originated in suggestions thus made. The Association also exercised an influence on the parliamentary proceedings via the activities of some of its vice-presidents. Indeed in connection with the Act and the various Government measures in the housing field noted above, the Association was engaged in negotiations with the Government for the greater part of the 1950s. It had, however, its domestic concerns to attend to as well.

The most substantial domestic change was made in 1959, when the conditions for membership were revised. There was a good deal of dissatisfaction with the regulation governing trustee status, which made it impossible for societies with total assets of less than £5 million to achieve that status. The Association responded by altering its rules, so that effectively the Registrar's regulations governing the grant of trustee status, became, with the exception of that requiring assets of £5 million, the conditions of membership of the Association. The time allowed by the Association for members to reach the required standards, regarding such matters as reserve ratios, was more generous than the Registrar had allowed. As a result membership of the Association should give the public the same guarantee of security in the case of small societies, that trustee status gives for larger societies.

Since the 1920s the possibility of the Association engaging in advertising campaigns on behalf of the movement generally had been discussed. The question was taken up again in the 1950s and eventually, in October 1957, a collective advertising scheme was started[58] and such advertising has continued each year since then. The expenditure is met by the voluntary contributions of members.

The growth in the size and national importance of building societies has ensured that their actions in relation to a variety of matters: interest rates, the conditions on which mortgage loans are granted, etc., are the subject of comment and criticism in the press and elsewhere.[59] Collective advertising has provided one means of replying to such criticism, which has sometimes been ill informed. Since 1955 the Association has published, about four times each year, *Building Society Affairs*, a pamphlet aimed at informing the public on matters of building society policy, and giving details of the financial position of the movement.

After some years of peace, following the introduction of district representatives in 1947, the Council was again under attack in the late 1950s on the question of its composition. Dissatisfaction was mainly centred on the stability of the membership of the Council.[60] Since the whole body of members votes at the election of members to the Council,[61] any sitting member is likely to be re-elected, for membership of the Council itself provides the main avenue by which a candidate can become nationally known. Indeed in 1957 the Council made a move to reinforce this tendency to re-election. A group of societies might hope to offset the disadvantage of their candidate being relatively unknown, by "plumping" for that candidate. The Council made suggestions that would have proscribed this practice, but dropped them in the face of opposition.[62] In 1959 a resolution from the Midland District requested that a larger proportion of the Council be elected on a district basis. The Council referred this suggestion to a committee and it was quickly decided that no change should be recommended.[63]

The attack was renewed more strongly in 1961,[64] when a resolution originating in the Metropolitan Association was carried, which called on the Council to submit proposals for changes in its constitution. The result was a series of proposals that were put to the 1962 conference. The main proposals were: (1) That the district associations elect sixteen members of Council instead of the current nine. (2) That the district members serve for three-year terms instead of the current one. (3) That members of Council retire on reaching age 70. (4) That the maximum number of co-opted members of Council be reduced from six to four.

A three-quarters majority in favour was necessary for these proposals to become effective and while there were substantial majorities in favour of all four of them, only numbers (3) and (4) above, received the requisite majority.[65] However, as part of a general revision of the Association's rules in 1963,[66] district (now renamed regional) associations were empowered to elect their representative to serve on the Council for three years, or a shorter term if they preferred; the balance between regional and national members was left unchanged. Given that over 60% of members voted to change this balance in 1962, it seems unlikely that the present balance will remain undisturbed.

During the last ten years the Council has exerted almost continuous pressure to reduce the tax burden of societies. This burden falls particularly heavily on the annual surpluses of societies; income tax and profits tax absorb more than half of any surplus. This situation has made it difficult for societies, reluctant to increase the spread between the interest rate paid on investments and that charged on mortgages, to halt the almost continuous fall in reserve ratios. As with so much that affects the affairs of building societies, the rules that govern building society taxation are embedded deep in the past. The development of these tax rules in the nineteenth century was outlined earlier.[67] Two world wars, and the rapid increase in the size of societies, have resulted in certain changes, although the present tax system rests basically on the arrangements first made in 1894. The two alternatives then offered to societies, Arrangements A and B, remained unchanged until rising taxation during World War One led to changes in Arrangement B.

That arrangement provided that at the option of societies, income tax liability of investors, resulting from the receipt of building society interest, could be met completely, by the society paying income tax at the current rate on one-half of the sum it distributed in interest payments. During World War One there was a reduction in the level of income below which people were not liable to tax and also gradations were introduced into the income tax scale. Thus in 1916, while the standard rate of income tax had risen to 5s. od., those with incomes up to £500 paid tax at the lower rate of 3s. od. If taxed individually many building society investors would have been liable to tax at this reduced rate, while the amount of tax levied on societies was still tied to the standard rate. Societies were reluctant to raise the matter with the authorities, partly from feelings of patriotism but also because of uncertainty as to the effect of the reduction in the level of incomes exempt from tax on their tax liability.[68]

In 1916, on the initiative of the revenue authorities,[69] there were negotiations with representatives of the Association. The result was that in future societies opting for Arrangement B, were to pay tax on half the interest distributed at one of the reduced rates—that applicable to unearned income not exceeding £500 per year—instead of at the standard rate. This 1916 settlement looked forward to a more detailed examination of the tax position of building society investors than was possible in wartime. The satisfaction of societies with the new agreement can be inferred from the fact that it led to thirty-seven new members joining the Association.[70]

The proposed examination of the position began in 1920. Societies had first to resist, as they did successfully, the proposal that the special arrangement for building societies should be discontinued. Agreement was not finally reached until October 1921 when it was decided that societies opting for Arrangement A could continue to do so, but no new admissions to this arrangement would be allowed. Those opting for Arrangement B would pay tax, as originally had been the case, at the standard rate on half the interest distributed.

In 1920 there was a threat of further taxation as a result of the introduction in the Budget of a special tax on company profits. The Finance Bill as originally published did not exclude building societies from liability to profits tax. As a result of the efforts of the Association, societies were granted exemption for three years and a further three years exemption was obtained in 1922.[71] In the event the tax disappeared before societies became liable to it.

The next revision of the income tax agreement came in 1924, becoming effective from 1925. The rapid rise in the assets of societies led the revenue authorities, rightly, to suspect that some investors were placing considerable sums with societies, raising the average rate of tax to which members should be liable. The situation was met by excluding interest paid to any investor with more than £5,000 invested in any one society from Arrangement B. Societies had to pay the standard rate of tax on interest paid to such investors. Account was also taken of the fact that limited companies were placing money on deposit with societies.[72] The interest paid to companies was also excluded from Arrangement B and was subject to standard rate. With these exceptions that arrangement was continued on the existing terms.[73] Some tax inspectors had been attempting to levy income tax under Schedule A on the offices of societies,[74] but the 1924 agreement confirmed that these premises were exempt.

The continued rapid growth of societies led to further discussions in 1930. For the first time an attempt was made to establish the true tax liability of building society investors by a detailed examination of a sample of 100,000 cases. This proved a lengthy matter and the draft proposals of a new agreement were not available until 1932, when they were placed before a special meeting of the Association in March. Essentially the existing Arrangement B, with the 1924 exceptions, was continued, but now the whole of the interest distributed was to be taxed, but at only two-fifths of the standard rate. In addition, tax was to be levied at the standard rate on the annual surpluses of societies, which had formerly been exempt. This change considerably increased the difficulties of rapidly growing societies, in their efforts to maintain adequate reserves. As part of the agreement societies undertook to obtain information from those making new or additional investments of £500 or over, to help the revenue authorities to establish whether such investors had total investments in excess of the £5,000 limit. The fact that a husband and wife were regarded as one person by the revenue and two persons by the societies was a source of trouble.[75] The new agreement, no longer Arrangement B, but Document 13A (1932) came into force in April 1932 and was to last for three years. A new investigation of investors' tax liabilities in 1935 led to no substantial change. The income tax rate for societies—the composite rate—was set at 1s. 8d., the standard rate then being 4s. 6d. The proportion between the two rates was to remain the same, in the event of any change being made in the standard rate. The new agreement was to last for four years and could be continued thereafter.[76]

During World War Two, the composite rate rose rapidly, reaching nearly 5s. 0d. in 1940 and eventually rising to 6s. 0d. Instead of being related only to the standard rate, lower rates in the tax structure also influenced the composite rate. Thus in August 1940 it was set at a proportion ($\frac{42}{90}$) of the standard rate of 8s. 6d., plus one-quarter of the difference between the reduced rate, 5s. 0d., and half the standard rate, making a total 49·85 pence.[77] When personal allowances were reduced in 1940, the resulting tax increase was credited to tax payers, and was to be repaid by the Treasury at some convenient date after the war. Since building societies paid tax on behalf of all their investors as a group, they too received "post-war credits", for part of their increased tax bill. The total of these credits held by societies eventually rose to nearly £2½ million before the scheme was discontinued. Building societies as a result of their special income tax arrangements were the only corporate bodies to receive these post-war credits. Personal holders of credits began to be repaid in 1954 as they reached retirement age, a criterion scarcely applicable to corporate bodies. Thus building societies became possessed of holdings of what might reasonably be called zero per cent Consols. A concession in 1959 meant that these credits would accumulate from that date at 2½% per annum. Eventually in 1962 the Treasury agreed to begin repayments to societies and since by that date 60% of personal holdings had been repaid, it was agreed that the same proportion of the societies' credits should be repaid.[78]

After the war, the composite rate fell, as income tax rates were reduced, reaching a low point of 4s. 3d. in 1948. The high level of post-war income taxation has ensured that the composite rate remained much higher than in pre-war days. Another factor has also been operative. As a result of the general rise in money incomes, the average tax liability of building society investors has increased, so that the composite rate has been a much higher proportion of the standard rate than was previously the case. This had led to some questioning of the utility of continuing the special tax arrangements of societies. Obviously, as the composite rate rises, building society investors with incomes so low as to attract little or no income tax, suffer a greater loss of interest as a result of these special arrangements. Equally the attraction of investing in a building society is weakened for those who are liable to income tax at the standard rate. Doubts about the equity of the "composite rate system" are not new; rising tax rates during World War Two produced protests on this score, especially from Walter Harvey.[79] These protests met little response. That societies generally approved of the existing system was demonstrated again after the war, when the Association strongly resisted the Board of Inland Revenue's suggestion that the special arrangements be discontinued:[80] indeed the outcome of the discussion was that statutory recognition was given to the arrangement, after fifty-seven years, in the Finance Act of 1951.

The advantages of the existing system are not as great, from the Board's point of view, as they once were. The liability for tax of the vast majority of building society investors has now to be assessed by the Board, irrespective of their receipt of interest. If the special arrangement were abolished the repayments of tax that would become necessary would involve extra work. However, the extra work would have been much greater, proportionately, if the special arrangements had been abolished in, say, 1920, when the resulting claims for repayment would have been the only contact of many investors with the authorities. None the less, to have to undertake an investigation of only a sample of building society investors' tax returns and negotiate with the Association must represent a saving compared with dealing separately with nearly $5\frac{1}{2}$ million interest payments by building societies.

Looked at from the societies' point of view, the question of whether the special tax arrangements are worth continuing is simpler. Ignoring considerations of equity, the important issue is whether such a change, which would increase the effective interest rate offered to investors paying low rates of income tax, would stimulate the inflow of funds more than the reduction in the effective rate, offered to those liable to the standard rate, would reduce that inflow. The answer would probably not be the same for all societies. Given that large investors are likely to be more sensitive to changes in interest rates, it is probably advantageous for societies to retain the existing system. From the investors' viewpoint, the problem presents itself most sharply when a person with a modest investment in a society retires from work, with a consequent sudden fall in his liability to income tax. Whether such investors respond by withdrawing their money from building societies is a question which those societies can easily answer.

In addition to income tax, building societies are also liable to profits tax, which originated as the National Defence Contribution in the 1937 Finance Bill. This was a levy of 5% on all profits, to last for five years to help pay for the rearmament programme. It seemed that for building societies which would be taxed on the whole of their income, less management expenses, the burden would be considerable. In June 1937, the Association appointed a deputation to meet the Chancellor of the Exchequer.[81] These representatives felt it would not be expedient to try and get complete exemption from the tax for building societies. The

Chancellor accepted that societies were in a special position compared with other trading concerns, but felt that to levy the tax only on building society surpluses would be to concede too much. The representatives were asked to suggest a formula giving a yield acceptable to both sides. In July a hastily convened meeting of the Council approved an offer that involved a tax of 1½% on the whole income of societies, less management expenses, and this offer was accepted by the Treasury.

As a result of the war, the National Defence Contribution was continued beyond the originally envisaged five years and in 1947, renamed profits tax, it became a more permanent part of the tax structure. The rate of tax levied on societies changed from time to time as a result of changes in the rate of profits tax. In 1958 the method of assessing societies for profits tax was changed, the interest paid to investors as well as management expenses were deducted from total income to determine the tax base, on which profits tax was to be levied at the same rate as for all other concerns. At the rate of tax then in force (10%) this change resulted in a substantial fall in profits tax payable, but subsequent increases in the rate of tax nullified this gain. As far as building societies are concerned, profits tax is essentially a tax on any surplus allocated to reserves and since reserve ratios for the movement generally have fallen considerably since the War, strenuous efforts have been made by the Association, in Parliament and elsewhere, to exempt societies from profits tax. So far these efforts have been unsuccessful.

A minor irritant was added in 1962, the tax on short-term capital gains. Gains realised on the sale of securities within six months of their purchase became liable to tax at the standard rate. Although building societies hold securities to ensure that they have adequate liquidity in much the same way as banks, the latter were excluded from liability to the tax, while building societies, in spite of the efforts of the Association, were not.

Chapter Fifteen

BUILDING SOCIETIES AND THE CAPITAL MARKET*

BUILDING SOCIETIES have always had to face competition from other institutions in their efforts to attract the savings of the public and, with the passage of time, the number of such competitors has increased. In particular the variety of investments offered by the National Savings Movement has grown a good deal since 1913. More recently the hire purchase finance houses and unit trusts have entered the field, widely advertising their attractions to investors. Table XXVII compares the progress of building societies with certain other institutions, showing that its growth rate has been much more rapid. The friendly societies, trustee

TABLE XXVII

The Growth of some Savings Institutions, 1903-63

£ million	1903	1913	1923	1938	1948	1963	A	B
Building Societies	66	66	125	759	1,038	4,331	65	4·2
Post Office S.B.	146	187	273	524	1,970	1,793	10	0·9
Trustee Savings Banks	52	69	103	243	764	1,591	23	2·1
Friendly Societies	—	53	80	152	206	260†	5	1·3
Ind. and Provident Societies	40	78	188	361	666	1,179	15	1·8
Collecting Societies	—	11	31*	85	166	340	31	2·0
Industrial Assce. Coys.	26	56	123	359	640	1,297‡	23	2·0
Other Life Assurance Coys.	274	380	—	1,322	1,478	4,240‡	13	3·3
Bank Accts. (Current and Deposit)	—	—	1,674	2,277	5,912	7,971	—	1·3
Defence Bonds	—	—	—	—	1,033	1,122	—	1·1
National Savings Certificates	—	—	445	519	2,104	2,685	—	1·3
Building Society Assets in real terms	113	100	102	647	357	864	—	—

Col. A. The 1963 total divided by the 1913 total, i.e. the growth factor, 1913-63.
Col. B. The 1963 total divided by the 1948 total, i.e. the growth factor, 1948-63.
* 1924;
† 1961.
‡ 1962.

Sources: Board of Trade Statistical Abstracts and Annual Abstracts of Statistics.

Notes on Table XXVII. Building Societies—Total Assets. Trustee Savings Banks includes special investment accounts except in 1903. Friendly Societies—Funds at the end of the year. Ind. & Prov. Socs.—Share capital and deposits in 1903, later years total assets. There is some duplication, with one society investing money in another. Other Life Assurance—Life funds of companies incorporated in the U.K. Banks Accts.—London Clearing Banks. National Savings Certificates include estimated accrued interest.

* *Notes on this chapter appear on page 312.*

savings banks, industrial and provident societies and the industrial life assurance companies, which were all of roughly the same importance as building societies in 1913, have been left far behind; none of them are now more than one-third the size of building societies. In both world wars national savings increased rapidly, but in peacetime this rate of growth has not been sustained. Comparisons over the period since 1948, show that building societies have grown at least twice as fast as their rivals, with the exception of life assurance undertakings.

The progress of building societies is rather less impressive if allowance is made for the changing value of money. For building societies this is best done by dividing the figures for total assets by an index of building costs;[1] and this is shown in the last line of Table XXVII, where comparisons are made on the basis of 1913=100, highlighting the fantastic growth of the inter-war years. Despite the rapid increase in total assets after 1945, societies did not regain, in real terms, their 1938 size until about 1960.

In recent years certain new competitors of building societies have emerged, and details of these are given in Table XXVIII, which also includes the special investment departments of the trustee savings banks.

TABLE XXVIII

Some Building Society Competitors

£ million	1950	1955	1958	1961	1963
Trustee S.B. Spec. Invests.	114	252	354	534	791
Finance Houses, Deposits		63	128	237	371
Local Authority Mortgages		596	973	1,441	2,028
Premium Bonds			216	352	437
Unit Trusts			100	319	353

Sources: Annual Abstracts of Statistics and Financial Statistics.

The progress of these departments has been notable and suggests that interest rates have become a more important factor, with trustee savings bank depositors, in recent years. Hire purchase finance houses do not rely very heavily on deposits from the public; less than 10% of their total deposits came from private persons at the end of 1957,[2] and this figure was about the same in 1963.[3] The decline in the importance of building society deposits noted earlier,[4] may owe something to the growing tendency of companies to place money on deposit with finance houses. Unit trusts are more serious competitors for building societies, since their money is nearly all drawn from the general public.

The increasing importance of local authorities as competitors derives from the restrictions that have been placed on their access to the Public Works Loan Board, especially since October 1955, for funds to finance capital investment.[5] The Radcliffe Committee found that a sample of fifty-six boroughs in England and Wales had, in March 1955, £10·9 million outstanding in mortgage loans from persons; this constituted 8% of all their mortgage loans.[6] By March 1958, the figure was £42·2 million, 20% of the total. The personal element in local authority borrowing, other than on mortgage loans, was small, only £1·4 million in 1958.

On the assumption that these fifty-six authorities are a representative sample of the whole body of such authorities then the total personal holding of local authority mortgage loans was about £190 million in 1958. Precise details of local authority borrowing from persons are not available until 1961; these show that in the three years 1961–63, the total of local authority borrowing from persons rose by £467 million. Clearly a new and keen competitor for the public's savings had emerged. Since local authorities' mortgages offer many of the advantages of building society shares, the above figures probably provide at least part of the explanation of the decline in the net inflow of funds into building societies in 1961 and 1962 after the high figure of £406 million in 1960; see Table XXIX.

The amount of saving that any institution can attract to itself must depend partly on the amount of saving by the public. Table XXIX gives details of gross personal savings and the yearly increase in the funds invested in building societies. Part of the explanation of the growth in building society funds stems from the growth in personal saving. However, the relationship between the two series is not close; the share of total personal saving going to any institution depends also on the attractiveness of the terms that institution offers to investors. There are three aspects of an investment which may attract savers; they are liquidity, security and the rate of return.

TABLE XXIX

Personal Saving and the Growth of Building Societies

£ million	1950	1953	1956	1959	1960	1961	1962	1963
Gross Personal Saving*	104	426	816	894	1,269	1,782	1,631	1,802
Net Investment in B. Socs.	110	157	154	270	406	203	361	497

Sources: National Income and Expenditure (H.M.S.O.) and C.R.R.

* Gross of depreciation and stock appreciation. These estimates of personal saving are liable to wide margins of error.

The ease with which invested funds can be withdrawn has long been one of the attractions that building societies have to offer and the strengthening of branch networks has served to add to this attraction. The importance of the liquidity aspect is borne out by Table XXX. This shows the amount withdrawn, including interest, by shareholders and depositors in certain years, as a percentage of share and deposit liabilities at the end of those years. Building society investors, especially depositors, make extensive use of the liquidity of their investments and the table suggests that this aspect has become a little more important in recent years.

The very high degree of security of money invested in building societies needs no proof; losses in this century (the exceptional case of the Birkbeck Bank apart) have always been very small in relation to funds

TABLE XXX

Withdrawals of Shares and Deposits

Withdrawals as a percentage of year-end balances

	1926	1930	1934	1938	1950	1955	1960	1963
Shares	15	14	10	12	10	13	15	15
Deposits*				24	23	29	28	26

Source: C.R.R.

* Figures are not available before 1937.

invested, and reserves, for societies as a whole, much more than adequate to meet losses. While investments are secure they have, in the nature of things, no prospect of appreciating. Inflation inflicts capital losses, in real terms, just as surely as commercial failures, if less dramatically. It would be surprising if the public did not move to protect its investments from losses through inflation. The growth of unit trusts no doubt owes a good deal to such fears. Recently this growth also owes something to another factor, the combination of life assurance with unit trust investment. There are clear possibilities here for building societies to combine life assurance with subscription shares, enabling subscribers to take advantage of the favourable tax treatment of life assurance premiums.

The third aspect of inter-institution competition concerns interest rates. Something of the sensitivity of building society investors to the rates of interest offered by societies and others is shown in Chart I. The continuous lines show the increase from year to year, in building society liabilities to holders of shares and deposits. The broken lines show the difference between the rate paid on building society shares, grossed up to include income tax at the standard rate, and the yield on Consols. If investors are sensitive to the relationship between building society rates and other rates, the two lines should move together, with societies growing more rapidly when they offer more attractive interest rates. Before 1939 the fit between the two series is fair, remembering that between 1930 and 1932, had investors wished to take advantage of the favourable rates offered by societies, they could not do so freely, because severe restrictions were placed on the amount of new money societies were prepared to accept. After the war the two series move well together. Again there were some restrictions on new investment until about 1950.

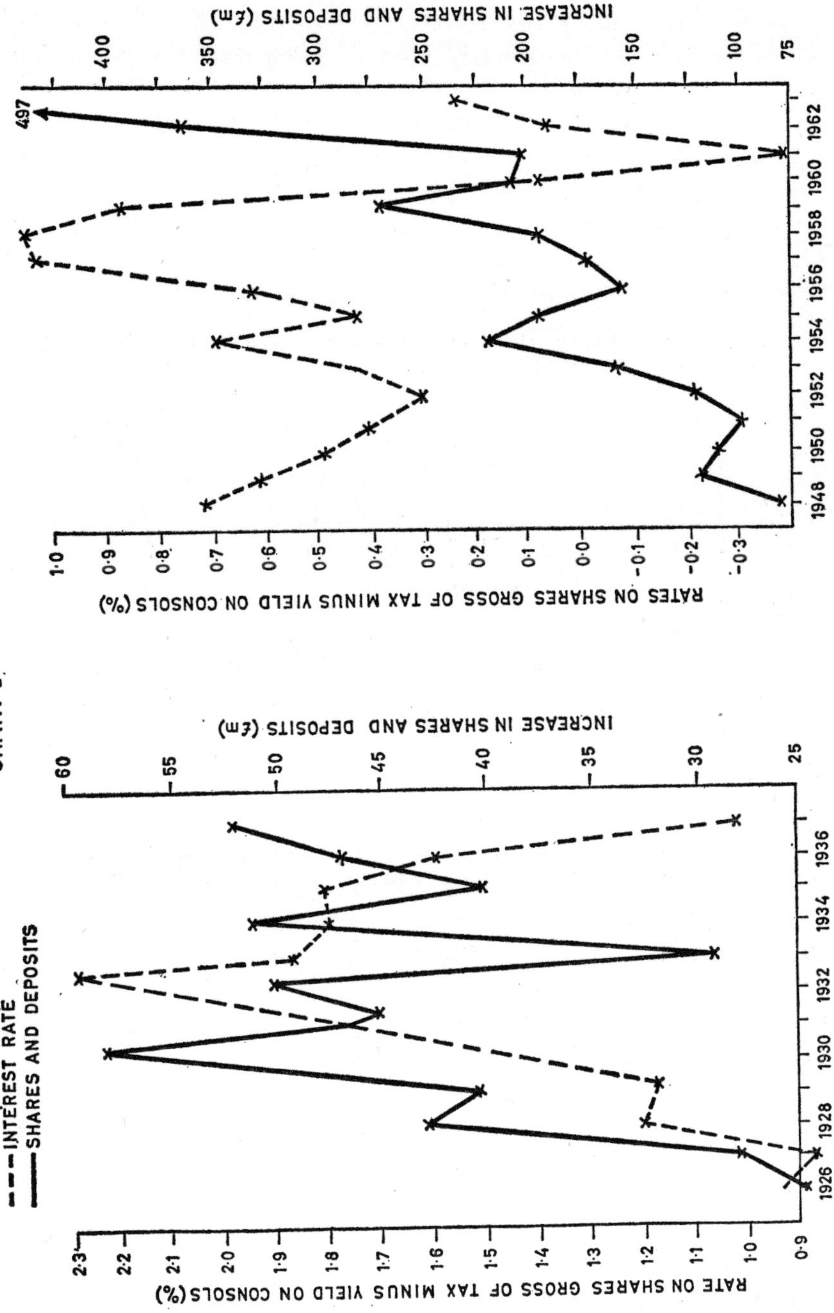
INCREASE IN SHARES AND DEPOSITS (£m)
RATES ON SHARES GROSS OF TAX MINUS YIELD ON CONSOLS (%)
497
INTEREST RATE
SHARES AND DEPOSITS
RATE ON SHARES GROSS OF TAX MINUS YIELD ON CONSOLS (%)

CHART I

The chart suggests that investors have become rather more sensitive to the rate offered by societies in recent years.

That at least a substantial number of investors are distinctly watchful of the relationship between the rates offered by building societies and others, is clear from Chart II. Here the continuous line traces the quarterly excess of new investment in building societies over withdrawals. The broken line gives the difference between the Building Societies Association's recommended rate on shares, grossed up to include income tax at the standard rate, and the yield on Consols, quarterly average. The relation-

CHART II

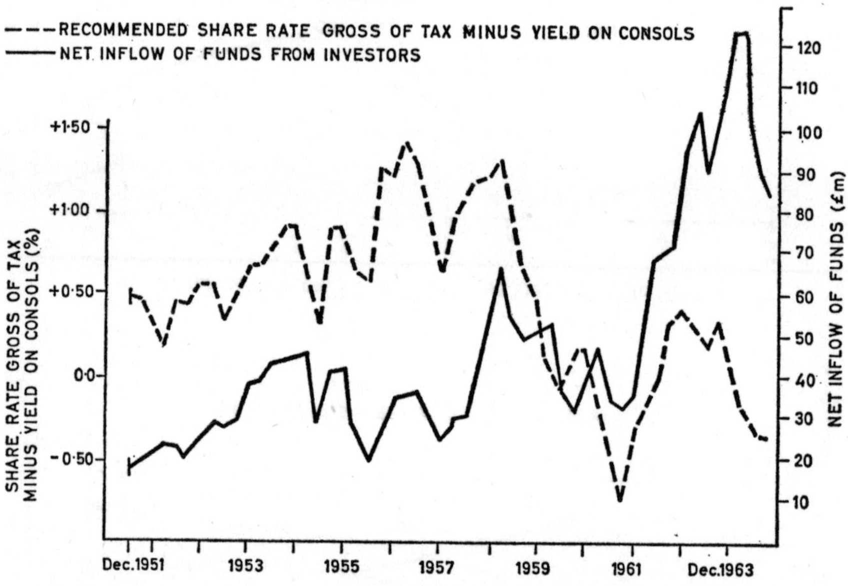

ship between the two lines is very close; they move in the same direction at almost all points, so that quite short run changes in the interest differential are reflected in changes in the net inflow of funds into societies. The share of the public's total saving invested in building societies depends a good deal on whether the interest rate offered is favourable in relation to that offered by competing institutions.[7]

In spite of this sensitivity of building society investors, societies have traditionally not been quick to change their interest rates when rates offered elsewhere are changing. This slow response has been possible because there has been a strong general upward trend in investment in societies. Not all investors move to withdraw funds when rates are unfavourable; indeed, as Chart II shows, even when the yield available elsewhere rises sharply, there is still some net inflow of funds into societies.

Thus the consequence of building society rates being low in relation to competitors is simply a check to their rate of growth. In present circumstances societies can afford to pause to ensure that any movement in interest rates is likely to endure, before they respond to it. However, if societies ceased to grow, then unfavourable relative interest rates would soon result in a net outflow of funds, and this would necessitate a much sharper response from societies.

In the market for mortgage loans building societies have fewer competitors than in the market for investment funds. An estimate of the size of the market for mortgage loans can be obtained by grossing up, at appropriate rates, the product of the stamp duty on mortgage deeds. At the 1947–63 rate of $\frac{1}{4}$%, £1 million received in stamp duty implies mortgage lending of £400 million. Unfortunately the published data on stamp duty receipts are not available for loans on houses as a separate category. The best category is "Houses and Land" which includes mortgages of industrial and commercial properties, as well as houses. Estimates are given in Table XXXI below.

The building societies' main competitors for mortgage business are the insurance companies, local authorities, banks and private persons. In evidence to the Radcliffe Committee the insurance companies estimated that at the end of 1957, 60% of their mortgage assets represented loans for house purchase.[8] On this basis that Committee estimated the net increase in insurance company house purchase mortgages for earlier years. Further details of the insurance companies activity in this field are available from 1962.[9] These show that, as a result of repayment of existing mortgages, the net increase in the insurance company holding of house purchase mortgages was 51% of the total advanced for this purpose in 1962, 32% in 1963 and 38% for the first nine months of 1964. This suggests that the Radcliffe Committee's figures for net advances by insurance companies need to be increased by a factor of 2 or 3, say 2·5, in order to get the yearly total of house purchase advances by insurance companies and this is done in Table XXXI. The contribution of the banks to the mortgage market is uncertain; little is known of the uses to which their loans to persons are put. The Radcliffe Committee did give details of the change in the banks' holding of house purchase mortgages for a few years in the mid-1950s. Local authorities also provide some finance for house purchase under the Small Dwellings Act and later Housing Acts. Table XXXI brings together the flow of funds from these various sources for house purchase.

The proportion of mortgage finance provided by building societies grew steadily during the inter-war years rising, in fact, to 41% in 1938. In the post-war years societies have achieved a still more important position, though their share of the total has fluctuated. In recent years competition from local authorities and insurance companies has increased a little. The high estimated figure for insurance company lending in 1961, gives some support to the Radcliffe Committee's view that these companies tend to lend more when building societies are having to restrict lending.[10]

TABLE XXXI

The Mortgage Market

£ million	1929	1936	1952	1958	1959	1960	1961	1962	1963
Total mortgage transactions*	273	365	556	755	1,073	1,180	1,283	1,395	—
Building Societies	75	140	266	375	517	560	546	613	849
Local Authorities		7	26	51	55	66	99	84	100
Insurance Companies				100	87	168	200	117	107
Banks			−13	22					
Each institution as a % of total:									
Building Societies	27	38	48	50	48	47	43	44	
Local Authorities		2	5	7	5	6	8	6	
Insurance Companies				13	8	14	16	8	

* Financial year beginning April.

The growing importance of institutional lending on mortgage suggests that personal lending on mortgage has declined. There is some direct evidence in support of such a view in the returns of estates subject to death duties in the Annual Reports of the Inland Revenue Commissioners. The total of mortgages held by estates on which duty was levied in the financial year 1938–39 was £13 million; in 1951–52 £12 million; in 1955–56 £10 million, and in 1961–62 £14 million. The raising of the exemption limit for estate duty in 1954 from £2,000 to £3,000 and the downward trend in death rates means that the figures for the later years would need to be raised a little to make them strictly comparable with the figure for 1938. However, the required adjustment would be small compared with the very large increase in the total of all mortgage loans shown in Table XXXI. Clearly private persons are now much less important as a source of funds for mortgage loans.[11] They have been replaced mainly by the expansion of building society lending, though local authorities and insurance companies have also played some part.

NOTES

References to certain sources have been abbreviated as follows:

R.C. 1. First Report of the Commissioners appointed to enquire into Friendly and Benefit Building Societies, with minutes of evidence. H.M.S.O. 1871.

R.C. 2. Second Report of the Commissioners. H.M.S.O. 1872.

R.C. 4. Fourth Report of the Commissioners. H.M.S.O. 1874.

C.R.R. Annual Reports of the Chief Registrar of Friendly Societies. From 1875 to 1894 a separate annual return was made to Parliament concerning building societies. Thereafter the Chief Registrar's work in relation to building societies is published as a separate section of his annual report covering all his duties.

B.S.G. Building Societies Gazette.

CHAPTER ONE

1. P. H. J. H. Gosden, *The Friendly Societies in England, 1815–75*, Manchester, 1961, p. 2.
2. A. Scratchley, *A Treatise on Benefit Building Societies*, London, 1849, p. 5.
3. W. Chambers, *Chambers Social Science Tracts*, No. 5, Edinburgh, 1862, p. 5. "The notion of applying the principle of the menage to a building society appears to have originated in the very high rents often paid by the humbler classes for a dwelling of a very insufficient kind."
4. *B.S.G.*, 1877, December, p. 152.
5. R.C. 4, Reports of Assistant Commissioners, p. 203.
6. The Leeds Building Club (1789) is an example of this type. See S. J. Price, *Building Societies*, London, 1958, p. 50.
7. In 1854 the town had at least nine societies and in 1874, fourteen. In 1886 H. F. A. Davies said that ". . . nowhere else in the United Kingdom is there a town which has so many building societies in proportion to the population as Swansea. . . ". (*B.S.G.* 1886, June, p. 79.)
8. Price, op. cit., p. 23.
9. Price, op. cit., pp. 59-67.
10. Copies of the rules of the following societies are in the Library of the University College of North Wales, Bangor: St. David's B.S., Manchester (formed November 12, 1822); St. John's B.S., Manchester (March 10, 1823); Medlock Friendly Society, Manchester (October 25, 1824); St. George's B.S., Liverpool (July 7, 1825); and Carnarvon B.S. (October 10, 1825). In addition that Library has copies of the rules of four other societies formed soon after the Carnarvon Society, in the same area, as follows: Bangor Benefit B.S. (July 31, 1826); Pentir B.S. (February 20, 1827); Carnarvon Union B.S. (October 10, 1827) and the Eryri B.S. (October 29, 1827). In his work *Happy Homes for Working Men* (Edinburgh, 1866), p. 115, James Begg, D.D., refers to a society at Hamilton and Stonehouse, Lanark, formed about 1820.
11. Societies formed in adjacent towns are grouped, thus Birmingham includes societies formed in Dudley, Wednesbury, Rowley Regis and Kidderminster. Where more than one society was formed in any year, the number of societies formed is given in the bracket.
12. The last two societies for Birmingham in Table II were at Wednesbury and Kidderminster.
13. R.C. 1, Q. 6456. Mr. Hosking was Secretary of a group of Liverpool Societies.

14. Price, op. cit., p. 27.
15. Ibid., p. 30.
16. *Aris's Birmingham Gazette*, February 18, 1782.
17. E. Naylor, *Bradford Building Societies*, Bradford, 1908, p. 22.
18. 15 East K. B. 551.
19. 33 Geo. 3, c. 54.
20. Op. cit., pp. 14, 15.
21. 4 & 5 Will. 4, c. 40, ii.
22. 15 East K.B. 511.
23. Loc. cit.
24. Loc. cit.
25. E. H. Phelps-Brown and S. V. Hopkins, *Economica*, N.S., Vol. 22, p. 205.
26. A. L. Bowley, *Wages in the United Kingdom*, Cambridge, 1900, p. 70.
27. *B.S.G.*, 1881, January, p. 13.
28. Price, op. cit., Ch. III, which gives a full account of the progress of the Longridge Society from its creation in 1793 to its termination in 1804.
29. H. Tompkins, *Building Societies*, London, 1845, p. 3. See also W. Stone, *A Treatise on Benefit Building Societies*, London, 1851, p. 20.
30. H. Bellman, *Bricks and Mortals*, London, 1950, facing p. 16.
31. Price, op. cit., p. 34.
32. *B.S.G.*, 1881, January, p. 13.
33. Naylor, op. cit., p. 16.
34. R.C. 1, Q.6318. W. Ashcroft.
35. Price, op. cit., p. 30.
36. *B.S.G.*, 1901, June, p. 91, citing an article in the *Dudley Herald*, May 18, 1901.
37. Price, op. cit., Ch. III.
38. Naylor, op. cit., p. 14.
39. Price, op. cit., pp. 63, 64.
40. Ibid., p. 61.
41. Naylor, op. cit., p. 64.
42. Price, op. cit., p. 576.
43. Tompkins, op. cit., pp. 4, 5.
44. Price, op. cit., p. 27.
45. Naylor, op. cit., p. 16.
46. Two of the twenty members of the Longridge Society placed their mark on the articles of agreement as did four of the twenty-eight members of the Amicable Society, Birmingham.
47. The St. John's Society, Manchester, allowed withdrawing members interest at 5% p.a.

CHAPTER TWO

1. Petition to Parliament of the St. Stephen's B.B.S., Salford, cited Price, op. cit., pp. 80, 1.
2. R.C. 1, Q. 6456.
3. Naylor, op. cit., p. 20.
4. Hansard Parliamentary Debates, 3rd Series, Vol. XXXII (1836, March 15), cols. 349, 350.
5. House of Commons Journal, Vol. 91, pp. 311, 323, 326, 347, 357 and 366.
6. R.C. 1, Q. 8161.
7. 57. Geo. III, c. 130.
8. R.C. 1, Q. 6456.
9. House of Commons Journal, Vol. 91, pp. 614 and 638.

10. "The original Act was not founded on the report of a select committee and slipped through Parliament unnoticed", R.C. 2, para. 22.
11. "In the Building Societies Act an intention is discernible of confining the interest of members to £150 each, but the language wholly fails to carry this out . . ." ibid., para. 77.
12. This office was created by the Savings Bank Act, 1817. He was originally the barrister appointed by the National Debt Commissioners to certify the rules of Savings Banks. His functions were extended to include the certification of the rules of friendly societies in 1829. His title was changed to Registrar in 1846.
13. Gosden, op. cit., p. 180.
14. "The Act of the 6 and 7 Will. IV, c. 27 read through the practice of the bulk of existing societies and the practice of those societies read through the text of the law, are almost equally unintelligible." R.C. 1, para. 21.
15. R.C. 2, para. 20.
16. Stone, op. cit., p. 19. See also H. F. A. Davis, *Law and Practice of Building and Land Societies*, 3rd ed., London, 1884, p. 4.
17. *Fleming v. Self*, 24 L.J.N.S., Ch., p. 33.
18. R.C. 2, Appendix I.
19. Ibid., para. 8.
20. *The National.* A weekly Family Journal of Politics, Literature, the Fine Arts and Record of Building Societies, 1847, February 6, p. 486.
21. R.C. 1, Q. 3026. W. R. Warner.
22. Loc. cit. J. Higham.
23. Ibid., Q. 4375. See also Q. 4419.
24. Ibid., Q. 7170.
25. Scratchley, op. cit., p. 6.
26. *Fleming v. Self.* 24. L.J.N.S., Ch. p. 40.
27. R.C. 1, Q. 4122.
28. E. von Plener, *English Building Societies*, translated by F. J. Faraday (Manchester, 1875). Dr. von Plener had been First Secretary at the Austro-Hungarian Embassy in London. An earlier work of his concerned English factory legislation. By 1875 he had returned to Vienna and was a member of the Austrian Parliament.
29. 18 L.J.N.S., C.P. 329.
30. See R.C. 1, Evidence of J. Higham, Qs. 3010–3020.
31. R.C. 2, para. 19.
32. R.C. 1, Q. 6150.
33. See *B.S.G.*, 1871, May, p. 40.
34. Tompkins, op. cit., pp. 6, 7.
35. Stone, op. cit., p. 130.
36. 20 L.J.N.S., Exch. 26.
37. R.C. 1, Qs. 2956, 7.
38. Ibid., Qs. 5752–5, W. Austin Lee, Secretary of the Burnley Society.
39. Ibid., Evidence of G. Lee, secretary of a group of Manchester societies. Q. 5859, "Do you mean you have used them [borrowing powers] whether you possessed them or not? A. Yes." See also the evidence of E. W. Brabrook, later Registrar, Q. 3306.
40. Scratchley, op. cit., 1867 ed., p. ix.
41. *In re Durham Counties P.B.B.S.*, 41, L.J.N.S., Ch. 124.
42. R.C. 2, para. 42.
43. 30 L.J.N.S., Ch. 785.
44. Section 1 of the 1836 Act only sanctioned the investment of a society's funds in mortgages.
45. R.C. 1, Q. 3940.
46. Ibid., Q. 5643.

47. Ibid., Q. 3755 and Q. 3972.
48. Ibid., Q. 5206.
49. *Morrison v. Glover*, 19 L.J.N.S., Exch. 20.
50. R.C. 2, para. 43.
51. *Laing v. Reed & others.* 39 L.J.N.S., Ch. 1. The Lord Chancellor said of the case ". . . I confess it appears to me, as I believe it does to the Lord Justice, that this is a bill which has been filed for the express purpose of obtaining the judgement of the Court on a point of law".
52. *In re the National Provincial P.B.B.S.*, L. Rep. 5, Ch. 309.
53. *In re The Victoria P.B.B.S.*, 39 L.J.N.S., Ch. 628.
54. 40 L.J.N.S., Q.B. 145.
55. The Lord Chief Justice's strictures must have seemed a little hard to Messrs. Williamson and Lawson, for Mrs. Richardson's son was the secretary of the Society!
56. R.C. 1, Q. 8234.
57. *In re The Sherwood Loan Coy*, 20 L.J.N.S., Ch. 177.
58. *In re The St. George's B.B.S.*, 27 L.J.N.S., Ch. 96.
59. 33 L.J.N.S., Ch. 520.
60. *In re the No. 3 Midland Counties B.B.S.*, 33 L.J.N.S., Ch. 739. This was the same society.
61. R.C. 1, Q. 3048.
62. *Mosely v. Baker*, 17 L.J.N.S., Ch. 257 (1847).
63. *Fleming v. Self*, 24 L.J.N.S., Ch. 29.
64. *In re The Victoria P.B.B.S.*, 39 L.J.N.S., Ch. 628.
65. W. T. Pratt, *The Law Relating to Benefit Building Societies*, 2nd ed., London, 1865, p. 17.
66. *Card v. Carr*, 26 L.J.N.S., C.P. 113.
67. *Parker v. Butcher*, 36 L.J.N.S., Ch. 552.
68. *Lovejoy v. Mulkerne*, 46 L.J.N.S., Ch. 630 (on appeal).
69. e.g., *Regina v. Evans*, 23 L.J.N.S., M.C. 100.
70. e.g., *Morrison v. Glover*, 15 Q.B. Rep. 103.
71. *Thompson v. Planet B.B.S.*, 42 L.J.N.S., Ch., p. 367.
72. *Dobinson v. Hawkes*, 16 Sim. 407.
73. *Walker v. Giles*, 18 L.J.N.S., C.P. 323.
74. *Morrison v. Glover*, 19 L.J.N.S., Exch. 20.
75. *Cutbill v. Kingdom*, 17 L.J.N.S., Exch. 177.

CHAPTER THREE

Statistical Note to Chapter 3

The House of Commons called for a return of all building societies registered at the end of 1869 and for certain details of their finances. These returns are analysed in Appendix A of the First Report of the Royal Commission on Friendly and Building Societies, 1871. As there was no central register in England and Wales, there were two stages to the process of getting returns. First, clerks of the peace who were responsible for enrolling societies on the court rolls were asked for particulars of all societies entered on those rolls, so that the second stage, distributing a questionnaire to the societies, could take place. The first stage "exemplified in a striking manner the unsatisfactory nature of any system of merely local registration unchecked by central authority".[47] Three counties recorded only the names of societies and elsewhere the amount of detail varied widely. When a set of rules was received, there was no general system of recording whether they were the rules of a new society, or a set incorporating alterations in the rules of an existing society. Both had to be certified by the Registrar and were then passed to the clerks for enrolment. The return showed 5,594 societies (or, more precisely, sets of rules).

There were four counties "which both indicate . . . alterations and are on the whole reliable". Fortunately these four: Lancashire, Middlesex, Stafford and Yorkshire, W.R., were all important centres of building society activity. Of the total entries on the rolls of 5,772, these counties account for 4,326 entries of which 1,713 were alterations to the rules of existing societies. Thus, for these counties a firm total of 2,613 actual societies emerges. Alterations as a percentage of total entries were, Lancashire, 25; Middlesex, 51; Stafford, 28; Yorkshire W.R., 41, giving an overall average of 40%. An unknown number of the 1,446 entries for the remaining counties were alterations. Assuming alterations were as frequent in the rest of the country as in the four counties (i.e. 40%) then the 1,446 entries yield 868 actual societies. This would give a total of 3,481 societies registered under the 1836 Act in England and Wales up to 1869.

The *Building Societies Gazette Directory* for 1874 gives 1,484 as the total number of societies in England and Wales in 1873. Of these 533 were permanents, of which nearly all would have been in existence in 1869. The Directory noted 951 terminating societies in England and Wales in 1873. Terminating societies were declining so there were probably more terminations than new societies formed during the period 1869-73. Thus the number of terminating societies in existence in 1869 was probably about 1,000. Adding this to the estimated 530 or so permanents, it means that of the 3,500 societies registered under the 1836 Act up to 1869, at least 1,500 were still in existence in 1869. To attempt estimates for earlier years requires a finer web of assumption. Assuming that the 500 or so permanent societies extant in 1869 were all that were ever formed—though there must in fact have been at least a few unsuccessful permanent societies—then the maximum number of terminating societies formed over the thirty-three years, 1836-1869 must have been about 3,000, of which about 1,000 were still in existence in 1869. We know that the estimated life of terminating societies was usually about ten years; some societies ran on for much longer, but also some died early. The Liverpool plan on which the London societies of the early 1840s were formed, involved a life of ten years. An even rate of formation of 100 societies a year for thirty years yields 3,000 societies and, with an average life of ten years, yields 1,000 societies at any point of time (after the first ten years). Such a hypothesis is at least consistent with the estimated data for 1869.

We know from Table III that societies were not formed at an even rate. That table will exaggerate the degree of variation, for it is probably a more accurate count of London societies than provincial, and we know that the building society idea arrived late in London, so that the London figures for formations in the mid-1840s are exceptional. While the number of societies in existence around 1850 is enlarged compared with 1869 by the recent formations of terminating societies, it is reduced by the lack of permanent societies at that date.

Taking all factors into account it seems unlikely that the number of societies in existence at any date was more than 1,500 and this figure, given the average life of terminating societies, was probably not reached until the early 1850s.[48] If the number of societies in the directory of 1874 is regarded as a substantial underestimation of the total in existence at that date, this would imply that 1,500 societies would be too high an estimate for the number extant in the 1850s. If an average life of terminating societies greater than ten years is assumed, then the estimate of societies in existence at any date would need to be raised, though a peak would not be reached until later, say 1856 or thereabouts. Even if an average of fifteen years is assumed (and this is surely high when allowance is made for societies registered which fail early) it is unlikely, if a figure of 3,500 societies is accepted as the total formed to 1869, that the maximum societies in existence simultaneously could ever have exceeded 2,000.

Appendix A of the Royal Commission's Report found the returns from societies so inadequate as regards details of their finances as to be not worth the bother of analysing, except as regards the number of members. This was not altogether the fault of the societies, "The resolution upon which the form of return has been framed appears to have been drawn up by someone who had very indistinct ideas as to the constitution of building societies".[49] Regarding membership, the returns from 1,024 existing societies showed an average membership of 207. The words "subscribing membership" were not consistently interpreted: borrowers sometimes, and depositors usually, seem to have been excluded. Taking the actual number of societies to be about 1,500 in 1869, and assuming the societies making returns were representative of the whole, then the total membership of societies would be a little above 300,000. This figure might be regarded as too high because large societies were more likely to make a return than small ones, though in London alone five societies with memberships of over 1,000 each made no return. If 1,500 is too low an estimate of the number of societies, then the estimate of total membership will be correspondingly low.

It is difficult even to make guesses about the relative importance of building societies in financing housing construction. The Royal Commission estimated the total assets of societies in England and Wales at £17 million, by assuming that the 124 member societies of the Building Societies Protection Association, for which the Commission had detailed information, possessed half the total assets of the whole movement. Assets in Scotland were put at £1·5 million and Ireland less than £0·5 million. A rough check that the Commission got at least the right order of magnitude can be made via the detailed figures available for societies in Sheffield. Sheffield showed a wide variety of sizes of societies among its 37 terminating and 12 permanent societies. Borrowers owed the 37 terminating societies £754,000. This total includes future interest and since the usual pattern of terminating societies was to lend only about £60 against total repayments over the years of £120, the actual amount lent by the 37 terminating societies would be only about half the outstanding debt, say, £370,000; an average of £10,000 per society. If the Sheffield societies are taken as a random sample of all the estimated 1,000 terminating societies around 1870, then the total lent by such societies would have been about £10 million.

Sheffield's 12 permanent societies were owed £292,000 by borrowers. This would represent somewhat more than was actually lent, the total being inflated by premiums. The average total of loans by each of the 12 permanents would thus be about £23,000. Again assuming the Sheffield societies to be representative of the whole, then the country's roughly 500 permanent societies would have lent, between them, about £11 million, making a grand total of a little over £20 million.

If the average term of loans was ten years this would mean that societies lent about £2 million per year. Such a figure is probably too low. First, then as now, many people, although contracting to repay their loan over ten years, did in fact repay more quickly. This point would apply more to permanent than to terminating societies. Ten years was certainly a common term, but some societies lent for longer periods.[50] Second, since the movement as a whole was growing, then new loans would exceed repayments. In the light of these considerations let us take £2·5 million as the annual amount lent by societies around 1870.

The next stage in the guessing game is to estimate the number of houses on which loans could be made with the £2·5 million. Information given to the Royal Commission on the average size of advances is not helpful because some of them were on industrial properties; there was also a good deal of borrowing on blocks of houses built to let. The 1836 Act suggests that at that time £150 was regarded as adequate to finance the sort of houses with which building societies were concerned. On the other hand the Rev. T. Thomas told the Royal Commission that £80 was sufficient to build a worker's cottage in Swansea; but not all advances were on workers' cottages. Maiwald[51] estimates that building costs around 1870 were a little over 60% of costs in 1930. The average cost of building local authority three-bedroomed houses in 1930 was about £400,[52] which would suggest a figure of £240 in 1870. Allowance must be made for some rise in housing standards over the years, so that a price per house of £150-200 seems a reasonable figure. Thus if all building society loans went to finance new houses, they would have financed the building of 12 to 18 thousand houses a year in the 1860s.

Weber has estimated[53] that 636,000 houses were built in Britain in the ten years 1861-70, an average of 64,000 houses a year, though the figures in fact fluctuate and increase sharply at the end of the period (1867, 65,300; and 1870, 85,900). Bearing in mind that some building society loans were on industrial properties, building societies, it may be very tentatively suggested, were financing the construction of one house in about every seven or eight built.

1. See note, p. 286.
2. Op. cit., p. 21.
3. Op. cit., p. 6.
4. Op. cit., p. 2.
5. Op. cit. (1869 ed.), p. 4.
6. *The National*, 1847, June 5th, p. 102.
7. *Directory and Handbook of Building and Freehold Land Societies*, London, 1874. Published by the *Building Societies Gazette*.
8. In fact there were at least 4 provincial permanents formed in 1846. The British Savings Fund and B.B.S., in Liverpool the Ramsbury Society, Marlborough, Wilts. the Wakefield Society, and one in Birmingham, see below, footnote, 29.
9. The isolation of this entry suggests that this society started life as a terminating society and later changed its rules to become a permanent one. This also almost, certainly applies to the permanent society in 1844. (See p. 47.)
10. The Scots total includes 35 Building and Investment Associations and Companies. It is not clear whether they were permanent or terminating. Evidence of the managers of a number of them to the Royal Commission suggests the vast majority were in fact permanent.
11. See p. 82.
12. *The National*, 1846, May 9th, p. 138.
13. Ibid., 1846, May 2nd, p. 124.
14. Ibid., 1846, June 27th, p. 226.
15. Ibid., 1846, May 16th, p. 155.
16. Ibid., 1846, May 30th, p. 188.
17. Ibid., 1846, July 25th, p. 269.
18. Ibid., 1846, July 25th, p. 261.
19. p. 35.
20. p. 25.
21. *The Reporter*, 1849, August, p. 155, November, p. 29; 1852, June, p. 122. The first annual meeting of this society was held in October 1849. J. H. James was this society's auditor in 1851.
22. p. 33.
23. See Price, op. cit., pp. 117-122, for a brief biography of Scratchley.
24. Other such Acts were 18 Geo. 2, c. 18 and 53 Geo. 3, c. 49.
25. *Marshall v. Bowen*, 14 L.J.N.S., C.P., 129.
26. *Hoyland v. Bremner*, 15 L.J.N.S., C.P., 133.
27. *Alexander v. Newman*, 15 L.J.N.S., C.P., 134. Five other cases immediately depended on the decision.
28. Stone, op. cit., p. 173.
29. The first permanent society had been founded in Birmingham a year earlier. G. J. Johnson, "On the Benefit Building and Freehold Land Societies of Birmingham", *Journal of the Statistical Society of London*, 1865, p. 507.
30. *The Reporter*, 1849, December, p. 44.
31. R.C. 1, Qs. 3973-5. The working of Taylor's society is described in his evidence, Qs. 3973-91.
32. *The Freeholder*, 1851, September 1st, p. 139.
33. Reprinted in H. Bellman, *Bricks and Mortals*, London, 1949, Appendix 2.

34. *B.S.G.* 1871, May, pp. 34, 35.
35. *The Freeholder*, 1850, January 1st, p. 8.
36. *Rouse's Benefit Building and Freehold Land Society Directory*, London, 1853, p. 53.
37. In its first four and a half years the National's income, net of withdrawals, was £498,000. G. Elkington, *The National Building Society, 1849–1934*, Cambridge, 1935, p. 19.
38. Elkington, op. cit., p. 15.
39. Elkington, op. cit., p. 14. Elkington cites an article in the Edinburgh Review early in 1852 as an example of such attacks.
40. *The Reporter*, 1850, December, p. 38.
41. Elkington, op. cit., p. 27.
42. R.C. 1, Q. 6139.
43. Ibid., Q. 6141.
44. *Mullock v. Jenkins*, 21 L.J.N.S., Ch. 65.
45. J. M. Ludlow and Lloyd Jones, *The Progress of the Working Classes*, London, 1867, p. 126.
46. Davis, op. cit., p. 336. *Robinson v. Dunkley*, 33 L.J.N.S., C.P., 57.
47. R.C. 1, Appendix A, p. 245.
48. *The Building Society Directory and Almanac for 1850*, published by Effingham Wilson (London), listed nearly 1,000 societies and after discussing the shortcomings of its own list estimated that there were in all 1,400 societies currently in operation. (*The Reporter*, 1850, January, p. 59.)
49. R.C. 1, Appendix A, p. 247.
50. See p. 75.
51. K. Maiwald, An Index of Building Costs in the United Kingdom, 1845-1938. *Economic History Review*, Vol. VII (December, 1954), p. 192.
52. M. Bowley, *Housing and the State*, London, 1945, p. 278.
53. B. Weber, A New Index of Residential Construction, 1838-1950, *Scottish Journal of Political Economy*, Vol. II, No. 2.

CHAPTER FOUR

1. Op. cit., pp. 34, 35.
2. Op. cit., 1849 ed., p. 41.
3. *The Building Societies Directory*, H. Brooks, ed., London, 1854, pp. 41, 2.
4. *The National*, 1847, September 25th, p. 21.
5. Davis, op. cit., 4th ed., London, 1887, pp. 16, 17.
6. R.C. 1, Q. 3222.
7. *The National*, 1847, October 30th, p. 51.
8. R.C. 2, para. 18.
9. *Directory of Building Societies*, 1885-6, H. Kent and V. M. Braund, eds., London, 1886, p. 451.
10. Op. cit., p. 42.
11. Op. cit., pp. 8, 9.
12. R.C. 2, para. 44.
13. Von Plener, op. cit., p. 29.
14. R.C. 1, Qs. 7163, 4.
15. Ibid., Qs. 3820 and 3864.
16. Ibid., Q. 5960, S. T. Woodhouse.
17. Ibid., Q. 4709, T. Y. Strachan.
18. Ibid., Q. 3569, W. R. Selway.
19. Ibid., Q. 5964, S. T. Woodhouse.
20. R.C. 2, para. 42.
21. R.C. 1, Q. 3319.
22. Ibid., Q. 2961, J. Higham.

23. R.C. 2, para. 25.
24. *Directory of Building Societies* [published by the *B.S.G.*], 1874, London, p. 11.
25. R.C. 1, Q. 3786, James Taylor.
26. S. J. Price, *From Queen to Queen*, London, 1954, p. 28.
27. Scratchley, op. cit., 1849, ed., p. 99. See also R.C.1, Qs. 6660-63. C. Lund and J. A. Binns.
28. Scratchley, op. cit., p. 73.
29. Tompkins, op. cit., p. 6.
30. R.C. 1, Q. 3094, J. Higham.
31. Op. cit., p. 78 ff.
32. J. McFarlane Gray, *Arithmetic of Building Societies*, Liverpool and London, 1864, p. 22.
33. *Building Societies and Their Traducers* by W., London, 1844, p. 8.
34. Ibid., p. 11.
35. Ibid., pp. 14, 15.
36. Ibid., p. 18.
37. Tompkins, op. cit., p. 6.
38. J. McF. Gray, op. cit., p. 26.
39. *B.S.G.*, May, p. 67.
40. Ibid., 1871, November, p. 142.
41. R.C. 1, Q. 4534, T. Thomas.
42. Ibid., Q. 2851, J. Higham.
43. *Chambers Social Science Tracts*, No. 5, W. Chambers, ed., Edinburgh, 1862, p. 10.
44. R.C. 1, Qs. 5512, 3. S. Andrew.
45. Ibid., Q. 8162, W. L. Harle.
46. Ibid., Q. 6244, W. Ashcroft.
47. Ibid., Qs. 5911, 2, G. Lea.
48. Op cit., p. 73.
49. *B.S.G.*, February 1869, p. 18, and January 1871, p. 7. Evidently sufficient support was forthcoming for the hall, Myddleton Hall, Upper St., was built and opened in January 1871.
50. R.C. 2, para. 47.
51. R.C. 1, Q. 4859, J. Campbell.
52. Ibid., Q. 2952, W. R. Warner.
53. Price, op. cit., p. 32.
54. R.C. 1, Qs. 2911-4, J. Higham.
55. Ibid., Q. 2949.
56. Ibid., Q. 3613, W. R. Selway.
57. Ibid., Q. 2908, J. Higham.
58. R.C. 2, Report of the Assistant Commissioner in Scotland, p. 52.
59. R.C. 1, Q. 4476, T. Thomas.
60. Ibid., Q. 6318, W. Ashcroft.
61. Ibid., Qs. 2918, 9, J. Higham.
62. Ibid., Q. 2929, J. Higham.
63. Ibid., Q. 7786, A. Allott.
64. Ibid., Q. 2933, W. R. Warner.
65. R.C. 2, Q. 12956, W. T. Ross.
66. Ibid., Q. 16308, J. Giusani.
67. R.C. 1, Q. 2923, J. Higham.
68. C. Egan, *The Law Relative to Benefit Building Societies*, London, 1847, p. 45.
69. Scratchley, op. cit., p. 55.
70. Op. cit., p. 61.
71. R.C. 1, Q. 4862.
72. S.C., Q. 1229, T. Fatkin.
73. O. R. Hobson, *A Hundred Years of the Halifax*, London, 1953, p. 27.

74. R.C. 1, Q. 4901, J. S. Parker.
75. Davis, op. cit., 1884 ed., p. 41.
76. R.C. 1, Q. 2994, J. Higham.
77. *The National*, 1846, April 4th, p. 58.
78. Hobson, op. cit., p. 31.
79. R.C. 1, Qs. 5982-89, S. T. Woodhouse.
80. Ibid., Qs. 5063-66, T. Fatkin.
81. R.C. 2, para. 13.
82. "At a later date when the idea [of the society itself doing the building] was revived the combinations were described as Building Clubs, the title 'Building Society' having become inseparably associated with societies which did not build," Naylor, op. cit., p. 35.
83. Scratchley, op. cit., 1867 ed., p. 7, see also Hobson, op. cit., Ch. 6.
84. R.C. 1, Q. 7372.
85. Ibid., Q. 6092.
86. Ibid., Q. 6796.
87. Ibid., Qs. 4301-4.
88. R.C. 2, Report of Assistant Commissioner in Scotland, p. 58.
89. R.C. 1, Q. 6831, J. Ryalls.
90. Ibid., Q. 7090, F. Ingoldby.
91. Ibid., Q. 7381, W. E. Whittingham.
92. R.C. 2, Q. 16304, J. L. le Mert.
93. R.C. 1, Q. 6092, H. J. Phillips.
94. Ibid., Q. 6055, H. J. Phillips.
95. G. Elkington, op. cit., p. 36.
96. R.C. 1, Qs. 5320-28, J. L. Jones and J. B. Reay.
97. Op. cit., 1849, pp. 67, 68.
98. Letter reprinted *The National*, 1846, March 28th, p. 47. See C. Egan, op. cit., pp. 3-6, for a full discussion of this point.
99. R.C. 1, Q. 8193, W. Harle.
100. Ibid., Qs. 7719 and 7895.
101. R.C. 2, report of Assistant Commissioner in Scotland, footnote to p. 7.
102. Stone, op. cit., p. 67.
103. R.C. 1, Q. 7862.
104. Ibid., Q. 2940, W. R. Warner.
105. Ibid., Q. 3101, J. Higham.
106. Ibid., Q. 3578, W. R. Selway and Qs. 8090, 1, F. Ravenscroft, Q. 7940, A. Allott.
107. Ibid., Q. 4029, W. Winterbothom.
108. R.C. 2, report of Assistant Commissioner in Scotland, Appendix, p. 54.
109. R.C. 1, Q. 4463, T. Thomas, Q. 5491, S. Andrew, Q. 6430, T. E. Priest and R.C. 2, report of Assistant Commissioner in Scotland, Appendix, p. 60.
110. R.C. 1, Q. 6503.
111. Ibid., Q. 5224, J. L. Jones.
112. Ibid., Q. 4811, T. Y. Strachan.
113. Ibid., Q. 6073, H. J. Phillips.
114. Between October and December 1870, the average for the Fourth City Mutual was £397 (R.C. 1, Q. 2906). T. Dawson gave the average for the Leeds Permanent as £350 (Q. 5029).
115. R.C. 2, Q. 13, 729, J. Glenn.
116. 17 L.J.N.S., Exch. 177.
117. *The Reporter*, 1849, April, p. 90.
118. Hobson, op. cit., Appendix 2. C. Brooks, *The First Hundred Years*, London, 1947, p. 45. R.C. 1, Q. 4948, J. Parker, Q. 2984, W. R. Warner.
119. R.C. 1, Qs. 3404, 5, E. W. Brabrook.

120. Naylor, op. cit., p. 50.
121. R.C. 1, Q. 2984.
122. Ibid., Q. 5271, J. B. Reay.
123. Ibid., Q. 5879, G. Lea.
124. Ibid., Q. 6672, C. Lund.
125. Ibid., Q. 6241, W. Ashcroft.
126. Ibid., Q. 2991, W. R. Warner.
127. Ibid., Q. 2998, J. Higham.
128. Ibid., Q. 2907, J. Higham.
129. Ibid., Q. 5720, W. A. Lee.
130. Ibid., Qs. 3484-86, E. W. Brabrook.
131. Ibid., Q. 7197. See also Q. 6034, G. Lea.
132. A. Scratchley and E. W. Brabrook, *The Law of Benefit Building Societies*, 2nd ed., London, 1882, p. 4.
133. R.C. 2, Report of Assistant Commissioner in Ireland, para. 22.
134. R.C. 1, Q. 3259.
135. Ibid., Q. 3077, W. S. Hoare.
136. Ibid., Q. 7118.

CHAPTER FIVE

1. J. M. Ludlow, Chief Registrar 1875-91, wrote, "framed as it was almost exclusively in the interest of the committees of the larger societies the Act of 1874 . . .", *Economic Review*, 1893, January, p. 72.
2. R.C. 1, Qs. 8161, 8162.
3. *The National*, 1847, February 6, p. 486.
4. Letter from Thomas Kergh, Assistant Secretary to the Board. *The National*, 1846, June 13, pp. 213, 214.
5. *The National*, 1846, August 8, p. 278.
6. Ibid., 1846, March 14, p. 10.
7. See below, Ch. 6.
8. *The National*, 1846, June 13, p. 214, and June 20, p. 319.
9. Ibid., 1846, July 25, p. 262.
10. Ibid., 1846, July 18, pp. 252, 253.
11. Ibid., 1848, February 26, p. 196; March 4, p. 205.
12. Ibid., 1849, January 20, p. 3. Half-yearly report of the Institute.
13. Ibid., 1849, January 20, p. 4 and January 27, p. 15.
14. Ibid., 1849, February 17, p. 56.
15. 18 L.J.N.S., CP 323. Giles was a trustee of the 3rd Temperance B.B. Association, London.
16. This case raised the issue more directly. It was "an action for use and occupation brought by the trustees of a building society against a tenant of mortgaged premises, and the mortgage deed was objected to on the ground that it had no stamp at all", 18 L.J.N.S., CP. 330, n.
17. Stone, op. cit., p. 135.
18. Stone, op. cit., p. 136.
19. *The Reporter*, 1849, December, p. 43.
20. Ibid., 1850, June, p. 144.
21. *B.S.G.*, 1869, March, p. 46.
22. Price, *Building Societies*, discussing the group, referred to by Higham, gives F. Davies, not R. Jesserun, as its secretary but unfortunately does not give the source of his information. In spite of this it seems to be the Institute that Price has in mind, for of the five men he refers to, as members of the group, three were reported as taking part in meetings of the Institute and one of them, E. J. Southwell, was for a time

joint secretary with Jesserun. (*The National*, 1848, July 22, p. 158.) Possibly Davies either acted as secretary at preliminary meetings before the formal organisation was created, or took over as secretary later. The latter possibility is unlikely for *The Reporter* makes no note of such a change at least up to February 1851, by which time the Institute was probably defunct.

23. Hansard, *Parliamentary Debates*, 3rd Series, Vol. CXXXVII (April 22, 1855), col. 1934. James Wilson, Financial Secretary to the Treasury.
24. Hansard, *Parliamentary Debates*, 3rd Series, Vol. CXXXIX (June 26, 1855), col. 118.
25. *Liverpool Courier*, 1855, July 18, p. 265.
26. *B.S.G.*, 1884, October, p. 129. Letter from T. E. Priest, who gave evidence, with J. Hosking, first chairman of the Liverpool Association, to the 1871 Royal Commission.
27. R.C. 1, Q. 6578. J. Hosking.
28. Hansard, *Parliamentary Debates*, 3rd Series, Vol. CXXXIX (June 26, 1855), col. 119.
29. E. Naylor, *History of the Building Societies Association 1869–1914*, London, 1915, published as an annex to the Annual Report of the B.S.A. for 1915, p. 71.
30. Naylor, op. cit., pp. 71, 72.
31. Price, op. cit., pp. 144-7.
32. R.C. 1, Q. 6638.
33. Naylor, op. cit., p. 73.
34. *B.S.G.*, 1869, May, p. 72.
35. See above, p. 37.
36. *B.S.G.*, 1869, September, p. 140.
37. Naylor, op. cit., p. 75.
38. e.g. *In re National Permanent B.B.S.*, L.R. 5, Ch. 309.
39. Naylor, op. cit., pp. 77, 78.
40. *B.S.G.*, 1870, July, pp. 99-102.
41. Price, op. cit., p. 195.
42. Naylor, op. cit., p. 79.
43. *B.S.G.*, 1871, September, p. 104.
44. R.C. 2, para. 19.
45. Ibid., para. 35.
46. Ibid., para. 36.
47. Ibid., para. 46.
48. Ibid., para. 53.
49. Ibid., para. 54.
50. Loc. cit.
51. In 1869 one of the two or three largest societies, the Planet, had promoted a private bill to vacate its registration under the 1836 Act and gain incorporation as a joint stock company, but the bill did not succeed. *B.S.G.*, 1869, December, pp. 192, 193.
52. R.C. 2, para. 68.
53. Ibid., para. 72.
54. Ibid., paras. 74-76.
55. Ibid., paras. 87-89.
56. Ibid., paras. 121-125.
57. Ibid., paras. 92-95.
58. Ibid., paras. 102-113.
59. Ibid., paras. 115-118.
60. Ibid., paras. 122-124.
61. *B.S.G.*, 1872, February, pp. 18-22.
62. Ibid., 1872, June, pp. 66, 67.
63. Ibid., 1872, July, p. 98.
64. Ibid., 1872, August, p. 119.
65. Ibid., 1872, March, p. 41.

66. Ibid., 1873, February, p. 24.
67. Naylor, op. cit., p. 87.
68. *B.S.G.*, 1873, June, p. 85.
69. Naylor, op. cit., p. 88.
70. *B.S.G.*, 1873, August, p. 118.
71. Ibid., 1873, September, p. 132.
72. Ibid., 1873, September, p. 133.
73. Cited *B.S.G.*, 1873, September, p. 134.
74. Ibid., 1873, November, p. 167. Letter from Messrs. Robarts and Hosking.
75. Ibid., 1873, August, pp. 122, 123.
76. Ibid., 1873, November, p. 167.
77. Ibid., 1873, December, p. 184.
78. Ibid., 1874, January, p. 5.
79. Naylor, op. cit., p. 91.
80. Hansard, *Parliamentary Debates*, 3rd Series, Vol. CCXIX (June 16, 1874), cols. 1743, 1744.
81. A. Scratchley and E. W. Brabrook, *The Law of Benefit Building Societies*, 2nd ed., London, 1882, p. 20.
82. *B.S.G.*, 1874, November, p. 146.
83. Ibid., 1874, November, p. 148.
84. Ibid., 1874, November, p. 157.
85. The Commission's recommendation that such societies should not be allowed to borrow was also ignored.
86. R.C. 2, para. 129.
87. *B.S.G.*, 1875, August, p. 99.

CHAPTER SIX

1. Bowkett, *Freehold Property for Mechanics*, p. 7.
2. Bowkett, *The Bane and the Antidote*, p. 334.
3. Bowkett, op. cit., p. 301.
4. Loc. cit.
5. Op. cit., p. 17.
6. Op. cit., p. 34.
7. *The National*, 1846, May 23, p. 162. See also the issue for 1846, April 4, p. 162, for an account of a slanging match at a public meeting between Bowkett and J. MacArthur.
8. Ibid., 1846, May 16, p. 146.
9. R.C. 1, Q. 4119.
10. Ibid., Q. 4126.
11. "If there be no other way let 1,000 men subscribe ½d. a week each that 50 or 100 of their number may be made freeholders and let all rejoice with their brothers whom they have made to rejoice. But let no man excuse himself with the plea that the rich will not help him." *Freehold Property for Mechanics*, p. 14.
12. Starr, in evidence, in *Starr v. Hardy*, reported *B.S.G.*, 1882, December, pp. 158-162.
13. In a preface to *Rules of a Starr-Bowkett Building Society*, London, January 1890, Starr refers to the 26th yearly balance sheet of his first society. In his evidence in *Starr v. Hardy* cited above, he said his first society was founded in 1859, but if this was so, progress must have been very slow at first for a *Directory of Building Societies*, 1885-86, H. Kent and V. M. Braund (eds.), London, 1885, gives 1863 as the founding date of the 9th Starr-Bowkett and 1864 for the 20th.
14. Kent and Braund, op. cit., give the founding date of the 165th as 1874.
15. C.R.R., 1892, p. 49.
16. *B.S.G.*, 1891, June, p. 95.

17. C.R.R., 1875, p. 2.
18. *B.S.G.*, 1869, March, p. 41.
19. R.C. I, Q. 4204.
20. Evidence in *Starr v. Hardy* cited above.
21. *B.S.G.*, 1882, January, pp. 4, 5, citing a letter from Starr to a prospective secretary.
22. Ibid., 1886, April, p. 57, citing evidence in *Starr v. Greenwood*, Queen's Bench Division, March 26, 1886.
23. Ibid., 1890, January, p. 5, citing evidence in *Starr v. Wall*, Q.B.D., December 11, 1889.
24. J. M. Ludlow, *Economic Review*, January 1893.
25. R.C. I, Q. 4231, T. E. Bowkett.
26. Hansard, *Parliamentary Debates*, 3rd Series, Vol. CCCXXXVIII (July 18, 1889), cols. 706, 707.
27. *Wallingford v. The Mutual Society*. 50 L.J., H.L. 50. The Mutual Society was not a Starr-Bowkett, but lots were drawn for appropriations, and part of Wallingford's case was that such a procedure was contrary to one of the Lottery Acts. Selborne L.C.J. commented "in my judgement this was not a gambling transaction within the meaning of that Act".
28. *B.S.G.*, 1881, December, p. 164.
29. E. W. Brabrook in a lecture to some accountancy students, ibid., 1887, September, p. 11.
30. Ibid., 1881, December, p. 161.
31. Ibid., 1882, April, p. 59.
32. R. B. Starr, *Why Pay Rent?* No date, a pamphlet.
33. Evidence given in *Starr v. Wall* cited above.
34. *B.S.G.*, 1869, July, p. 108.
35. C.R.R., 1908 and 1909. In 1908, seven of the eight new building societies formed in New South Wales were Starr-Bowketts.
36. International Union of Building Societies, *Proceedings of the Ninth Congress*, London, 1963, p. 53.
37. *B.S.G.*, 1895, February, p. 27.
38. Ibid., 1882, February, pp. 24, 25, and May, p. 88.
39. Op. cit., p. 185.
40. *B.S.G.*, 1882, January, p. 10.
41. Ibid., 1885, October, p. 126.
42. Ibid., 1880, January, p. 7. Letter from a correspondent.
43. Ibid., 1882, July, p. 112. See *B.S.G.*, 1883, January, p. 27, for a description of one such angry meeting.
44. e.g. *Starr v. Greenwood* and *Starr v. Wall*, cited above and *Starr v. Buckley*, *B.S.G.*, 1886, August, p. 101.
45. S.C., Q. 3993, W. H. Pearce.
46. *Rules of a Starr-Bowkett Society*, London, 1885.
47. Connor described his method of operation to the Select Committee of 1893, see his evidence Qs. 3484-3658.
48. Letter from J. W. Campbell, *B.S.G.*, 1890, February, p. 19, where further details of these societies are given.
49. *B.S.G.*, 1889, February, p. 19.
50. Ibid., 1883, August, p. 110.
51. S.C., Qs. 4318-4430.
52. C.R.R., 1884, p. 46.
53. C.R.R., 1886, pp. 54, 55.
54. C.R.R., 1891, p. 37.

55. Details of these societies were given to the Select Committee by Horsley, Qs. 3795-4110.
56. *B.S.G.*, 1892, July, p. 104.
57. Ibid., 1891, August, p. 124.
58. S.C., Qs. 3280-3283.
59. Evidence elsewhere (see above p. 109) suggests that the first "Models" and "Self Helps" were formed in 1882. Possibly some societies had been formed but were not registered until 1883.
60. Including ballot and sale societies.
61. In 1890 incorporated societies had total assets of £51·5 million and 646,000 members.
62. *Journal of the Statistical Society of London*, 1885, p. 48. Commenting on a paper by E. W. Brabrook.
63. Loc. cit., p. 50.
64. *B.S.G.*, 1890, November, p. 170.
65. S.C., Q. 40, E. W. Brabrook.
66. E. W. Brabrook, *Building Societies*, London, 1906, pp. 136-137.
67. See his article in the *Economic Review*, 1893, January, and his evidence to the Select Committee, Qs. 510-607.

CHAPTER SEVEN

1. K. Maiwald, An Index of Building Costs in the United Kingdom, 1845–1938, *Economic History Review*, Vol. VII, December, 1954, p. 192.
2. E. Naylor, op. cit., p. 99.
3. The annual return to parliament included information on the number of years each society had been in existence. From this it is possible to distinguish societies which existed before 1874 and which later incorporated. Thus, in the return for the year ending December 1876, any society that had been in existence two years or more must almost certainly have existed before the 1874 Act, for the first incorporations under that Act did not take place until December 5, 1874.
4. Including December 1874.
5. *Statistical Society of London Journal*, 1875, p. 209. T. F. Peacock was a London solicitor interested in building societies, who read a paper on the subject to the British Association in Bristol in 1875.
6. *B.S.G.*, 1878, February, p. 38.
7. *Directory of Building Societies*, 1885-1886, ed. H. Kent and V. M. Braund, London, 1885, p. xi.
8. *B.S.G.*, 1875, April, p. 50. A correspondent pointed out that no penalties were laid down for directors failing to make up accounts, failing to have them audited or for including prospective interest as an asset.
9. Ibid., 1876, July, p. 84.
10. C.R.R., 1889, p. 78.
11. S.C., Q. 4853. E. W. Brabrook was Assistant Registrar until 1891, then Registrar until 1904.
12. In 1890 the courts effectively eased the limit by interpreting Section 15 of the 1874 Act as meaning two-thirds of all sums due to the society from mortgagors, including interest and fines, not two-thirds the outstanding principal which had been the generally accepted interpretation among societies. *Neath Permanent Building Society v. Luce*, 59 L.J., Ch. 3.
13. *B.S.G.*, 1889, May, p. 73.
14. Ibid., 1888, March, p. 40.
15. S.C., Q. 664, C. Binyon.
16. *Cunliffe Brooks & Co. v. Blackburn & District B.B.S.*, 54 L.J. Ch. 376.
17. C. Brooks, op. cit., p. 68.

18. S.C., Q. 4712, James Higham.
19. Ibid., Q. 55, E. W. Brabrook.
20. C.R.R., 1891, p. 37.
21. This lower limit is taken to exclude societies just formed and the small promoter societies where deposits were often prohibited.
22. *B.S.G.*, 1880, June, p. 78.
23. Ibid., 1880, August, pp. 113-120, December, p. 167.
24. Ibid., 1883, June, p. 81.
25. Ibid., 1890, March, p. 45.
26. Ibid., 1885, March, p. 37.
27. Ibid., 1875, April, p. 63.
28. Ibid., 1890, August, p. 124.
29. S.C., Qs. 2873-2875, W. B. Peat, Liquidator of the Onward B.S.
30. *B.S.G.*, 1890, February, p. 24.
31. Ibid., 1875, August, p. 119.
32. H. F. A. Davis, op. cit., 1887 ed., p. 71.
33. Report of an investigating committee, *B.S.G.*, 1889, November, p. 172.
34. *B.S.G.*, 1878, February, p. 18.
35. Ibid., 1878, April, p. 47, and May, p. 70.
36. Ibid., 1878, May, pp. 62 and 70.
37. Ibid., 1878, December, p. 154.
38. Ibid., 1888, September, p. 138.
39. Ibid., 1882, November, p. 147.
40. Ibid., 1877, December, p. 152. Comment in a letter.
41. Ibid., 1889, May, p. 77.
42. Ibid., 1884, April, p. 50.
43. Ibid., 1885, February, p. 22.
44. Ibid., 1884, August, p. 104.
45. Loc. cit.
46. Ibid., 1883, September, p. 125.
47. Ibid., 1887, October, p. 123. Editorial comment.
48. In 1883 the directors had lent £4,500 to a colliery company in which some of them had an interest, although the society's solicitor had said the title was not good. *B.S.G.*, 1883, February, p. 20.
49. S.C., Q. 2311.
50. *B.S.G.*, 1879, January, p. 3, and April, p. 47.
51. Ibid., 1891, January, p. 2, concerning the Fourth City Mutual Society.
52. Ibid., 1891, July, p. 108.
53. C. J. Lowe, *A Half Century Record*, Bristol, 1901, pp. 128, 129.
54. S.C., Q. 34, E. W. Brabrook.
55. Letter to *B.S.G.*, 1884, June, p. 78. Davis was the foremost legal commentator of the day on building societies.
56. Ibid., 1887, May, p. 99.
57. *Sheffield and S. Yorks. B.S. v. Aizlewood*, 59 L.J., Ch. 34.
58. *B.S.G.*, 1886, November, p. 135.
59. Ibid., 1891, January, p. 2.
60. Ibid., 1878, November, pp. 136, 137.
61. Ibid., 1879, January, p. 13.
62. In an article "Building Societies", *Economic Review*, 1893, January, p. 80.
63. Notices of withdrawal bring stagnation and stagnation brings anxiety was the sequence put to the Select Committee of 1893 by the Chairman of the Building Society Protection Association, Q. 775, C. Binyon.
64. *B.S.G.*, 1884, March, p. 39. Chairman of the Municipal Society.
65. Ibid., 1885, October, p. 123, Chairman of the Richard Green Society.

66. Ibid., 1886, January, p. 10. Meeting of the Rock Building Society.
67. S.C., Q. 1395, E. Wood, Chairman of Temperance Building Society. This attitude was odd in view of the response of the Temperance Society to the Liberator crisis the previous year. See below.
68. A letter to the *B.S.G.*, 1890, May, p. 74, claimed that this was a frequent practice.
69. S.C., Q. 2699, C. J. Steward, liquidator of the Liberator Society.
70. *In re N.W. Perpetual Building Society, B.S.G.*, 1888, July, p. 112.
71. S.C., Q. 34.
72. The 10% sample yielded 71 societies, but 8 either made no return or were in process of dissolution.
73. 56 L.J., P.C. 57.
74. C. J. Lowe, op. cit., p. 121.
75. S.C., Q. 207.
76. L. Rep. 8, App. Cas. 235. In *Tosh v. North British Building Society*, L.J., 11, App. Cas. 489 the same view was taken.
77. *B.S.G.*, 1889, April, p. 60.
78. S.C., Q. 1229.
79. *B.S.G.*, 1882, August, p. 109.
80. Ibid., 1877, April, p. 47.
81. S.C., Qs. 313–342 and 29–32, E. W. Brabrook.
82. C. J. Lowe, op. cit., p. 82.
83. Op. cit., p. 123.
84. *B.S.G.*, 1890, September, p. 136.
85. Ibid., 1876, November, p. 30.
86. See above, p. 125.
87. S.C., Q. 1148, T. Fatkin.
88. Ibid., Q. 1105, T. Fatkin.
89. Naylor, op. cit., pp. 96, 102.
90. Ibid., p. 115.
91. Ibid., p. 122.
92. Ibid., p. 101.
93. Ibid., p. 114.
94. Ibid., p. 119.
95. *B.S.G.*, 1897, August, p. 121.
96. Building Societies Act, 1874, S. 16.
97. *B.S.G.*, 1876, December, p. 138.
98. 53 L.J., Q.B. 290; L. Rep., 9 App. Cas. 260.
99. Naylor, op. cit., p. 106.
100. Price, op. cit., p. 274.
101. Section 2.
102. See above, p. 77.
103. Naylor, op. cit., p. 100.
104. Ibid., p. 101.
105. *B.S.G.*, 1887, May, p. 59.
106. The Association's membership was not normally given in its annual report, though it was sometimes revealed incidentally at meetings. Naylor gives no membership figures for these years in his history of the Association: the figures given are taken from the *B.S.G.*, 1873, December, p. 184; 1877, March, p. 37; 1885, April, p. 42, and 1888, June, p. 193.
107. *B.S.G.*, 1880, August, p. 100.
108. At the 1881 Annual General Meeting, *B.S.G.*, 1881, November, p. 148.
109. See above, p. 108.
110. L.R. 17, Q.B. 66.

111. e.g. October 1880, p. 144; December 1880, p. 167; July 1883, p. 94; May 1886, p. 67; June 1886, p. 78.
112. Committee meetings were held at the offices of the Fourth City Mutual and later at those of the Temperance Society.
113. *B.S.G.*, 1885, April, p. 42.
114. Ibid., 1886, June, p. 75.

CHAPTER EIGHT

1. H. Bellman, *Bricks and Mortals*, London, 1949, p. 69.
2. *B.S.G.*, 1884, December, p. 55.
3. Ibid., 1887, February, p. 18.
4. "The Relation of the State to Thrift", *Stat. Soc. of London Journal*, 1885, see especially pp. 35, 36.
5. An address to the Chartered Accountant Students Association, reported in *B.S.G.*, 1886, June, p. 78.
6. Ibid., 1889, May, p. 75. The Building Societies Bill introduced in January 1887 (*House of Commons Journal*, 1887, pp. 17 and 23) was not a reform measure. It sought only to legalise advances made by societies on property held on statutory tenancies under the Land Law Ireland Act 1881. It did not become law.
7. Ibid., 1890, December, p. 187.
8. Select Committee, Appendix 18, Observations by W. Edmonds, one of the liquidators, on the causes of failure of the Portsea Society, p. 280.
9. S.C., p. 282.
10. Ibid., p. 281.
11. Loc. cit.
12. Loc. cit.
13. Loc. cit.
14. *B.S.G.*, 1892, June, p. 91.
15. The history of the Liberator has been the subject of many works. S. J. Price gives an excellent concise account in Ch. XVI of *Building Societies*. For a fictional treatment see W. T. Stead, Two and Two make Four, *Review of Reviews Annual*, 1893.
16. *B.S.G.*, 1893, July, p. 110. M. Theobald, a Liberator auditor at the public examination of the directors.
17. Ibid., 1879, August, p. 106.
18. Price, op. cit., p. 290.
19. The Liberator, and the Municipal Society founded in 1874, had spectacular growth records, good agency systems and used extensive publicity. In this (though fortunately in the Liberator's case little else) they pointed the way for other societies in the future.
20. *B.S.G.*, 1889, January, p. 4. A profile of the Liberator at the height of its powers. Viewed retrospectively this article included a nice piece of unconscious humour. "The progress of the Society under Mr. J. S. Balfour's management was unprecedented and might, without exaggeration, be termed extraordinary."
21. S.C., Q. 2607. Evidence of C. J. Stewart, official liquidator of the Liberator.
22. Ibid., Q. 2604, C. J. Stewart.
23. *B.S.G.*, 1885, August, p. 97. See also 1886, August, p. 105.
24. S.C., Qs. 2691-2696, C. J. Stewart.
25. *B.S.G.*, 1888, April, p. 51.
26. S.C., Qs. 2615, 2616. C. J. Stewart.
27. *B.S.G.*, 1886, August, p. 105.
28. Ibid., 1892, March, p. 35.
29. Ibid., 1891, March, p. 35.
30. S.C., Q. 2605, C. J. Stewart.

31. *B.S.G.*, 1892, March, p. 35.
32. S.C., Q. 1004, F. Ravenscroft, manager of the Birkbeck Society.
33. S.C., Q. 1003, F. Ravenscroft.
34. *B.S.G.*, 1892, October, when a special supplement described the run.
35. Lowe, op. cit., p. 10.
36. Naylor, op. cit., p. 123.
37. *B.S.G.*, 1893, February, p. 19.
38. Ibid., 1892, December, p. 185.
39. Ibid., 1893, March, p. 42.
40. Ibid., 1893, August, p. 125.
41. Naylor, op. cit., p. 128.
42. Price, op. cit., p. 318.
43. Naylor, op. cit., p. 128.
44. *Kent v. Tabernacle P.B.S.*, 63 L.J., Q. B. 33; [1892] 2 Q.B. 613. The decision in this case had required a building society arbitrator to do so.
45. Hansard, *Parliamentary Debates*, 4th Series, Vol. XXVIII (August 17, 1894), col. 1372. The Stirlingshire Building Society was the society in question, though, in the event, it incorporated in 1896.
46. Annual Report of the B.S.A. for 1894. Naylor, op. cit., p. 130.
47. At the Annual General Meeting of the B.S.A., *B.S.G.*, 1896, March, p. 34.
48. *B.S.G.*, 1896, March, pp. 34, 35.
49. S.C., Qs. 4713, 4714, James Higham.
50. *B.S.G.*, 1893, August, p. 126.
51. C.R.R., 1897, p. 13.
52. The return of the Birkbeck Society was excluded from the calculation for 1900 and 1910; its high ratio of deposits was the result of its banking activity and would distort the comparison, especially since the Birkbeck was unincorporated and thus made no return in 1890.

CHAPTER NINE

1. e.g. J. S. Watts, *The Truth about the Liberator*, London, 1892, ". . . instead of the 'Liberator' its name should have been 'Ensnarers Investment Coy.—Unlimited' ". *The Greatest Crime of the Nineteenth Century*, London, 1897, ". . . under the cloak of religion the worthiest among our working class have been ruthlessly robbed of their thrifty savings".
2. The assets of the Birkbeck society (unincorporated) were excluded from these calculations: it was substantially a deposit bank and not a building society.
3. For a discussion of these matters see H. O. Horne, *A History of Savings Banks*, London, 1947, Ch. 15.
4. e.g. *B.S.G.*, 1905, June, p. 83. Edward Wood's report as chairman of the B.S.A.
5. Ibid., February, p. 25.
6. Ibid., 1909, August, p. 108, a suggestion first made in 1900, ibid., July, p. 109.
7. Ibid., 1899, May, p. 80.
8. Ibid., 1906, October, p. 141.
9. Ibid., 1902, March, pp. 44, 45. In contrast to the U.S.A., where by 1900 the Hartford Life Insurance Company had created a special department to deal with such policies, ibid., 1902, February, p. 24.
10. Ibid., 1905, July, pp. 100–102.
11. Eventually the Companies Act 1929 restricted the use of the description *building society* to societies registered under the Building Societies Acts.
12. Naylor, op. cit., p. 180.
13. Building societies were not alone in this; other entrepreneurs advertised the advantages of what they had to offer with brutal frankness. An undertaker, offering his

business for sale, stressed the advantages of his location thus: "Sanitary arrangements much neglected; mortality from fevers excessively high. Total death rate 107; higher than any town within a radius of 50 miles; one trade competitor (carpenter) only. Excellent opening for energetic man willing to put his heart in the business." Cited, *B.S.G.*, 1900, November, p. 164.

14. C. Brooks, op. cit., p. 121.
15. Hobson, op. cit., p. 59.
16. Ibid., p. 69.
17. The Co-operative Permanent claimed precedence in the introduction of Home Safes. A. Mansbridge, *Brick on Brick*, London, 1934, p. 65.
18. Hill put forward his ideas in two papers read to the B.S.A. conferences of 1908 and 1911.
19. In the Temperance Society in 1854, "As an inducement to Directors 'to expend their time in the advancement of the Society's interests' it was decided that they be paid the usual agency commission on all shares disposed of by them. . .". Price, *From Queen to Queen*, p. 29.
20. *B.S.G.*, 1906, August, p. 114, and 1907, March, p. 36.
21. C. Brooks, op. cit., p. 82.
22. e.g. *B.S.G.*, 1906, August, p. 114.
23. The Northampton Town and Country Society was one such. *B.S.G.*, 1902, March, p. 41.
24. Ibid., 1910, October, p. 135.
25. C. Brooks, op. cit., p. 110.
26. *B.S.G.*, 1899, December, p. 183.
27. Excluding the figures for the Birkbeck Society.
28. Actually, there were two Birkbeck societies. One started business as a land society and, while it was still extant in 1911, the overwhelming proportion of the business had become concentrated in what had started as a straightforward building society in 1851.
29. *B.S.G.*, 1899, August, p. 120.
30. Ibid., 1910, December, p. 168.
31. The annual average yield on Consols was rising, 2·90% (1908), 2·97 (1909), 3·16 (1910) and 3·23 (1911).
32. *B.S.G.*, 1911, November, p. 139.
33. Ibid., 1912, June, p. 86.
34. Ibid., 1915, March, p. 26.
35. G. Bishop, Secretary of the Society, outlined the action taken in a pamphlet for the benefit of his colleagues in other societies. Passages from this are cited in C. Brookes, op. cit., pp. 103-109; see also *B.S.G.*, 1903, May, pp. 73, 74.
36. 1849, April, p. 90.
37. Scratchley, op. cit., 1849 ed., p. 141.
38. *The National*, 1848, September 9, p. 4.
39. Hobson, op. cit., p. 38.
40. Price, *Building Societies*, pp. 484, 485.
41. *B.S.G.*, 1869, April, p. 57.
42. Ibid., 1869, December, p. 185.
43. Ibid., 1881, November, p. 148.
44. Ibid., 1874, April, p. 146.
45. In a letter to the *B.S.G.*, 1878, September, p. 116.
46. Ibid., 1881, November, p. 148.
47. Davies, op. cit., 1887 ed., p. 108.
48. *B.S.G.*, 1883, November, p. 145.
49. Ibid., 1884, February, p. 20.
50. Ibid., 1884, April, p. 51.

51. Hansard, *Parliamentary Debates*, 3rd Series, Vol. CCXCIV, cols. 630, 631.
52. Ibid., 3rd Series, Vol. CCCIV, cols. 432, 433, and Vol. CCCV, cols, 5, 6.
53. *B.S.G.*, 1886, June, p. 78.
54. Ibid., 1886, October, p. 186.
55. Ibid., 1887, April, p. 53.
56. This owed something to the arrangement previously negotiated between George Bishop (Woolwich Equitable) and the tax authorities. Ibid., 1916, July, p. 98.
57. Ibid., 1888, February, p. 12.
58. Loc. cit.
59. Price, op. cit., p. 490.
60. *B.S.G.*, 1881, November, p. 148.
61. As was the case in some Birmingham societies, see *B.S.G.*, 1901, July, p. 110.
62. J. J. Millar, *Building Society Finance and Statistics*, Edinburgh, 1905, pp. 38, 39.
63. Naylor, op. cit., p. 133. A similar suggestion had been made by W. Saunders (Principality) in 1889, *B.S.G.*, 1912, April, p. 72.
64. In 1894 S. Davies (Leicester Permanent) had been appointed to the Committee but resigned after a year because of the difficulty of attending meetings.
65. Naylor, op. cit., p. 138.
66. *B.S.G.*, 1895, July, p. 105.
67. Ibid., 1899, May, p. 73, and June, p. 84.
68. Ibid., 1906, July, p. 94.
69. Naylor, op. cit., pp. 147-149.
70. *B.S.G.*, 1907, July, p. 91.
71. Ibid., 1909, July, pp. 94-98.
72. Ibid., 1911, July, p. 86.
73. Ibid., July, p. 92.
74. Ibid., July, p. 93.
75. Ibid., 1911, April, pp. 49-50, and June, p. 73.
76. e.g. Enoch Hill had referred in a letter to the *Gazette* (1911, January, p. 6) to the "apparent apathy of the Executive . . . whose attitude is now causing widespread dissatisfaction amongst the officials of the societies in union. . . . There is no apparent benefit to be derived from a deputation of picked men, who with gentle words and compliments plead with a Chancellor of the Exchequer that he will be merciful with the savings of the industrious and thrifty".
77. *B.S.G.*, 1911, July, p. 90.
78. Ibid., 1911, April, p. 50.
79. Ibid., 1911, September, pp. 111-114.
80. Ibid., 1912, June, p. 81.
81. Ibid., 1913, June, pp. 82-85.
82. Ibid., 1914, July, p. 98.
83. The idea of district organisations first appeared soon after the Association was formed, being suggested by J. E. Enion (London Road Permanent, Manchester) in 1873. *B.S.G.*, 1873, February, p. 23. The suggestion was made again in letters to the *Gazette*, 1897, June, p. 85 (Arthur Webb) and 1905, September, p. 138.
84. *B.S.G.*, 1915, June, p. 87.
85. Ibid., 1915, June, p. 74.

CHAPTER TEN

1. C. Brooks, op. cit., p. 128.
2. Problems arising from the War. *B.S.G.*, 1916, January, p. 10.
3. Hobson, op. cit., pp. 73, 74.
4. *B.S.G.*, 1917, June, p. 78, and 1918, May, p. 64.
5. Ibid., 1914, October, p. 147.

6. Ibid., 1914, September, p. 133.
7. Ibid., 1916, January, p. 11.
8. Ibid., 1918, July, p. 90.
9. Report of C. F. Saunder (a member of the Committee) to the board of the Principality Society, December 10, 1915. Cited, A. Noakes, *The Principality Building Society*, London, 1960, p. 34.
10. Hansard, *Parliamentary Debates*, Fifth Series, Vol. LXXVI, cols. 2299, 2300.
11. *B.S.G.*, 1915, December, p. 155.
12. Op. cit., p. 157.
13. Mansbridge, op. cit., p. 75.
14. *B.S.G.*, 1912, August, p. 118.
15. Ibid., 1916, January, p. 10. E. Wood.
16. Hobson, op. cit., p. 74.
17. *B.S.G.*, 1915, November, p. 143.
18. Ibid., 1915, January, p. 3.
19. Ibid., 1916, February, p. 20.
20. E. A. Scratchley, in one of his regular contributions to the *B.S.G.*, 1916, May, p. 69.
21. *B.S.G.*, 1917, July, p. 85.
22. Mansbridge, op. cit., p. 69.
23. *B.S.G.*, 1914, December, p. 171.
24. Ibid., 1915, August, p. 107.
25. *B.S.G.*, 1916, July, p. 196.
26. Loc. cit.
27. Ibid., 1917, December, p. 147.
28. Ibid., 1916, May, pp. 62, 63.
29. Ibid., 1917, June, pp. 82, 83.
30. M. Bowley, *Housing and the State*, London, 1945, pp. 10-12.
31. Price, *Building Societies*, p. 394. *B.S.G.*, 1918, June, p. 70, and July, pp. 82-86 and 90.
32. December, p. 219.
33. 59 L.J., Ch. 34.
34. E. W. Brabrook, *Building Societies*, London, 1906, p. 107.
35. *B.S.G.*, 1921, June, p. 118.
36. Cmd. 1447.
37. Bowley, op. cit., p. 22.
38. Ibid., p. 24.
39. Ibid., p. 27.
40. H. Bellman, *Bricks and Mortals*, London, 1949, p. 219.

CHAPTER ELEVEN

1. As a result of the war, the report was not published until 1944.
2. The Committee estimated that about 7,500,000 pre-1914 dwellings were still occupied in 1938.
3. 1939, August 26th, p. 394.
4. Bowley, op. cit., p. 98.
5. Bowley, op. cit., p. 130. Building costs were such that, even with the government subsidies, the rents of local authority houses were out of reach of the poorer groups.
6. Ibid., p. 227.
7. Ibid., p. 274.
8. *B.S.G.*, 1933, April, p. 238.
9. Op. cit., pp. 88, 89.
10. B. Mitchell, op. cit., p. 353. "The figure for money incomes is the average income of a man in normal full-time employment, including periods of sickness and recognised holidays but not periods of unemployment." The index of real incomes relates the data for money incomes to the Ministry of Labour's cost of living index.

Real wages probably rose rather less than the figures indicate, because the price of food fell more than that of other items in the cost of living index, and food was overweighted in that index.

11. Until 1928 the Registrar published only a figure of total members and in many societies, this included borrowing members and depositors. However, knowing the number of shareholders in 1928, if the increase in shareholders between 1927 and 1928 can be established, the number of shareholders in 1927 can be deduced, and also the proportion of shareholders to total members for 1927. For the three years 1928 to 1930, the number of shareholders increased thus—135,000; 184,000 and 128,000. The increases in balances due to shareholders for the same years, in £ million, were: 37, 52 and 39. The ratio between the increase in balances (in £ thousand) and the increase in members was therefore fairly stable: 3·6; 3·6; and 3·3. The increase in balances between 1927 and 1928 was £40 million; which suggests that the increase in members for the same year was about 140,000 (using a ratio of 3·5). This suggests that actual shareholders totalled 990,066 of the 1,416,456 members, 70%. Total shareholders for years before 1927 can be estimated by taking 70% of the Registrar's figures of total members.
12. H. Bellman, Building Societies—Some Economic Aspects, *Economic Journal*, March, 1933, p. 17. My table regroups Bellman's data to form a smaller number of classes.
13. Sources: Mitchell, op. cit.; C.R.R. and *The Economist*.
14. Elkington, op. cit., p. 55.
15. Until 1928 certain other liabilities were included in the total of deposits, the most important of these being bank loans. Thus the figures for 1922 are not strictly comparable with those for 1938. Given the very liquid position of societies in 1922, the exclusions were probably not very significant at that date. If allowance could be made for these the increased dependence of societies on deposits would be a little greater than the figures imply.
16. The number of depositors and the average size of deposits are not available before 1928.
17. *B.S.G.*, 1932, June, p. 419.
18. *The Economist*, 1932, July 16, p. 134.
19. *B.S.G.*, 1923, August, p. 163.
20. See Hobson, op. cit., Ch. 21, on the Halifax's use of publicity.
21. Hobson, op. cit., p. 91.
22. Bellman, *Bricks and Mortals*, p. 125.
23. Mansbridge, op. cit., p. 116.
24. ". . . I submit that collateral security has been forced on building societies by post-war property and monetary conditions. Older more rigid opinions and practice have of necessity been relaxed to some degree." W. Harvey, *B.S.G.*, 1924, September, p. 189.
25. *Building Societies Yearbook*, 1928. Article by W. Harvey, p. 307.
26. In 1932 Hill claimed that the Halifax Society had an arrangement for the employees of certain firms to have 100% advances, guaranteed by the employer "over 70 years ago". (*B.S.G.*, 1932, June, p. 413.) He was probably referring to arrangements with Messrs. Ackroyd and Crossley, see *Eighty Years of Home Building*, Halifax Building Society (1937), pp. 15–18.
27. *B.S.G.*, 1924, January, p. 16.
28. Ibid., 1923, December, p. 243.
29. e.g. The South Wales and Mon. Society (ibid., 1924, July, p. 137).
30. Ibid., 1924, July, pp. 133, 134.
31. Ibid., 1924, December, pp. 241, 242.
32. *Building Societies Yearbook*, 1928. E. Hill, p. 191.
33. Bowley, op. cit., p. 84.

34. Memorandum of the Housing Committee of the Association's Council to the Ministry, *B.S.G.*, 1932, October, p. 746. See also the Association's annual report for 1934, ibid., 1935, June, p. 447.
35. H. Bellman, *Three Thrifty Millions*, London, 1935, p. 128.
36. *B.S.G.*, 1933, December, p. 900.
37. e.g. The Temperance. Price, *From Queen to Queen*, p. 85.
38. Hobson, op. cit., p. 111.
39. 1935, January 19, p. 136.
40. If houses exceeded a certain maximum laid down in the Act, they were not eligible for the subsidy. Minimum standards of size and equipment were also prescribed.
41. *B.S.G.*, 1924, December, p. 244.
42. 1939, February 18, pp. 347, 348.
43. *B.S.G.*, 1919, November, p. 123.
44. Ibid., 1920, July, p. 68; 1921, May, p. 94, and June, p. 112, and 1922, July, p. 136.
45. Ibid., 1922, July, p. 135.
46. Ibid., 1922, July, pp. 132, 133.
47. Rule 3 of the Association.
48. *B.S.G.*, 1932, July, pp. 428-432.
49. Price, *Building Societies*, p. 436. This may have been a response to a plea from S. E. Platt, another building society actuary, for the creation of a central actuarial body for building societies. (*B.S.G.*, 1876, August, p. 93.)
50. In 1916 detailed suggestions for such an institute were put forward by J. B. Annan, including details of the subjects which should be included in the institute's examinations. (*B.S.G.*, 1916, August, p. 117.)
51. Ibid., 1920, July, pp. 84, 85.
52. Ibid., 1920, September, p. 108.
53. Ibid., 1920, December, p. 145.
54. Ibid., 1921, May, p. 87.
55. Ibid., 1930, March, p. 171.
56. Ibid., 1930, February, p. 88, and July, p. 483.
57. Ibid., 1934, January, p. 6.
58. Ibid., 1934, April, p. 272, and October, p. 886.
59. Ibid., 1934, October, p. 889.

CHAPTER TWELVE

1. *B.S.G.*, 1921, June, p. 119, and July, p. 156.
2. Ibid., 1921, July, p. 135.
3. Ibid., 1925, January, p. 10.
4. H. Bellman, "Building Societies—some Economic Aspects", *Economic Journal*, 1933, March, p. 11.
5. To eliminate the influence of the merger of the two largest societies, the Halifax Permanent and Equitable Societies, which took place in 1928, it may be thought appropriate to take the nine largest societies in 1930; this would reduce the figure for 1930 from 53% to 51%.
6. In the Temperance Society ". . . normally [loans] were granted to those living in London and its immediate environment". In 1940 this society began to open branches outside London, a ". . . reversal of the policy of the previous half century". Price, *From Queen to Queen*, p. 84 and p. 105.
7. "A Statistical Analysis of Building Societies", *Journal of the Royal Statistical Society*, Vol. XCIV (1931), Part II, p. 183 and p. 189. The figures above result from combining Brace's date for his Northern Counties and Yorks, with those for Lancashire and Cheshire.

8. See above, p. 72. The Leeds Provincial Society, formed in June 1849, had 25 branches by the end of 1850. (*B.S.G.*, 1941, December, p. 760.)
9. *The Economist*, 1932, April 23, p. 919.
10. Loc. cit.
11. *B.S.G.*, 1930, April, p. 256.
12. Ibid., 1930, July, p. 499. H. W. L. Lester (Hastings P.B.S.).
13. Ibid., 1933, December, p. 900.
14. Ibid., 1930, March, p. 146.
15. Ibid., 1939, April, p. 302. W. Harvey.
16. Ibid., 1930, July, p. 499.
17. Ibid., 1933, July, p. 548, and 1935, May, p. 398.
18. Ibid., 1935, March, p. 183, and August, p. 696, and 1936, June, p. 530.
19. Ibid., 1931, September, p. 661.
20. Ibid., 1942, April, p. 191. A letter from an insurance company official.
21. Ibid., 1932, January, p. 35.
22. Ibid., 1930, May, pp. 316, 317, and 1932, January, p. 35.
23. Ibid., 1931, June, p. 442. H. W. L. Lester.
24. Price, *Building Societies*, p. 410.
25. *B.S.G.*, 1932, January, pp. 64-66.
26. Ibid., 1931, June, p. 444.
27. Ibid., 1932, January, pp. 33, 34 and 64.
28. Ibid., 1932, February, p. 111.
29. Price, op. cit., p. 412.
30. *B.S.G.*, 1932, September, p. 600.
31. Price, op. cit., p. 413.
32. *B.S.G.*, 1933, March, p. 173.
33. 1933, February 25, p. 419, and March 18, p. 591.
34. *B.S.G.*, 1933, July, p. 525 and p. 530.
35. Ibid., 1933, July, p. 533.
36. Ibid., 1934, June, p. 549.
37. Ibid., 1934, January, p. 4, and February, p. 95.
38. Ibid., 1934, May, p. 378. Annual Report of the Association.
39. Ibid., 1934, June, pp. 542-544.
40. Ibid., 1934, July, p. 607, and August, p. 678.
41. Ibid., 1934, October, pp. 815, 816.
42. Ibid., 1935, February, p. 95.
43. Ibid., 1935, March, p. 175.
44. Ibid., 1935, May, p. 366. Editorial comment.
45. *The Economist*, 1935, April 13, p. 860.
46. Price, op. cit., pp. 419, 420.
47. *B.S.G.*, 1936, July, p. 606.
48. Price, *From Queen to Queen*, p. 91.
49. *The Economist*, 1936, April 11. Building Societies Special Survey, p. 12.
50. *B.S.G.*, 1922, January, p. 7.
51. Ibid., 1937, July, p. 678.
52. Ibid., November, p. 1008.
53. Ibid., 1936, July, p. 586.
54. Ibid., p. 585.
55. It was the issue of the code that led the N. Staffs. societies to break with the Midland District Association and form their own organisation in January 1936.
56. *B.S.G.*, 1937, June, p. 504. Editorial comment.
57. Ibid., 1938, January, p. 7. Editorial comment.
58. Ibid., April, p. 228.
59. Ibid., 1937, December, p. 1055.

60. Ibid., 1940, June, p. 516.
61. Ibid., 1940, June, pp. 496-498.
62. Price, op. cit., p. 93.
63. *B.S.G.*, 1924, May, p. 91.
64. H. Bellman, *Three Thrifty Millions*, London, 1935, p. 89.
65. *B.S.G.*, 1934, February, p. 95.
66. The changes are described by J. H. Robertson, *Building Societies Yearbook*, 1937, London, pp. 315-336.
67. *B.S.G.*, 1937, March, p. 191.
68. *C.R.R.*, 1932, p. 6.
69. *C.R.R.*, 1938, pp. 6, 7.
70. Hansard, *Parliamentary Debates*, Vol. CCCXXXVII, col. 1267 (June 23, 1938).
71. *C.R.R.*, 1938, p. 4, and *B.S.G.*, 1936, July, p. 614.
72. *B.S.G.*, 1933, September, p. 730.
73. Ibid., 1935, July, p. 630.
74. 1 A.E.R. [1939] 481; on appeal 1 A.E.R. [1940] 302 and the further appeal to the House of Lords, 2 A.E.R. [1941] 205.
75. *B.S.G.*, 1939, June, pp. 500, 501. See also *The Economist*, 1939, February 18, pp. 347, 348.
76. Ibid., 1938, December, p. 1061. In 1937 the *Gazette* (March, p. 194) reported the formation of an earlier owner-occupiers' association at Romford.
77. The Society's action none the less failed because the mortgage deed produced could not be proved to be that executed by Mrs. Borders.
78. See above, p. 181.
79. This decision followed the Appeal Court's earlier decision in *Halifax P.B.S. v. Salisbury* (4 A.E.R. [1939] 427) where the same point was raised and decided in favour of the Society, again without the Court having to pass judgement on the validity of pool arrangements.
80. Hansard, *Parliamentary Debates*, Fifth Series, Vol. CCCXLVI, col. 379.
81. Ibid., col. 377.
82. *B.S.G.*, 1935, March, p. 254.
83. Bellman, *Bricks and Mortals*, p. 130.
84. *B.S.G.*, March, pp. 122, 123.

CHAPTER THIRTEEN

1. *B.S.G.*, 1939, July, p. 582, W. Harvey.
2. Bank loans and other liabilities rose from £11½ million in 1938 to £13½ million in 1939.
3. C. Brooks, op. cit., p. 152.
4. Hobson, op. cit., p. 116, and *B.S.G.*, 1939, October, p. 858.
5. Hobson, op. cit., p. 116.
6. 1941, June 7, p. 762.
7. 2 & 3 Geo. 6. c. 67 and c. 71 respectively. Both Acts received the royal assent on September 1, 1939.
8. *B.S.G.*, 1942, August, p. 368.
9. R. S. Sayers, *Financial Policy*, 1939-45, H.M.S.O., 1956, p. 175.
10. *B.S.G.*, 1941, July, p. 477.
11. Ibid., 1947, January, p. 6.
12. C. Brooks, op. cit., p. 163.
13. *B.S.G.*, 1941, August, p. 557.
14. Ibid., 1937, February, p. 92.
15. Hansard, *Parliamentary Debates*, Fifth Series, Vol. CCCXXXVI, cols. 209, 210.

16. Ibid., Vol. CCCXLV, cols. 27, 28.
17. *B.S.G.*, July 1939, p. 634.
18. Ibid., 1941, July, p. 475.
19. Op. cit., pp. 159–161. See also Price, *From Queen to Queen*, p. 100; Bellman, *Bricks and Mortals*, p. 132, and Hobson, op. cit., p. 121, for details of some other societies.
20. Hobson, op. cit., p. 120. This concession cost the Halifax Society well over £100,000.
21. *B.S.G.*, 1944, March, p. 76.
22. *C.R.R.*, 1938, p. 5.
23. 1874 Act s. 33 modified by s. 19 of the 1894 Act.
24. *B.S.G.*, 1961, July, p. 608, where a later Registrar, Sir Cecil Crabbe, discussed the considerations that influenced him in the exercise of these discretionary powers.
25. Ibid., 1942, August, p. 362. Something of the thinking that lay behind these moves is given in the then current pamphlet by Arthur Webb, *Signposts of Building Society Finance*.
26. Ibid., 1942, August, p. 362.
27. Ibid., September, p. 400. The Council had recently appointed a Reconstruction Committee to consider the post-war position of societies.
28. Ibid., October, p. 444.
29. Ibid., May, p. 227.
30. Ibid., 1943, January, p. 7.
31. C. Brooks, op. cit., p. 163.
32. *B.S.G.*, 1942, July, pp. 316–338.
33. Ibid., 1944, July, p. 234.
34. Ibid., 1944, June, p. 199.
35. Ibid., 1942, April, p. 177.
36. For the definition of "dwelling house" used, see above, p. 184.
37. *B.S.G.*, 1944, April, p. 110.
38. Ibid., 1943, July, p. 230, and 1944, August, p. 279.
39. Ibid., 1945, October, p. 382.
40. See below, p. 275.
41. *B.S.G.*, 1949, January, p. 23.
42. *The Banker*, 1948, May, p. 96.
43. *B.S.G.*, 1949, April, p. 178.
44. Ibid., 1944, December, p. 421.
45. Ibid., 1945, February, p. 48.
46. Ibid., 1945, April, p. 120, and May, p. 161.
47. Ibid., 1948, July, p. 398.
48. Ibid., 1946, July, p. 266, and *The Banker*, 1946, April, p. 102.
49. "Encouragement" of a different sort was also possible. With the prevailing housing shortage and the lack of knowledge that many tenants had of their legal position as controlled tenants, threats of large rent increases could help to persuade the tenant to purchase his house on the terms offered.
50. *B.S.G.*, 1946, July, pp. 265, 266.
51. Ibid., 1942, March, p. 123.
52. Participation in the scheme grew rapidly; by 1943, 110 societies, representing 83% of the movement's assets, were taking part.
53. Price, *Building Societies*, p. 560.
54. Apart from recommending a 4% rate for borrowers in September, 1945, after a number of societies had already reduced their rate.
55. *B.S.G.*, 1945, December, pp. 428, 429.
56. Ibid., 1944, December, p. 417.
57. Ibid., 1946, July, pp. 254, 255.
58. Ibid., 1947, July, p. 281.

59. Ibid., 1944, December, p. 421, and 1945, June, p. 205.
60. This figure was raised to 50% in 1961, at the same time as the basic subscription was raised for societies with assets over £200 million.
61. *B.S.G.*, 1949, August, p. 445.
62. Ibid., June, p. 331.

CHAPTER FOURTEEN

1. *B.S.G.*, 1953, June, p. 362.
2. 1954, May, 8, pp. 477, 478.
3. *B.S.G.*, 1959, April, p. 259.
4. Ibid., 1955, June, p. 369.
5. Committee on the Working of the Monetary System, Minutes of Evidence, H.M.S.O., 1960, Q. 7377 (F. Bentley).
6. The Rent Act, 1957, Report of Inquiry (Cmd. 1246, 1960).
7. Cmd. 571 of Session 1958–59.
8. See p. 256.
9. *B.S.G.*, 1959, May, p. 365.
10. Hansard, *Parliamentary Debates*, Fifth Series (H.C.), Vol. DCLVII, col. 978 (April 9, 1962).
11. Ibid., Vol. DCVII, col. 65. (D. Heathcoat Amery, June 15, 1959.)
12. Progress was slow, by 1963, from the earmarked £25 million, projects involving a total of £5 million had been approved, and those for a further £3 million were under consideration. (Cmd. 2050—1963.)
13. *B.S.G.*, 1963, July, p. 583.
14. Loc. cit.
15. See Table XXIII.
16. The index of house prices is the unweighted average of the three indices (four since 1960) compiled by the Co-operative Permanent Building Society, which show the changes in the prices paid for existing houses in three price ranges. They represent national averages. There have, of course, been wide variations in the course of house prices between different parts of the country. Between 1958 and 1963 prices in London and the South-East rose by 60% compared with only 25% in the North-East. (*B.S.G.*, 1964, March, p. 209.)
17. In 1945 the Halifax Society, the largest building society, held 16·5% of the movement's assets and in 1950 13·2%.
18. *B.S.G.*, 1958, January, p. 36. (The Council had long frowned on this practice, see its Annual Report for 1951, *Building Societies Year Book*, London, 1951, p. 257.)
19. *The Banker*, 1958, p. 325.
20. Committee on the Working of the Monetary System, Minutes of Evidence, Qs. 7344–7346 (F. Bentley and A. Meikle).
21. E.g. loc. cit., Qs. 7361–7363, and *B.S.G.*, 1958, March, p. 151.
22. Ibid., 1956, June, p. 423.
23. *C.R.R.*, 1959, pp. 6–9, where the Registrar discusses the exercise of his powers.
24. Loc. cit.
25. E.g. Securities valued at book values and Post-War Credits were included in reserves.
26. *B.S.G.*, 1958, June, p. 392, see also Committee on the Working of the Monetary System, Minutes of Evidence, Qs. 7339–7340.
27. *The Banker*, 1958, pp. 778, 779.
28. These figures express specific and general reserves plus provision for future taxation as a percentage of total assets. If the figures were calculated according to the Registrar's definition of reserves for trustee status purposes they would be lower. The information is not available for such a calculation.

29. *B.S.G.*, 1964, October, p. 881.
30. *C.R.R.*, 1963, p. 12.
31. These societies held 98·8% of all building society assets in 1963.
32. The data given in the Registrar's reports does not make it possible to calculate this figure before 1961.
33. *B.S.G.*, 1960, May, p. 342.
34. The Halifax Society was not alone among the large societies in not following the Association's recommendations. See *B.S.G.*, 1960, June, p. 442.
35. *B.S.G.*, 1955, June, p. 375.
36. Ibid., 1956, August, p. 556.
37. The Association had in fact already recommended that members should not allow deposits from companies to become important in their finances (ibid., p. 557).
38. *B.S.G.*, 1956, August, p. 556.
39. Loc. cit. See also *The Banker*, 1957, May, pp. 315, 316.
40. P. 240.
41. *C.R.R.*, 1960, Appendix III. Report of the investigation into the affairs of the State Building Society, p. 9.
42. *C.R.R.*, 1956, p. 1.
43. From the passing of the Prevention of Fraud (Investments) Act in 1939 until the end of 1952, the Registrar made seventeen investigations. Between 1953 and 1959 he made thirty-three investigations.
44. *C.R.R.*, 1954, p. 5.
45. Ibid., 1959, p. 15.
46. *B.S.G.*, 1956, September, p. 648.
47. *C.R.R.*, 1959, p. 15.
48. *B.S.G.*, 1962, December, p. 1066.
49. Loc. cit.
50. The Registrar has power to increase this figure, as he did, to £7,000 in December 1963 in the Building Societies (Special Advances) Order, S.I. 1963, No. 2112.
51. See above, p. 258.
52. The 1960 Act was consolidated with the unrepealed portions of the earlier Acts to form the Building Societies Act, 1962.
53. Given these circumstances, Mr. Bentley's successful effort to join the Halifax Board in 1957 (above, p. 260) is all the more remarkable.
54. Hansard, *Parliamentary Debates*, Fifth Series (H.C.), Vol. DCXXV, cols. 41-43, and Vol. DCXXVII, cols. 959-960, and ibid. (H.L.), Vol. CCXXIII, cols. 527-535.
55. *B.S.G.*, 1961, July (Conference Issue), p. 583.
56. Ibid., 1964 (Conference Issue), p. 462.
57. Building Societies Act, 1962, s. 7.
58. Some of the district associations had earlier taken the initiative in this field.
59. See, for example, the debate on the second reading of the 1960 Act in the Commons. (Hansard, *Parliamentary Debates*, Fifth Series, Vol. DCXXV, cols. 33-155.
60. Cf. above, p. 169.
61. Except in the case of the nine members elected by the district associations.
62. *B.S.G.*, 1957, April, p. 238.
63. Ibid., 1961, June, p. 463.
64. Ibid., 1961, July, pp. 587-595.
65. Ibid., 1962 (Conference Issue), p. 497.
66. Ibid., 1963 (Conference Issue), p. 469.
67. Above, pp. 158–64.
68. *B.S.G.*, 1915, September, p. 131.
69. Price, op. cit., p. 494.
70. *B.S.G.*, 1917, June, p. 79.
71. Ibid., 1920, July, p. 66, and August, p. 95, and 1922, July, p. 130.

72. This was not entirely a post-war phenomenon. The Principality Society had received such deposits before the war. *B.S.G.*, 1915, January, p. 3.
73. *B.S.G.*, 1924, October, pp. 206, 207.
74. Ibid., 1924, August, p. 167.
75. Ibid., 1932, April, p. 227.
76. Ibid., 1935, September, p. 760.
77. Ibid., 1940, September, p. 687.
78. Hansard, *Parliamentary Debates*, Fifth Series, Vol. DCLXVI, cols. 739, 740.
79. E.g. *B.S.G.*, 1940, April, p. 225; 1941, April, p. 266; and August, p. 557.
80. Ibid., 1961, April, p. 291.
81. Ibid., 1962, August, pp. 666-668, where Sir Harold Bellman, a member of the deputation, gives an account of these events.

CHAPTER FIFTEEN

1. The index was obtained by linking three indices of costs; Maiwald's index for the period to 1938, the *Economist* index for 1938-39 and the Co-operative Permanent Society's index from 1939.
2. Committee on the Working of the Monetary System, Minutes of Evidence, p. 964.
3. *Financial Statistics*. (H.M.S.O).
4. Above, p. 251.
5. Committee on the Working of the Monetary System, Report, para. 93.
6. Ibid., Memoranda of Evidence, Vol. 2, p. 173.
7. See J. E. Powell, *Savings in a Free Society*, London, 1961, p. 61, where the proportion of gross personal savings going to building societies is shown to move closely with the attractiveness of the interest rate offered by societies.
8. Committee on the Working of the Monetary System, Memoranda of Evidence, Vol. 2, p. 221.
9. *Financial Statistics*. (H.M.S.O.).
10. Committee on the Working of the Monetary System, Report, para. 248.
11. E. V. Morgan, *The Structure of Property in Great Britain*, Oxford, 1960, p. 72, on the basis of estate duty returns, estimates the personal holding of mortgages fell from £500 million in 1953 to £438 million in 1955.

BIBLIOGRAPHY

Books.

Ansell, C. *A Treatise on Friendly Societies*. London, 1835.

Argent, E. *A Preparatory Introduction to a System for the Better Regulation of Building Societies*. London, 1848.

Ashworth, H. *Housing in Great Britain*, 2nd ed., London, 1957.

Bacon, R. K. *The Life of Sir Enoch Hill*. London, 1934.

Barry, W. W. *A Treatise on the Law and Practice of Benefit Building Societies*. London, 1866.

Begg, J. *Happy Homes for Working Men*. Edinburgh, 1866.

Bellman, H. *The Building Society Movement*. London, 1927.

The Silent Revolution. London, 1928.

Building Societies: Retrospect and Prospect. London, 1930.

Three Thrifty Millions. London, 1935.

Bricks and Mortals. London, 1949.

Bowkett, T. E. *The Bane and the Antidote*. London, 1850.

Bowley, M. *Housing and the State*. London, 1945.

Brabrook, E. W. *Building Societies*. London, 1906.

Bradford Equitable Building Society. *Second Thoughts* (a history of the Society). 1951.

Brooks, C. *The First Hundred Years* (a history of the Woolwich Equitable Society). London, 1947.

Brooks, H. (ed.). *Building Society Directory*, 9th ed. London, 1854, 10th ed. 1855.

Brown, R. G. *How to Use a Building Society*. London, 1937.

Cohen, J. *Building Society Finance*. London, 1933.

Cole, G. D. H. (ed.). *Studies in Capitalism and Investment*. London, 1935.

Building Societies and the Housing Problem. London, 1942.

Coventry, W. F. *Problems in Building Societies Operating Branches*. London, 1951.

Davis, H. F. A. *The Law and Practice of Building and Land Societies*, 2nd ed. London, 1874.

Building Societies, Their Theory, Practice and Management. London, 1887.

Detheridge, F. *A Handbook of Building Societies*. London, 1874.

Egan, C. *The Law Relative to Benefit Building Societies*, 1st ed. London, 1847.

Elkington, G. *The National Building Society*, 1849-1934. London, 1935.

Fawcett, A. *A Practical Manual on Building Societies*. London, 1893.

Friedlein, C. D. A. *Building Societies and Borrowers*, 1st ed. London, 1872.

Gilzean-Reid, H. *Co-operative Building Effort in Glasgow*. Alex. Gardner, Glasgow (?) *circa* 1894.

Godwin, N. *Building Societies Auditors' Companion*. London, 1882(?).

Gray, J. McF. *The Arithmetic of Building Societies*. Liverpool and London, 1864.

Halifax Building Society. *The History of the Halifax Building Society*. London, 1903.

Eighty Years of House Building. 1937.

Halifax Equitable Building Society. *The Halifax Equitable Building Society*. Halifax, 1921.

Harkin, F. J. *Building Societies*. Londonderry, 1915.

Hodgson, L. G. *Notes on Building Society Management and Book-keeping*. London, 1925.

Building Societies; Their Origins, Methods and Principles. London, 1929.

Hobson, O. *A Hundred Years of the Halifax*. London, 1953.

Houghton, D. *Building Societies at Your Service*. London, 1945.

James, J. H. *A Guide to Benefit Building Societies*. London, 1849.

On the Cost and Right of Redeeming Property Mortgaged to Building Societies. London, 1854.

Jones, T. *Every Man His Own Landlord*, 4th ed. London, 1870.

Kent, H., and Braund, V. M. (eds.). *Directory of Building Societies*, 1885-86. London, 1885.
Leaver, J. B. *Building Societies, Their Past, Present and Future*. London, 1942.
Lees, J. F. *Book-keeping for Terminating Building Societies*. London, 1895.
Lowe, C. J. *A Half Century Record* (a History of the Bristol and West Society). Bristol and London, 1901.
Ludlow, J. M., and Lloyd Jones. *The Progress of the Working Classes*. London, 1867.
McArthur, J. *Building Societies Simplified and Improved*. London, 1845 (?).
McGovern, J. H. *Buy Your Own Home*. London, 1886.
Mansbridge, A. *Brick on Brick* (a History of the Co-operative Building Society). London, 1934.
Naylor, E. *Bradford Building Societies*. Bradford, 1908.
A History of the Building Societies Association, 1869-1914. Published as an annex to the Association's annual report for 1915.
Noakes, A. *The Principality Building Society, 1860-1960*. London, 1960.
Peters, C. R. *Building Societies Explained and Compared*. London, 1883.
Platt, S. E. *Building Societies*. Aylesbury, 1887.
Plener, E. von. *English Building Societies* (translated, F. J. Faraday). London, 1875.
Powell, E. T. *Evolution of the Money Market—Letters to a Small Investor*, 3rd ed. London, 1916.
Powell, J. E. *Savings in a Free Society*. London, 1961.
Pratt, J. Tidd. *The Law Relating to Friendly Societies*, 3rd ed. London, 1838.
Pratt, W. T. *The Law Relating to Benefit Building Societies*, 2nd ed. London, 1865.
Price, S. J. *From Queen to Queen* (a History of the Temperance Building Society). London, 1954.
Building Societies. London, 1958.
Riley, G. S. *Building Society Practice*. London, 1935.
Rouse, R. *A Building Society Almanack*. London, 1853.
Building and Freehold Land Society Directory. London, 1871.
Building Societies and Borrowers. London, 1874.
Sanderson, W. H. *Plunder: The Truth about House Purchase Companies*. Bridlington, 1908.
Scratchley, A. *A Treatise on Benefit Building Societies*, 1st ed. London, 1849.
The Warning to Building Societies Conveyed by Recent Legal Decisions. London, 1872.
The Law of Land Societies, 3rd ed. London, 1880.
Scratchley, A. and Brabrook, E. W. *The Law of Benefit Building Societies*, 1st ed. London, 1875.
Southam, A. D. *Building Societies as Investments*. London, 1929 (?).
Stanesby, J. T. *Auditing Considered in Relation to Building Societies*. London, 1875.
Stone, W. *A Practical Treatise on Benefit Building Societies*. London, 1851.
Strachan, T. Y. *Building Society Legislation*. London, 1869.
Stubbins, T. K. *Practical Treatise on Building Society Matters*. London, 1905.
Thompson, J. *The Law and Practice of Benefit Building Societies*. London, 1850.
The Times. *British Homes: The Building Society Movement*. London, 1938.
Tompkins, H. *Building Societies*. London, 1845.
Valance, A. *Very Private Enterprise* (an Account of the Liberator collapse). London, 1956.
Wrigley, E. *How to Manage a Building Association*, 6th ed. 1874.

Pamphlets.

Bowen, J. *Building Societies and their Traducers*. London, 1844.
Bowkett, T. E. *Freehold Property for Mechanics*. London, 1843.
Alchemy or the Art of Turning Base Metals into Gold. London, 1844.
Chambers, W. Chamber's Social Science Tracts, No. 5. *Building Societies*. Edinburgh, 1862.
Fairchild, E. C. *Building Societies: Their Reform and their Future*. London, 1945.
Foster, J. *Building Society Mismanagement*. Newcastle, 1872 (?).

James, J. H. *Benefit Building Societies; their Advantages if Legitimately Considered.* London, 1845.
Rider, J. *The Starr-Bowkett Building Societies.* Leeds, 1887 (?).
Starr, R. B. *Starr-Bowkett Societies as They Are.* London, 1878.
Why Pay Rent? London, 1880s.
Watts, J. S. *The Truth About the Liberator.* London, 1892.
The Greatest Crime of the Nineteenth Century. London, 1897.
The Return of Jabez Balfour. London, 1897.
Webb, A. *Signposts of Building Society Finance.* London, 1942.
Wilson, R. McN. *Financial Freedom for Housing.* London, 1945.
W. *Letter to Greenway Robbins.* London, 1844.
A.R.W. *Do Building Societies Benefit Borrowers?* London, 1871.
Anon. *How to Purchase a House Sooner through a Building Society.* London, 1871.
Bristol Building Societies. 1878.
All's Well That Ends Well (A Starr-Bowkett pamphlet). 1884.
Rules of a Starr-Bowkett Building Society. London, 1885.

Articles.

Bellman, H. Building Societies—Some Economic Aspects. *Econ. Journal*, Vol. 43, 1933.
Brabrook, E. W. Friendly Socs. and Similar Institutions. *Stat. Soc. of London Journal*, Vol. 38, 1875.
The State in Relation to Thrift. Ibid., Vol. 48, 1885.
The Progress of Friendly Societies and Similar Institutions, *Journal of the Royal Statistical Society*, Vol. 58, 1895; Vol. 68, 1905, and Vol. 78, 1915.
Brace, J. A Statistical Analysis of Building Societies. Ibid., Vol. 94, 1931.
Bray, J. F. L. Small Savings. *Econ. Journal*, Vol. 50, 1940.
Hamilton, R. Thrift in Great Britain. Ibid., Vol. 2, 1892.
Johnson, G. J. On the Benefit Building and Freehold Land Societies of Birmingham. *Stat. Soc. of London Journal*, Vol. 28, 1865.
Ludlow, J. M. *Building Societies. Economic Review*, Jan., 1893.
Maiwald, K. An Index of Building Costs in the U.K. *Econ. Hist. Rev.*, Vol. 7, 1954.
Moos, S. Building Societies and Building Finance. *Bulletin of Oxford Institute of Statistics*, June, 1945.
Murphy, G. W. Some Aspects of Building Society Finance. *Manchester School*, Vol. 24, 1956.
Preston, E. Personal Savings through Institutional Channels. *Bulletin of Oxford Institute of Statistics*, September 1950 and September 1951.
Russell, H. The Borders Case. *Land Economics*, Vol. 15, 1939.
Stead, W. T. Two and Two Make Four (a fictional account of the Liberator collapse). *Review of Reviews Annual*, 1893.
Sykes, J. A Note on Building Societies. *Yorkshire Bulletin*, Vol. 9, 1957.
Weber, B. A New Index of Residential Construction, 1838-1950. *Scottish Journal of Political Economy*, Vol. 2.

Periodicals.

The National, March 14, 1846, ceased publication probably in March 1849.
The Reporter, January 1849, still extant at the end of 1852.
The Freeholder, January 1850 to February 1852, continued as *The Freeholder and Commercial Advertiser*, ceased publication August 28, 1852.
The Building Societies Gazette, January 1, 1869, still extant.
The Building Societies Journal, May 1881, discontinued June 1881.
The Building Societies Review, February 1894, discontinued March 1894.

INDEX